THE **NEW** COMPLETE BOOK OF BICYCLING

---

by Eugene A. Sloane

Simon and Schuster
New York

Copyright © 1970, 1974 by Eugene A. Sloane
All rights reserved
including the right of reproduction
in whole or in part in any form
Published by Simon and Schuster
A Division of Gulf & Western Corporation
Simon & Schuster Building
Rockefeller Center,
1230 Avenue of the Americas
New York, New York 10020

ISBN 0-671-27119-9
Library of Congress Catalog Card Number 73-9362
Designed by Irving Perkins
Manufactured in the United States of America

4 5 6 7 8 9 10 11 12 13

CONTENTS

PREFACE

As the world becomes more mechanized, the need for walking diminishes to the point where we drive our cars to the corner drugstore for a gallon of ice cream or the Sunday paper. As our legs threaten to go the way of our appendix as useless appendages, the medical profession becomes increasingly alarmed at the incidence of cardiac failure due more or less directly to lack of exercise. Paradoxically, it seems that the very civilization that has brought unprecedented economic wealth to Americans has also made life so physically easy that it can be fatally disabling.

There is hope, however. In addition to other good things, such as pizza pie and continental car styling, World War II G.I.'s brought home a desire for a better type of bicycle than had been available in this country before the war—the so-called "English racer." While a far cry from an actual racer, this bicycle does have three gears and is considerably lighter than the balloon-tired seventy-five-pound monsters the G.I.'s had dragged around as children. After the war, bicycling became something grown-ups could enjoy, too. Pedaling was a lot easier, and we adults could even look dignified on a bike.

During the postwar baby boom, it became a common sight to see a child being carried on the back of its mother's bicycle to the store where she did the family shopping, or simply for a pleasant ride on a summer afternoon. Soon, entire families were pedaling around town, in the parks, and even on extended trips.

Today, thanks to the eminent cardiologist Dr. Paul Dudley White, the efforts of the entire bicycle industry (especially the Bicycle Institute of America), and to a growing realization on the part of the public of the need for regular exercise, a genuine bicycle boom among adults is here.

In this book, you will learn about quality, ultralightweight bicycles that make cycling much easier than you dreamed possible, with gears that let you take the steepest hills sitting down. We hope that by describing top-rated bicycles, we will be able to convince the novice cyclist of the worth of a good machine, whose frame seems almost alive and responsive to the thrust of the leg muscles. A fine bicycle can become a part of you, an extension of your torso and your arms and legs. Its ten or fifteen gears will shift instantly and surely, and its brakes will stop you safely and smoothly.

For experienced cyclists, the book offers tips for maintaining all kinds of bicycles, and guides to aid you in the selection of everything from the bicycle itself to accessories, tools, and camping equipment. We hope that the book will bring to the sport of cycling much the same dedication those who enjoy other sports give to equipment selection and to play of the sport itself. The chapters on camping and touring are the sum of the experiences of dozens of knowledgeable cycle tourists.

Most important, for children as well as adults, there is a chapter on cycling safety in both city and country.

And cycling is fun! This book can make bicycling a source of genuine enjoyment for you and your family, and you'll find there's much more to bicycling than just good exercise. The cyclist is open to nature, to the sound of the cricket in the field, the distant farm tractor, the wind as it rushes through a forest or field.

While much of this material has been prompted by my personal experiences, some points have grown out of other riders' years of cycling. I am particularly indebted to and want to dedicate this book to the late Oscar Wastyn, Sr., Chicago, one of the last great custom bicycle builders in the United States; Gene Portuesi of Detroit, Michigan, an American Olympic Cycling Team coach; Dr. Clifford Graves of La Jolla, California, President of the International Bicycle Touring Society; Dr. G. Douglas Talbott of Kettering, Ohio, Director of the Paul Dudley White Research Laboratory; Al Stiller of Chicago; Jim Rossi, twice United States national cycle-racing champion; Peter Hoffman, of *Bicycling!* Magazine (formerly *American Cycling*); Fred DeLong of Hatboro, Pennsylvania; and my good friend Robert Wahlgren of Winnetka, Illinois, whose extensive library of old books and magazines on bicycling was of inestimable help in writing the chapter on history.

Credit must also go to my wife, who typed the first edition of this book, and who in this second edition finally receives the warm thanks she should have had in the first writing. I wish also to thank Mary Dell Onley of Wilmette, Illinois, who, with the single exception of my wife, is probably the country's most photogenically efficient secretary, and who typed all of the revised data in this second edition. Finally, I thank my good friends Fred DeLong of Hatboro, Pennsylvania, and Mike Waldron of Detroit, Michigan, for their technical advice and assistance; Thomas W. Chlapecka, Research Associate, National Safety Council, Chicago, for his help in revising the chapter on Safety; medical student Ms. Jean Lewis of Wilmette, Illinois, for her surgical assistance in tubular tire repair; and Ms. Kendra Massey, formerly a top woman racer, for her contributions in general to this revision. I would also like to take this opportunity to thank the literally hundreds of readers who so kindly wrote to me over the past three years with their own bicycling experiences and suggestions for improving this book. Let it be said that these ideas have been and will continue to be gratefully received. Those so far received have, whenever possible, been incorporated in this edition.

This second edition, revised as of 1973, goes to press on the crest of a bicycle boom in the United States of unprecedented proportions. In 1972, for the first time in U.S. history, more bicycles (a whopping 20 percent more) were sold in this country than passenger cars. (May Allah grant this trend to continue and even accelerate!) About 13.5 million bikes were sold in 1972, and by 1974, 27 percent of the population in this country will be riding around on bicycles.

With the bike boom has come a minor shortage of bicycles, particularly in the higher priced brackets. And at the same time, with visions of a lucrative market here, importers from all over the world have begun to ship bicycles into the U.S. Unfortunately, an alarming number of bicycles designed for the low-priced market (ten speeds under $100.00) are of rather dubious quality, and will do nothing to make cycling the joy and pleasure this sport can become. I have visited the two major international bicycle shows and conventions in 1971 and 1972, in Milan, Italy, and Cologne, Germany, respectively, and the 1972 and 1973 U.S. major bike shows in New York. I can tell you that bicycle component suppliers of high quality derailleurs, brakes, tubing, rims, hubs, chains and the like tell me they are virtually sold out through at least 1974, and many are tied up through 1975. All of which indicates a continuing shortage of quality bicycles (price ranges from $250.00 to $650.00 and up). Bike prices have risen at least an average of 10 percent a year, and this trend will continue.

Young, and even older people have already discovered that the bicycle is a fine way to meet each other. I recall a recent writing assignment on Chicago's bikeways for *Chicago* Magazine, for which I biked over some 250 miles of city streets set aside as bike routes, and over the Windy City's beautiful Lake Shore bike trails along Lake Michigan. On this jaunt I carried a small cassette tape recorder in a rear bike bag, and had the mike strung around my neck. As I proceeded up the Lake Shore bike path northward from the Loop, I approached sweet young things on this fine summer Sunday, also cycling their beauteous way in the same direction. Upon overtaking them I asked how they felt about cycling, their bike commuting habits, how far they rode, how they liked the bike paths, etc. One gal said to me: "Frankly, sir, I don't believe you really have a tape recorder in your bag. I think that mike's a dummy and that it's a great way to meet girls." She then said cycling actually was a fine way to meet men, an observation amply born out by this writer and other cyclists of both sexes and all ages, later. It seems that when you're on a bike you already have a lot in common with other cyclists, and starting up a conversation with a fellow cyclist (I use the term "fellow" loosely) can be on such innocuous terms as "Isn't your rear tire a bit low?" or, "My, that's a really fine bike you have there!" But you have to be careful. Once I was overtaking a lovely "girl" with long, flowing coppery red hair, who from the rear exhibited a most enticing "ankling" technique. As I came abreast I said to "her": "I just have to congratulate a girl who has such a great ankling technique," at which point I noticed that the red tresses in the rear were matched by an equally bushy red beard in the front. So much for unisex cycling.

But I am glad that cycling is an accepted enthusiasm for the young. What more healthful path to youthful dalliance than a tour on bicycles built for one, or two? Anticipation of the tenting to come can only be matched by shared enjoyment of the beauty of the day, the blue sky overhead, the trees and pastures all around, the earthy aroma of field and orchard. At nightfall, every fiber of every muscle will be keenly in tone, a rewarding natural aphrodisiac from a healthful day's outing of fifty or seventy-five miles.

Finally, along with the bike boom, the flood of low quality imports and quality bike shortages, has come a proliferation of bike stores, a trend I applaud. However, it's a lot easier to open a bike store than it is to train a bike mechanic, and so you will find an even greater shortage of skilled repairmen. It will cost far more and take longer for your bicycle to be repaired than ever before. All of which is good reason to read the chapters on bicycle maintenance in this book carefully so you can do your own repairs. If you can ride a bike, you can fix it, short of frame repairs or work requiring costly and scarce tools, which account for only around 2 percent of repairs in any case.

Finally, as a sport, I am happy to report that bicycling has grown at a rate of more than 70 percent over its nearest competitor, boating; and about 65 percent greater than camping. Bicycling indeed has actually contributed to the spurt in camping, with more Americans than ever before taking to the road on their bikes, panniers filled with camping gear, carriers loaded with sleeping bag and tent, cycling happily through the land in this country and abroad. Airlines have seen the trend and they now have (finally) made it easy and practical for you to take your bike with you on domestic and foreign flights (see page 225 for details). Airlines such as Swissair with their Wings and Wheels program, KLM, Sabena and others have actually planned bike trips abroad for Americans, and we should soon see Europeans touring America on similarly planned tours.

One more observation. Since this book appeared, as author of the only modern book on bicycling available at the time, I have been a guest on numerous network and local TV and radio programs and have been interviewed in the newspapers. A constantly recurring question has been "Why the bike boom? How come so many millions are taking to bikes—even more so than when there were no cars—when cars and public transportation are so available?" In the past three years I have talked to hundreds of cycling enthusiasts, new and experienced, old and young, and it's my judgment that the basic reasons for the bike boom are an increasing awareness of the importance of exercise and its vital contribution to good health, plus a related sense of boredom with other forms of exercise such as jogging. The threatened shortage of gasoline, if it drives gas prices up markedly (I think $2.50 a gallon would be fine), should also save lives by making nongas-using, nonpolluting cyclists out of overweight, under-exercised commuters. An enjoyment of bicycling for its own sake comes at the head of many reasons for the bike boom. In an age when so many of us feel relatively powerless to change the course of human events, the fact that we can at least go relatively great distances (upwards of 80 to 100 miles daily on tour) on our own pedal power gives one a rare feeling of accomplishment. And the sudden realization by hundreds of thousands of hitherto chairbound commuters that cycling is a fun, nonpolluting, inexpensive way to get to work has added many cycling devotees to this growing and healthy sport. So, to all my readers, Happy Cycling!

EUGENE A. SLOANE

March, 1973
Evanston, Illinois

THE **NEW** COMPLETE BOOK OF BICYCLING

1

CYCLING YOUR WAY
TO BETTER HEALTH

The right kind of physical exercise can add years to your life. It can also make you feel better daily, and prepare you to compete in today's demanding world, where sheer stamina and resistance keep one out front.

The right kind of exercise, according to Dr. Paul Dudley White, is sustained for at least an hour and is vigorous enough to produce a mild sweat. Cycling is just such exercise.

A number of studies have been made to determine the relationship between cycling, exercise, and health. A quick review of these facts will, I'm sure, convince you of the importance of exercise.

First, however, I must say a word about conditioning. No beginner should hop on a bicycle and pedal 15 or 20 miles at top speed right away. Everyone, however, even octogenarians, can do this, if they keep themselves in good physical condition.

According to Dr. Clifford L. Graves, a well-known cycling expert, a trained cyclist in good physical condition should be able to ride 25 miles in between an hour and a quarter and an hour and a half, no matter what his age. Records of the Veterans Time Trial Association (a time trial is a race against the clock) show that seventy-two-year-old Billy Steer rode a 25-mile time trial in one hour, fourteen minutes, seventeen seconds, and when he was seventy-four rode 190 miles in twelve hours. At sixty-four, E. A. Butt covered 439 miles in a twenty-four-hour trial.

Every year the Cyclists' Touring Club of England holds a century (100-mile) ride for men over fifty and women over forty, in which hundreds of people participate. In 1966 the oldest rider, who was eighty-five, completed the 100-mile run without pain or strain.

"What all this amounts to," says Dr. Graves, "is that a healthy person can engage in vigorous physical activity well into his old age."

It is no coincidence that most heart attacks occur when the victim has been sedentary for a number of hours. Dr. Graves states that there has yet to be a heart attack during the thousands of time trials held by the VTTA. On the contrary, he says, "Heart attacks are much more apt to come during inactivity, because it is during inactivity that the blood pressure drops and the coronary circulation slows down." [1]

Dr. Paul Dudley White is justifiably unhappy about many Americans' lack of exercise. We spend all evening watching TV, take the car to the drug store, use electric appliances, and end our days too tired for the extra effort and exercise that could save our lives. [2]

Dr. White states that no one should sit down for more than an hour without getting up and moving about, preferably jogging in place for a couple of minutes. This is the way to keep a heart healthy and blood pressure down.

Vigorous exercise like bicycling will also:

· Improve the blood flow to the brain, keeping it operating at full capacity.
· Induce a state of *healthy* fatigue—a wonderful antidote to the nervous stress and strain of modern life.
· Reduce the possibility of a slipped disc by strengthening back muscles.
· Add as much as five years to life expectancy (according to Dr. Jean Mayer, Professor of Nutrition at Harvard University's School of Public Health). [3]
· Reduce the incidence of all types of degenerative vascular disease, responsible for or associated with heart attacks, strokes, and high blood pressure. (This accounts for approximately 55 percent of all deaths that occurred in the United States in 1968, as opposed to 18 percent due to cancer and 11 percent due to auto accidents.) [4]

[1] Clifford L. Graves, "A Doctor Looks at Racing," *American Cycling* (now *Bicycling!*), December, 1966, pp. 18–27.
[2] Paul Dudley White, "For Fun and Fitness Get Back on a Bike," New York: Bicycle Institute of America.
[3] American Heart Association, "Lack of Exercise and Life Expectancy," *Heart Research Newsletter*, Vol. XIII, No. 2 (Spring, 1967), p. 3.
[4] G. Douglas Talbott, "Medical and Health Aspects of Bicycling," Kettering, Ohio: Cox Coronary Heart Institute, 1967.

DR. RODAHL'S EXPERIMENT

Fred DeLong, who writes for Schwinn's (one of the most prominent domestic bicycle manufacturers) dealer publication, described, in one of his articles, the research of Dr. Kaare Rodahl, in Philadelphia. Dr. Rodahl took telemetered cardiograms of a number of men while they were cycling on a stationary bicycle, at various levels of activity. From the cardiograms, Dr. Rodahl determined each man's tolerance for exercise. Based on this tolerance level, he set up a program of hard physical exercise of varying duration for each man.

Participants in this program were executives who ranged in age from twenty-nine to forty-two; follow-up examination of each participant by Dr. Rodahl revealed that the men were rewarded for their rigorous regimen with as high as 10 percent over-all increase in physical capacity. Pulse rates were better, and the executives reported that they were more alert on the job and had more energy left for home activities. They all agreed that physical deterioration so common to men over thirty had in their cases not only been checked, but reversed.

FATIGUE AND EXERCISE

We have all read about fatigue that comes about with no apparent physical cause. How many times have you come home exhausted after "a hard day at the office," where all you did was sit hour after hour at your desk? And, how often do women complain to their husbands of feeling "tired all the time"?

Nothing fights fatigue after a tension-filled day in the office or around the house better than getting on a bicycle and pedaling for all you are worth.

Dr. Theodore Klumpp, a New York specialist participating in an American Medical Association panel on geriatrics, stated, "Fatigue is the greatest obstacle to a happy, useful life for oldsters. Its best antidote is physical activity when one feels tired. Over and over again it has been demonstrated that physical activity at the end of a trying day brings a degree of freshness and renewed energy that nothing else can equal."[5]

[5] "Ride A Bike to Health," *New York World Telegram,* Vol. 126, No. 291 (August 29, 1959).

And a recent study of fatigue[6] showed that this is a primary complaint of executives. In a survey of 165 top-level executives, 43 percent said they often feel tired. They ascribed their fatigue to job pressure (61 percent), increasing age (46 percent), and excessive work load (25 percent).

Dr. John E. Vaugh, Vice President of Fairleigh Dickinson University, observes that some executives feel thirty years old at 9:00 A.M. and sixty at 5:00 P.M. Other observers of executive life note that the ability to build up and keep a full head of steam all day long is crucial if job and career goals are to be met. Therefore, regular exercise on a bicycle not only can prolong your life; it can also promote your career.

Jogging Can Be Dangerous

"Jogging is murder . . . unless the individual over thirty-five has an electrocardiogram first and repeats it every year," says Dr. Meyer Friedman, director of cardiovascular research at Mount Zion Medical Center, San Francisco. He said that a recent study of coronary deaths among men of middle age or younger show that there is a clear danger in heavy exercise for anyone over thirty-five. Besides pointing out that many such deaths can be predicted, Dr. Friedman's observations point up the rising heart attack death rate for men. Since 1950, the heart attack death rate for men twenty-five to forty-four has risen 14 percent and for men forty-five to sixty-four, only 4 percent (so if you live to forty-five you must be doing something right, such as bicycling).

Jogging, as noted, has doctors worried, especially if you just decide to start jogging without a medical examination first. Jogging imposes severe stress on the heart, whereas cycling can be off to a tapered, easy start and gradually built up in intensity.

A WORD ABOUT PHYSIOLOGY

Why does exercise promote health? Let's look for a moment at the heart and lungs.

The Heart

The heart is a fantastically efficient machine. It pumps 5.2 quarts of blood in a minute in a person at rest. It can pump as much as 31.7 quarts

[6] "Get Rid of That Run-Down Feeling," *Nation's Business,* July, 1967, pp. 82–83.

a minute during exercise. The blood is a transport vehicle that carries off wastes and supplies nutrients to muscles and other tissues.

Arteriosclerosis and exercise

Arteriosclerosis is a disease in which the walls of the arteries become hardened and calcified. In extreme cases, the arteries become pipelike, bonelike tubes. Hardening of the arteries begins at birth, but exercise helps delay its progress. Blood that flows rapidly will not permit deposits to settle in the walls of the blood vessels as quickly as blood that flows slowly.

Take a pipe two millimeters in diameter. If this pipe can pass one cubic milliliter of water per second, a pipe twice the diameter (four millimeters) can pass four times that amount. The resistance to flow in a pipe is inversely proportional to the fourth power of the pipe diameter, all of which simply means that *a very small decrease* in the diameter of your veins and arteries due to calcification will result in a *great decrease* in the amount of blood these vessels can carry. To compensate, the heart must pump harder and the blood pressure goes up. High blood pressure is a common cause of stroke or rupture of a blood vessel in the brain.[7]

Atherosclerosis

Atherosclerosis occurs when fatty substances are deposited in the lining of the blood vessels. This is why a low-fat diet is advisable in middle and old age. The fatty deposit comes in contact with the flowing blood and can start a blood clot which, in turn, may plug up the arteries that feed the heart. This plugging of the coronary arteries (thrombosis) is a major cause of heart attack. Such a blood clot may also block arteries that lead to the kidneys and cause kidney damage, or it may block an artery in the brain and cause a stroke.

Exercise, by keeping the blood flowing swiftly, helps prevent these dangerous symptoms.

The Respiratory System

One measure of lung efficiency is vital capacity—the difference between the maximum amount of air that can be taken into the lungs and the maxi-

[7] Arthur C. Guyton, *Function of the Human Body.* Philadelphia: W. B. Saunders Co., 1959.

mum amount forced out. Your ability to breathe deeply depends on the strength of your respiratory muscles.

Exercise strengthens respiratory muscles and, by inducing regular deep breathing, can help keep vital capacity high.

WEIGHT CONTROL

You can also use your exercise program to get rid of excess weight. The only problem here is that after a brisk bicycle jaunt, people tend to overeat. They rationalize, using the exercise as an excuse. I admit that there's nothing like a bicycle ride to make a person wolf down a meal. But, if exercise is going to help control your weight, you must use self-control. Remember that next to cycling the best reducing exercise is placing both hands firmly on the edge of your dinner table and pushing hard.

Calories and Exercise

Let's consider the relationship between caloric intake and exercise. For a medium-sized male, five feet, nine inches tall, a reasonable weight would be 150 pounds. You probably know your own best weight. Multiply your optimum weight by 20 and you have about the number of calories you should consume daily with light work or moderate exercise. For our medium-sized man, this would be 150×20 or 3,000 calories per day.

Mild cycling uses up an average of 5 calories per minute or 300 calories per hour. Vigorous cycling, which you need to do to go up a hill, will use up approximately 10 calories per minute, or 600 per hour.

CYCLING REGIMEN

As I have already cautioned, if you are not used to strenuous exercise, take it easy on bicycling in the beginning. Do not tackle a cycle tour without conditioning yourself first. Keep your bicycle in the lowest, or next to lowest, gear and ride slowly, without strain, three or four miles a day for two or three weeks. Build up your cycling stamina gradually by increasing your daily rides by two or three miles each week. If you are in good health (and you should have a complete physical every year to be sure about this), you will probably find that ten miles or so a day will keep you fit and trim.

WINTER EXERCISE

If you live in what is laughingly called the Temperate Zone, skating, skiing, and just plain dog-trotting are all fine winter workouts to keep you fit when ice and snow on the streets make cycling too difficult and dangerous. Cycling, skating, and skiing are complementary sports, each keeping you fit for the other.

There will be days during the winter when the weather is so bad or your schedule so limited that you do not have time to go outside for exercise. When this happens, there are a number of good bicycle-like exercisers on the market. I prefer the Model 951 Ergometer made by Jonas Oglaend of Sandnes, Norway.

If you can't find the Ergometer in your local bike shop, ask the importer, Intersport, Inc., P. O. Box 1241, Bellevue, Washington, for the name of a store near you that sells it. Incidentally, many ski resorts have a bike exerciser you can use to warm up on before braving the cold, a practice I applaud as a heart saver.

When using this or any similar exerciser, set the load (which should be adjustable) to a level at which you can feel resistance, and pedal at your normal cadence (sixty-five to eighty-five pedal revolutions per minute) for three or four minutes. Rest for the same period, then pedal another three or four minutes. Repeat this for about twenty minutes.

Start training by following this program twice a week for two weeks; increase frequency to three times a week for the next two weeks, and, thereafter, exercise four times a week. Finish each session by flexing your muscles lightly.

Or, ride for ten or twelve minutes at a time in front of the television set. The noise level of the Oglaend unit is low enough to permit fast and furious use without interfering with TV viewing. This machine is fitted with SKF ball-bearings and a special tire to keep the noise low. The Oglaend unit costs around $95.00. I have a book-holder with light set up in front of my Ergometer, and my experience shows I get about six miles per chapter of the average book, with a fairly stiff workload set on the exerciser.

Schwinn, too, makes a good bicycle exerciser, with built-in speedometer, mileage indicator, and adjustable pedal resistance. It lists for about $100.00 and is available from any Schwinn dealer.

A word of caution about home fitness equipment. Forget about any gadget that purports to condition or tone your muscles without work. Gadgets that claim to give you exercise by "remote muscle control"— electronic stimulation or motor-driven apparatus—are, in my opinion, useless. You've got to move those muscles yourself. Save the money these gadgets cost and buy a good bicycle exerciser that you pedal yourself.

If you can't find the Oglaend or Schwinn units, test out the exerciser you do find by riding it. Does it feel rickety or "junky"? Is there an easily adjustable friction or other idler to decrease or increase pedal resistance? Is it quiet? If not, keep looking.

WHAT ISN'T EXERCISE

Besides workouts on electric or motor-driven gadgets, other activities are touted as good exercise but are in fact not. Golf, for example, is not adequate exercise—not even eighteen holes. If you carried your own bag and *ran* between strokes, you might approximate a half-hour of bicycling. For youngsters, according to Dr. Dale L. Hanson, Associate Professor of Physical Education at the University of Maryland, Little League baseball involves very little exercise—"So minimal," he states, "that it should not be considered a major factor in the development of cardiovascular-respiratory fitness." Dr. Hanson reached this conclusion by telemetering the heart-rate response of players (excluding the pitcher and catcher) in Little League games. The results proved that, unlike many other sports, baseball consists of a great deal of watching and waiting.

You are not exercising either when you travel in an airplane or on a train, no matter how tired you feel at journey's end. In fact, long flights alarm Dr. Paul Dudley White, who has proposed equipping planes with a bicycle exerciser for such flights. He believes the exerciser would help keep the pilot relatively immune from heart attacks, and keen and alert enough to meet emergencies. It would also maintain circulation in the legs, states Dr. White, where blood clots sometimes form. The airlines probably wouldn't like this idea, but I am in favor of the passenger getting up and walking up and down the aisle during the flight.

Studies made by Dr. Jeremy Morris of London, England, showed that bus drivers, who work sitting down, have twice as many heart attacks as bus conductors, who go up and down the aisles and stairs to collect fares. Other studies have shown that sedentary postal employees have more heart attacks than mail carriers who walk most of the day.

If you've been skipping around in this book for more than an hour, it's time to put it down and go for a quick bike ride!

2

PRACTICAL TIPS FOR
BICYCLING SAFETY

If you read and follow the suggestions in this chapter on cycling safety, you need never have a bicycle accident. The recommendations are based on my own observations during fifteen years of city, country, night and day, winter and summer bicycling, and on those of others with the same background.

A summary of bicycle accidents is given at the end of this chapter, a review of which should show you why cycling safety is so very important.

GENERAL SAFETY HINTS

In the first place, a cyclist is far more likely to *run into* a car or other object than to have it run into him. I will begin, therefore, with a few general rules *you* should observe, which apply to all types of cycling, before getting into specifics of safety, its seasonal aspects, city versus country riding, and night versus day riding.

LEGAL ASPECTS

From the viewpoint of obedience to traffic regulations, most public officials look upon bicycles as a motor vehicle. Police regularly give tickets to cyclists who violate these regulations, and, in my judgment, they *should*.

It is tempting to run a stoplight or stop sign if there is no visible cross-traffic. You can whip a bicycle quickly around a line of stopped cars, and it can give you a satisfied feeling to leave the automobile at the light as you wend your way down the next block. But this is a hazardous undertaking; you simply cannot tell when a car might shoot out of a hidden intersection, alley, or driveway and come barreling down the street toward you. A bicycle simply cannot move out of the way fast enough. And if you are run into after having violated a traffic regulation, you will have a mighty tough time collecting on the other guy's insurance!

Here are general cycling safety tips:

- *Always ride* WITH *the traffic, never* INTO *the traffic.* Riding with the traffic reduces the relative speed difference between you and moving traffic, and thus reduces the impact if an accident should occur. You'll feel a bit nervous at first with all that traffic coming from behind you, but you'll get used to it. If your city *requires* bicyclists to ride *into* (against) the stream of moving traffic, then you and your fellow cyclists in that city had better have the law changed. Surely the law is designed to protect citizens; a law that *endangers* cyclists should be ignored and repealed.
- *Never ride on a city street where parking is not allowed!* There is simply no room for you between the traffic and the gutter on streets where car parking is forbidden. Such streets are high-traffic through streets. Cars might drive you right into the curb, or drive behind you honking madly because your bike is moving too slowly.
- As a corollary to the above, *always ride on city streets where car parking is allowed* and, in fact, where cars are parked. By law, traffic is supposed to allow from thirty to thirty-six inches, up to a full three feet, on streets where cars are parked, to allow for the doors of parked cars to open easily. (Unfortunately, this is not always adhered to.) If you are a reasonably skilled cyclist and can ride straight, thirty inches will be all you will need. You'll even have room to spare.
- *Watch out for car doors opening ahead of you when riding on streets with parked cars!* Discourteous drivers have whipped in ahead of me, parked their cars, and opened the door on the driver's side, all in one motion, forcing me to veer out into the stream of traffic to avoid running into them. As you cycle on streets with parked cars, keep a close watch on the cars as far ahead as you can see. I have trained myself to watch parked cars for a block ahead, and to notice what's going on in all the parked cars on that block.
- *In particular, watch through the rear windows and look at the sideview mirrors of parked cars.* These will help you know if a driver or passenger is about to open a door. You may notice a driver who appears immobile and waiting, but I have found that this does not mean that he won't suddenly

Fig. 1: Here are a few of the thousands of bicycle touring enthusiasts who participate in the mammoth annual Tour of the Ohio River Valley (TORV), the country's
largest such group tour, and, like bicycling itself, growing in popularity by leaps
and bounds, or, should we say, by huffs and puffs? As you can see, everyone's in
the act; men and women of all ages, bicycles of all descriptions. In case you're
wondering where the baggage is, it's carried by "sag wagons," which follow the
tour and also pick up any sagged riders and broken-down bikes.

leap out of his car. Some cities and states have an ordinance that makes the driver liable for any accidents caused by his opening a door on the traffic side, but you will still be better off if you can avoid running into a car door any time. Watch out especially for children in cars; they are always unpredictable.

The whiplash protector above car seats can hide the actions of a driver who may be about to open a door, since it covers much of his head area. So be doubly careful; assume that any car in which you can't see the driver's side may have an occupant who's about to open his street-side door in front of you.

· *You're not car size* on a bike. Many drivers fail to see anything smaller than a car on the road, because they're not used to looking for anything smaller. A friend of mine wound up with a two-month stay in bed from severe internal injuries because he assumed that an elderly female driver saw him. She and he were coming in opposite directions on a narrow street on which cars were parked. She was in the middle of the road and he assumed she would move over as she approached him. She didn't, and later she said she never saw him, despite his brightly colored clothing. Elderly drivers *are* to be considered dangerous to cyclists, as I have said elsewhere in this book. They often have bad vision, poor depth perception, confused color discrimination, slow reflexes, and they are frequently terrible drivers to begin with. (Pretty soon I'll fit into that category.) Too many states do not require stiff annual physical examinations of drivers over sixty-five. But elderly cyclists are *good* cyclists . . . they have to be, to have survived.

As you cycle, be alert for the same situations you would be concerned about if you were driving a car. These include:

· Children chasing a ball into the street.
· Adults coming out from between parked cars.
· Cars leaving a parking place without signaling.

I have found, in fact, that my extreme caution as a cyclist has made me a much safer driver of automobiles, because now, instinctively, I drive more defensively.

· *Beware of the "Sunday Driver."* Drivers who don't drive regularly can be dangerous to cyclists. Whenever I hear behind me the squeal of power brakes and wheels being turned rapidly, usually followed by a horn blowing, it almost always seems to be an inexperienced driver who cannot decide what to do about me. Watch out for these people at intersections. They may appear to be waiting patiently for you to pass, but they seem to be unaware that an experienced cyclist in good physical condition may be coming at fifteen or twenty miles an hour, and they will suddenly charge out in front of you. Also, I have found that these drivers will come uncomfortably close to me when they pass.

Men and women who drive to work every day are usually safe to be around on a bicycle. And teenagers who have taken driver education courses in high school are often safe drivers. But watch out for the suburban housewife or the older driver! Give them a wide berth. Don't rely on their hand or automatic turn signals—they are not necessarily indicative of their next move.

· *Approaching an intersection calls for judgment.* If it's a suburban through street with a stop sign in your favor, do not assume that traffic will stop because of the sign. Sometimes drivers will barrel up to stop signs, slow to a running crawl, and speed up again, even though you as a cyclist have the right of way and are already into the intersection. Teenage male drivers are particularly untrustworthy in this respect, with or without driver education.

I have found that the safest procedure to follow upon seeing a car waiting for me to pass through an intersection, whether the car is to the left or the right, is to move over to the center of the road as I approach the corner, provided there is no traffic behind me. In this position I have a better chance of swerving right or left to avoid a collision if the driver at the intersection decides to force his way through. From the center of the road, I have room to turn the corner right or left as necessary to avoid being hit. If I were to go through the intersection next to the curb, it would be impossible to turn at the sharp right angle necessary to escape collision. Get into the habit of starting up with the traffic as the traffic light changes, so a vehicle is on your left to run interference for you. I also like to cross all intersections with a vehicle on my left; it's good protection, just so you are *sure* the vehicle isn't going to turn right, right into you.

Cultivate the habit of cycling in an absolutely straight, unwavering line at all times, and continue to do so while you quickly turn your head as necessary to check traffic behind you. If there is no traffic, try cycling down the center of the dividing line on the street. You'll be surprised to find that after a little practice you'll be able to steer straight down the line. Accurate steering is vital in city cycling, because the clearance between traffic and parked cars is ample only if you can cycle straight, without weaving from side to side.

· *Watch out for child cyclists.* Children on bicycles usually weave from side to side, turn unpredictably without signaling, and cannot be counted on not to run into you even when you are passing them. I watch children on bicycles very closely as I approach them from the front or the rear, and I am ready to take evasive action at all times.

Incidentally, while cycling in the city, you should have your hands on or next to the brake levers at all times, so that you can stop instantly if you have to. Also, keep toe straps loose. I'll never forget the time I forgot to loosen my toe straps on a city ride. It was during rush-hour traffic at the major intersection in Detroit, and I came to a traffic light with cars all around me. I stopped quickly, but with my feet strapped tightly in the pedals, I toppled slowly and ingloriously to the side.

Apropos of motorists' attitudes, there seems to be a curious relationship between the time of day and the attitude of the driver toward cyclists. For example, I used to cycle from my home in Grosse Pointe Farms to my office in downtown Detroit, a distance of twelve miles. The route took me through the car factory area, and I found that if I cycled before 8:00 A.M. motorists were quite discourteous and careless about my well-being. When I left home after 8:00 A.M., however, I found everyone quite courteous. During evening rush hours, though, no holds are barred and courtesy to cyclists doesn't seem to exist.

If you want to cycle on a Friday or Saturday evening, try to avoid main traffic routes, and watch out at all times on any roads for a drunk driver or a teenager late for a date or showing off to his girl.

- *A word about city cycling routes.* If you want to cycle to work (a good idea), I recommend that you get out a large-scale map of the city and carefully chart your route downtown. Plan to use only streets that are parallel to main arteries, so that the stop signs will be in your favor, but the streets will not be heavily traveled in rush hours.

I often ride my bicycle from my home in Evanston to Chicago's Loop, a distance of about fourteen miles. I have charted a rather devious route which avoids all main arteries, yet gives me streets quite safe all the way downtown. I use it summer and winter, except when it is raining or there is snow or ice on the street. All the streets I use for this trip have parked cars on them, or permit such parking. It takes me about one hour to get downtown, which is not bad when I consider that it takes nearly an hour to get there via public transportation. In my judgment, the extra time is well spent for the exercise involved.

- *Right of way.* Remember that cars on your right, at intersections, have the right of way; in any case, don't argue. Pedestrians have the right of way at all times. I would advise you to give the right of way to anyone who wants it.
- *Driveways can be a hazard,* particularly if they are hidden by shrubbery or parked motor vehicles. Women drivers in particular have a habit of shooting backward out of residential driveways into the middle of the street. So be

ready to veer away. It's a good practice to look back over your shoulder frequently so that you always know the overtaking traffic situation, and whether or not it's safe to swerve to the left to avoid an accident at any given moment. Watch out especially for cars and trucks emerging from shopping-center parking lots.

· *As you approach a stoplight, watch out for cars next to you that want to turn right.* Although it infuriates drivers, I veer left into the traffic line if the traffic light turns red as I approach it, to prevent motorists from pushing me to the curb. Since there are no parked cars at intersections, right-turning cars tend to hug the curb at stoplights, or as they approach intersections. Once you have stopped, you can move out of the way to let traffic by when the light changes. Be especially careful about buses. Bus drivers must pull over to the curb to let passengers on and off. If you're following a bus, remember that it may stop at *any* corner, and it is definitely unsafe for you to be between the bus and the curb at a corner. Stay behind a bus, even if its diesel fumes tempt you into taking chances on passing. You can watch your opportunity and pass the bus between intersections or, if traffic permits, you can pass it on the left while it is stopped. Do this slowly and carefully, watching out for cars and pedestrians who may suddenly appear in your path from in front of the bus. Once you have passed a bus, you should be able to stay ahead of it.

· *At extremely busy intersections, if it's possible, use a truck or a bus to run interference for you.* Just stay to the right of the truck, and anyone coming from the left will run into the truck instead of you.

In my many years of cycling through city traffic, I have never had any kind of traffic accident. There was one mishap, but it was ridiculous— and my fault. I was cycling home on a pitch-black, very cold January evening about 6:30 P.M. The street was deserted, without traffic or a pedestrian in sight. Because it was ten degrees below zero, my feet were getting cold, and I looked down for a moment to check the connection between my electrically heated socks and the battery strapped to my seat post. Before I could look up, I found myself spread-eagled on the roof of a parked car. On that dark night, the black car was invisible a few feet away. I wasn't hurt, but I wrecked a front wheel rim and bent a fork. Fortunately, I was wearing a hard crash helmet, so if my head did hit anything I was not aware of it. Since that incident, I have always checked my gear while at a standstill.

· *Consider safety equipment.* A great many cities and/or states now require motorcyclists to wear approved hard crash helmets. I see little difference in falling off a motorcycle or a bicycle—you might strike your head on a concrete pavement, a curb, or any other unyielding surface, in either case. A motorcyclist goes faster and can hit an immovable object harder, but the relative speed of impact is of little concern, since you can just as easily receive a skull fracture by falling from a stationary bicycle.

I always wear a protective crash helmet of some kind for city cycling. In winter I prefer the "Hard-Nok" trooper hat (Fig. 2) made by G & R Distributors, which sells for around $15.00 in sports and snowmobile stores. This hat is a hard crash helmet disguised as a trooper or hunter's hat, with pile-lined warm ear flaps and a chin strap to hold the hat on. (I should point out that *any* hard hat you wear *must* have a chin strap, because a minor jolt can knock a hat off before your head hits the curb.) The G & R trooper hat weighs only 14 ounces and comes in a variety of colors, the safest being a highly visible international orange. If you can't find this hat, write to G & R Distributors, 3015 N. California Avenue, Chicago, Illinois 60618, for a dealer near you.

In summer a good protective hat is a professional hockey helmet, which is open and so relatively cool to wear. So far, no one has come up with a really cool summer crash hat for cyclists, who work up a sweat even without a hat. The Cooper SK100 for around $5.00 and the junior Cooper for a child is one version of a hockey hat that seems to offer reasonable

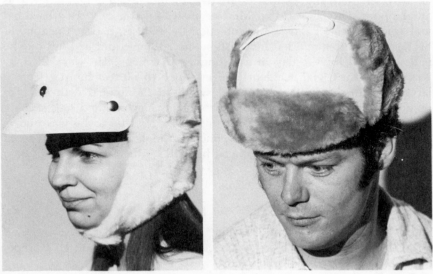

Fig. 2: This trooper hat, in male and female versions, offers crash-helmet security with winter cycling warmth. Made by G & R Distributors, Chicago, and available in sporting goods stores.

protection. The so-called "monkey hat" of a latticework of leather-covered foam, worn by racing cyclists, offers little more than psychological protection, in my opinion. The orthopedic and neurological surgeons to whom I have shown this "racing" hat say it is virtually useless for protection against skull fracture and brain damage, though it might prevent skin abrasion in a very minor fall, if there is such a thing.

To quote from the National Safety Council's *Family Safety* Magazine (Spring, 1972), Dr. Stephen E. Boyd notes that "The brain is a delicate structure. It floats in a closed hydraulic system. A sudden jar and the brain hits the skull, causing hematoma or concussion." In other words, the type of injury so very likely to occur when falling even from a slow-moving bicycle, when the head strikes the hard street or curb, or part of a car, can cause permanent brain damage and related psychological, physical, and emotional involvement. Or death.

A poignant note was added to the increasing need for head protection by cyclists with the untimely death of William W. Sheets, who, when he died, was president of the 350-member Rochester, New York, Bicycling Club. Mr. Sheets, forty-one, was killed in a bicycle accident a few years ago. He was an ardent, experienced, and physically capable rider who felt very strongly about the use of the bicycle as a vehicle for commuting, as an intelligent and viable alternative to the urban blight known as automobiles. The point is that Mr. Sheets, who normally wore a hard hat and who advocated this head protection for cyclists, had at the time of his death forgotten and left his crash helmet at home and had left one he had borrowed for the day in a restaurant that noon. He was killed by what seemed a trivial accident, one in which to protect himself from a large German shepherd dog he had swung at the animal with his bike pump. At the same time he lost control of his machine and fell, striking the pavement. He died a few hours later in a hospital as he was undergoing surgery. It is to be hoped Mr. Sheets' passing was not in vain, for if his case can save the lives of others, his will be the larger contribution.

HELMET SAFETY TIPS

Since this book came out in October, 1970, I have had a lot more time for cycle touring and, as a consequence, have toured all through Europe, the U.S. and in the Canadian Northwest. I have found that the more cycling you do, the more likely you are to have a serious accident, usually when you expect it least. For example, one lovely spring afternoon in May I was peacefully and happily cycling across the Hood Canal

Bridge over Puget Sound, my mind on a hamburger and a malted milk at that noontime hour. The wind was gusting to around 30 knots from the side. I was warned, before going over the bridge, by the toll-booth keeper, that many cyclists had cracked up in the middle of the bridge, where the openable span joins the fixed section of this structure. I was barrelling down an incline into the movable section of the bridge, marveling at the beauty of the Cascade Mountains on one side, the Olympic Mountains on the other, whose snow-capped peaks gleamed in the distance. I did not watch carefully enough for cracks in the pavement, and suddenly found myself flying through the air, over the bars. I landed about 15 feet down the road on my right shoulder and suffered a rather painful separation. The bicycle simply broke in half at the top tube, so my trip was ended even had I not been hurt. I wound up in the hospital reflecting that evening, between bouts of pain, that instead of my shoulder it could just as easily have been my head I landed on and, thinking about my carelessness, that perhaps it should have been. My front wheel had slipped into the 2-inch-wide crack between the spans, right up to the axle, and the bike stopped dead, as I almost did. This accident was not entirely in vain, however, since I spent considerable time while in bed the next day complaining loudly to the Washington State Highway Commission about the need for protection for cyclists at the joints of this bridge. The bridge tender who picked me and my bike up after the accident regaled me with stories of other cyclists who had come to the same mishap in the same spot, which still did not make me feel one whit better. A few weeks after I had returned home I received a letter from the Highway Commission informing me that as a result of my accident they were going to put a thick rubber mat strip over the joints. Friends from Seattle have since told me this has been done and now cyclists can cross this bridge without being exposed to this quite hazardous situation. Since this squeaky wheel got the grease, I would suggest you squeak loudly to the proper authorities any time you see a road hazard condition of any type, on behalf of future cyclists who will come that way.

A few months later, on another bicycle, I was bending hard over the handlebars, getting up steam, when I suddenly found myself straddling the top roof of a parked large American car. Again my bicycle broke in half at the top tube. Aside from the fact that I was rapidly running out of bicycles, I wound up with a badly sprained left wrist. Again, I was not wearing a crash helmet of any kind. And, again, I could have been killed, and probably would have been, had I hit a truck instead of a car with an ample trunk over which I could slide instead of hitting something as solid as the back of a truck. Now I have helmet religion, and I would no more think of getting on a bike, even for a ten-foot ride, without don-ning a crash helmet, than I would of riding Lady Godiva style at minus 40°F (or at any other temperature).

In addition, then, to the data that precedes the recounting of these two idiotic accidents of mine, both of which were entirely preventable had I, in the first incident remembered the bridge toll collector's warning in time, and in the second, looked up more frequently or better yet never taken my gaze from the road ahead, I would like to add more information about crash helmets. Most of this current news about helmets comes from experienced cyclists who read about my two accidents in the *Bulletin of the League of American Wheelmen* and wrote me about their own head jarring accidents, and of their conversion to and experience with, crash helmets.

I made the round of safety equipment stores and hockey and sporting goods establishments to try out and test whatever I could find by way of helmets that could be used for warm-weather cycling. For cold-weather cycling, any good motorcycle helmet will do, as well as the Trooper cap noted above. But for warm weather you want something with ventilation and no ear flaps. A chin strap is a "must" to keep the hat on your head in a collision.

I now like the Cooper HK 300 hockey helmet, which at this writing sells for around $9.95. It comes in small, medium and large sizes, and though I take a 7⅛ size hat, I found the large size most comfortable. A drawback to this helmet is that it depends on foam padding inside the plastic helmet for protection and this padding is not sweat absorbent. But it is more comfortable than the CCM Model 504325 hockey helmet, which sells at this writing for around $15.00. It's adjustable in four direc-tions and the lining will absorb sweat but it's not a suspension-type lining. Suspension-type helmets I think would be safest, since they use a bridge of nylon webbing at the top of the helmet that keeps the head separated by about an inch from the plastic outer helmet shell, with foam lining on sides. Jockey helmets, worn by professional jockeys and by equestrians in general, have such a suspension system. These are light, and while expensive, are excellent and can be purchased from any riding apparel and equipment shop (look in your Yellow Pages) for about $30.00. The "Caliente" model is excellent and is mandatory at race tracks. Much above 60°F outside though and this helmet gets too warm and you have to switch to one of the hockey helmets. Bell, a well-known California motorcycle helmet maker, reports it has a cycle helmet for pedal shovers, but I haven't been able to get one as yet for test. Clarke Ross, who is a long-time cyclist and Denver bike and ski store proprietor, reports *his* favorite helmet is a Romer Kayak professional helmet, made in Germany and imported by White Water Sports, P.O. Box 9406, Denver, Colorado, 80209. This helmet has a thick nylon shell with a suspension interior. Mr. Ross reports several mountain descent high-speed bike accidents in which cyclists fell hard on their heads, landing in ditches amidst rocks, with the only damage some scratches on the helmet exterior. The Romer sells for around $20.00, is a full suspension job with no rubber padding and so should be cooler than the rubber-padded types.

Nestor Johnson Mfg. Co. makes a Model 704 hockey helmet that has several noteworthy features of interest to bicyclists. The helmet has a nylon strap webbing at the top, which can be adjusted to any head size and which keeps the head about an inch from the outer plastic shell. Between the suspension web and the head there is also a half-inch layer of dense foam. Around the lower periphery of the helmet is an inflatable air chamber, which can be blown up so the helmet fits snugly, and which acts as a shock absorber. A quarter inch of dense foam is on the inner surface of the air cell, between the cell and the head. A heavy ¾-inch dense plastic foam layer is at the back of the helmet. A chin strap holds the helmet on the head. This helmet sells for around $14.00 in sporting goods stores. I have found this helmet to be quite cool and comfortable.

- *Lights are a vital necessity* if you cycle at night, on any road anywhere. Rear lights are especially important, and these should be clearly visible to over-taking traffic from at least three blocks away. A wide choice of lights is available—most of them poor. (For a full discussion of bicycle lights, turn to page 284, in the chapter on accessories.) Just remember that the largest tail-light is the best; it should be visible from the rear and both sides from at least 500 feet away.

  A new French-made light is available, which can be strapped to the left leg, just above the calf, below the knee. It costs about $1.50, is very light-weight, has a white front light and a red rear light, and can also be seen from the side. The up-and-down motion of the leg as you pedal adds two-way visibility to this light for the motorist, and it is an excellent back-up system to your main lights if they should fail.

- *Reflectors* are also a safety back-up to lights. The bigger the reflectors, the better. Use a three-inch-diameter round reflector. Another good reflector is Minnesota Mining's reflective pressure-sensitive tape. Stick strips of this tape on the back of cycling shoes, on fenders, belts, helmet, frame, pedals, and handlebars. You can also add glass-bead type reflectors to pedals, even those with toe clips. These reflectors are highly visible at night as pedals move around the arc, up and down. Glass bead reflectors should also be attached on the rear of the bike, under the saddle or on the rear fender or carrier, and on both sides of the fork (blades).

· *About horns.* A mechanical horn, such as a squeeze-bulb type, takes up too much room for the noise it makes. Tinkle bells are about all you need if you do a lot of sidewalk riding. If you really want noise, try a Freon-powered boat horn, which can be heard for five blocks. When they were new on the market, I bought one and put it in a bottle carrier on my handlebar, where I could get at it quickly. It sounded rather like a diesel freight train coming down the highway. The first time I used it, I was between a squad car and the curb, and it caused the squad car to leap forward with dome light flashing. The second time, I tried it on a woman driver coming at me from an intersection. She came to a satisfying, screaming stop. The third time, I blew it at a driver who opened a car door in front of me, and it frightened him into closing the door rather quickly. By the time he did, I was long past him. But since I find my lung power about as good a horn as I need, I discarded the Freon horn and its pound of gas. In general, it's far better to be alert at all times to what's happening around you and be prepared to take evasive action than it is to count on a horn to get you out of trouble. Freon horns won't work below 45°F.

The miniature Freon-powered horn weighs but a few ounces, comes with a clip for handlebar mounting, and is available in bicycle, sports, and some department stores. When not in use cycling, the horn can be pocketed for emergency signaling. A typical such horn (Fig. 3) costs around $4.50, and gives about 100 blasts from the replaceable aerosol can (at two for $3.50).

· *Cycling in parks.* Cycling at night is usually safe enough if you can be seen, but even lights won't help if you are foolish enough to cycle in city parks at night—especially in big cities like Chicago, New York, or San Francisco.

Fig. 3: This small Freon-powered horn is light, fits on handlebars, and makes a loud blast.

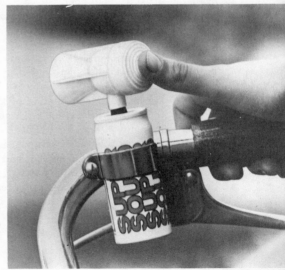

Avoid dark parks, ill-lighted streets, and shore paths where police protection is spotty or nonexistent. On my first trip to Chicago, I was foolish enough to be lured by the summer evening solitude of a lakeshore park area and, in one wooded section, I was confronted by a gang of young hoodlums. Fortunately I had my Freon-powered boat horn with me, so I simply bent over the handlebars to get up speed, and when I was a few feet from them, I sounded the horn. The sudden blast made the kids leap out of the way as though I were firing a machine-gun. I was no more than ten feet away when they realized they had been had, but by that time, I was doing thirty miles an hour.

· *Making turns on a bicycle* is a bit different than in an automobile. If there is traffic around, you should, of course, signal turns. A left turn from a busy street or at a busy intersection can be made in two ways. The safest method is to cross the street to the other side of the intersection, stop and wait for the light to turn, and walk across with pedestrians. This is the way children should be taught to cross. Never attempt to make a left turn from the right curb position; this is as bad as trying to turn left in a car from the right lane of a four-lane highway.

I prefer to make my left turns by moving to the center of the road as I approach the intersection, signaling my intention, and making sure traffic will permit this move. I either make my left turn at once, if coming traffic will permit, or I wait at the intersection until the traffic clears. If the traffic is extremely heavy, I go to the far side of the intersection, wait until traffic clears, and turn left in the pedestrian cross-lane. Again, letting a truck run interference on a left turn is a good protective measure.

· *About clothing.* Clothing worn on any type of bicycle trip should, ideally, be brightly colored. International orange is a good color if it's a bright, clear shade; a light windbreaker of this color is ugly but ideal. You can also buy jackets made of light-reflective or light-phosphorescent safety orange of the color you see on traffic police gloves, school crossing-guide belts, or road-workers' vests. For availability, check with any safety supply store listed in the classified directory of the telephone book. These phosphorescent vests glow when light strikes them, so they are particularly useful at night.

I like the Glo-Jo reflective belt (Fig. 4) which costs only $1.50 and which rolls up to handkerchief size and can be stuffed in a pocket when not in use. If you can't find this belt in your bike shop, write to the Gladd Company, 32 Luvergne Avenue, Minneapolis, Minnesota 55419. For greater reflective protection, the Bicycle Safvest (Fig. 5) has more reflective material than the Glo-Jo, costs around $4.50 for the adult size and $4.00 for the child size, and is made by Safety Flag Company of America, 390 Pine St., Pawtucket, Rhode Island 02862. This vest is of nylon mesh so is suitable for summer. For winter use, a solid Day-Glo fluorescent vest offers excellent daytime protection. Frankly, I would never ride, day or night, without a reflective, highly visible vest of some kind on. The Day-Glo Blaze Orange Vest by Safety Flag costs $4.25.

Fig. 4: This reflective belt is inexpensive, light, rolls up into a pocketable ball, and offers excellent nighttime reflective visibility, and daytime eye-catching safety.

Fig. 5: Safety vest is available in cool mesh for summer, solid for winter, and has nighttime reflectivity and daytime color to attract motorists' attention.

I always wear gloves when cycling. One fall without gloves removed some skin from the palm of my hand and taught me never to go out without gloves of some sort. If your bicycle has tubular tires, you should wear Italian cycling gloves in the summer and ski mittens in the winter. Italian gloves have double thick palms so that you can reach down and brush off any glass or other impedimenta your tires may have picked up. It's a good idea to do this whenever you think you have run over something that could cause a flat. I prefer ski mittens to ski gloves for winter cycling because mittens are much warmer, yet not too bulky for gripping brake levers.

WINTER CYCLING COMFORT

The only mystery to winter cycling that appears to puzzle noncyclists is how to keep warm. I do a lot of riding in all weather, and as the temperature drops I pile on more clothes, starting with thermal underwear.

Cold feet in particular seem to plague most cyclists in cold weather, which is natural, considering the distance blood has to travel to keep these extremities warm. For the cyclist, around 38°F seems to be the cut-off point, below which feet are prone to painful, or at least irritating, cold. I have tried electric socks and find them workable but not worth the expense and bother of battery replacement, plus the weight of the battery. The best solution I have found for cold feet is a pair of thermal "sub-zero" ski socks, 60 percent wool, 20 percent nylon. The "Kitzbuhel" Wigwam brand I found for $3.50 a pair in a large Chicago Loop department store work very well for me. On the bottom of the sock it says "Designed for plastic boots." These are thick socks, so you'll need shoes at least a size larger to accommodate them. If you find the ball of your foot isn't just where you want it with the longer shoe, shim out the toe clip about ⅛ inch.

The ideal shoes for winter cycling, of course, would be the weatherproof and fleece-lined short boots, made with reinforced inner soles for cycling. Conventional summer cycling shoes are made this way, with four-point steel shank supports to minimize foot fatigue over long distances. I have not been able to locate a winter cycling shoe in the United States, but after a good deal of searching and correspondence with European sources, I finally found one.

The winter cycling boot I like is a short boot, chukka style, completely fleece lined, including the inner sole and uppers. The entire shoe is waterproofed, has a medium heel, and is cut and styled to permit free ankle movement. This little boot costs, with duty and postage, about $18.00—

a reasonable price for warm feet in cold-weather cycling, in my opinion. These shoes can be obtained from W. F. Holdsworth, Ltd., 132 Lower Richmond Road, Putney, S.W. 15, England.

For the hands, double-palmed ski mittens are about as warm as electrically heated gloves. The rest of a good winter cycling outfit consists of Italian-made wool shorts with chamois lining in the crotch, overlaid with thermal underwear, followed by a cotton track suit. A sweater or two and a leather jacket, a hard helmet with earflaps or a knit cap with ear muffs, and a scarf complete the outfit. When it gets down to −10°F, I substitute down-filled pants for the cotton track suit. They're a bit bulky, and you may have to lower the saddle about ¼ inch to compensate, but you'll never get cold. But it *is* fun to cycle around in −30° MET (mean effective temperature, an index reading of wind velocity, air temperature, and relative humidity) in perfect comfort, to the consternation of shivering pedestrians, and heart-attack-prone physically soft motorists.

When it gets down to 30°F, I like a down-filled short jacket, such as the "Comfy Game Coat," which sells for around $70.00. This is a particular favorite of mine, because it comes in two pieces, an inner down-filled jacket of water-repellent nylon, and an outer shell of water-repellent 50 percent polyester and 50 percent cotton which acts as an excellent windbreaker and has roomy pockets. Either can be worn alone, so if it warms up, or you warm up, you can shed either for comfort. Comfy is a division of Olin Manufacturing Company, located at 310 1st Avenue, Seattle, Washington 98104. Another excellent down-filled jacket I have used is sold by L. L. Bean (see Appendix for address) called a "Jac-Shirt," which sells for around $33.00, weighs only fifteen ounces, and can be folded compactly into its own inside pocket. It has a zipper front, insulated collar, and two hand pockets. The bright orange color is most visible.

What about snow? You can ride in snow if you're careful. For winter snow cycling I use 27-inch x 1¼-inch tires rather than thinner tubulars. The thicker and wider tread gives a bit more road-holding stability. Of course, this means a complete change of wheels, because tubulars and clincher tires are not interchangeable on the same rim.

Do not ride on light snow with ice underneath, or on ice-covered streets. You can ride in snow until it gets up to about two inches deep, after which the going gets a bit rough. The roads are usually plowed soon after most snowfalls, so if you get up early enough in the morning, you can ride down the center of the road until traffic becomes heavy.

A TRIKE FOR WINTER CYCLING

An adult tricycle can take much of the skid hazard out of winter cycling; in fact, it can make slippery street cycling an enjoyable and challenging experience. We discuss adult tricycles in more detail on pages 134–138.

However, I would like to cover some of the safety aspects of tricycles. First, brakes are often inadequate, because U.S.-made adult trikes are heavy and awkward, and on a downhill run can be hard to stop, as I found out when I had to jump a curb and stop in a beckoning clump of bushes. No harm done, but I put dual caliper brakes on the front wheel right away. Also, the U.S. heavy trikes in some cases develop a dangerous front end wobble or shimmy and are hard to steer accurately. I by far prefer the trike I made from an old but still good lightweight bike and an adapter kit (Fig. 56, page 136) made in England and supplied by Holdsworth (see page 497 in Appendix for address), for around $65.00. It comes with hubs only, so you will have to lace the rims on yourself, or have it done. I should also note that a tricycle ride is much softer than a two-wheeler because there's an extra wheel to absorb road shock.

A word about riding a trike safely. When an adult cyclist tries to ride a tricycle for the first time, the result is usually quite ludicrous and can be dangerous. This is because the experienced cyclist leans *into* the direction of turn, and if the trike seems to be going the wrong way he leans the other way and expects the trike to turn like a good little bicycle should. But compensating for oversteering by leaning away from the direction of turn on a trike simply makes it turn the wrong way faster. Adding to the problem is that the cyclist thinks he's on a two-wheeler, and is afraid to *wrest* the handlebars where he wants to go because his experience is that if he does that the bicycle will fall over. But a trike is more like a car than a bicycle in its handling characteristics, and steering is largely a matter of turning the handlebar where you want to go and forgetting about falling over. However, since the outer wheel tends to rise off the ground and unbalance the trike on a turn, you should always lean slightly *away* from the direction of turn to make the trike turn accurately, which is exactly opposite to what you should do on a bicycle. One other safety hint for riding a trike: When you first start out as a novice tricyclist, go very slowly at first. Beware of cycling on a right angle to an incline, such as when you're riding on a sidewalk and come to a driveway. An incline to right (or left) tends to make the trike turn in the direction of incline, and you could (as I did) wind up in the street in the middle of busy traffic. Just don't *let* the thing turn!

RIDING IN THE RAIN

Riding in the rain can be fun if you're equipped for it. When I think it's going to rain, I take along a light rain outfit, cape, or poncho.

Cycling in the rain is safe enough if you don't try to take corners too fast. Pavements are especially slippery when the rain has just begun to fall. In the autumn, when leaves begin to drop, remember that the only thing slicker than wet leaves is wet ice. You can take a rather nasty spill if you try to cut around a corner fast and run into a patch of wet leaves.

Remember, too, that you are going to be less visible to motorists when it's raining or snowing. Therefore, you should be doubly careful to stay away from high-traffic streets and roads, to listen for oncoming traffic, and to be alert at all times.

In summer, fall, and spring, wet-weather cycling does require that you have some sort of waterproof clothing, because at 10 or 15 mph quite a breeze blows over you. This amount of air can, by evaporative cooling effect, chill you down quite a bit, even excluding the heat transfer effect from your skin to the colder rain water itself. It takes some time for rain to soak clothing, but when it does you can get quite cold, even in the summer. Plastic rain capes that cover the handlebars are a bare minimum of protection, but they are cheap and can be rolled up compactly. I find them a bother because they flop around and get quite sticky and clammy underneath as skin moisture condenses on the inside of the cape. Condensation is unavoidable with any rain garment that's water*proof,* since if it keeps rain from your skin, it also keeps moisture from your body from evaporating. One excellent jacket designed for the cyclist and which is water*proof* (not just water *resistant*) is Schwinn's Tuff-N-Dry jacket, (Fig. 6) which has "breather" vents under the arms to let at least some of the condensation out. This jacket tucks up into a small round ball into its own pocket when not in use. Best of all, perhaps, it has a hood which tucks up into its own collar, and has reflectorized racing-style safety strips front and rear. The bright orange color is most visible. This jacket sells for $17.95 at the Schwinn dealer. With matching waterproof nylon pants, $24.95. These are 1973 prices and may rise.

An inexpensive pair of light blue or yellow sunglasses will keep rain

Fig. 6: This light waterproof nylon jacket has pants that roll up into the jacket, so jacket can be used alone as a windbreaker. Available at Schwinn stores.

out of your eyes, if you don't wear glasses. I prefer light yellow glasses; they make dark days look a lot cheerier.

Last, and perhaps most vital to your safety, remember that bicycle caliper brakes, like auto brakes, do not stop you as well when they're wet, especially if they are out of adjustment in the first place. Brake shoes should grab both sides of the rim evenly (see page 380 for details on brake maintenance and adjustment). In wet weather, begin your stop sooner than normal, and bike more defensively and carefully so as to avoid the necessity for panic stops. Whenever I hear of a cyclist who tells me (usually from his hospital bed) that he fell off his bike while avoiding a motorist, I always ask myself what he was doing that he had to avoid the car so suddenly in the first place. There are bad drivers, hazardous to cyclists, true, but that's the greater reason for extreme caution on the part of cyclists at all times.

REAR-VIEW MIRRORS

A *rear-view mirror* can be almost worthless or a lifesaver, depending on what kind you use. The type that mounts on the handlebars is no good, in my opinion, first, because the bike bounces so much it's hard to use the mirror, and second, you have to look down and to the left to see out of it, thereby removing your eyes from what's ahead for a few seconds, a dangerous lapse of cycling vigilance during which you could hit a car. The best rear-view mirror is one that mounts on the ear piece of your eyeglasses (Fig. 7). As with bifocal lenses, the eyeglass-mounted mirror takes a bit of getting used to, but once you have, you'll find it indispensable to country or city riding. I have been using this type of mirror for two years, and find now that I can no more cycle without it than I can drive without a rear-view mirror on my car. Mounted on the eyeglass ear piece, it takes but a momentary flick of the eye to check the entire road behind for oncoming traffic, without having to bend or move your head

Fig. 7: A tiny rear-view mirror that clips onto your eyeglasses or cap visor can be a lifesaver because you can tell what's coming up from behind without having to look around over your shoulder. Versions are made for thin temple glasses, wire frames, and cap visors. About $3.50. Order from Ultra-Light Shop, Box 308, Brinkhaven, Ohio 43006.

more than a degree or two, if that. In the country, especially when careening down steep, curving hills at high speed, you can *only* tell what's coming behind with this type of mirror, because at 45 to 50 mph downhill you can't risk unbalancing yourself by looking around over your left shoulder far enough to see behind. Yet it's very comforting to know that you can hold to the middle of the road at high speed, so you have plenty of room to manoeuvre if anything, such as a blow-out, should go wrong with the bike. I really do urge you to equip yourself with this little gem of a mirror, which is made to fit metal frames, wide-temple glasses, or to clip on the visor of a cap (tell which one you want). The mirror costs about $3.50 and can be ordered from the Ultra-Light Shop, Box 308, Brinkhaven, Ohio, 43006. It is *not* a gimmicked-up dentist's mirror, but is made by an experienced cyclist and maintenance genius, Chuck Harris, for cyclists, out of one-piece aluminum and high-quality mirror. In city cycling it's wise to know what's behind, so you always know whether or not you can swerve out into traffic to avoid a car door being opened in your face by a thoughtless motorist, or to avoid a child, dog, or pedestrian. Or a human being. It's usually quicker to swerve than to try to stop, if you can swerve safely.

WATCH OUT FOR STORM SEWERS

Storm sewers with grated street covers are a little-recognized but very real hazard in city cycling, particularly in suburbs. Many makes of these drains are designed with sufficient width between the grating members to permit a bicycle wheel to drop down between them (Fig. 8). Some of these gratings are round, and it would be a simple matter to have them all turned with the grating perpendicular to the curb. This danger should be pointed out to the city street and road commissioner, or a similar official.

If the grating is not round or square, and the openings are parallel to the curb, the best thing to do is to inform the police or fire department, or whichever local agency issues bicycle permits, so those who apply for bicycle licenses can be warned about the danger. A cyclist going at fifteen or twenty miles an hour can be seriously injured if his front wheel drops into a storm-sewer grating.

Fig. 8: This is how you can get hurt on the grated storm sewer covers found in many cities in the United States. If you or your children should happen to run into such a storm sewer grating, be sure to get the name of the grating manufacturer for use by your attorney. Many large bridges have similar hazards in the form of an expansion joint, that is, the point at which road meets bridge.

BRIDGE EXPANSION JOINT HAZARDS

I found myself in a predicament similar to the sewer-grating situation on my first trip over the bridge between Detroit and Windsor, Canada. I didn't notice it going over, because I had a bad head wind and was going fairly slow. But on the way back, with a strong tail wind, a steep hill, and the bridge arched down to meet the land, I barely had time to swing my wheel to the slight angle needed to avoid dropping the wheel between the bars of a grated expansion joint, where two sections of the bridge meet. Afterward, Gene Portuesi, former Olympic team cycling coach, told me that on the day the bridge opened many years ago, unsuspecting cyclists were thrown and hurt when they passed over this grating at high speed.

So, watch out for expansion joints on bridges, especially suspension bridges over wide rivers. *These joints usually run the entire width of the bridge.*

COUNTRY RIDING

Never, but never, ride on freeways, toll roads, or major arterial highways. I know there are a number of touring cyclists who argue that it is perfectly safe to cycle on interstate highways because the shoulder is broad enough to keep them away from the main traffic stream. No doubt this is true—the shoulder is wide enough, and it is paved. The trouble is that should an accident occur anywhere near you at the seventy-mile-an-hour-plus speeds common to interstate routes, you could be involved. At those speeds, it would take only a passing brush by a motor vehicle to send you spinning off into the wild blue yonder. Also, highway shoulders are frequently littered with broken glass and other hazardous material.

There are other tips on country cycling in the chapter on touring (pages 195, 204, 207). Here, let me just say that you should plan your route using roads parallel to main routes. You will be amazed at how well paved many of the less-used back-country roads are, and these roads have little traffic and almost all the beauty. In general, avoid any road bearing a state or federal route number. Many states have cross-state bicycle routes, which are simply hand-picked, well-paved roads bearing little motor traffic. (See Chapter 7.)

If you have to ride on dirt roads, be very careful about cornering on sandy or pebbly surfaces, watch out for potholes that can send you sprawling and bend a wheel, and keep your eyes and ears open for oncoming traffic.

Country riding does have one special hazard: people who habitually drive on back-country roads are almost never alert for cyclists, or, for that matter, for any other traffic. Consider the sight of a silo or a barn to be a danger signal, and be alert for a truck or tractor to come right out on the highway from a hidden intersection, without regard for oncoming traffic, including cyclists. Farmers seem to regard the roads in front of their homes as their personal driveways, and they are prone to drive in and out of their property as though no other traffic exists.

On any country road, whether paved or not, keep your ears open for traffic coming in either direction. It's quiet in the country, and you can hear motor vehicles coming from at least a mile away. And on dusty dirt roads, you can often see as well as hear evidence of approaching traffic. Rural drivers may be on any part of the road as they approach you, so if you have just rounded a corner and you hear a car coming up fast behind you, either stay on the far right side of the road or ride well to the left, on the shoulder, to let the car by. If you're cresting a hill, keep alert to traffic behind you. After you pass the crest, if there is no oncoming traffic, cross to the left side of the road for a block or so, so upcoming cars won't zoom over the hill into you, since your presence cannot be observed below the crest.

Rural Intersections

Where two rural roads meet, any stop signs generally are not observed, so be prepared to stop as you approach intersections. Be aware, at all times, of the surrounding territory so that you will know the best place to go to steer yourself out of trouble.

For example, if as you approached an intersection a car suddenly shot out at you from the right, where could you go? There's usually a ditch at these intersections, with little or no shoulder. Or, if there is no other traffic, you could cross the lane or even make a 180-degree turn.

If you're with a group of cyclists, it's wise to have an experienced rider at both ends of the line. The rear cyclist can listen for and size up potential hazards from oncoming traffic, and the lead rider can analyze the situation from up front, such as intersections, approaching traffic, curves, and hills.

If you're cycling in mountainous terrain, or plan such a trip, double check the maintenance of brakes beginning on page 380. Be sure your brake cables are in good shape, brake blocks are fresh and new, and brakes properly adjusted, with levers where you can grab them quickly.

RADIOS NOT RECOMMENDED

Because ears as well as eyes must be used in any type of cycling, I definitely do not recommend listening to a radio while cycling. I have seen cyclists pedaling along with a tiny earpiece plugged into one ear, completely oblivious to the sound of traffic around them. A radio takes away from cycling enjoyment, in any case. In the country especially, how can one possibly enjoy the sound of the wind and the birds, or simply the wonderful silence, when a radio is on?

SAFETY TIPS FOR YOUNGSTERS

The following tips could save your child from serious injury or worse. Insist that he or she learn these rules and observe them without exception:

- Ride only on streets where cycling is permitted, never on streets where signs say cycling is not allowed.
- Never ride on a street unless there are parked cars in evidence, and then watch out for car doors opening in front of you.
- Never ride at night without a good headlight and a good taillight. The rear light should be visible to motorists from two to three blocks away. Your bicycle should also be equipped with a two-to-three-inch-diameter reflector.
- Brakes should always be in good working condition.
- Always signal your turns. Left arm straight out with index finger straight out means left turn; left arm straight up means right turn.
- At street intersections, give everyone the right of way, including cars, trucks, buses, and people.
- Never turn left, while mounted, at a *busy* intersection, or at one where there is a stoplight. *Always* dismount, walk to the far side of the street, across the intersection, wait till the light turns, and *walk* your bicycle across in the pedestrian lane.
- Obey all stoplights, stop signs, and other road signs, just as though you were driving a car.
- *Never* try to hitch a ride by holding onto a truck. You never know which way the truck will turn or how suddenly it will stop. Trucks often have air brakes that enable them to stop so fast that you would not be able to hold on. If the truck stops that quickly, there is probably an emergency reason which would also apply to you. The truck driver may not realize you are hanging on, and brush you against an object such as a parked car.
- Never ride two on a bicycle unless you have a tandem. Riding two on a bicycle built for one makes it hard to see where you are going, hard to stop, and easy to spill.
- Always go *with* the traffic, not against it. When you ride along with the traffic, you give the drivers of cars behind you a better chance to steer out of your way, and they're more likely to see you than if you unexpectedly appear in front of them going the wrong way.
- Steer straight; don't weave all over the street; stay close to parked cars at all times.
- *Don't fool around on a bicycle.* Many boys and girls think it's fun to rear the bicycle back on the rear wheel and go off down the street with the front wheel off the ground. Fun and games and trick riding on a bicycle can be

dangerous if you are thrown off balance into the path of a car, or if you fall and strike your head on a concrete curb. You can have fun on small-wheeled bicycles, because they're so manoeuverable, but I would advise playing bike polo or bike hockey only on a school parking lot.

ABOUT DOGS AND OTHER ANIMALS

A dog may be man's best friend when both are afoot, but there's something about a man on a bicycle that brings out the worst in a dog. For years I have been wondering what it is about a man on a bicycle that turns friendly dogs into snarling beasts. Perhaps the bicycle emits some infuriatingly high-pitched sound that only a dog can hear. Or it may simply occur to the dog that he has a human being at a disadvantage.

Whatever the reason, you should always be on the alert for an attack by a dog of any size, shape, and description, at any time, in any place. I find myself reacting instantly to the tinkle of a dog collar and watching shrubbery and front yards in the suburbs and farm yards. All dogs are potential enemies. In the country, you can usually outrun a dog, which is the best advice I can give you, if this is possible. But if the dog comes at you from the front, or cheats by cutting across a yard as you round a corner, you might be in for a bad bite.

The dog problem is a serious one for cyclists, and it occupies a lot of space in bicycling magazines published in both this country and abroad. Reviewing the experience of a number of cyclists, the best defense, if you are not able to get away, seems to be a slender whip fastened to the handlebar stem, somewhat like an old-fashioned buggy whip. A cyclist can have it in his hand in an instant. One quick blow across a dog's nose will make even the most vicious animal think twice about further pursuit.

Other types of protection I have seen used include a standard bike water bottle filled with liquid household ammonia and equipped with a spray nozzle from an old bottle of window cleaner; a standard oil spray can, clip mounted to the stem and filled with ammonia; a starter's blank pistol, which seems to scare dogs away; and a "Hot Shot" dog-trainer prod, something like a cattle prod, which gives a harmless but painful electrical shock of high voltage but almost zero amperage. The "Hot Shot" (Fig. 9) is 36 inches long, has a tip the entire head of which shocks, weighs 24 ounces and is also available in 24-inch and 48-inch long models. The 24-inch model, at $15.65, is more easily carried in a clip on the top tube

Fig. 9: "Hot Shot" cattle prod is good for protection against dogs. The twenty-four-inch model is more practical for bicyclists.

(which you'll have to make out of old bike clips). The "Hot Shot" is made by Hot-Shot Products Co., Inc., 440 W. Nixon St., Savage, Minnesota 55378.

You can also buy a small aerosol spray can of "dog repellent" for about $2.50 from most hardware stores, which can shoot a thin stream of chemical about ten feet. The active ingredient in the spray is Oleoresin Capsicum, a pepper derivative. The trouble with this protection is that by the time you fish the can out of your pocket, aim it, and press the button, you could already be bitten. However, if you have time to stop, and the dog is close enough, the spray will discourage him from any further interest in you. Incidentally although the effects are potent, there is no permanent damage done to the animal. The Capsicum is called "Halt" and if you can't find it, you can order cans by mail from the manufacturer, Animal Repellents, Inc., P. O. Box 168, Griffin, Georgia 30220, for $2.50 per can plus 15¢ for shipping. Be sure to ask for the plastic clip so you can fasten this little aerosol can to your stem or fork stay.

A word of caution about using "Halt." Do not use this spray if you are cycling into the wind and another cyclist is behind you. On one trip I was on a cyclist did just that, and sprayed into a 20-mph headwind, missed the dog completely, but succeeded in having the wind whip the spray up and deflect it right into the eyes of a girl cyclist behind him. It took three full water bottles to wash out her eyes, and a lot of love to get that girl back on her bike.

Sometimes, with smaller dogs, you can intimidate them by growling at them viciously as you approach them, even swerving your bike right at them. I have had some dogs turn tail and run in front of me in fright. Finally, after a few blocks, they collapsed in fear in the gutter. But don't try this on a German shepherd police dog, or a Weimaraner. I sprayed a German shepherd with "Halt" once, and I think he laughed and swallowed the spray like a child gulping down a piece of candy; if I'd thrown the can at him he'd have eaten it, "Halt" and all, for dessert. Perhaps the worst thing about dogs, other than the fact that their bite can put you in the hospital, is their tendency to throw themselves at, or under, the front wheel of a bicycle. Even very small dogs try to bite the front wheel, and have caused a cyclist to run into the dog, lose control and crash. A number of cyclists have been killed this way. Some ardent cyclist dog haters carry a starter's pistol loaded with 22-caliber blanks and report the loud discharge scares dogs away; frankly, I'd rather rely on more positive measures and not risk a bite for a bang.

Don't Use Weapon

Other cyclists I know have come so close to serious injury because of dogs, especially in the country, that they are seriously thinking of carrying a small 22-caliber pistol, or a CO_2 pellet gun. I strongly advise against taking these steps, first, because in most states they're illegal to carry as a concealed weapon without a license; second, the dog owner may fire back if he hears or sees you; third, it's extremely difficult to aim accurately from a moving bicycle and you may hit a fellow cyclist. You can make an effective defense out of a 30-inch piece of electric conduit, or a section of an old metal fly rod. But I still think "Halt," as its big brother "Stinger," is a good defense, and won't do permanent damage to the dog. Both sprays are essentially the same, except "Halt" sprays for about eight feet in still air and costs about $2.50; "Stinger" sprays about fifteen feet in still air, costs about $6.50 from sporting goods stores, holds about twice as much as "Halt," and is made by Penguin Industries, Parkesburg, Pennsylvania 19365.

A problem to be aware of with dogs is that they tend to attack the first cyclist that passes by. If this cyclist is at the head of a family group, or a stream of ten or more cyclists, chances are good that the dog, concentrating on the first cyclist, will get in the way of following cyclists and cause a domino-type accident, with cyclists crashing into one another. I have even had two dogs chase a lead cyclist and almost cause a crash as following cyclists tried to get out of their way. As a leader, you can stop, dismount, and keep the dog interested in you until your group is safely out of range. The dog, however, will attack you the second you sling one foot over the top tube. So it's best, in this situation, to get the dog close enough to spray him with "Halt" and *then* jump on your bike and get underway fast.

The old adage that barking dogs don't bite cannot be trusted, I have found, but be doubly suspicious of the dog that comes up to you silently and stands there looking at you. He's just waiting for you to get back on the bicycle so he can get you at a disadvantage. A friend of mine who is an experienced cyclist spent two months in the hospital because of just such an incident. One evening she was cycling alone about thirty miles from home. A snarling dog chased her down a dead-end street, where she dismounted. The owner of the dog was in his yard nearby, but made no move to call the animal back. The dog waited until my friend had climbed back on the bicycle and, as she was mounting sank his teeth in her calf, penetrating all the way to the bone, through heavy jeans. Not realizing how serious the bite was, my friend rode home and attempted to treat it herself. By the time she got to her doctor, the wound was so badly infected that she not only had to be hospitalized for two months, but she has suffered minor but permanent impairment of leg movement, which affects her riding ability.

My heart goes out to children who are chased by dogs and badly frightened—or bitten. Most cities do not permit dogs to be at large anymore; they have to be either tied up or penned in the yard. In the country, of course, farm dogs are seldom tied and are almost always ready and willing to attack the passing cyclist.

What to Do If Bitten

To avoid a painful series of rabies inoculations, if you are bitten, remember to try to find out who owns the offending animal. Your child should be instructed to do the same thing if he is bitten. A dog will usually run home after an assault, and if you can manage it, and there is no one in the immediate vicinity who can tell you who owns the animal, try to follow it home. You can then warn the owner to keep the dog locked up for the period of time recommended by your doctor. If at the end of that time the dog has not developed rabies, you or your child will not need rabies shots.

If you are in the country and are bitten, and you cannot follow the animal to its home, try to memorize what he looks like: his size, shape, markings, and general appearance. A neighbor in the vicinity may recognize your description and help you locate the dog and avoid rabies inoculations.

In any case, if you are bitten by a dog, *always* get immediate treatment as soon as possible from a doctor. Then call the dog warden and your lawyer, in that order. You have all the legal redress in the world, because people should keep a dog that will attack a cyclist under restraint. Even if you yourself aren't bitten, you will be doing a favor to the rest of the cycling fraternity if you take note of the address where the chase began as the probable home of the animal, and call the dog warden as soon as you get home. I think dogs attack out of a sense of duty, feeling that the territory around their house is their exclusive property.

Other animals sometimes bite, too, though more rarely than dogs. Squirrels, woodchucks, and raccoons, if they think they are cornered. or are crazed by rabies, will bite. If you're bitten, it's important to capture the animal, if at all possible, so it can be held for observation to see if it develops rabies. Don't kill it, because rabies may be in the undetectable stage. The World Health Organization states that if you're bitten by an animal that *cannot* be held for observation for rabies development, you *must* undergo rabies inoculations, which is an ordeal.

If you camp out on a bicycle tour, observe all the usual precautions about snakes and other animals. Keep a simple first-aid kit with you. If you fall, clean your scratches and cuts with tap water from a canteen or flask, and apply antiseptic ointment. Then bandage lightly. If the cut did not cause a lot of bleeding or sever a muscle, there's no need to end the trip or wait for the wound to heal. If you want to cycle-tour, you'll have to get used to a few bumps and bruises and take them in stride.

CARRYING A CHILD SAFELY

There are a number of good seats especially designed to permit you to carry a small child on a bicycle, as long as he can sit up. Be sure to use a seat that is fitted with side rails and a restraining strap. (See page 302 in the chapter on accessories for full details on child seats.)

A word of caution: I do not recommend a child-carrier seat that fastens to the handlebars. The weight of a child on the handlebars creates a dangerously unbalanced bicycle and makes accurate steering practically impossible. In the event of an accident, the child has no protection. When the child is in a rear-wheel carrier, you are between him and any object ahead.

What I have noted about carrying a child also applies to packages. Use baskets or panniers to lug groceries or carry gear on a trip. If you must carry more than will fit into your carriers, be sure to use a bag especially designed to fit handlebars, with a front spring-clip carrier to support its weight, or a bag designed for use without a carrier. (See page 208).

A fairly recent development which I feel adds considerably to bike child-carrying safety is a trailer which hitches onto the back of a bicycle and which can be fitted with a molded plastic seat (Fig. 10) with room

Fig. 10: Bike trailer doubles as child carrier with built-in safety belt. Plastic seat is removable so carrier can be used for shopping, camping, or utility hauling such as newspaper delivery. Available from bicycle stores.

for two or three toddlers. A safety strap holds the children in place. The trailer, with seat removed, can be used for shopping or camping. It hitches onto the seat post and can be quickly attached and removed. The trailer adds stability; but its main advantage is that children can be towed safely behind the bicycle, rather than balanced precariously on the bike itself. The trailer alone, with zippered nylon bag (for groceries, etc.) that closes against the weather, costs around $49.95 (less the bag, about $39.95), and the child-carrying seat costs another $20.00 or so. The seat can be added to the trailer with the zippered nylon bag in place. Both are made by Cannondale Corporation, 35 Pulaski Street, Stamford, Connecticut 06902.

GENERAL SAFETY TIPS

During the time since this book first appeared, I have bicycled extensively in this country and in Europe, and have picked up a number of experiences and ideas which can be vital, I believe, to your safety and comfort.

· *Downhill cycling* can bring you to speeds as high as 50 or 55 mph. If the phenomenon known as front wheel "wobble" or "shimmy" occurs, with amplitude and frequency of the swings increasing every second, you can easily lose control of the bike and crash into a tree, a car, or fall over and hit the pavement. For the reasons noted below, the wobble shakes the handlebars almost uncontrollably. You should know how to hold the handlebars so the wheel can't wobble. On high-speed downhill runs, hold the handlebars just *below* the brake levers, with the inside of the forearm, just above or at the wrist (your hands firm but relaxed), firmly against the *rear* of the handlebars at the point where the bars begin to curve downward (above brake levers), as in Fig. 11. In this safety position, both the side of the arms and the hands are holding the handlebars firmly. I can tell you from experience how horrifying it is to have this happen. I was going down a fairly steep hill in the Greinalp section of Austria, at about 50 mph, when my front wheel suddenly began shimmying. To my right was a straight unguarded drop-off of about 2,000 feet; to my left a dense forest of unfriendly hard trees behind a ditch; to my rear thirty-nine other cyclists careening downhill equally as fast; and ahead a heavily laden oncoming truck. I consider myself very fortunate in having been able to react fast enough, at about the third widening shimmy, to be able to stop. My initial tendency, about a microsecond long, was to fight the shimmy and keep on, which in the experience of others would have caused me to crash, and not unlikely to the right where the lake at the bottom of the 2,000-foot drop would have

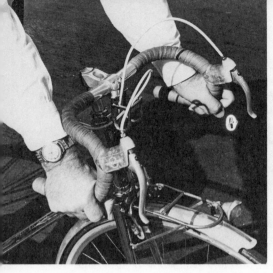

Fig. 11: This grip, in my opinion, is safest for downhill high-speed cycling, at speeds where front wheel shimmy can develop which could cause you to crash. Grip handlebars firmly, but where you can quickly reach brake levers. Inside of wrists should be locked against handlebars, as shown, for added firmness of grip. (*Photo courtesy Dr. Clifford Graves, La Jolla, California*)

been cold comfort as a shock absorber. (Water, as any boy knows who has jumped off a high diving board feet first, is for all practical purposes fairly incompressible.)

What causes high-speed wobble or shimmy? A number of things contribute. A tubular tire glued on crooked; spokes too tight on one side and too loose on the other (as when you try to correct for a rim flat spot); a bent fork (which in my case baggage "smashers" at the airlines were responsible for); a loose headset cone; unbalanced panniers front or rear; possibly even a loose front-wheel hub cone. As noted, my shimmy was due to a bent fork blade. You can avoid bent forks and stays by blocking them with wood or with a dummy axle bolted on both sides of dropouts when shipping via airline or railroad.

· *Brakes Get Hot.* In downhill high-speed riding, brakes have to be used at curves, or to prevent hitting a slower cyclist or car ahead, or simply to slow up. When brakes are constantly applied, friction between brake shoes and rim can heat the rim to the point where the glue that holds tubular tires on the rim can be melted soft and so cause the tire to slide off. In the case of clincher wired-on tires, the rim can get hot enough to cause air in the tube to expand and blow the tube out. (I have had both tubular and clincher tires startlingly blow out on me when the bike was standing still. When exposed to hot summer noontime sun on a hot sidewalk, air in the tire heated and expanded.)

To prevent rim heat build-up on downhill runs, brake with rear and front brakes alternately and lightly; try to keep speed under control so you don't have to brake hard. Sometimes, if the tire doesn't come off the rim entirely (if you're lucky), the tire will simply slide around the rim, so the valve is ripped loose and you get a flat, slowly sometimes, and a blow-out at other times. Always be prepared for a blow-out downhill in any case. You never know what your tire picked up earlier that can cause a blow-out at high speed, which is another good reason for holding onto handlebars with your hands as described above.

· *Toe clips,* which are discussed elsewhere, are also a safety aid because they keep feet from slipping off pedals. A number of accidents are on record which have been caused by the rider's foot slipping off pedals in traffic, causing the cyclist to lose control and steer into traffic; or by a foot slipping on a hill climb so steering control is lost and the bike falls over or hits the curb or an oncoming or passing car; or, when feet slip, the cyclist can be injured by falling on the top tube (a male cyclist, anyway).

While on the subject of tires, if you have tightened a spoke, always make sure the sharp spoke head hasn't been poked up past the nipple where it can eventually puncture the tube on clincher rims.

· *Cycling in a high wind* can be as dangerous as sailing in one. I distinctly recall one frightening ride from my office in Chicago's Loop to my suburban Evanston home twelve miles distant during a windstorm of hurricane proportions (the ESSA weather bureau clocked winds gusting to 65 mph that day). I was riding on Clark Street, a fairly wide two-lane major city street during the rush hour. The first thing I noticed were pieces of debris, such as plywood sheets from building sites, pieces of paper, and whatnot flying through the air, which fortunately missed me. Then I began to be blown over to one side so I was leaning about fifteen degrees to the right just to be able to keep going forward in a straight line. Then, suddenly, the pressure would ease and I had to lean the other way fast to keep from falling to the right. Then the wind would shift and I would have to lean the other way. I quickly discovered that while the wind may be directionally steady (if gusty) on the open plains, ocean or lake, when large buildings are in the way, wind direction can change unpredictably; such are the dynamics of air flow. So if you *must* ride in a high wind in the city, be prepared for violent and sudden changes in wind direction and velocity so you aren't propelled all over the street, as I was for the first six blocks. Remember, when cycling in a high wind, to watch the road ahead of you for blowing leaves or pieces of paper, which will tell you in advance where the wind is coming from, so you can take action if necessary, such as bracing yourself or gearing down. When the wind is gusting much above 40 mph, I strongly suggest that you not try to buck the wind, particularly a shifting wind, without gearing down to at least two or three gears below your normal riding gear. I have, at times, been bowled along at a great clip, practically sailing, with the wind at my back, but within seconds the wind would shift so that it was coming from the front or from the side. When the wind was coming from the side or from a seventy-five-degree angle, I had to gear down in order to control the bike properly. The danger, if you are in traffic and the wind is gusting, is that you might be tossed into the stream of traffic, which is definitely an unhealthy situation.

· *Stem and seat post* must be in their respective tubes far enough so you can't break them off. If you will remove your handlebars you'll notice that the stem skirt is split, so that a wedge or beveled cone-shaped nut can hold the stem tightly in place against the surrounding steering head metal by expanding the skirt. Handlebar stem must always be far enough inside the head tube so that the split section is *at least 2 inches below the top of the head tube* (Fig. 12). Otherwise, if the skirt split shows, it's easy to break off the stem where the stem is weakest, at the split. Same applies to the seat post, which, while not split, must have *at least* 2½ inches of seat post metal *inside* the seat tube (Fig. 13). If you have to raise the saddle any higher than that, you need a bigger frame bike or, at the very least, a longer seat post (which you can buy from your bike shop). For the beginning or the occasional rider if you can't raise the handlebars to about the level of the saddle without exposing the stem skirt split, you definitely need a larger frame (see page 144 for discussion of frame size selection). Remember that if the split shows, handlebar stems can break while you're straining uphill, which can be dangerous since you immediately lose all steering control except what you can get (if you're lucky) by leaning to one side or the other. Brakes don't work very well either when handlebars are dangling loose in your hands.

CYCLING SAFETY—BEHIND THE NUMBERS

Cyclists are becoming safer pedalers, if figures don't lie. Data from the National Safety Council for 1964 and projected figures for 1972 show that total bicycle-related fatalities rose 55 percent, whereas total bicycle sales rose 118 percent and total number of bicycles in use (more or less) rose

Fig. 12: To prevent handlebar stem from breaking under stress, always have two inches of the stem above the split skirt, as shown below, inside the head tube below the head set locknut.

Fig. 13: You must have at least 2½ inches of the seat post inside the seat tube, as shown below, to prevent the seat post from breaking under stress.

TABLE 1: It's obvious that most of the percentage increases in bicycle-related fatalities was in the 15-to-24-year-old group. Their quicker reaction time alone was not enough to save them; perhaps judgement was a factor in this increase.

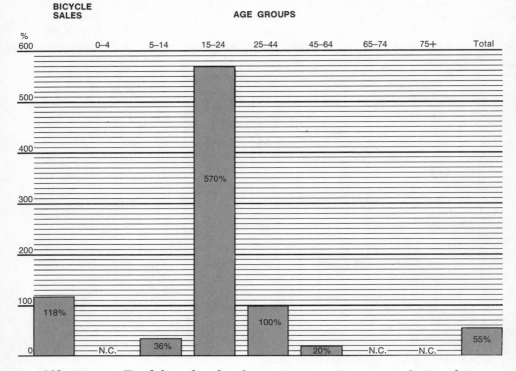

BICYCLE
SALES   AGE GROUPS

139 percent. Total bicycle-related injuries rose 41 percent during this period.

However, *total* increases by age group point up some interesting relationships. Table 1 shows that most of the increase in fatalities, a whopping 570 percent, were in the 15- to 24-year-old age group; Table 2 shows that the greatest increase in accidents was in the 25- to 44-year-old age group, which was up 260 percent.

Most of the fatalities were still accounted for by the 5- to 14-year-old age group in both years: 63.8 percent in 1964 and 79 percent in 1972. So by all odds, children 5 to 14 represent the age group most likely to be killed or injured in all such bicycle-related accidents. Accordingly, it would seem that the greatest educational job in terms of bicycle safety still must focus on children 5 to 14, and special attention must also be given to age groups 15 to 24 and 25 to 44.

TABLE 2: Bicycle-related injuries rose 260% for the 25-to-44-year-old group, which suggests that more of them are cycling than ever before and so total exposure to accident is greater. Evidently, bicycle safety education should also be aimed at this group, as well as the 5 to 14 and 15 to 24 age groups.

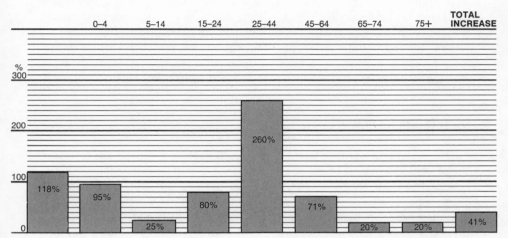

That the greatest *percentage* rise of bicycle-related deaths (1964 vs. 1972) was in the 15- to 24-year-old group (570 percent vs. only 100 percent increase for ages 25 to 44, and 20 percent for ages 45 to 64) suggests that the quicker reaction time of the younger group alone was not enough to keep them from being killed; whereas the experience of the older groups may have kept more of them alive in 1972.

When it came to bicycle-related injuries, things changed, however, and this time the 25- to 44-year-old age group (Table 2) had the greatest percentage increase, 260 percent (reflecting greater use of bicycles by this group) compared to 80 percent for the 15 to 24-year-olds, and 71 percent for the 45- to 64-year-old group. And more toddlers are being injured, up to 95 percent since 1972 as a percent of the totals.

Finally, in 1964 there were 690 bike-related fatalities and 34,000 bicycle-related injuries versus 1,070 deaths and 48,000 injuries in 1972.

Types of Injuries

A check of hospital emergency rooms in 1970 showed that 8.5 percent of all product-related injuries were due to bicycles, that these injuries involved lacerations above the neck, skull fractures and concussions, and injuries to the groin area. Several of the groin injuries were documented as having been due to the victim's feet slipping off the pedals while pressing hard, causing a fall on the top tube of a boy's bicycle (which is why I advocate toe clips on rattrap pedals). The same report cautions that projections such as gear shifts on handlebar stem or top tube, and high-rise handlebars leading to instability, can cause serious injury. Banana seats, which invite "doubling up" of riders, were also cited as having caused serious accidents. The report, by the Bureau of Product Safety, Food and Drug Administration, is titled "A Staff Analysis of Bicycle Accidents and Injuries" and is dated March 24, 1972.

Bicycle-Spoke Injuries

The danger of a child's foot being caught in bike spokes, with resulting major and deep lacerations to the child's leg and loss of control of the bike with injury to the cyclist, has been pointed out by Dr. Fredric D. Berg, a pediatrician. While at Children's Hospital in Chicago, Dr. Berg's attention was drawn to this hazard by cases being brought into the hospital's emergency room. Further investigation proved that such injuries were caused either by carrying the child on the top tube, handlebars, or rear fender. In one case, the parent had neglected to install leg guards on the child carrier seat, although even these guards did not always prevent such an accident.

Defensive Cycling and Statistics

With the boom in bicycling has come a number of stories in major newspapers pointing up the rash of bicycle accidents which seem to the reporter writing the story to reflect an increasing hazard to the cyclist. Yet an analysis of each accident points up, for the most part, that while it may well be perfectly true that the motorist was at least partly at fault, nevertheless the chances for such an accident could have been markedly reduced by the cyclist. For example, the August 15, 1972, issue of the *Wall Street Journal* cites a few bike accidents which bear discussion. The *Wall Street Journal* noted the case of one woman who rode her bike eight miles from her home to her job. All went well until one day, as she approached an intersection, "a fast-moving car," to quote the *Journal*, "swerved in front of her." While she missed the car, she slammed on her brakes so hard she fell over and suffered severe cuts, a concussion and partial amnesia, and had vertigo for several months. The *Journal* does not state whether the car was coming from her rear, or from either side, but in any case, cars do drive at high rates of speed and the cyclist should be very wary while cycling on roads where this is possible. I assume the car passed and cut in front of her, perhaps to escape an oncoming vehicle, perhaps out of sheer rage at having to cope with a cyclist.

In another instance, the *Journal* related the case of a family of four who were all killed by a car, the driver of which said he never saw them. To have killed *four* bicyclists, the motorist must have been speeding pretty fast. Again, it's dangerous to ride on highways where cars can zip by you at high speed, and if you must, as on an otherwise peaceful country road, you should at least be aware that a car is coming up fast (use an eyeglass-mounted rear-view mirror) and so be able to take evasive action if you think he doesn't see you. And to make sure the driver *does* see you, you should make yourself highly visible by wearing a reflective band or vest, or brightly colored clothing that stands out from the surrounding foliage and countryside.

In this article, the *Wall Street Journal* goes on to tell about a man who was making a long-distance ride with other bike enthusiasts. They were riding on the shoulder of a four-lane highway when a passing trailer truck left a wake of strong wind which knocked the cyclist over, causing a broken hip, clavicle, and slight concussion, and putting him on crutches for six months. Well, you know the answer to that one by now, I hope. What in heaven's name was this bunch of bike nuts doing riding on a four-lane highway? Even on the shoulder? A big trailer truck at high speed (45 mph or more) pushes a load of air in front and creates a suction of air behind. The wake of air, like a boat wave, plus the inrushing air that fills the suction, produces a push-pull air situation that can unbalance and knock over a cyclist. Which is why you should be braced for a blow of air as a truck passes you, which won't be often if you stick to side roads.

The *Wall Street Journal* also cites the case of a man who ran into a suddenly opened parked car door. Now he wears a crash helmet. You *may* not be able to see *all* the drivers who are about to open closed doors in front of you. I keep a wary eye on parked cars and know what's coming up from behind me, so I know whether or not I can swerve safely into the street to evade suddenly opened doors, and I have both brake levers in hand at all times in city traffic. If I even remotely think there's a possibility of someone opening a car door I either stop, slow down while screaming at the top of my lungs, or go around the door by swerving out into the street. And in one final story, the *Wall Street Journal* tells of the man who, most regrettably, died after falling off his bike after being attacked by a dog. Well, dogs do jump unexpectedly out of hedges and you can't always see them coming, but do try to anticipate this situation by keeping a keen eye out for our four-footed "friends" (what cyclist could have better enemies?) and outwit them by speeding up, curbing them with a spray of "Halt," or striking them hard on the nose with a whip.

With four accidents that had definite lethal potential within the past twelve years, all my own fault and totally preventable, I can afford to sound a bit self-righteous in discussing the mishaps of other cyclists. I admit *mine* were avoidable; I simply want *you* to keep from having to say the same.

Where and When Accidents Occur

According to a National Safety Council Survey, instances of collisions between vehicles and bicycles occurred about as follows:

- Well over half at intersections.
- Seven out of ten during daylight hours.
- Four-fifths involved a violation on the part of the motor vehicle operator.
- One out of five bicycles involved had some mechanical defect.

Most common traffic violations by bicyclists are:

- Failure to yield right of way. (In most cases, the cyclist did not see the car; in others, he simply infringed on the motorist's right of way.)
- Riding in the center of the street.
- Speed too fast for conditions.
- Disregard of traffic control devices.
- Riding against the flow of traffic.
- Improper turning.

Injuries, not involving motor vehicles, were caused by falls on ice or otherwise slippery or bumpy roads, or by a defective mechanical condition of the bicycle, improper use of the bicycle, and/or overloading.

MODEL CITY BICYCLE ORDINANCE

While on a bicycle tour of Vermont, I picked up a then-new bicycle ordinance which has been approved by the Rutland, Vermont, City

Council and which is law in that city. I think it covers all the bases so far as bicycle safety is concerned. I particularly like Section 4981(b) putting the onus on parents; Section 4982 requiring registration; Section 4990 applying traffic laws to cyclists; Section 5000 requiring lights; and last but not least, Section 5001 establishing a bicycle court for juveniles under the aegis of the chief of police.

I do disagree, though, with Section 5000(c) which requires that bicycles be equipped with a brake that can be so operated as to make the bicycle skid. This requirement may be fine for coaster brakes, and most of these brakes can be so actuated. But they are on only one wheel. Caliper brakes, on the other hand, are on both wheels and do not have to be able to lock the wheel so as to cause it to skid. In fact, the skid requirement, even for a coaster brake, can be downright dangerous, especially on a slippery surface such as gravel, ice or wet leaves. Far better to be able to bring the bicycle to a controlled, safe stop within a reasonable distance from the point at which brakes are first applied. Braking efficiency varies widely on bikes, with the better side and centerpull brakes quite effective and the cheaper caliper brakes very poor and dangerous. A good ordinance would establish bike brake power on some empirical ground of reasonableness. Since there is no published data I could find on bicycle brake stopping power, I would suggest to ordinance writers that a bike should be stoppable completely within one foot for every mile per hour it travels up to 12 mph and algebraically greater for every mph over that speed. At 12 mph you should be able to stop in 12 feet but "g" forces cut this stopping power drastically above 12 mph. Here's the Rutland ordinance in full; may all other cities emulate Rutland.

CITY OF RUTLAND BICYCLE ORDINANCE

CITY OF RUTLAND
CITY COUNCIL
NO. 43: AN ORDINANCE REPEALING TITLE 27, CHAPTER 3, SUB-CHAPTER 11 OF THE REVISED ORDINANCES OF RUTLAND, 1967, AND SUBSTITUTING THE FOLLOWING SECTIONS THEREFOR REGARDING THE REGISTRATION AND REGULATION OF BICYCLES IN THE CITY OF RUTLAND, AND ESTABLISHING A BICYCLE COURT.
PURSUANT TO SECTION 44, (XXXVII), OF THE CHARTER, CITY OF RUTLAND, 1963:
Be it ordained by the City Council of the City of Rutland as follows:

SECTION 4981. EFFECT OF REGULATIONS; MISDEMEANORS; PARENTS AND GUARDIANS

(a) It is a misdemeanor for any person to do any act forbidden or fail to perform any act required in this subchapter.

(b) The parent of any child and the guardian of any ward shall not authorize or knowingly permit any such child or ward to violate any of the provisions of this subchapter.

(c) These regulations applicable to bicycles shall apply whenever a bicycle is operated upon any street or upon any public path set aside for the exclusive use of bicycles, subject to those exceptions stated herein.

SECTION 4982. REGISTRATION REQUIRED

(a) The term "bicycle" means and indicates a light vehicle without a motor, having two wheels, usually tandem, having handle bars and a saddle, seat or seats, and propelled by the feet acting on pedals connected with cranks or levers.

(b) No person who resides within this city shall ride or propel a bicycle on any street or upon any public path set aside for the exclusive use of bicycles unless such bicycle has been registered and a registration tag is attached thereto as provided herein.

SECTION 4983. REGISTRATION APPLICATION

Application for a bicycle registration and registration tag shall be made upon a form provided by the city and shall be made to the chief of police. An annual fee of 50 cents shall be paid to the city before each registration or renewal thereof is granted.

SECTION 4984. ISSUANCE OF REGISTRATION; RECORD MADE BY CHIEF OF POLICE

(a) The chief of police upon receiving proper application therefor is authorized to issue a bicycle registration which shall be effective until the next succeeding first day of May.

(b) The chief of police shall not issue a registration for any bicycle when he knows or has reasonable ground to believe that the applicant is not the owner of or entitled to the possession of such bicycle.

(c) The chief of police shall keep a record of the number of each registration, the date issued, the name and address of the person to whom issued, and the number of the frame of the bicycle for which issued, and a record of all bicycle registration fees collected by him.

SECTION 4985. ATTACHMENT OF REGISTRATION TAG

(a) The chief of police upon issuing a bicycle registration shall also issue a registration tag bearing the registration number assigned to the bicycle, the name of the city and the calendar year for which issued.

(b) The chief of police shall cause such registration tag to be firmly attached to the bicycle for which issued in such position as to be plainly visible.

(c) No person shall remove a registration tag from a bicycle during the period for which issued except upon a transfer of ownership or in the event the bicycle is dismantled and no longer operated upon any street in this city.

SECTION 4986. INSPECTION OF BICYCLES

The chief of police, or an officer assigned such responsibility, shall inspect each bicycle before registering the same and shall refuse a registration for any bicycle which he determines is in unsafe mechanical condition. The chief of police or the officer designated by him, may delegate the duty of inspection to authorized persons or agencies.

SECTION 4987. RENEWAL OF LICENSE

Upon the expiration of any bicycle registration the same may be renewed upon application and payment of the same fee as upon an original application.

SECTION 4988. TRANSFER OF OWNERSHIP

Upon the sale, transfer or other disposal of a registered bicycle the registrar shall remove the registration tag and surrender the same together with his registration certificate to the chief of police, who shall issue in lieu thereof, at the current rate, a new registration certificate and tag to another bicycle owned by the applicant.

SECTION 4989. RENTAL AGENCIES

A rental agency shall not rent or offer any bicycle for rent unless the bicycle is registered and a registration tag is attached thereto as provided herein and such bicycle is equipped with the lamps and other equipment required in this subchapter.

SECTION 4990. TRAFFIC LAWS APPLY TO BICYCLE RIDERS

Every person riding a bicycle upon a roadway shall be granted all of the rights and shall be subject to all of the duties applicable to the driver of a vehicle by the laws of this State declaring rules of the road applicable to vehicles or by the traffic ordinances of this city applicable to the driver of a vehicle, except as to special regulations in this subchapter and except as to those provisions of laws and ordinances which by their nature can have no application.

Cross references. Operating of vehicles, rules of the road, and other provisions relating to vehicles and traffic, see 23 V.S.A. Sec. 1001 et seq.

SECTION 4991. OBEDIENCE TO TRAFFIC-CONTROL DEVICES

(a) Any person operating a bicycle shall obey the instructions of official traffic-control signals, signs and other control devices applicable to vehicles, unless otherwise directed by a police officer.

(b) Whenever authorized signs are erected indicating that no right or left or U turn is permitted, no persons operating a bicycle shall disobey the direction of any such sign, except where such person dismounts from the bicycle to make any such turn, in which event such person shall then obey the regulations applicable to pedestrians.

SECTION 4992. RIDING ON BICYCLES

(a) A person propelling a bicycle shall not ride other than astride a permanent and regular seat attached thereto.

(b) No bicycle shall be used to carry more persons at one time than the number for which it is designed and equipped.

SECTION 4993. RIDING ON ROADWAYS AND BICYCLE PATHS

(a) Every person operating a bicycle upon a roadway shall ride as near to the right-hand side of the roadway as practicable, exercising due care when passing a standing vehicle or one proceeding in the same direction.

(b) Persons riding bicycles on a roadway shall not ride more than 2 abreast except on paths or parts of roadways set aside for the exclusive use of bicycles.

(c) Whenever a usable path for bicycles has been provided adjacent to a roadway, bicycle riders shall use such path and shall not use the roadway. The chief of police may designate a sidewalk as a usable path. A sidewalk so designated shall be suitably marked for the safety and convenience of pedestrians.

SECTION 4994. SPEED

No person shall operate a bicycle at a speed greater than is reasonable and prudent under the conditions then existing.

SECTION 4995. EMERGING FROM ALLEY OR DRIVEWAY

The operator of a bicycle emerging from an alley or driveway or building, shall upon approaching a sidewalk or the sidewalk area extending across an alleyway, yield the right of way to all pedestrians approaching on said sidewalk or sidewalk area, and upon entering the roadway shall yield the right-of-way to all vehicles approaching on said roadway.

SECTION 4996. CLINGING TO VEHICLES

No person riding upon any bicycle shall attach the same or himself to any vehicle upon a roadway.

Cross references. Similar provision, see Section 4940.

SECTION 4997. CARRYING ARTICLES

No person operating a bicycle shall carry any package, bundle, or article which prevents the rider from keeping at least one hand upon the handle bars.

SECTION 4998. PARKING

No person shall park a bicycle upon a street other than upon the roadway against the curb or upon the sidewalk in a rack to support the bicycle or against a building or at the curb, in such a manner as to afford the least obstruction to pedestrian traffic.

SECTION 4999. RIDING BICYCLES ON SIDEWALKS

(a) No person shall ride a bicycle upon the sidewalks located within the business district of the City of Rutland as defined by the ordinances of the City as posted by said City.

(b) No person shall ride a bicycle in a residential district except juveniles under the age of twelve (12) years, exercising due care may ride upon a sidewalk, but they shall yield the right-of-way to any pedestrian, and shall give an audible signal before overtaking and passing said pedestrian.

(c) This section shall not apply to established bicycle paths.

SECTION 5000. LAMPS AND OTHER EQUIPMENT ON BICYCLES

(a) Every bicycle shall be equipped with a lamp on the front which shall emit a white light visible from a distance of at least 500 feet to the front and with a red reflector on the rear of a type which shall be visible from all distances from 50 feet to 300 feet to the rear when directly in front of lawful headlamps on a motor vehicle. A lamp emitting a red light visible from a distance of 500 feet to the rear may be used in addition to the red reflector. This section shall be effective April 1, 1973.

(b) No person shall operate a bicycle unless it is equipped with a bell or other device capable of giving a signal audible for a distance of at least 100 feet, except that a bicycle shall not be equipped with, nor shall any persons use upon a bicycle any siren or whistle.

(c) Every bicycle shall be equipped with a brake which will enable the operator to make the braked wheel skid on dry, level, clean pavement.

SECTION 5001. POWERS OF CHIEF, BICYCLE COURT

The chief of police may make further rules and regulations in regard to bicycles as he may deem necessary for the safety of the public. He shall have the authority to establish bicycle patrols in the various schools of the City and to maintain a bicycle court for the trial of juvenile offenders under this ordinance.

SECTION 5002. BICYCLE COURT PENALTIES

The bicycle court authorized by this ordinance shall have the authority to impose one or more of the following sentences:

(a) Reprimand or suspended sentence.

(b) Preparation of a composition of two hundred to one thousand words on various aspects of safety, for example, "Reasons for Safe Riding Rules."

(c) Impounding a bicycle at City Hall for a period or from seven to thirty days.

(d) Requesting parents to deprive an offender of the use of his bicycle from one to thirty days.

(e) Ordering bicycle to be immediately registered.

(f) Copying of a specific section of the bicycle ordinance from one to twenty-five times.

(g) Recommendation to chief of police to revoke or suspend license.

SECTION 5003. REVOCATION AND SUSPENSION OF REGISTRATION: APPEALS THEREFROM

The chief of police may revoke or suspend any registration for just cause. An appeal to the Juvenile District Court may be had by any person so penalized under this subchapter. It shall be unlawful for any person to operate a bicycle while the registration thereof is revoked or suspended. By the adoption of this ordinance, it is not intended that this penalty is the exclusive one but should be construed with other state statutes governing the use of vehicles on highways.

SECTION 5004. SAVINGS CLAUSE

If any provision of this ordinance or the application thereof to any person or circumstances is held invalid, such invalidity shall not affect other provisions or applications of the ordinance which can be given effect without the invalid provision or application and to this end the provisions of this ordinance are declared to be severable.

Submitted to the City Council this 5 day of July, 1972.

J. FRED CARBINE, JR.
President

ATTEST:

JOHN W. BARRETT
Rutland City Clerk

Approved by his Honor the Mayor on the 6 day of July, 1972.

WILLIAM H. FOLEY, SR.
Mayor

Published this 22nd day of July 1972.
Effective August 12, 1972.

BIKE ROUTES

We'll have lots more to say about cross-country bike routes in the section on camping and touring (see page 184). Right now I'd like to point out that many cities, such as Chicago, Boston, and Washington, D.C., under pressure from bicycle commuting groups have put signs, generally green with a white bicycle, on certain fairly low traffic-density city streets; the signs say "Bicycle Route," or words to that effect. These signs are supposed to tell the motorist to be aware that he is sharing the street with bicycles, and the bicyclist that this is a street on which the motorist may be expected to give him elbow room. So far, my experience in a great many cities with these bicycle routes has been that after a few weeks the signs become invisible to motorists, and the situation is as before, with cyclists battling for street room, motorists giving way grudgingly, and the accident rate (see page 59) steadily climbing as more new, inexperienced cyclists of all ages ride to and from work during rush hours. A word of optimism tempered by experience. You should be able to commute even during rush hours, if you exercise reasonable care, and if you can ride in a fairly straight line. Thousands of us do so every day, even in winter months.

A note of hope has been struck in Chicago for commuting bicyclists. On one busy street, the city has partitioned off a lane wide enough for

Fig. 14: Typical bicycle path in Holland. A wide, fairly smooth pavement, physically separated from the road, characterizes these bike trails which parallel roads in Holland, and, to a lesser extent, in Belgium, France, and Germany.

two cyclists abreast, with cars forbidden to drive or park in this lane. Better yet, of course, are physically separated lanes, as in Belgium and, even more so, in Holland, (Fig. 14) where wide, smoothly paved bike trails wind through quiet sylvan woods and fields, far from the noise and stench of auto traffic; or at least separated from the highway by a few hundred feet of grassy, wooded strips in many cases, or winding along a canal or stream.

One more country cycling hazard I should mention is the attitude of native yokels toward cyclists. One rarely finds gratuitous nastiness from city motorists, but it is not unusual to find country bumpkins who go out of their way to make cycling hazardous for tourists. I have had yokels try to run me off the road with their camper pick-up trucks in Washington state, scream insults from farm trucks in rural Vermont on otherwise quiet, peaceful country roads. Friends from Kentucky tell me cycling life can be made miserable by hillbilly types who throw beer bottles at them from car windows or veer toward them as they pass, horns blowing, passengers screaming. Dogs hate cyclists, too, and I think bumpkins have the same attitude, for some of the same reasons: something different, intrusion on their "private" roads; they consider it an activity somehow "unmanly" and "childish" for adults and therefore an object of legitimate ridicule. So when cycling in the country, watch for cars coming from behind that seem to be heading for you, be ready to take evasive action and, above all, try to get their license number and if you have friends along, use them as witnesses if you can for charges of assault with a deadly weapon, the automobile. Try above all to remember what the driver looks like, although I know this is difficult.

3

SO YOU WANT TO
BUY A BICYCLE!

Now you've made up your mind. You want to buy a bicycle. But what kind of bicycle should you get? New or secondhand? Coaster brakes or caliper brakes? A three-speed "racer" (Fig. 15) or one of those fancy jobs with turned-down handlebars (Fig. 16) and lots of gears and things hanging from the rear wheel? Where should you buy your bicycle? Do you go to a discount house or a bike shop? How about a take-apart bicycle (see Fig. 52, page 128)—handy to store in the trunk of the car, neat, too—very "camp." And how can you tell a top-grade bicycle from a piece of junk that will give you nothing but trouble and needless expense?

This is going to be a difficult chapter for me to write. I have tried everything—the cheap new three-speed, the better new three-speed, the really expensive three-speed "English racer," and the moderately priced ten-speed turned-down handlebar job. I have finally found the only bicycle I can live with—the best one money can buy (but not the most expensive). This is simply to point out that you need to be rather careful and selective in your analysis of what kind of bike you want, how much you can afford to pay, and selection of the bicycle itself. As the bike boom in the U.S. continues, bike makers abroad and bicycle importers here are marketing a very, very wide range of bicycles of makes never before imported into the U.S. Whatever price range you decide on (and I urge you to consider spending at least $200.00 for a reasonably good machine), it pays to shop around for the best bike in any given price bracket. I would have saved a lot of money, and enjoyed cycling a lot

Fig. 15: A well-built "English racer" type bicycle. Not a racer, of course, but it's durable, and suitable for young teens who bang bikes around. Has coaster brake rear, hub brake front.

Fig. 16: This well-made medium-weight, medium-price bicycle weighs twenty-eight pounds, has ten speeds, and front and rear center-pull caliper brakes.

more from the beginning, had I not had to learn from experience the shortcomings and deficiencies of all the various makes and models.

Over the years, I have tried all these bicycles, for both short and long trips. Now I know that I would never invest in anything but a good quality ten-speed or, for long trips and in mountainous country, fifteen-speed bicycle, with turned-down "racing" handlebars.

But I don't want to scare you away from cycling altogther, or have you put down this book right now and write me off as just another cycling nut. I must confess that, at first, the idea of paying $200.00 for a bicycle with dropped handlebars, complicated gears, and apparently flimsy wheels and frame seemed to me to be sheer madness. But I want to tell you immediately that if you intend to get serious about cycling, for health, for the pure pleasure of getting out of doors, or for family trips and touring, you will eventually wind up paying *at least* $200.00 for a new ten-speed machine. I recommend, therefore, that you seriously consider this purchase now. Cycling as a fun thing to do may not appeal to you at first, but I warn you, once you start, you'll more than likely be bitten by the bug.

Today, almost 95 million Americans own bicycles and, presumably, ride them occasionally. Bicycle sales practically doubled between 1960 and 1966. According to the Bicycle Institute of America, sales rose from 3.8 million bicycles in 1960 to 6 million in 1966 and are estimated to be 14 million in 1972 and 1973 and 17 million in 1974. It looks like bike sales are going up a lot faster than the rate of population increase.

Part of this upward trend in bike sales can be attributed to the publicity surrounding President Eisenhower's first heart attack, and subsequent statements by his physician, Dr. Paul Dudley White, who encourages daily bicycle riding to promote good health (see the chapter on health for a full discussion, page 15).

I am convinced that the 35 percent of the bicycles sold today to adults are purchased mainly for health reasons. And there's no telling how many grown-ups sneak their child's balloon-tired monster out of the garage and wheeze it around the block a few times an evening. But this type of cycling—on the heavy, rusty, rattling monstrosity that passes for a bicycle in America—may keep you from truly enjoying cycling, which is the best argument for you to try this growing sport on a good machine.

But you may not want a bike for yourself. You might want to buy one for your child. What type, size, and make should you buy? Far too often I have seen children completely frustrated by a bicycle that is too large, too complicated, and too unwieldy for their age and physique. A ten year old should not be expected to be able to mount and ride a twenty-six-inch wheel, three-speed, caliper-brake (handlebar-mounted brake levers) machine. The frame is too big for him to get up on the saddle easily, and when he does, he can't reach the pedals. And once in motion, he can't stop because he's too weak to grasp the brake handles.

Further on in this chapter (Table 3, page 87), you will find a selection of bicycles for children from ages two to sixteen, based on size, design, and price. But first, let's look at a few problems that are common to any bicycle purchase.

WHERE TO BUY A BICYCLE

First, let me recommend categorically that you buy a bicycle *only* in a bicycle store. Let me tell you why. I have spent a good many hours examining bicycles in discount shops and department stores. Although you *can* save a few dollars in such places, chances are that if the bike's not a cheap brand that will fall apart within a year, you will spend far more time getting it ready to ride than you will have saved.

For one, I have never seen a skilled bicycle mechanic on duty in a discount or department store. The assembly job that store clerks do is mute testimony to this fact. Wheels are badly out of line, caliper brakes unworkable, and handlebars askew. If the bicycle on display is the best the store's "mechanic" can do, then what will the bicycle you buy be like if the store assembles it for you? And if the store does not assemble it for you, and it comes "almost fully assembled" in a carton, you will have a long, difficult task ahead when you try to put the bicycle into riding condition.

To prove my point, I am going to tell you what happened when I chose, at random, a "fully assembled" cartoned bicycle from the stock of a discount house, indicating the time I spent making it ready for the road. (Remember, I can work a bit faster on bikes than the average person; I have the correct tools, some experience, and a lot of interest.) Here is what I found in the carton:

- Frame and fenders covered with protective gum tape, which I had to remove. (eight minutes)
- Front wheel badly out of alignment. One spoke nipple stripped, spoke loose. Had to remove tire, replace broken spoke, replace tire, realign wheel. (thirty minutes including trip to bike shop for new spoke)
- Front-wheel hub cones binding, wheel hard to turn. Readjusted hub cones. (fifteen minutes)

- Rear wheel badly out of alignment; realigned. (fifteen minutes)
- Gear-shift handle not installed. Gear-shift cable not installed. Rear three-speed hub not adjusted because cable not installed. Installed and adjusted gear shift and cable. (twenty minutes)
- Fenders not installed. (fifteen minutes)
- Front light not installed; no batteries. (eight minutes)
- Pedals on reversed. Normal for shipment, but had to remove and reinstall correctly. (eight minutes)
- Caliper brakes not set correctly. (ten minutes)
- Bottom bracket (crank) bearings binding; chainwheel turned tightly. Readjusted bottom bracket cone. (six minutes)
- Front fork binding. Readjusted headset cone. (five minutes)
- Handlebars and seat not adjusted for rider. (fifteen minutes)

Assembly time totaled two hours and forty minutes, which, at $9.50 an hour, the going rate for bicycle mechanics, amounts to nearly $25.00.

Bicycle stores, on the other hand, will sell you a bike that is fully assembled and ready to ride safely. And if it isn't in tip-top shape, there's always a trained mechanic on hand to fix it. In addition, under the warranty you can always take a bicycle back to a bicycle store for small adjustments. Department and discount stores cannot honor a warranty because usually they have no one on hand to repair a bike.

Further on in this chapter I am going to give you pointers on what to look for when you buy a new bicycle, in terms of both quality and the method for checking, to make sure all is in good working order before you leave the store.

ALL ABOUT FRAMES

This information on frames is rather technical, but it will be valuable for the cycling enthusiast who wants to get the best possible frame construction.

Bicycle frames are made of a number of different kinds of steels and tubing. The garden-variety, inexpensive, coaster-brake or three-speed bicycle is usually made of seamed tubing—a strip of steel wrapped into tubular form by rollers and then automatically welded electrically into a tube. Such tubing is straight gauge, meaning that it is not reinforced where it joins other parts of the bicycle. Typically, the tubes of this type of frame are simply stuck into each other and welded at the joints. The problem with a frame of this sort is that electric welding is done at high temperatures, which causes stresses at the joints that can weaken them. Simply sticking frame members into each other and welding them makes the weakest type of frame construction. Unfortunately, the vast majority of bicycles are made this way.

The best bicycles are made with Reynolds '531' double-butted, cold-drawn, seamless manganese-molybdenum steel. This tubing combines lightness with high strength and resistance to "fatigue," and high tensility for maximum resilience with a feeling of "liveliness" in the frame.

The average cyclist cannot tell if a frame is double-butted just by looking at it. Double-butting means that the metal is thickened at both ends where maximum stress occurs, without changing the outside diameter of the metal tube (Fig. 17).

There are a number of different combinations of Reynolds '531' tubing, so a Reynolds decal on a frame does not necessarily mean that it is a superior bicycle. Read the label or decal carefully to know exactly what you are buying.

Here is what the various Reynolds labels or decals (Fig. 33, page 102) mean:

The label that says "Reynolds '531' Frame Tubing" means that the top tube, seat tube, and down tube are made of Reynolds '531' plain gauge (*not* double-butted) steel.

The decal or label that says "Guaranteed built with Reynolds '531' plain gauge tubes, forks, and stays" means that all the tubing in the frame is Reynolds '531' *plain* gauge (*not* double-butted) steel.

The decal that says "Guaranteed built with Reynolds '531' butted frame

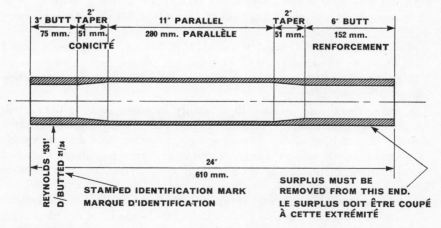

Fig. 17: Best bicycle frames are made of Reynolds '531' double-butted tubing, shown here. See Fig. 33 for a complete description of various types of Reynolds '531' tubing.

tubes" means that the top, seat, and down tubes of the frame are of Reynolds '531' double-butted tubing.

The label that says "Guaranteed built with Reynolds '531' butted tubes, forks, and stays" means that the frame is all Reynolds double-butted. This is the most costly and best frame you can buy. But even this type of frame is not the best possible one unless it is brazed properly, and finest quality, precision-made, hand-filled lugs are used.

The Reynolds manufacturer specifies that the best brazing is done by hand, using low-temperature bronze brazing materials with a melting point no higher than 850 degrees Centigrade. Look for bicycle frame specifications that say "all-lugged, low-temperature, bronze-brazed" or words to that effect. High-temperature brazing makes joints brittle at the point of stress, which can negate the good tensile qualities of the Reynolds steel.

A Word About Other Tubing

Really cheap bikes have frames of seamed, welded, low-carbon steel tubing with a "joined" or "yield" strength (after having been welded) of about 22,000 pounds per square inch, which seems strong but really isn't. These frames are heavy and stiff, and give a spine-jolting ride.

In the low- to medium-range bikes, frames are seamed, welded, high-carbon steel, with a joined strength of around 32,000 pounds per square inch.

We have already discussed Reynolds '531' tubing, which has a joined yield strength of around 80,000 pounds per square inch, and contains 1.45 percent manganese, 0.25 percent molybdenum, 0.29 percent carbon and 0.35 percent silicon.

A frame metal also used on high-quality bicycles, such as the Cinelli line, is the famous Italian Columbus tubing. This is a high-quality chrome molybdenum tubing which gives a somewhat stiffer ride than Reynolds '531,' and hence is favored for track and road-racing machines. A similar metal is made in Japan and used in their top bicycles, such as the Fuji line.

Schwinn uses three different types of tubing, depending on the quality of their bicycle. The top line Paramount series is made of double-butted Reynolds '531' tubing. Schwinn's second line, such as the Super Sport and Sports Tourer models, are of 4130 chrome molybdenum steel tubing with a yield strength of around 75,000 pounds per square inch. Other Schwinn bicycles are of 18- to 20-gauge cold drawn welded steel tubing, made in their own tube mill. The 18- to 20-gauge steel explains why Schwinn lower-priced models are a bit heavier than comparable bikes; Schwinn puts more steel into their frames for strength, while some other low-priced bicycles are of light-gauge welded steel tubing. When it comes to lower-priced models, as for youngsters of ten to fourteen, a stronger frame is more desirable, particularly if the bike is to be handed down from child to child in the family. I should point out that my stricture about nonlugged frames does not apply to the Schwinn chrome moly frames, which are gas-welded and built up at the joints. It is also, of course, possible to build beautiful '531' or Columbus butted frames without lugs, and without detracting from strength, and in fact some fine machines are built that way. These are usually tailormade frames to individual order. The frames that bother me are the low carbon tubes simply stuck into each other and high temperature machine-welded on a mass production line. These frames tend to be poorly aligned, and, as noted, weak and unresponsive.

An aluminum riveted lug construction bicycle has been successfully made in this country by Hi-E Engineering Company, Nashville, Tennessee. I have one of these bicycles (Fig. 18) and I like it very much. The ride, with hi-flange hubs, is softer and more comfortable than a conventional chrome moly or Reynolds '531' tubing bike, and so I plan to use

Fig. 18: All-aluminum frame and riveted construction, made by Hi-E Engineering Company, Nashville, Tennessee. Frame weighs about 3½ pounds, which makes up into a road bike of under 22 pounds.

the Hi-E for touring. The frame weighs about three pounds less than conventional frames, so the complete bicycle is that much lighter than ordinary machines. When you consider how much work and planning goes into reducing the load carried on tour, the three pounds saved by the Hi-E machine can make a lot of difference. I found that out on one backbreaking tour of Vermont's Green Mountain country; specifically, that even lightening a load by one miserable little pound makes hill climbing measurably (muscularly) easier. The Hi-E "Cosmopolitan" bike frame is made of high-strength aluminium alloy and riveted construction, with strength comparable to high carbon steel. Hi-E's chainwheel is a standard T.A., but the bottom bracket is their own, and has precision, deep-groove sealed bearings needing no maintenance for 1,500 hours at least, longer if bicycle is not raced under load conditions. The headset is similarly designed. Cost of the complete bike is in the $500 area; the frame alone is around $300.

Titanium is a new alloy in restricted use for bicycle frames. This metal has a tensile strength and rigidity comparable to Reynolds '531' butted tubing, but is lighter. A complete frame, less bottom bracket, weighs about three and a half pounds, so it is possible to make up a complete touring bike with wide-range gears, triple chainwheel, etc., and yet have a machine that weighs about eighteen pounds. Titanium is a true space-age metal, having nuclear age chemical and medical applications due to its great corrosion resistance. The frame metal has a natural high-polish finish on the order of stainless steel, only brown, and it can also be colored any color by anodizing. Titanium is expensive; welding must be done in an inert gas atmosphere, so the frame is quite costly, around $500 for the frame alone. So when you add other components such as wheels, hubs, saddle, seat post, bars and stem, gears, bottom bracket and headset, you would have a bicycle the total cost of which could be well over $700.00! But you'd have an ideal touring frame that should last a life-time and that would be virtually impervious to corrosion. Titanium frames are made by Speedwell Gearcase Company, Ltd., Tame Road, Witton, Birmingham B6 7HR, England, and Teledyne Liniar Engineering, 651 W. Knox Street, Gardina, California 90248. The Teledyne people make both road and track frames and have told me that their road frame is also designed for touring. The Teledyne titanium frame, at this writing, should retail for around $350, complete with fork assembly.

This is also a warning about titanium frames! I bought one for touring from a bike supply house. When it came I spent three hard working days meticulously assembling this frame with high-test grade components. When finished, I had about $800 invested in it. But what a disappointment when I took it out on the road! I had expected a superlight, highly responsive machine weighing around 19 or 20 pounds. I had the weight down, all right, so touring would be that much easier. But the frame was so "whippy" that every time I shook the handlebars the rear brake would grab. The frame was so flexible that it would have been extremely prone to front wheel wobble, especially with a pannier load. I then discovered this was a time trial frame, designed for gentle acceleration and lightness up to maximum speed against the clock or over a measured course. Needless to say this frame was returned, but I wasted three days' time. I am going to be exceedingly skeptical about titanium or any other metal than good old Reynolds '531' or Columbus tubing from now on.

A *plastic frame bicycle* has been made of carbon fiber reinforced plastic (CRFP), which in the raw state costs about $50.00 a pound. The English Carlton Cycle firm has such a machine on test, using this plastic with aluminum lugs and poly resin joining the plastic tubing. Tensile strength range of this plastic is said to be somewhere between 100,000 and 300,000 psi and it is claimed to offer a stiffer ride than comparable strength metal tubing. Given the high raw cost of this plastic, it should be possible to make a complete touring bike for about $800.00. Such a machine would weigh about nineteen pounds. But I'd hate to have to make frame repairs on this bike; and as for the aluminum or titanium frames, repairs would be virtually out of the question at the dealer level due to the equipment needed. Whether the respective factories would undertake such repairs is a question, since they are so far behind on frame orders. But since we bike freaks have always wanted the best (are we like camera bugs?), there will no doubt be a steady if small market for these exotic machines.

Dow Chemical has made a magnesium die-cast frame weighing about two pounds, but of fairly weak material with a yield strength of only 23,000 psi. Dow appears to have abandoned this project.

One final note about frame metal. I have been asked questions about Cantiflex tubing from time to time. This tubing is made by Reynolds for Horace Bates Cycles, Ltd. Bates says it is made exclusively for them, to their patent. Cantiflex tubing has inside and outside diameters which are greater toward the middle, while at the same time metal thickness is increased at the end. Bates claims that this construction reduces energy wasting frame "whip" by increasing frame rigidity and resistance to bending strain. Frame metal is standard Reynolds '531' composition. Bates also has their own patented '531' forks which they call "Diadrant," with a twin radius they claim reduces impact shock to arms and related loss of power caused by reduced leverage and coordination between arms and legs as weight is lifted momentarily from pedals. The Diadrant forks absorb this shock and permit steady uninterrupted pedaling, according to Bates. This firm makes only custom-built frames and delivery time is rather long, at the very least six weeks and more likely three months or longer.

A Word About Custom Frames

There has been a lot written about how to order custom frames, with advice on frame geometry such as rake of front fork, angle of seat and down tubes, wheelbase length, etc. This is all fine for engineering types who know what they're about and probably make a good living designing bikes. I feel that the hours you spend agonizing over these details could best be spent on a more healthy activity, such as riding a bike.

The Appendix (page 501) lists a handful of selected British builders and one French one. I could have added Italian and Belgian frame builders, but in my opinion, those I have selected do just as good a job. They speak English and understand our system of measurement, so you won't have to convert everything to metric when you send in your body measurements.

These firms can build you a frame, or a complete bicycle, to meet your exact bodily dimensions and the type of cycling you plan to do. If you're a tourist, all you need do is specify the gear range you have in mind, suggest the make and model of rim, hub, bottom bracket and crankset assembly, make and model of handlebars, and stem and brakes you'd like. The frame builder will need your inseam measurement from floor to crotch bone as measured in stocking feet, leg length, length of arm from shoulder to knuckles, shoe size, over-all height, torso length, and your body weight, as shown by Fig. 19. For a discussion of gears, see page 179. With your measurements send a check for $150 for frame alone or $300 for complete bicycle, and ask to be billed for the balance.

HOW TO CHECK YOUR NEW BICYCLE'S CONDITION

Whether you buy a new or a used bicycle, there are certain things you should look for to make sure the bicycle will be safe to ride and will give you reasonable satisfaction. Gene Portuesi, who has his own bicycle shop in Cadillac, Michigan, says that even top-quality imported machines must be removed from their cartons, assembled, adjusted, and then disassembled and repacked before shipment to the customer.

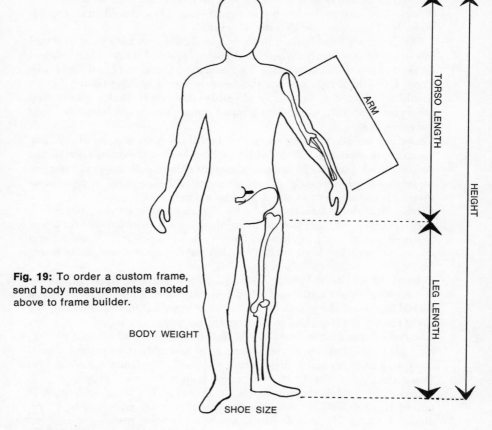

Fig. 19: To order a custom frame, send body measurements as noted above to frame builder.

Points for you to check are:

- *Wheels:* Spin wheels. Put a finger or pencil on the frame while wheels turn; watch for out-of-roundness. Pay no attention to tire, watch rim only. Wheels should be perfectly true from both side-to-side and concentrically as to roundness. In checking display bicycles, I found that 90 percent of them had wheels way out of round.
- *Spokes:* "Pluck" spokes or "twing" them as you would strings on a guitar. Spokes should give about the same musical pitch all around, and should show about the same degree of tightness. Even if wheels are aligned, loose spokes will cause them to go out of round soon.
- *Hubs:* Spin wheel slowly. Wheel should come to a stop gradually. If wheel stops suddenly, hub cone needs readjustment.

Grasp wheel between fingers and, holding the bicycle frame firmly, move wheel from side to side. If wheel has side play, hub cones are too loose.

· *Brakes:* Test coaster brakes on an actual ride. They should grab enough under hard back pressure to make wheel skid.

Check caliper hand brakes. Brake blocks should grab both sides of wheel rim squarely and evenly. When hand lever is released, brake blocks should be clear of rim sides and not rub. Test on a ride, trying front and rear brake alone. Each should show about the same degree of braking ability. Levers should be adjusted to fit your hand (cable adjustment). Brakes should stop evenly and smoothly, even when gripped tightly, should not "shudder," grip unevenly, or squeal.

· *Gears:* See trouble-shooting section on both hub gears and derailleur (ten-speed gears on pages 353 and 461). A bicycle should exhibit none of the defects listed and should operate smoothly through all the gear changes. Make sure a three-speed gear hub is lubricated before riding a new three-speeder because oil evaporates in storage and in transit.

· *Frame:* Sight down fork and frame for alignment. Check frame where fork goes through head tube; look at the paint. If paint is wrinkled slightly where top tube and steering head meet, the bicycle has been in an accident and frame has probably been bent. Wrinkled paint indicates metal movement under stress, such as collision with a brick wall.

· *Fenders:* Should be on tight and not rattle. Try a road test. In fact, on a road test nothing should rattle, and when you coast over a bumpy road all you should hear from the bicycle is the sound of the wind in your ears and the slight click of the freewheel pawls from the rear, as you coast.

· *Chainwheel and bottom bracket:* Check bottom bracket adjustment by slipping chain off chainwheel and spinning the assembly. Chainwheel should come to a stop gradually, move easily and freely. It should not come to a stop suddenly, or "bind." Have someone hold the frame steady and push cranks from side to side. You should be able to feel or see no side play. If any of these defects are present, the bottom bracket cone should be re-adjusted. Check chainwheel for alignment by rotating pedals and sighting down the side into the teeth of the chainwheel. If the chainwheel is "wavy" it can be straightened; if wavy and a ten speed, the chain will rub in spots on the chainwheel and front derailleur cage. If too wavy, it may jump off the chainwheel. (See page 368 for more information.)

· *Pedals:* Should turn freely, not bind, and should have no side play.

· *Handlebars and Saddle:* Should be adjusted to fit the rider, and be tight. (See pages 84 and 144 for details on fitting.)

· *General check:* Just because a bicycle, of any make or model, is brand new, right out of a crate, and you have bought it from a bicycle dealer, you have no guarantee that nothing can go wrong (or is wrong) with it.

The sad fact is that you or your bicycle dealer *must* check *every* bolt, nut, cable adjustment, derailleur adjustment, and everything else that can come loose or go out of whack, before you ride the new bicycle out of the shop. This is true regardless of *how* much the bicycle costs or *what* make it is.

Let me give you an example. Recently I bought a fine, rather costly, derailleur-equipped bicycle expressly designed for touring. After giving it a most cursory inspection, I set off on a short trip. After a few miles, while I strained up a steep hill, the chain suddenly slipped off the center of the three chainwheels. I was mildly annoyed at the time, but if I had given it proper thought, I would have stopped cycling right there and walked home. (A chain does not simply slip off the center chainwheel! Off the smaller or larger wheel, possibly, if the front derailleur is maladjusted. But slipping off the center chainwheel meant that something was drastically wrong.) All I did, however, was slip the chain back on the wheel (which was rather difficult because it had gotten firmly wedged between the center and outer chainwheel). About fifty feet farther, the chain slipped off again. This time I studied the chainwheel closely, and I found, to my horror, that a center bolt, spacer, and nut had fallen out entirely in two places out of the five, and the other three bolts were loose. This time the chain was wedged in firmly, and the center chainwheel was badly warped from the wedge pressure of the chain.

To give you another example, a friend of mine rode a brand-new expensive bicycle out of a showroom, and after cycling about five miles, the rear derailleur cable slipped right out of the derailleur cable clamp. The clamp bolt had fallen out as well, which meant a long ride home over hills in top gear. Incidentally, if you should break a cable on the road and don't have a replacement on hand, you can adjust the rear derailleur so it stays in an intermediate gear, thus avoiding having to ride in top gear all the way home.

These are trivial mechanical troubles in the showroom, but on the road, they can spoil a trip. Replacement parts can be obtained only in the bike shops specializing in high-quality bicycles. Parts for these machines are almost always made in Europe and nuts are threaded on the metric standard. So check *everything* before you leave the bicycle store.

One final word of advice. If the mechanic needs any special tools to remove the freewheel or adjust the derailleur, for example, buy the tool while you are in the shop. (See page 216 for a list of tools you should always carry.)

A WORD ABOUT PRICES

Bicycle prices have nearly doubled since 1966, and are still rising. Therefore I have decided simply to select certain bicycles as representative of top quality machines in various broad price categories and/or juvenile age categories, and let you shop around. Bear in mind that component prices (brakes, gears, rims, tires, etc.) are going up every six months or so during this bicycle-boom-created shortage. I am hopeful that the price rise situation will level out when, as, and if bicycle component manufacturers are able to increase production to meet the demands of the bike boom. Prices on parts or bikes quoted are probably going to be higher by the time you read this far.

THE CHILD AND THE BICYCLE

It is very important to fit a bicycle to a child—to buy him one that fits him, and that he can handle safely and pedal easily. Beyond that, you should consider how much bicycle you get for your money, and here it is very easy to go wrong.

To help you make the right decision, I have carefully examined and reviewed the specifications of dozens of makes of bicycles, ending up with a selection of those makes that I believe represent the most bicycle for the least money. There are less expensive bicycles on the market, but the models I have recommended will, with reasonable care, greatly outlast less costly makes. For this reason, it is worth investing a few dollars more.

Table 3 (page 87) gives you bicycle selections for the two-to-five, five-to-seven, seven-to-twelve, ten-to-thirteen, and ten-to-sixteen-year-old child, respectively. Models for both boys and girls are included. But before you buy a bicycle, I urge you to study the following general recommendations for type of bicycle by age group. They will help you understand why the particular models in each group were selected.

Children from Two to Seven

Because, with proper care, a relatively inexpensive bicycle can last for five or six years, even when subjected to the rigors of a child's use, it pays to ignore the toy-like fixed rear hub, solid tire bicycles and start with a fairly decent bicycle your child can grow with. (After all, the seat and handlebars can be raised as your child grows.)

For children aged two to seven, therefore, I recommend a 10- to 20-inch-wheel bicycle with a coaster brake (Fig. 20). Definitely do *not* get your small child a gear-shift bicycle with hand-lever caliper brakes. He hasn't the strength to operate either, and you'll only frustrate him.

I also do not recommend that children from two to seven have a bicycle with "high-riser" handlebars. (In fact, I deplore high-rise handlebars for

TABLE 3 · Bicycles for Children

AGE CHILD	MAKE AND MODEL	SPECIFICATIONS
2–4	Schwinn Lil' Tiger	Sturdy frame, chrome fenders, removable top bar, training wheels (you don't need them), 26 pounds.
2–5	Schwinn Sting-Ray Pixie	Convertible top tube, 16-in. x 1¾-in. tires, 27 pounds.
2–5	Vista M-90	Convertible top tube, coaster brake, 28-spoke wheels, 20-in. x 1¾-in. pneumatic tires, 40 pounds. Not light, but tough.
2–5	Raleigh DL-80	28-spoke, 20-in. x 1⅜-in. wheels, mattress saddle, coaster brake. Not convertible, 26 pounds.
5–7 BOYS	Schwinn Speedster	Coaster brake, 20-in. x 1⅜-in. tires, sturdy frame, 31 pounds.
5–7 GIRLS	Schwinn Breeze	Same as above, except girl's frame.
5–7 UNISEX	Huffy 2056	Convertible top tube, 20-in. x 1¾-in. wheels, coaster brake. Converts to girl's model by removing bolted-on top tube.
7–12	Schwinn Varsity Sport	Handsome 24-in. wheel, rugged, ten speed meets need of more knowledgeable (about bikes) youngsters who won't settle for a one-speed or three-speed machine. Worth the rather high price, in terms of sturdiness and good design. Down-turned bars, narrow racing saddle. Boy's frame, 36 pounds.
10–13	Falcon 58	24-in. wheels, 18-in. frame, five speeds, center-pull brakes, lightweight at only 28 pounds.
10–13	Murray Ohio 2-6670	Ten speeds, side-pull brakes, 24-in. x 1¾-in. wheels, down-turned bars, narrow racing saddle.
10–13	Murray Ohio 2-6470	For the taller child, has 26-in. x 1⅜-in. wheels, otherwise similar to 2-6670.
10–16	Schwinn Heavi-Duty	Designed for delivering newspapers, groceries, etc. Built like a truck, with 26-in. x 1¾-in. "tractor" tires, heavy-duty saddle and spokes, cantilever frame.

Fig. 20: For the child of five to seven, this sturdily made bicycle will last through a family of growing children. Top tube removes to convert to girl's model. Take off the training wheels, though; they slow up cycle learning process.

anybody; they're awkward, hard to use, and lead to an unbalanced situation, which makes them downright dangerous.)

Training wheels actually slow a child's learning time. Your job as a parent is to help the child learn to balance, and training wheels won't do it. You should run alongside the child, explaining that as the bike goes one way he should lean the other. After a few hours practice, your child should be able to balance on a soft grassy surface that cushions falls.

Remember, until your child is a mid-teenager (fourteen and up), a bicycle is basically a toy. If he wants a fake motorcycle engine, banana seat, or fake motorcycle tank, humor him. It's a cumbersome toy, but at least it's a safe one, if he stays off the street and rides on the sidewalk only. And 20-inch x 1¾-inch balloon tires can take quite a lot of punishment.

Children, thanks to grown-up advertising, think of a bicycle as an automobile; hence, bicycle manufacturers use names such as "Roadmaster," "Jet Pilot," and "Sport Shift."

Children from Seven to Nine

For children from seven to nine, I recommend a 24-inch-wheel bicycle with 1¾-inch tires and coaster brakes on the rear wheel, as shown in Fig. 21. You can find cheaper models, but the quality will be inferior, and if you have younger children who will want to use the bicycle later on, the better model will still be around when the first child graduates to something bigger.

Fig. 21: The child from seven to nine or ten will like this well-made bicycle with 20-inch wheels and coaster brake.

Fig. 22: For ages nine to twelve, this sophisticated little machine with 24-inch wheels features child-proof ten-speed shifting mechanism with 5½-inch cranks to fit the child. Weighs 36 pounds.

Children from Nine to Twelve

The small, 20-inch frame, 26-inch-wheel bicycle with a three-speed rear hub and caliper brakes front and rear, is a nice little machine for the nine-to-twelve age group (Fig. 22). This bike should have 1¾-inch tires. Again, though, I'd avoid high-rise handlebars; they are really dangerous. Because hands must be raised elbow high to steer, good balance is hard to hold and the bicycle isn't easy to steer.

Children from Twelve Up

As ever, emulating their parents, youngsters today are becoming so knowledgeable about bikes that they are beginning to reject the one-speed balloon-tired monsters they used to prefer, and even the small-wheeled jobs with hi-rise bars and banana saddles. Now you'll more than likely have to buy your child at least a five-speed derailleur bicycle, or, more likely, a ten-speed. You can buy very good ten-speed bicycles that will fit children from 12 to 14, such as the Schwinn Varsity Sport, a scaled-down version of a conventional ten-speed, with downturned racing bars and a narrow saddle (Fig. 23). If your child of 12 to 14 is really "into" bikes, or you want him to be equipped with a higher-performance small frame bike, you can even buy him a fairly expensive model with Reynolds '531' tubing, 24-inch clinchers, and center-pull brakes, such as made by Frejus. Or you could have one of the custom frame builders (see Appendix) make him up a custom-fitted machine with tubular tires, either for road or track racing, or for touring.

In the first edition of this book I said that as soon as young people arrived at high school, they turned their backs on bicycling as "kid stuff." A few years ago, this was true, and my own children's bicycles languished in the garage after they left eighth grade. But all has changed now, and the bike boom, with adult participation, is reflected in the youth movement toward bicycles in high school, on college campuses, in more AYH tours for ecological and just fun reasons. So you should consider (you may *have* to consider) a fairly decent ten-speed for your youngster of fifteen and up. Your child may wish a $250 bicycle, for example, and if he or she can contribute some of the cost through earnings, fine. Make sure, though, that if you *do* spend a lot of money for a fine bicycle for

Fig. 23: For teenagers, an inexpensive ten-speed bicycle, such as shown here, is suitable for commuting to school, on campus, or touring. Models available weigh 38 to 41 pounds, with the lighter bikes more expensive but still under $100 (at this writing).

your youngster, that the child has reached maximum growth, so the bicycle can't be outgrown.

A word about lights. If he's a teenager, you are not going to be able to keep your child off the streets after dark. Therefore, any bicycle you buy him should have a good front and a good rear light. I recommend the generator light for a child's bicycle because it eliminates the possibility of a dead battery. The generator is ready to provide light at all times. For the really fine bicycle, however, where long after-dark trips are involved, the matter of lights is a separate problem altogether. (See page 284 for a discussion of lights.)

For a young person who has the inclination and the mechanical ability to take proper care of his bicycle, you might spend a bit more and buy him a five-speed derailleur bicycle.

Fig. 24: For adults or teenagers who care, here's a better grade ten-speed than shown in Fig. 23. It has alloy chainwheels, rims, and hubs; a wide gear range for hill climbing; a chrome molybdenum seamless steel tubing frame; and it weighs around 31 pounds.

TABLE 4 · **Top-Quality Three-Speed Bicycles** *

MAKE AND MODEL	SPECIFICATIONS
Schwinn Speedster	Conventional diamond frame, flat handlebars, spring saddle, side-pull caliper brakes, 26-in. x 1⅜-in. tires. Good feature is wide range of frame sizes, 17 inch, 20 inch, 22 inch, and 24 inch to fit all heights. 38–41 pounds (depending on frame size) and at low end of price scale of these bicycles.
Raleigh DL-24	26-inch wheels. Front wheel has Dyna-hub that powers front and rear lights on this bike. Rear carrier, fenders, front and rear side-pull caliper brakes, pump, key lock on front fork. 21- and 23-inch frame sizes in men's model, 21-inch in women's model (DL 22L). For very tall folks, the DL-1 and DL-1L (men's and women's frames) have 28-inch wheels with 24-inch frame on men's and 22-inch frame on women's models. DL-24 weighs 42 pounds (about 6 pounds of accessories).
Columbia 6616	Generator, front and rear lights, rear carrier, 27-inch wheels with lighter tires (27-in. x 1⅜-in.) account for lighter weight at 36 pounds.
DBS Oglaend Spesial	New on the U.S. market is this fine machine from Norway. Features exceptionally good brakes, with DBS hub brake on front wheel, coaster brake on rear wheel. 22-inch frame size only, 26-in. x 1⅝-in. tires, has fenders, flat bars, spring saddle, internal wiring for lights, but no lights. Tool set, excellent finish. About 36 pounds. DBS women's model, the "Sport," has 20-inch frame, same specifications as men's "Spesial."

* Three-speed models with internal rear hub (not derailleur). Fairly heavy models for around-town use, not suitable for touring. The kind used by British postmen on their appointed rounds, with fenders, flat handlebars, coaster and/or caliper brakes. While model numbers and names may change from year to year, there's fairly little difference in the bicycles.

I have seen literally hundreds of teenagers on the road within the past two years, ten-speeds loaded down with tent, sleeping bag, and other camping gear, in small groups unsponsored, or in larger groups on trips sponsored by the American Youth Hostel organization. Bicycling has become an "in" thing in this age group.

Bicycles have sprouted on college campuses throughout the nation, and where before a fond parent would give a child a new watch as a send-off college gift, the gift is now likely to be a shiny new ten-speed bicycle.

Now that cycling is an accepted teen-age and young adult interest, what kind of bike is best suited to this age group? My answer is the same bike suited to the adult, with the single exception being that an adult can (usually) afford to pay more for a bike than a student can. Yet I find even twelve year olds unusually knowledgeable about bicycles. I'll never forget the time I was in Minneapolis, having been invited by Dayton's, a large department store in that city, to talk about bikes and cycling to local citizens. About 500 people showed up, of which about 10 percent were under fifteen. The question-and-answer period was fast and intense, and indicated that the cycling public had become far more sophisticated than it had been just a few years ago. I think the high point of this session was the question asked by a twelve-year-old boy, who wanted to know what kind of bicycle Belgian professional racer Eddy Merckx rode when he won the Tour de France in 1972 for the fourth time. I told this knowledgeable young man that I thought it was a Kessels, a custom-built Belgian bike, although Eddy used to ride a Masi, from another small builder in Milan, Italy, and a Colnago at other times. Therefore, since the first edition of this book appeared in October, 1970, I have noted an almost complete reversal of the then typical teen-age disdain for bicycles as "kid stuff." No question about it, bicycles have become as much an interest of young people as they have of adults. Teenagers today devote the same kind of loving care and attention to their expensive, beautifully made ten speeds as we older folk used to lavish on our "jalopies" of an earlier era. I think it's a step in the right direction for young people to be so selectively enthusiastic about material things, and perhaps this is a step toward a happier, carless society.

How to Fit the Bicycle to the Child

Since 26-inch-wheel bicycles come in a variety of frame sizes, ranging from 18 inches to 24 inches, you should try to fit the bicycle to the child. By age fourteen, for example, your child will be almost fully grown, as far as his legs are concerned. The simplest way to fit a bicycle to a boy is to buy the largest size frame he can straddle comfortably with both feet on the ground and crotch over the top tube (the bar running from handlebars to seat). For a girl, buy the frame size that, with seat properly adjusted (see pages 159–164), will permit her to get on and off the bicycle easily.

A WORD ABOUT QUALITY

There are several bicycle manufacturers in the United States, and large numbers of bikes are imported from England and Japan. It is interesting to note that there is quite a variety in quality, but not much difference in price, between domestic bicycles and imports. Let me tell you a few things to look for to help you select the best quality for the least money. (You should study this section if you are interested in a really top-quality machine for long rides, club tours, and general cross-country cycling for pleasure and health, because none of the bicycles discussed till now are really suitable for this type of cycling.)

THE FRAME: Where frame tubes meet, they should be brazed into lugs at their joints (Fig. 25). Frame construction where tubes are inserted into each other (Fig. 26) is not nearly as strong as the lugged and brazed

Fig. 25: The hallmark of a good bicycle is a lugged frame, as shown here. A lug is a fitting into which frame tubes are fitted and brazed.

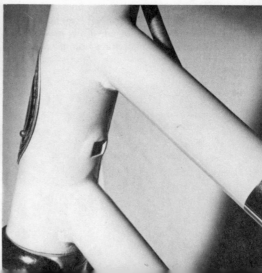

Fig. 26: This frame construction found on less expensive bicycles, is not as strong as that shown in Figure 25.

frame, except as noted earlier. However, there are lugs and lugs. The very plain lugs, that look like pieces of sawed-off pipe in a "T" shape, are more than likely simply cast steel, whereas the cut-out decorative looking lugs on the finer bicycles are forged steel, the latter being of course much stronger as well as lighter. The poorly welded, unlugged frame tends to come apart at the joints, as shown in Figs. 27, 28, and 29.

Fig. 27: Here's what can happen to a cheap bike frame, where tubes are simply stuck into one another and welded in place. The owner of this bike was unpleasantly surprised when he suddenly found himself riding a "collapsible" bicycle, one that self-destructed into two pieces, with the fork and headset going one way, and the rest of the bike another. Note that welds simply parted at the headset, with the top and down tubes breaking at the joints. This was a brand-new bike, perhaps a month old.

Fig. 28: Close-up of the two main tubes that broke off a cheap bike, also shown in Fig. 27. Note that welds were inadequate, which can be a problem with automated machine welding.

Fig. 29: Close-up of headset of bike in Fig. 27. Note that welding is practically nonexistent on this cheap frame, which is another good reason to buy only a lugged frame (except for Schwinn, Oglaend and Lambert frames, which are well built up).

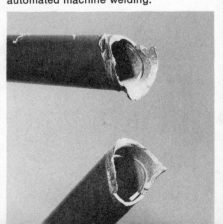

SIDE-PULL

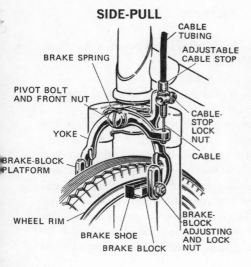

CABLE TUBING

BRAKE SPRING

ADJUSTABLE CABLE STOP

PIVOT BOLT AND FRONT NUT

CABLE-STOP LOCK NUT

YOKE

CABLE

BRAKE-BLOCK PLATFORM

WHEEL RIM

BRAKE-BLOCK ADJUSTING AND LOCK NUT

BRAKE SHOE

BRAKE BLOCK

Fig. 30: Side-pull brakes are usually found on less costly bicycles, hence are more widely used. To adjust, loosen locknut, turn cable stop so brake blocks barely clear rim. Give wheel a twirl. If wheel is badly out of line, straighten it by adjusting spoke tension (see page 449 for instructions on wheel alignment). Otherwise wheel will bind at spots where it rubs on brake blocks. Retighten nut. If only one brake block contacts rim when brake lever is squeezed, tap down lightly on brake spring opposite side where block binds. Brake blocks must not touch tire when brake is applied!

CENTER-PULL

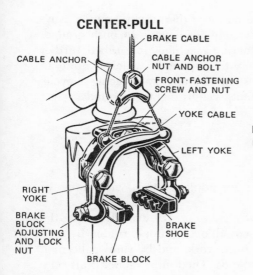

BRAKE CABLE

CABLE ANCHOR

CABLE ANCHOR NUT AND BOLT

FRONT·FASTENING SCREW AND NUT

YOKE CABLE

LEFT YOKE

RIGHT YOKE

BRAKE BLOCK ADJUSTING AND LOCK NUT

BRAKE SHOE

BRAKE BLOCK

Fig. 31: Center-pull brakes are found on medium- and high-cost bicycles.

CALIPER BRAKES: There are two basic types of caliper "hand" brakes— side-pull, Fig. 30, and center-pull, Fig. 31. Until recently, only inexpensive bicycles had side-pull brakes, because until some of the new cam-action designs came out, side-pulls were considered inferior because they pull up from one side only, and would not work as positively as center-pull designs. Cheap bikes still use cheap side-pulls, but expensive bicycles use highly engineered, polished aluminum alloy brakes such as those made by Campagnolo, Shimano, and Universal.

HUBS: Should be one-piece machined. Avoid the stamped-metal type.

WHEELS: Should have thirty-six spokes in the rear wheel and no less than thirty-two spokes in the front wheel; except English bicycles with three-speed rear hubs, which have forty spokes in the rear and thirty-two in the front. Other lightweight models have thirty-six spokes front and rear. An exception are the smaller bicycles, twenty-four-inch wheels and down, where twenty-eight spokes front and rear should be installed. Any fewer number of spokes than those listed above will give you a weak wheel that won't stand up under rough handling. Spokes should be double-butted, which means they should show a slight thickening at both ends for added strength.

WEIGHT: Fully equipped, should be no more than thirty pounds. Anything heavier is just too much dead weight for anyone to push around. The better quality road-racing and touring machines (described further on) weigh around twenty-two to twenty-three pounds, which is quite an energy-saver on long rides. The finest hand-made track-racing bicycle, without brakes and stripped to the limit, weighs eighteen pounds.

BICYCLES FOR ADULTS

There are only two types of bicycles for adults, with a wide range of quality and prices within these types.

There is the so-called "tourist" bicycle (see Fig. 15) which is really the common, garden-variety bicycle one sees all over Europe, ridden by men and women around town and to and from work, and by rural policemen and mail carriers on their appointed rounds. The tourist model is also the bike the American Youth Hostel cycle shops and other cycle shops usually rent out. This machine is one step away from the balloon-tired heavyweight bicycle so popular among children in the United States. It is also known as an "English racer," though as a racing machine it's about as suitable as a wheelbarrow.

For the adult who wants a reasonably reliable bicycle for tootling around town, the English racer is quite adequate when it is equipped with a three- or five-speed rear hub and caliper brakes.

However, for really serious cycling fun and for long trips, the ten-speed, derailleur-equipped bicycle with turned-down handlebars is a must. If you think there's a lot of performance difference between the fifty- to sixty-pound balloon-tired monster and the English tourist racer, then you're in for a delightful surprise when, after riding the heavy English racer, you try a lightweight twenty-two-pound high-performance road bicycle with a good selection of derailleur gears (Fig. 32). You'll find, as I did, that there's by far more difference between the English racer and the ten-speed job than there is between the English racer and the balloon-tired bicycle. It's like changing to a hot sports car from a worn-out, six-cylinder, cheap compact car. Actually, I think the difference is even greater than that, but the novice may not appreciate such a tremendous improvement. Perhaps the best way to test this difference is to go on an all-day jaunt with a friend riding the twenty-two-pound, ten-speed bike and you the forty-five-pound, three-speed English tourist type. If you are both in about the same physical condition, the first hill you meet is going to see you down at the bottom while your friend is sailing over the top, and after about ten miles, you'll want to rest while your friend cycles around you in circles.

At this point, swap bicycles with your friend. You'll find the fine steel frame of the ten-speed feels like a spirited colt after the heavy frame of the tourist. Also, the ten-speed bicycle goes exactly where you want it to in contrast to the imprecise steering of the tourist model. And when you shift down to low speed on the first steep hill and find you can go right up the grade sitting down, you'll wonder how you ever finished ten miles

Fig. 32: Typical of top-grade touring bicycles in the $365 to $500 bracket, this all-handmade frame of '531' double-butted Reynolds tubing is Campagnolo-equipped has center-pull brakes, clincher tires, aluminum alloy hubs and wide range gears; weighs around 26 pounds.

on the tourist. Also, you'll find your cycling efficiency increased by about 40 percent because of the "rattrap" toe clips that enable you to pull up with one foot while you push down with the other. More about toe clips later.

While the turned-down handlebars on the ten-speed may worry you at first, you will quickly discover that it's actually more comfortable than the conventional tourist handlebars. When you bend over slightly instead of sitting straight up, you cut wind resistance considerably. Also, this new position lets you use your back and stomach muscles in addition to your arm and leg muscles. Later on, I will discuss dropped or turned-down handlebars versus conventional handlebars again, because you can get either kind with any type of bicycle.

If your limited cycling needs will be satisfied with a tourist or English racer type of bicycle, I have listed several good ones in Table 4, with their specifications itemized. I have checked these models, and they will all give you excellent service. Some are a bit better than others, with better brakes, seat, and frame; in general, the more expensive models will last longer and need less maintenance.

A note about the various makes of bicycles I mention in this chapter. By no means do they represent all the fine makes available. I have had to limit my list to a few bikes in each category, and have tried to pick those makes which are made in quantity and are generally available throughout the country. Also, the market changes every day, with new models and parts being introduced constantly. If your bicycle store does not carry these particular makes, or if you are interested in buying a specific bike which is not listed here, you can use the specification tables to check the quality of the bike you are interested in. A great variety of machines can be bought in this country.

DERAILLEUR TEN-SPEED BICYCLES

When you take your first look at derailleur-equipped bicycles, you will probably be puzzled at the broad price range, since all these bicycles look pretty much alike.

The old saw, "you get what you pay for," applies here. The price depends on the quality of steel used in the frame and the type of equipment the maker selects to hang on the frame.

Therefore, in buying a derailleur-equipped bicycle, you should examine its specifications *very* carefully. Below are a few pointers to guide you in your selection. You won't always find the parts equally matched; for example, you may find a frame of the very finest steel equipped with low-cost components, a selection of gears you don't particularly want, or tube tires when you prefer tubular tires.

Later on in this book (page 179), you'll find a complete discussion of gears and gear ratios to help you in selecting the right combinations for the type of cycling you want to do, and to fit your own physical ability. You might read this data now before making your final decision.

A Warning About Road-Racing Bikes

A road-racing bicycle has a shorter wheel base, less fork rake, and a stiffer frame than a touring bicycle. Road-racing bicycles are designed with stiff frames, so more pedaling energy goes into forward movement, less into frame "whip" or "give." Road bikes are hard riding, tough on arms, hands, and bottoms. The problem is that unless you are an old hand at bicycling, you may not be able to tell a road-racing from a touring machine. Yet the finest road machines, such as those made for European professional racing cyclists, sell from $600 and up. You may go into a bike shop, with no budget in mind, looking for the very best, with someone's recommendation that "Masi" or "Cinelli" is the top machine. Well, they are certainly among the world's finest machines, all hand-crafted, of top-grade components. But unless you are careful, your $600 plus will get you a bicycle fine for the Tour de France, but a back-buster for touring. Good touring bicycles are the Schwinn "Paramount P-15" or "P-13"; Motobecane "Grand Record"; Frejus "Super Corsa" fifteen speed; Fuji "Newest" or "Finest"; Bianchi "Gran Premio" and "Corsa Special." There are many other fine, fairly expensive touring bicycles. Road-racing bicycles, such as the Cinelli, Masi, or Motobecane "le Champion," *can* be used for touring, but the ride will be stiff. It would be like driving a souped-up, road-racing car versus a softer, deluxe-riding Rolls Royce. It all depends on what you want . . . for myself, I prefer a softer ride for distance touring. To make sure you get what you want, take a yardstick and a twelve-inch ruler with you to the bike shop and measure fork rake and wheel base, as shown in Fig. 59, page 145. Measure fork rake by holding the yardstick about on the centerline of a fork blade, then measure perpendicular distance from the yardstick to the centerline of the fork dropout. Road-racing bicycles have about 1¾-inch rake. Touring bicycles have a longer rake, generally around 2 inches, and a track bike, for smooth surfaces, has a 1-inch to 1¼-inch rake. The wheel base of road-racing bicycles is 39 to

39½ inches; the wheel base of touring machines is longer, about 40½ inches in today's bicycles (touring bikes made a few years ago had longer wheel bases, up to 42 inches). You check wheel base by measuring the distance between the centerline of front and rear dropouts (the place where wheel axle fits on rear stays and front fork).

THE FRAME: The best quality bicycles use Reynolds '531' tubing. The Reynolds trademark (Fig. 33) bearing this number will be on the frame and fork. Reynolds '531' metal is made only in Great Britain, but it is used

Only the Top Tube, Seat Tube and Down Tube of a frame with this transfer are made from REYNOLDS 531 Tubing—plain gauge.

All the tubing in a bicycle with this transfer is REYNOLDS 531 — Frame Tubes, Chain & Seat Stays & Fork Blades, but it is all plain gauge tubing.

The Top Tube, Seat Tube and Down Tube of a frame which bears this transfer are REYNOLDS 531 BUTTED tubing.

This transfer signifies that the bicycle is an aristocrat, a thoroughbred — made throughout of REYNOLDS 531 tubing BUTTED for lightness with strength.

Fig. 33: '531' tubing varies by type and use. Study this illustration and the remarks made about each grade of tubing to understand what you are getting when you buy an expensive bicycle. The best bicycles, of course, come with the bottom decal transfer signifying that top-grade Reynolds '531' is used throughout. See also page 76 for more data on frame steels. Please note that Columbia tubing, used on some Italian bicycles, is comparable to Reynolds.

by top bicycle manufacturers all over the world (including the U.S.S.R., which ordered a carload to make its own track bicycles for the 1964 Olympic races). Also, as noted in the section on frames on page 76, Columbus tubing is of quality equal to '531,' but a bit stiffer and used more for track and road-racing machines. Japanese bicycles, such as the top-line Fuji, and Schwinn "Super Sport" and "Sports Tourer" models also use a good grade of chrome molybdenum seamless cold-drawn steel.

RIMS: The best rims are made of aluminum. Mavic, Weinmann, Fiamme, and Milremo are all high quality. Steel rims are a sign of lower quality. Generally, special orders aside, machines with tubular tires (sew-ups) indicate a more expensive machine.

HUBS: Although Campagnolo aluminum alloy hubs (Fig. 34) are considered among the best, there are other hubs of equal quality available. The Phil Wood aluminum alloy hub, made in California, is one of the better hubs on the market, in my opinion. It costs no more than the Campagnolo Record hub, and has the added advantage of being smoother running, with cartridge bearings sealed against water and dust and requiring no maintenance for about five years. Another excellent hub made in the U.S., by Hi-E Engineering Company, Nashville, Tennessee, is also

Fig. 34: Campagnolo hubs, among the finest money can buy, are a hallmark of quality in any bicycle, are used for both track and road racing, and are also found on fine touring bicycles.

Fig. 35: Ultra-lightweight sealed bearing hub made by Hi-E Engineering Company, Nashville, Tennessee, weighs only 3.1 ounces, is sealed for around 1,500 miles before needing maintenance.

sealed, very smooth-running, and needs no maintenance for 1,500 miles or three years (Fig. 35). Both Phil Wood and Hi-E hubs can be dismantled for relube. The Hi-E front hub, at only 3.1 ounces, is the lightest on the market (but use a Campagnolo cam skewer instead of the Hi-E, it holds better).

Another excellent and quite unique hub is the Cinelli "Bi-Valent" hub. This unit separates the freewheel from the hub. The freewheel rear gear cluster is mounted on the right rear dropout, separately from the hub. The hub is designed so it can be dropped into the gear cluster in a second, making a five-second wheel change possible. It also makes removing the rear wheel simpler since you can pull it out without tangling in a mess of chain, derailleur, and freewheel (your hands stay clean). Also the front and rear wheels become interchangeable, so no "dishing" (see wheel alignment, page 433) of the rear wheel is needed. You can also change freewheels for different gear ratios easier. You would have to buy a set (two hubs, freewheel, or skewers) of these hubs, which are low flange. The rear hub, instead of being threaded for a freewheel, is splined so it fits into the freewheel. If you want extra-wide ratio gears you would have to have your bike shop make them up for you by changing the gears that come on the Cinelli unit, which are narrow ratio for road racing.

For a very good, smooth-running alloy quick-release hub I like the Triplex Super Olimpic. This hub comes in both low and high flange, and is quite reasonably priced. Incidentally, I really can't tell you where to buy any of the hubs listed here. If your bike shop doesn't have them at the moment, try one of the mail-order bike stores listed on page 497 in the Appendix, which includes sources in Great Britain. The bike boom of the seventies has normal channels of distribution for parts and bikes pretty much in a turmoil and state of change.

TABLE 5 · **Available Hubs**

MANUFACTURER	MODEL	MATERIAL	FLANGE	WEIGHT (oz.) FRONT	REAR	QUICK RELEASE
CAMPAGNOLO	Record	Alloy	High	9¼	12¼	Yes
CAMPAGNOLO	Record (Track)	Alloy	High	9¼	12¼	No
CAMPAGNOLO	Record	Alloy	Low	8¼	10¾	Yes
PHIL WOOD	Phil	Alloy	High	Not Available		Yes
HI-E	Hi-E front	Alloy	Low	3.1	N.A.	Yes
SHIMANO	QR	Alloy	High	Not Available		Yes
SHIMANO	WN	Steel	High	Not Available		No
SANSHIN	Sunshine	Alloy	High	Not Available		Yes
SANSHIN	Standard	Alloy	High	Not Available		No
TRIPLEX	Super Olimpic	Alloy	High	Not Available		Yes
TRIPLEX	Super Olimpic L	Alloy	Low	Not Available		Yes
ZEUS	Gigante	Alloy	High	9	12	Yes
ZEUS	Gran Sport	Alloy	Low	8¼	10½	Yes
ZEUS	Pista (Track)	Alloy	High	8	11	No
ZEUS	Standard (Track)	Alloy	Low	7¼	10	No
NORMANDY	Luxe	Alloy	High	9.5	13	Yes

Steel vs. Aluminum Alloy, or vs. Solid Axles

Hubs for ten-speed bikes come in both aluminum alloy and steel (Table 5). The aluminum alloy is lighter, generally more precision-made, and costs a lot more. Steel hubs are heavier but stronger, and are found on the less expensive bikes. Best hubs on road bicycles come with quick-release cam-actuated skewer so you can remove wheels from bike frame in a jiffy (so can thieves), with a hollow axle for the skewer to pass through. Track hubs have solid axles and hex bolts so wheels can be locked to dropouts to withstand terrific pressures from racing athletes.

LUGS: Lugs are the sleeve braces by which the tubes of the frame are joined together (Fig. 25). The trade name "Nervex" indicates high quality. Even though some lugged frames are stronger than unlugged frames, this is not always so. If lugs are simply cast-iron hunks of metal, little better than water pipe, about all they do is add weight to the bicycle, and give it the vague appearance of a more costly machine. You can tell a cast lug

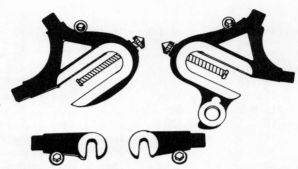

Fig. 36: These Campagnolo forged steel fork (bottom) and rear frame tips (top) are brazed into fork blades and seat and chain stays, respectively.

(as opposed to a forged steel lug on fine bikes) by filing it; the file will bite easily into the metal. The dealer won't take kindly to your filing into a new bike, though. Instead, you can usually, though not always, tell if the lug is cast and not forged because it will look something like a simple cast-iron pipe "T" or "L," with straight unadorned edges. A good forged lug is generally cut away in fancy curves, has smooth edges, and often in the very best bikes, hand-applied striping at lug edges.

DERAILLEURS: We will talk more about derailleurs in the chapter on Gears (page 179). Here we will simply list some of the best models, found on higher quality bicycles, in descending order of quality by manufacturer. First, though, I would like to point out that, until 1971, Campagnolo pretty much had the quality market all to itself. Till then, Campagnolo was, justifiably, considered the best in derailleurs, dropouts, shift levers, bottom bracket and chainwheel sets, pedals, and seat posts. Today the situation has changed, and in my opinion, there are other manufacturers' products comparable or even superior to Campagnolo and they cost considerably less. So if you're planning to switch derailleurs, it pays to check some of the other derailleurs listed here for price. (In the first edition of this book I gave a lot of prices on parts and bikes. Since then prices have almost tripled and are still rising, so I will try to stay away from being specific about prices, but rather concentrate on quality comparisons and let you do the price shopping.) The derailleurs listed below are in descending order of quality (and price) by manufacturer. That is, in the Campagnolo line, for example, the best model is the Nuovo Record front

Fig. 37: This new wide-range derailleur, the Shimano GS, is lightweight, quick-responding, and costs much less than the comparable Campagnolo GT. Other good wide-range derailleurs are made by Huret and Sun Tour.

derailleur and the least expensive is the Sport model. The Gran Turismo is their wide-range derailleur found on touring bicycles with a broad gear range. However, at 13 ounces I find this model fairly heavy, and prefer the Shimano Crane GS (Fig. 37) at 8.5 ounces and at substantially less cost. The Sun Tour V-GT is another excellent derailleur, although it's heavier at 12.1 ounces. In general, though, the top models of all derailleur lines are roughly comparable in performance.

Campagnolo has until recently, possibly along with Zeus and Stronglight, been considered the top line of chainwheel, crank, and bottom bracket assembly. Relative newcomers, who also make good quality aluminum alloy cotterless cranks (Fig. 38), chainwheels, and bottom brackets,

Fig. 38: Typical cotterless crankset of polished aluminum alloy.

TABLE 6 · **Derailleur Specifications**

| | | **REAR DERAILLEUR** | | |
| | | NO. TEETH | WEIGHT | MATERIAL |
MANUFACTURER	MODEL	CAPACITY	(ounces)	(body)
CAMPAGNOLO	Nuovo Record	13–30	8¼	Al. Alloy(P)*
"	Gran Turismo	13–34	13	Steel
"	Valentino	13–30	11	Steel
"	Sport	13–30	12½	Steel
SHIMANO	Crane	13–28	9	Al. Alloy(P)
"	Crane GS	13–34	8.5	Al. Alloy(P)
"	Titlist	13–28	8.8	Al. Alloy
"	Titlist GS	13–34	9.9	Al. Alloy
"	Tourney	13–28	9.5	Al. Alloy
"	Tourney GS	13–34	10.6	Al. & Steel
"	Eagle SS	13–34	13.4	Steel
"	Eagle GS	13–38	14.1	Steel
"	Eagle STO	13–34	13.1	Steel
"	Eagle GTO	13–38	14.1	Steel
"	Lark STO	13–34	12.7	Steel
"	Skylark	13–34	11.3	Steel
"	Lark-W	13–34	12.7	Steel
HURET	Jubilee	13–24	4.7	Alloy(P)
"	Allvit	13–30	11	Steel
"	Super Allvit	13–34	13	Steel
"	Svelto	13–24	11	Steel
"	Super Touring	13–41	11	Steel
SIMPLEX	Prestige	13–28	8.75	Plastic
"	Criterium	13–28	10.25	Plastic
ZEUS	Criterium-69	13–31	9	Al. Alloy(P)
"	Alfa-Jr.	13–28	8.5	Steel
TRIPLEX	Sport	13–28	10	Steel
"	Super	13–28	9.5	Steel
SUN TOUR	Sun Tour V	13–24	8	Al. Alloy
" "	Honor	13–28	13.3	Steel
" "	V-GT	14–34	12.1	Al. Alloy
" "	GT	14–34	14.1	Steel

* Polished and buffed to a smooth, fine finish.

MODEL	FRONT DERAILLEUR NO. CHAINWHEEL CAPACITY	WEIGHT (ounces)	MATERIAL (body)
Record	3	4	Al. Alloy(P)
Valentino	3	5	Steel
Titlist	3	4.9	Al. Alloy(P)
Thunderbird	3	6.7	Steel
Thunderbird GTO	3	6.5	Al. & Steel
Jubilee	2	2.8	Al. Alloy(P)
Allvit	3	8	Steel
Super Allvit	3	9	Steel
Svelto	3	8.5	Steel
Super-Competition	3	4.5	Plastic
Criterium	3	4.5	Plastic
Criterium-69	3	4.75	Al. Alloy
Alfa-65	3	6.25	Steel
Sport	3	5.5	Steel
Extra	3	5.5	Steel
Compe-V	3	5.25	Al. Alloy
Sport	3	5.8	Steel

include Sugino (their five-pin crankset) and Shimano Dura-Ace. Sugino five-pin chainsets are now coming on European-made high-quality bicycles, due to shortages of European-made cranksets.

T.A. also makes alloy chainsets, but I've had trouble with them due to pins holding the cranks together coming loose, so that the chainwheel flattens (irretrievably) under cycling pressure. After tightening loose pins on a replacement T.A. crankset I had no further trouble, though. Nervar also makes a fairly good alloy chainset. Sugino makes a three-pin alloy crankset, but their five-pin is stronger and more likely to stay in alignment.

BRAKES: Until Campagnolo came along a few years ago with their expensive side-pull caliper brakes (Fig. 39), center-pull designs such as Mafac "Competition" (Fig. 40) were thought to be superior to side-pull. Center-pull brakes pull up evenly from the center, whereas side-pull brakes pull up from one side only and generally don't work as smoothly. Campagnolo brakes, however, are excellent, though they cost as much or more than an entire bicycle in the low price range, and four or five times as much as the best center-pull brake. The Campy side-pulls, frankly, aren't four or five times better than Mafac "Competition," Mafac "Racer," or Universal center-pulls, and Mafacs stop better than the Campy (heresy though this may be!). In fact, I have found only one brake I consider better in terms of stopping power than Mafac, and it isn't

Fig. 39: Campagnolo side-pull brakes are quite expensive; they were designed for the road-racing cyclist who wants minutely accurate braking control.

Fig. 40: Mafac center-pull alloy brakes offer fingertip stopping power, very good braking, and are reasonably good in wet weather. But don't trust any brakes on a wet pavement; cycle so you know you can stop in an emergency.

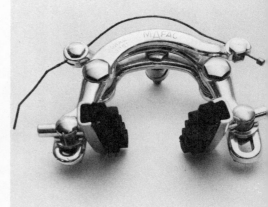

Campagnolo. Besides, I, with others, have had trouble with squeaky Campagnolo brake blocks. And replacement blocks alone on Campy brakes cost a small fortune, dollars compared to cents, for ordinary, non-royal blocks. Campy side-pulls are beautifully made, though, so if you're a real bike buff, well, go to it. They also have the only really easy-to-use quick-release lever I've seen. Your brakes should have quick releases because the rim is always narrower than the tire. Since brakes have to grip the rim, and the tire is *above* the brake block, you either have to let air out of the tire (if you remove the wheel) or risk pulling a brake block loose as you scrape the wider tire past the blocks. (If the tire goes by easily, brake blocks are too far from the rim.)

Shimano has come out with a side-pull all-alloy brake that looks very much like a Campagnolo side-pull, handsome finish, quick release, and all, which works quite well and costs considerably less (see Fig. 239, p. 385).

Weinmann 999 alloy center-pull brakes are also excellent, as is their Japanese counterpart, Duo-Compe center-pulls. But there are some center-pulls on cheap ten speeds, made God knows where, that are really horrible; which means the ultimate test is riding, and price. You won't find really awful components, for example, on a bike that costs $250.00 and up (to $1000.00, as of this writing, which has to be the ultimate in two-wheeled conspicuous consumption).

"Safety" Levers Aren't

On some bikes you'll find two sets of brake levers. One set is the standard kind that stick up above the handlebars, on the curve of the bars. The second set is flatter, connected to the same brake lever as the first, but the lever is parallel to and just underneath the top, flat part of the handlebars. I have used these "safety levers" and in my opinion they're anything but safe. They can, in fact, mislead you into thinking you can stop when in fact you cannot. The reason is because the "safety levers" do not have the distance of "travel" the standard levers do. Thus, unless wheel rims are almost perfectly true, and brake shoes adjusted so they are no more than ⅛ inch from the rims, "safety levers" won't pull up enough to force the brake shoe against the rim for a safe stop, especially a successful panic stop. Brakes get out of adjustment easily, rims won't stay aligned forever, brake cables stretch, so a "safety lever" that stopped you safely once may not do so when you need it. My advice is to go to your bike shop and have these unsafe safety levers removed, or do it yourself by unscrewing the nut holding the safety lever, removing the spacer, and replacing it with a shorter spacer (from your bike dealer) and screwing the nut back on again. True, safety levers are attractive to short-fingered women, who feel more secure with them. If this is so, it's much better to install "touring" handlebars with brake levers parallel to the top of the bar already installed, but specially made so you can get plenty of lever travel (see Fig. 62, page 149).

Oh yes, I mentioned one brake that stopped me better than Campagnolo. That's the Shimano *hydraulic* brake. Yes, I said *hydraulic* (Fig. 41). This brake has a master cylinder and two brake cylinders which force caliper brake arms apart and brake pad against the rim. The master cylinder is separately ported so the back brake stops a second or so before the front brake. Best of all, both brakes are actuated by a single brake lever, which can be positioned underneath the handlebar flat, if you don't mind using a rattail file to enlarge the diameter of the master brake cylinder block to fit downturned bars. (These brakes were made for in-

Fig. 41: New Shimano hydraulic caliper brake. (A) master cylinder; (B) brake lever; (C) rear brake cylinder; (D) front brake cylinder; (E) caliper arm; (F) brake shoe; (G) extra brake fluid; (H) hydraulic line clips; (I) hydraulic line; (J) mounting clip for handlebar mounting.

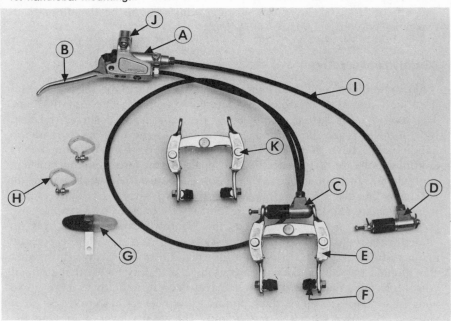

expensive bikes with flat bars; for racing, a two-lever system should be used.) But I think they are the best in the world, and certainly inexpensive. Nothing has ever stopped me as well, and they seem to work almost as well in the rain as when it's dry. True, the hydraulic lines are a bit bulkier than cables and cable covers, the finish of the lever and calipers is not up to bike-buff standards, and the calipers are steel, not aluminum. But boy, do they stop! And with one finger, yet. Shimano (at this writing) hasn't been able to sell them to American bike makers because they cost a bit more than low cost side-pull brakes, but if we all holler at once, I think Shimano will at least have them available at bike wholesale supply houses that supply retail bike shops. And there's no reason why the cosmetics of buffed aluminum calipers and master cylinder can't be designed into these brakes, for us bike freaks.

TIRES: In general, you will find the more expensive, higher quality bicycles fitted with 27-inch wheels and tubular (sew-up) road-racing tires (Fig. 153). But you can, if you wish, specify tube-type (Fig. 42) 27-inch x 1¼-inch wheels and tires. Tubular tires are more prone to flats in city-street cycling, and they are more difficult to repair because the casing is sewn up all the way around. But they and the wheels they are used on are lighter and more responsive, making cross-country pedaling easier and more enjoyable. Tube-type wired-on tires and the wheels they are used on are heavier. However, tube tires are easier to repair because the tube is readily accessible. On the other hand, tubular sew-ups can be changed in a few minutes, and they are so light that several spares can be carried compactly. Repairs can always be made after a trip.

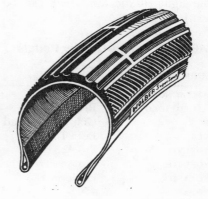

Fig. 42: These tube-type lightweight tires are easier to repair than the sewn-up "tubular" type. They are heavier and less responsive than tubulars, but fine for touring. (See Figure 194 for location of inner tube and rim.)

A new clincher tire recently introduced removes most of the objections to these as compared with tubulars. The new clinchers are 27 × 1⅛ inches, as compared with the 27 × 1¼ inches of conventional clinchers, so they offer rolling resistance about as low as tubular tires, which are also 27 × 1⅛ inches. The new clinchers are still a bit heavier than most tubulars, although they compare favorably in this respect with heavier training and touring tubular tires. These new clinchers will, in my opinion, take away a lot of the attractiveness of tubulars for touring, such as light weight, low rolling resistance, and better feel of the road. And with the new clinchers, as with the old, puncture repair is simplicity itself, as compared to the hassle of unsewing, patching, and restitching the tubulars. And the new clinchers are a good deal less prone to flats than tubulars. If you switch to the new clinchers (27 × 1⅛ inches) you will also need to switch to new 27 × 1⅛-inch tubes. (Zefal has recently introduced a very good pump with a Schraeder valve head, thank heaven!)

PEDALS: All the better bicycles have pedals made of light, forged-aluminum alloy barrels and with alloy or steel rattrap sides. And, of course, they are all rattrap (Fig. 43) design, with toe clips and straps so feet can't slide off. (Accidents leading to injury and fatality have been attributed to feet slipping off pedals and resultant loss of balance and fall.) Cheaper bikes have rubber and steel pedals, or all-steel rattrap pedals, usually without toe clips and straps, although they can be fitted on. Cheap pedals are wider, and either bind as they turn or are so loose there's obvious sideplay, and are comparatively heavy, around ten ounces each. See Table 7 for a quick review of some of the better pedals. (Incidentally, remember to add pedal reflectors, a highly visible safety item, since at this writing suppliers haven't as yet been required to add them. The light plastic kind that can be fitted to *both* sides of pedals are best.)

TABLE 7 · High-Quality Pedals

MANUFACTURER	MODEL	MATERIALS	WEIGHT (each, oz.)
CAMPAGNOLO	Record Road	Alloy and Steel	8
CAMPAGNOLO	Record Track	Alloy and Steel	7½
ZEUS	Gran Sport, Road	Alloy and Steel	7⅓
ZEUS	Pista Track	Alloy and Steel	7
KYOKUTO	Pro Ace Road	Alloy and Steel	8
KYOKUTO	Pro Ace Track	Alloy and Steel	7½
LYOTARD	Platform #23	Steel	6½
LYOTARD	45CS	Alloy and Steel	5.63

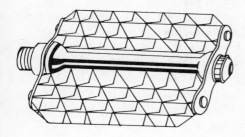

Fig. 43: The three basic types of pedals. Top, conventional rubber tread pedal, for city and knock-about use; center, road-racing pedal, also fine for touring, and bottom, track-racing pedal, light-weight, with teeth for gripping shoes.

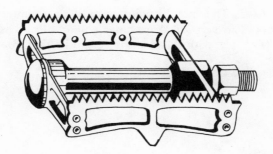

HEADSETS: The headset on a bicycle is the set of bearings, cones, top washer, and locknuts which hold the fork in place and permit it to turn accurately and smoothly. Headsets on good bicycles have their maker's name stamped on them, usually on the top locknut. To check headset adjustment (or for cheap headset), lift front wheel off floor and turn fork by front wheel, feel for binding or roughness. Hold bike down, handlebars held firmly, wheel on floor, and lift handlebars to rear and front of bike to check for sideplay looseness. Cheap headsets often have cracked lower cups, which you can't detect in the assembled bike. If in doubt, disassemble headset (see page 430) and check top and bottom cups for tiny cracks and imperfections, and for shiny "galled" spots showing wear at misaligned points.

Better headsets are made by Campagnolo, Stronglight, and Zeus.

UNISEX FRAMES: Years ago, when women's clothing was more voluminous and no "lady" wore slacks, a girl's frame bicycle, sans top tube, was a necessity to permit females to ride, mount, and dismount easily and safely. But today, when women and girls wear pants (or shorts) routinely, the heavy, cumbersome girl's frame is on the way out. Bicycle dealers report that they are selling almost as many bikes with top tubes to women as they are to men, and that they're selling four times as many men's frames (with top tube) as women's frame bikes. The Women's Lib movement can only have had a beneficial effect on bicycling, for the extra cable lengths for gears and brakes make controls more sluggish on women's frames (bicycles, that is) and these bikes are harder to control accurately. So far as I know, men aren't complaining.

STEMS AND BARS: The best bicycles come with aluminum alloy stems and handlebars. The very best machines come with recessed stem bolt design stems (Fig. 44), with the stem bolt head hidden from view. This is

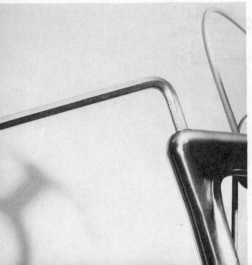

Fig. 44: Best handlebars on top-quality bicycles have dressier recessed stem bolts. You will need a 7-mm. Allen wrench (shown) to adjust this stem or to remove it. Stem shown is made by Cinelli.

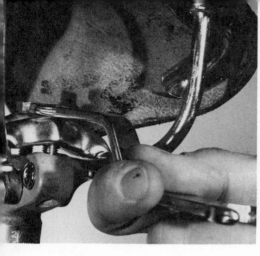

Fig. 45: A typical high-quality aluminum-alloy seat post with microtilt adjustment of the saddle.

mostly a cosmetic advantage, though the lack of a protruding stem bolt can add to safety. But you'll need a 7 mm. Allen key wrench for the stem bolt, which is one extra tool to carry on trips you would not need with conventional stem bolt design. Recessed stems are handsome, though, especially the stem and engraved bars made by Cinelli, Dia-Compe, Sakae Ringyo, Ltd., and t.t.t.

SEAT POSTS: Seat posts on fine bicycles are made of aluminum alloy and have a unique microtilt adjustment (Fig. 45) that lets you move the saddle up or down in as small an increment as you wish, to accommodate the curves of your you-know-what. These seat posts are made by Campagnolo, Zeus, Unica-Nitor, t.t.t., and Sakae Ringyo, Ltd.

DROPOUTS: The slotted fitting where the wheel axle fits in on the fork blades and stays is called a "dropout," because when you loosen axle bolts or quick-release skewer, the wheel "drops" out. Cheap bikes with fairly flimsy construction use stamped dropouts, often just stuck into the fork blade and welded there (Fig. 46), and pressed and spot-welded into rear stays (Fig. 47). Compare these dropouts with the strong, forged-steel brazed-in-place dropouts in Fig. 48 and Fig. 36 on page 106.

Fig. 46: Stamped-fork dropout.

Fig. 47: Weak chainstay dropout of spot-welded, stamped construction.

Fig. 48: Forged, brazed, very strong dropout found on better bicycles.

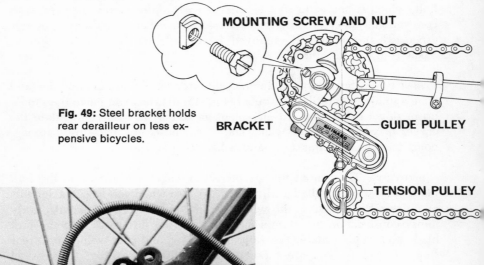

MOUNTING SCREW AND NUT

Fig. 49: Steel bracket holds rear derailleur on less expensive bicycles.

BRACKET

GUIDE PULLEY

TENSION PULLEY

Threaded ear for derailleur

Fig. 50: Threaded "ear" on rear dropout on good bicycles receives rear derailleur axle for accurate alignment and ease of derailleur removal for cleaning.

Fig. 51: Kickstands add useless weight, can damage chainstays if tightened too much.

On cheap bikes the rear derailleur is held in place by a steel bracket (Fig. 49) that is held on by the axle lock bolt or quick-release skewer and a small nut and bolt at the rear of the bracket. On good bikes, the rear derailleur axle goes into an integral threaded "ear" on the rear derailleur (Fig. 50).

KICKSTAND: You'll never find a kickstand on a good bicycle for at least four reasons. First, if the kickstand is bolted on chainstays (Fig. 51), it will eventually loosen and when you tighten it, you squeeze and weaken the stays. Second, if it's welded on, stays are weakened at the weld due to heat stress. Third, kickstands, even aluminum ones, add weight. Fourth, a good breeze, or a passerby, can knock over a bike propped up by a kickstand, with possible damage to derailleur, finish, brake levers, or handlebars; it's much better to *lean* the bike against a wall. And you can't conveniently chain a bike to a telephone pole or fence and still have it held up by the kickstand, and in any case the chain will hold the bike in place. So please wipe that look of dismay off your face because good bikes are "missing" a kickstand; it's a negative feature.

SELECT THE BICYCLE YOU WANT

Only you can select the right bicycle to fit your purse and the kind of cycling you plan to do. However, to help you buy the best machine, I have selected, from the hundreds of makes and varieties of derailleur bicycles available today, a few of the best models in three price ranges: fairly good-quality, low-priced models (Table 8); higher-quality, medium-priced machines (Table 9); and top-quality, precision-made bicycles where price isn't a factor (Table 10).

TABLE 8 · Low-Cost, Quality Derailleur Bicycles*

SPECIFICATIONS	PEUGEOT UO-8
FRAME	Seamless lightweight tubing, special lugs, chrome fork, tips, and head
FRAME SIZE	21 in., 23 in., 24 in., and 25 in.
DERAILLEURS	Simplex "Prestige" No. 537
CRANKS	Nervar, steel, cottered design
CHAINWHEEL	10-speed 36 x 52 teeth mountain gear; steel; double chainwheel
HUBS	Normandy dural wide flange with Simplex quick-release axles and skewers
FREEWHEEL	Atom 14, 16, 19, 22, and 26 teeth
RIMS	Rigida dural rims, 27 in. x 1¼ in.
SPOKES	Double-butted stainless steel
TIRES	Hutchinson 27 in. x 1¼ in. tube type
HANDLEBARS	AVA alloy stem, Maes bar (drop)
SADDLE	Black butt leather racing type
BRAKES	Mafac center-pull "racer" with covered levers
PEDALS	Lyotard No. 36 rattrap
ACCESSORIES	Pump, Mafac toolbag, tools
WEIGHT	27 lbs. complete

* While model numbers change from year to year, the basic bicycle remains about the same. Special note: Due to bike-boom-induced parts shortage, bicycles in this Table may come with other parts, such as derailleurs and crankset. Specifications listed are from manufacturers' catalogues and are subject to change without notice.

GITANE GRAN SPORT	RALEIGH RECORD DL-130
Seamless lightweight steel, Bocama lugs, chrome fork, tips, and stay ends	Seamless, lugged high carbon steel
Men's: 19½ in., 21½ in., 22½ in., 23½ in., 24½ in., 25½ in. Women's (Mixte frame): 19½ in., 21½ in., 22½ in.	19½ in., 21½ in., 23½ in.
Simplex "Prestige"	Huret "Allvit"
Nervar, steel, cottered design	Nervar, steel, cottered design
Durax 36 x 52 dual (40 x 52 optional)	Steel, 40 x 52 teeth
Normandy Sport dural with quick release	Atom Alloy
14-26 (optional, 14 to 28)	Maillard 14-28 teeth
Rigida dural	Endrick
Butted stainless steel	Butted stainless steel
Michelin 50 27 in. x 1¼ in. clincher	27 in. x 1¼ in. gum wall
Pivo Maes bend	Maes Pattern
Narrow, leather	Men's: leather racing; women's: mattress
Mafac Racer center-pull	Weinmann center-pull No. 144
Lyotard No. 36	Steel rattrap
Tool kit	None
29 lbs.	29 lbs.

Other excellent low-cost derailleur bicycles include: Oglaend DBS "Winner"; Schwinn Varsity Sport; Motobecane "Nobly"; Atala "Gran Prix"; Nishiki "Olympiad"; Azuki.

TABLE 9 · Moderate-Cost, Good Quality Derailleur Bicycles

SPECIFICATIONS *	RALEIGH SUPER COURSE	SCHWINN SPORTS TOURER
FRAME	Reynolds '531' plain-gauge tubes with Nervex lugs. Chrome fork tips	Chrome molybdenum seamless drawn tubing, not lugged but strongly brazed. Chrome fork tips
FRAME SIZE	21½ in., 23½ in., 25½ in.	22 in., 24 in., 26 in.
CRANKS	Stronglight steel	T.A. alloy cotterless crankset
CHAINWHEEL	Stronglight steel cottered; 40-52 teeth	T.A. double chainwheel, alloy, 40-52
HUBS	Normandy alloy with quick release	Alloy, wide flange
DERAILLEURS	Huret Luxe (or Simplex)	Campagnolo G.T.
FREEWHEEL	14-28 teeth	14-34 teeth wide range, Shimano alternate tooth design
RIMS	27 x 1¼ alloy	27 x 1¼ alloy
SPOKES	SS **	SS
TIRES	27 x 1¼ lightweight, amber wall	27 x 1¼ HP gum wall
HANDLEBARS	Maes alloy	Maes
SADDLE	Brooks leather B-15	Brooks P.15 or similar
BRAKES	Weinmann 999 with quick release (center-pull)	Weinmann 999 center-pull alloy
PEDALS	Atom alloy rattrap	Alloy, with toe clips and straps
ACCESSORIES	None	None
WEIGHT	27 lbs.	31-33 lbs. depending on frame size

* Specifications above are from manufacturers' literature and are subject to change without notice.

Other excellent bicycles in this range are: Fuji S10-S; Jeunet "610"; Ferrari "Superfast"; Bottechia "Special"; Atala "Competizione"; Anquetil "Tour de France"; Gitane "Hosteler."

** Stainless steel.

MOTOBECANE "GRAND TOURING"	BIANCHI GRAN PREMIO
1020 steel tubes, M.B. lugs, tubular deluxe fork with chromed crown and tips	Bianchi alloy steel tubes throughout, chromed fork crown and headset
21 in., 22 in., 23 in., 24 in., 25 in., 26 in.	22 in., 23 in., 24 in.
Stronglight alloy cotterless	Campagnolo cotterless alloy
Stronglight alloy, 40-52 teeth dual	Campagnolo alloy dual, 42-52 teeth
High-flange Normandy alloy, quick release	Bianchi special high-flange alloy
Huret Allvit Lux, wide range	Campagnolo Velox
14-32 teeth wide range	Regina 14-28 teeth
27 x 1¼ alloy	Nisi Corsa alloy, tubular
SS	SS
27 x 1¼ HP gum wall	Pirelli Gran Premio 27 x 1⅛ tubular
Maes alloy	TTT Maes alloy
Ideal 80, alloy seat post	Seamless nylon
Weinmann or Mafac Lux center-pull, quick release	Universal side-pull alloy
Lyotard alloy with reflectors, toe clips and straps	Bianchi special, extra light, quill type, with toe clips and straps
None	Silca pump, water bottle, and cage
27 lbs.	24 lbs.

TABLE 10 · Highest Quality Derailleur Bicycles *

SPECIFICATIONS ** RALEIGH PROFESSIONAL MARK IV

FRAME	Reynolds '531' double-butted throughout. Carlton lugs. Chrome tips on fork blades and stays. Low temperature brazed. Forged integral sloping fork crown. "Victor" direct seat stay cluster.
FRAME SIZE	20½ in., 21½ in., 22½ in., 23½ in., 24½ in., 25½ in.
CRANKS	Campagnolo alloy 6¾ in. cotterless
CHAINWHEEL	Campagnolo double plateau, alloy, 44 and 52 teeth
HUBS	Campagnolo Record, high-flange alloy with quick-release
DERAILLEURS	Campagnolo Nuovo Record polished alloy
FREEWHEEL	13-24 teeth, 6-speed Regina
RIMS	AVA Sprint, alloy, 27 in. for tubular tires
SPOKES	Robergel
TIRES	27 x 1⅛-in. Clement Criterium silk tubulars
HANDLEBARS	G. B. Maes style, alloy, with TTT recessed alloy stem
SADDLE	Brooks Professional Team Special; Campagnolo alloy seat post
BRAKES	Campagnolo Record side-pull
PEDALS	Campagnolo Super Leggers Strada with toe clips and straps
ACCESSORIES	Pump
WEIGHT	22 lbs.

* Cost virtually no object.
** Specifications from manufacturers' literature subject to change without notice. Where possible, touring models have been selected, such as the Schwinn P-15. Other fine, highest-quality bicycles include: Masi (very limited production); Bottechia "Professional"; Panasonic Fuji "Newest" and "Finest" models; Atala "Record"; Gitane "Tour de France"; Mercian "Campianissimo," "Olympic Road," and "King of Mercian" models.

PEUGEOT PX-10E	SCHWINN PARAMOUNT P-15
Reynolds '531' double-butted seamless tubing; Nervex lugs; Simplex ends	All tubes and fork of Reynolds double-butted '531' tubing. Chrome trim on head lugs, fork crown, rear stays, and fork blades. Two-inch fork rake, Campagnolo sport fork tips. Head and seat mast at 73° angle to wheelbase center line.
21 in., 23 in., 24 in., and 25 in.	20 in., 21 in., 22 in., 23 in., 24 in., 25 in., 26 in.
Stronglight Super 63 Competition cotterless dural	Campagnolo Nuovo Record Alloy 6¾ in. (170 mm.) cotterless
Double Stronglight dural, 45 and 52 teeth	Triple plateau Campagnolo Nuovo Record alloy, 36/49/54 teeth
Normandy luxe competition alloy; Simplex high-flange with quick-release	Campagnolo Record, high-flange alloy with quick-release
Simplex Prestige 537	Campagnolo Gran Turismo wide range
Competition grade, 14, 16, 19, 20, and 23 teeth	Regina D'Oro, 14, 16, 19, 25, and 31 teeth
Mavic Montlhery, reinforced spoke holes, 27 in.	Weinmann alloy 27 in.
Robergel double-butted	Chrome plated, .080–.060 gauge
27-in. tubular road-racing	27 x 1¼ HP clinchers; tubular optional
AVA dural bars and stem	Maes style, Cinelli alloy bars and stem
Brooks Professional with Simplex seat post	Brooks Professional leather (factory broken in); Campagnolo alloy seat post
Mafac Racer center-pull, alloy; Hooded levers	Weinmann 999 alloy center-pull
Lyotard 45CA dural with toe clips and straps	Campagnolo Record with Christophe toe clips and Binda straps
Dural road-racing pump	Campagnolo tools for cranks, saddle, seat post, and derailleurs
About 21 lbs.	25 lbs. (may vary according to frame size)

Prices are not given because they fluctuate; anyway, you will do better by comparison shopping. You may have up to an 18-month wait for some models.

TABLE 10 · **Highest Quality Derailleur Bicycles** (continued)

SPECIFICATIONS	FREJUS RECORD SUPERCORSE 15 SPEED
FRAME	Reynolds '531' double-butted 19/22 gauge tubing throughout. Handmade, low-temperature brazed frame. Head and seat mast angles 73° parallel, cutaway pro-lugs, Campagnolo stay ends, plated. Fork is butted oval to round blades, pro-crown, and plated Campagnolo fork ends.
FRAME SIZE	21 in., 22 in., 23 in., 24 in., 25 in.
CRANK	Campagnolo Nuovo Record cotterless alloy
CHAINWHEEL	Campagnolo Nuovo Record triple plateau, 36/49/54 teeth
HUBS	Campagnolo Record high-flange, quick-release, alloy
DERAILLEURS	Campagnolo Nuovo Record front and rear
FREEWHEEL	Regina 14 to 22 teeth *
RIMS	Fiamme tubular 27 in. alloy
SPOKES	Double-butted 14-gauge stainless steel
TIRES	Pirelli Gran Premio 16 oz., aged for longer life, 27 in. x 1⅛ in. tubular
HANDLEBARS	Alloy bar and stem, recessed stem bolts
SADDLE	Butt leather racing saddle
BRAKES	Universal center-pull with quick-release and hooded levers
PEDALS	Campagnolo Record alloy
ACCESSORIES	None
WEIGHT	23 lbs.

* I recommend changing to 14/34 Shimano freewheel, and changing to Campagnolo Gran Turismo or Crane GS wide-range rear derailleur, for wider range gearing.

GITANE "GRAN TURISMO"

Reynolds '531' double-butted frame throughout. Prugnat lugs; '531' Campagnolo fork ends; chrome tip stays, fork crown, and fork tips.

21½ in., 22½ in., 23½ in., 24½ in., 25½ in.
Campagnolo alloy cotterless
Campagnolo alloy triple plateau 36/46/52 teeth
Campagnolo Record, quick-release
Campagnolo Gran Turismo wide range
14 to 31 teeth
Dural Mavic for clincher tires
SS butted
Michelin 50 27 in. x 1¼ in. clinchers

Pivo Dural Randonneur (for touring), alloy. Pivo Pro stem, alloy
Butt leather, Campagnolo 26.4 mm. alloy seat post
Mafac racer center-pull, deluxe
Campagnolo alloy, with toe clips and straps
Generator light front and rear, lightweight stainless-steel fenders; T.A. bag supports front and rear
25 lbs.

MINI-BIKES—NOTES AND COMMENTS

There are dozens of so-called "mini-bikes" on the market. Some are heavy and cumbersome, some are fairly light and responsive. Many have take-apart features, some of which are more trouble than they're worth.

Mini-bikes have utility advantages. The good ones are reasonably light and easily taken apart, so you can stuff them in a car trunk or apartment closet. Good ones have quick-release seat post and handlebar adjustments, so a six-foot father can adjust it to himself for an evening jaunt, and his four-foot young child can readjust it to suit himself in a few minutes. They are very maneuverable, and the best of them have powerful brakes, such as the Oglaend unit shown in Fig. 52. Test any mini-bike for braking power before purchase, though; since the small diameter wheels offer less braking action, brakes don't work as well. Mini-bikes aren't for touring, but they are ideal for shopping, for college campus use, evening jaunts, commuting distances under five miles, and for bicycle polo (page 259).

Fig. 52: Here's a good quality mini-bike, made in Norway by Oglaend, and available in this country in many bicycle shops. Features coaster brake rear, internal drum brake front, concealed wiring for front and rear lights (but no lights), two-speed hub, 20 x 1.75-inch tires, quick take-apart and seat post and handlebar adjustment. At about 35 pounds, it weighs less than most take-apart small wheelers.

A TANDEM CAN BE FOR YOU!

A little further on I will discuss the various types of tandems, but let's look at them for a minute, and consider some of the advantages and dis-advantages of tandem cycling.

First, the advantages. One of the difficulties in family cycling with two or more bikes is that too often one member of the family is less expert than the other and can't keep up. One person always lags behind, and the good cyclist is forced to slow down his pace in order to stay within shouting distance. Tandems end this problem, although there are certain back-seat driver situations that can take its place. Tandem riding lets you and your partner chat about the day and the scenery, and the fun of working together as a team in cycling can add to the enjoyment of family life in general.

Tandem cycling can be a lot of fun for two riders for a number of reasons. A tandem is a lot easier to pedal than a single bicycle, in terms of energy exerted. I can recall being on my tandem with my wife on a very windy, gusty day, cycling into the wind. We were with other riders on single bikes, and we consistently led the pack, sometimes by as much as a quarter mile, yet we are not particularly strong riders. While the other riders were being blown about and had trouble cycling in a straight line due to unpredictable and violent gusts of wind, we on our tandem went straight as an arrow. We consistently tandem-cycle long distances, seventy-five to eighty-five miles a day on trips, and arrive at our destina-tion not half as tired as we used to be riding a single bike.

On a tandem, the total weight of which is around forty-five pounds (for a good one), two riders are pushing less steel, and putting more pedal muscle power into moving forward, than is possible for one cyclist on a single bicycle to apply. So the going is appreciably easier on a tandem than on a single bike. Further, the riders, being close together, can enjoy a conversation much better than the hurried shouts between single cyclists. And tandem riders, working in harmonious pedaling, simul-taneously partake of the joys of cycling, the passing scenery, and the healthful vigorous activity as no two single cyclists ever could.

On the negative side, if the riders are unevenly matched, so that one has to do most of the pedaling; if one rider simply cannot or will not learn to pedal smoothly along with his or her partner; if one rider persists in suddenly, without warning, stopping pedaling with feet still in the pedals, thus locking them and throwing the other rider off balance, and even causing him to hurt his ankle as his foot slips out of the pedal, or causing him to wobble and lose steering control; if the rear rider cannot accept the need for adopting the pedaling rhythm, mounting, dismounting, and starting style of the front rider; or is not content to enjoy the advantages of the rear cyclist in worry-free pedaling, with the ability to watch the scenery without concern for steering or braking, then tandeming is not for you.

There is a strong indication that Women's Lib has about put the male/female tandem out of business. Just about every young woman cyclist I have discussed riding a tandem with tells me that she is not about to "take a back seat to any man, particularly on a bike." I agree that this attitude will kill the tandem business, because it does take a particular turn of mind and personality to ride second fiddle on one; I know, I have tried it and while I don't consider myself particularly docile or masochistic, I can understand how the Women's Lib women feel. To make tandeming feasible, the rear rider must adapt herself (or himself) to the pedaling of the front rider. If the front man starts and stops from his right foot, the rear cyclist must also. The rear rider must pay some attention to road hazards in order to anticipate a need for coasting prior to a stop, as in approaching a stop sign or stoplight, and, when cornering sharply, be ready to lean slightly in the direction of the turn. Otherwise, however, the rear rider must be content to let the front man (or woman) do all the steering, braking, and gear changing.

The front rider, on the other hand, must be considerate of the rear cyclist. He must tell the rear rider when to coast, when he is about to come to a complete stop, when he is about to make a turn, and when he is about to brake. He must use the gears so as not to fatigue the rear rider, if he is the stronger. He must shift down before going uphill, and must at all times be in a gear that is comfortable for the rear cyclist and well within her or his physical capacity. The front man must not insist on riding a big gear and complain that the rear rider is not pushing hard enough or fast enough.

There is a lot of enjoyment to be had from riding a tandem, and in my opinion the rear rider can have just as much fun as the front man. True, the rear rider has to have a certain adaptability in relating to what the front rider is doing, and it would help if the rear cyclist is a totally submissive person. However, even the most aggressive, hard-driving person (of either sex) can enjoy being at the rear of a tandem, such are the joys of this variation of cycling. You don't *have* to feel put down if you're a woman and are riding the rear saddle. If you do, swap places with the front rider for a while. It's done all the time.

About the Tandem

There are two types of tandems made, the eighty-five-pound monster that's suitable for around-the-block riding and feels like a truck about to fall apart, or the precision-made, light (forty-five pounds or so) tandem that's made like the finest bicycle. Whatever you do, don't buy the clunker in hopes you might enjoy tandeming and will trade it in for a good one. Trade-in value is negligible, and a clunker will unsell you on riding a tandem permanently. If you're not sure about a tandem, borrow a good one and ride it for a minimum of 100 miles before you say no. Less mileage than that will not give you a chance to learn how to tandem, and believe me, riding a tandem takes a different skill and practice before the rear rider stops grabbing for nonexistent brake levers and learns to trust the judgment of the front man. A first ride on a tandem, even for experienced cyclists, can make you feel like you're on a trick bike, balanced on a wire high over Niagara Falls, and are about to fall off any minute. An experienced cyclist has trouble riding rear saddle on a tandem because he hasn't learned that the worst thing you can do, on a start-off, is to try to balance. All you need do as a rear rider is sit on the saddle, concentrate on getting your feet into the toe clips, and pedal hard to get the thing going so you don't wobble and the front man has enough speed up so he can steer straight. You should both start off with the same foot, e.g., put the right foot in the pedal clips, pull up to about eleven o'clock, push down, at the same time hump up into the saddle, pedal two or three strokes with the left foot still out of the toe clips to get up speed, stop pedaling for a second while you both get the left foot in the left pedal clips, then take off. Once learned, starting and stopping a tandem is an exercise in rhythm which is very much like learning to dance all over again (the kind where you actually hold the partner).

Back to the tandem itself. You can buy a combination woman's mixte frame in the rear and man's frame up front, or one with a man's frame front and rear. Schwinn's very fine Paramount Tandem, for example, comes in two sizes, the T-19 has a 19-inch rear mixte frame and a 22-inch front. It also comes in a 22-inch rear and 24-inch front frame, both men's.

Adjustment of saddle height and handlebars is critical on a tandem. The rear handlebars are usually attached to the front seat post, so if you move the front seat up or down, you will have to readjust the rear handlebars separately, which can be done. Most tandems come with flat rear handlebars, curved to allow for the front rider's thighs on the down stroke of the pedal. Trouble with these flat bars is that the rear cyclist has only one place to put his hands. If he moves them around, he has to put them under the front man's buttocks, which may be pleasant enough under some circumstances, but can lead to problems in others. I would substitute the rear flat bars for downturned handlebars, which gives the rear man a choice of handle locations. Otherwise, with the flat bars, the rear cyclist will soon put enough pressure on blood vessels in the palm of his hands to stop circulation and cause them to tingle with what is popularly known as "pins and needles." Weight cannot be put on the center lower part of the palm for very long without shutting off circulation. It's also very important that the rear rider's bars be adjusted up or down so he can absorb road shock partly by leaning on the bars, and partly through the saddle. The rear rider is subjected to a lot more road shock than the front rider because the rear man rides almost right over the rear wheel, whereas the front man is in the middle of the tandem. It's also vital that the rear man's saddle be comfortable and well broken in. Avoid a plastic saddle; they can't be broken in and the rear rider will be in agony after two hours. Use a well-worn leather saddle, at least on the rear. The rear man should learn to put more weight on his arms than he's used to as a single cyclist, to absorb the added road shock. The front cyclist should learn to tell his rear man about bumps coming up so his partner will be ready for them. Finally, and I will repeat this warning because it's so important to the joy of tandem cycling, neither cyclist should suddenly stop pedaling without warning the other man, nor should either man suddenly shift weight about so as to throw the other off balance, without giving advance warning.

Once two matched riders (temperamentally, at least) learn to cycle in tandem, harmoniously and in rhythm, tandem cycling will be a rewarding way to go; far easier, faster, and physically and emotionally closer than single cycling. But if you're always battling about who's not pedaling hard enough; if one rider is always throwing the other off balance; if you can't learn to coordinate getting feet in pedals, or starting and stopping, then tandeming definitely is not for you. Like teaching the other to drive, tandeming can put a strain on a marriage unless you're compatible cyclists; if you're not, perhaps a marriage counselor can improve both your marriage *and* your tandem riding.

Fine, lightweight, precision-made tandems are made by Schwinn (as noted), by Jack Taylor of England, by Follis, and by Gitane.

If you want a tandem, and togetherness is a good reason to buy one, you should get a tandem you can enjoy. I would buy only a tandem built as a high-quality ten-speed derailleur machine, with ten-speed gear shift and lightweight road-racing wheels and tires. This machine will weigh

Fig. 53: Best high-performance, lightweight tandem made in the U.S. is Schwinn's T-19, above, with woman's frame rear, man's frame front.

about forty-three or forty-four pounds, compared to the eighty-nine or ninety-pound weight of a balloon-tired tandem, and will be much easier to pedal.

The Schwinn tandem as of this writing has the following specifications. There are two models: T-19 (Fig. 53) has a 19-inch rear frame size with a woman's mixte frame design and a 22-inch front man's frame size. T-22 (Fig. 54) has a 24-inch front and 22-inch rear man's frame design, or is available with a 22-inch rear and front, or a 24-inch frame rear and front. Frame and fork are chrome molybdenum seamless drawn steel. Wheels are clincher 27 × 1¼-inch tires, Campagnolo alloy hubs, Weinmann alloy rims. Handlebars are alloy road-racing dropped front, rear semiflat alloy. Brakes are Mafac tandem cantilever design. Frame tube ends are reinforced with pressed-in sleeves. Frame is hand assembled. Cranks are

Fig. 54: Basically the same as T-19, this Schwinn model T-22 has man's frame front and rear.

alloy cotterless; pedals are Campagnolo alloy with toe clips and straps. Rear derailleur is Campagnolo Gran Turismo wide-range, front is Campagnolo Record. Freewheel is Regina D'Oro with 14, 16, 19, 25, and 31 teeth. Saddles are Unica-Nitor nylon with waffle top, on Campagnolo seat posts. Weight is around forty-three pounds. Tools are provided. Rear T.A. chainwheels have 52- and 36-tooth driving wheels.

Naturally, tandems are also raced. Track tandems, like their track single bike counterpart, are brakeless, with ultralight tires and rims without brake flats, stiff frames with little fork rake and short wheelbase. Track tandems are single-purpose machines, designed for whirling around an oval track at high speed, with sensitive steering and efficient power transmission (fixed gear). The frame is so short, in fact, that the rear rider's chin practically rests on the front man's back (see Fig. 115 on page 240 in the racing chapter).

ADULT TRICYCLES

If you're beyond the age when you think you can learn how to ride a bicycle, or if, for some reason, you cannot or should not balance yourself on one, adult tricycles might be the answer for you.

There is a wide variety of these tricycles, however, and it's important to get a good one, because with these bikes, the best costs so little more. In this market, you're paying a larger price because of the small demand and limited production.

Actually, a good tricycle isn't much less efficient than a good bicycle. In England, there have been racing events in which tricyclists have attained speeds of forty miles an hour or better.

The real difference between a bicycle and a tricycle of equal quality lies in the greater maneuverability of the two-wheeler and the consequent greater skill it takes to ride one.

Still, rather than give up the joy of outdoor pedaling, a tricycle can be an excellent compromise. One sees great numbers of tricycles in retirement areas.

Three Types of Tricycles

There are three basic types of tricycles available. One is a rather heavy (around eighty-five pounds) unit with 26-inch tires, complete with detachable rear wire utility basket; a trike conversion unit so you can convert a reasonably good ten-speed into a fairly lightweight (thirty-eight pounds or so) ten-speed trike; and a tailormade tricycle with any gear ratio you wish, made of Reynolds '531' butted tubing and also with ten speeds.

For those who want a tricycle because they have a balance problem, and who will use it for little more than shopping or gadding about town, I recommend the Schwinn Tri-Wheeler as the best-made unit of this type. You can get it as a one-speed model with coaster brakes, or as a three-speed model. Sears Roebuck also has a similar model (Fig. 55).

If you want a tricycle for other uses, such as winter cycling where the three-wheel stability lets you ride safely over ice and through snow up to three or four inches deep, or on a frozen lake surface. when a two-wheeler would be extremely hazardous, then you want a lightweight, high-performance machine comparable to your good two-wheeler. An inexpensive route to such a trike would be a good conversion unit, such as is made by Higgins and is available from Holdsworth in England (see Appendix for address), which lets you convert your good ten-speed to a ten-speed trike, yet easily and quickly reconvert it back to a two-wheeler when the roads are unclogged of ice and snow. The Higgins unit is made to fit a brazed fitting on the seat stay so it won't lift up and smack you in the back as you pedal. Since I did not want to braze anything on my

Fig. 55: Typical adult tricycle. This is a heavy machine, not particularly easy to pedal, but suitable for use by those with a balance problem for shopping, short trips of a mile or two, running errands, etc. It has a three-speed gear, 1.5 cu. ft. wire basket, 24-inch wheels, coaster brake rear and caliper brake front. This model is sold by Sears Roebuck.

Fig. 56: Close-up of trike tandem adapter unit. This unit can also be used to convert a single bicycle to a trike. Note that where unit is bolted into dropout, there are two bolts. Conversion unit came with only one bolt, the long one that spans the stays. Another hole was drilled in the adapter unit so it would stay put in dropout and not wind up somewhere around rider's neck. Note that derailleur had to be moved to the left to line up with freewheel gears. Note the alloy Shimano Crane "GS" wide-range derailleur, which does a good job of holding chain tension and shifting, despite the rather extreme angle of chain with respect to chainwheel and front derailleur guide cage.

good bike frame, I drilled another hole in the conversion unit (Fig. 56) so two bolts hold it in the rear dropout. I had, of course, to add six or seven links to my chain to compensate for the gear cluster now further away, but I could use my derailleur without moving it.

How to Ride a Tricycle

Tricycles can be dangerous! Yes, *very* dangerous, if at first, without due caution, you just climb up into the saddle and take off. I have let dozens of people of all ages and strengths try my tricycle, and, without exception, each one would have run into a tree, or a bush, or even lost control right out in traffic, had I not started them off in the center of a huge school yard on a Saturday. I'm not clear in my own mind exactly why even highly seasoned cyclists have such trouble coping with a three-wheeler. I know I did. My first ride on a trike was in Central Park in New York City, and the first thing I did—ridiculously, I thought at the time—was turn and hit a tree. I just couldn't control the thing. I got on again, and ran right off the sidewalk into the middle of the street. Fortunately, it was on a week end, a day when only muscle-powered vehicles are allowed on Central Park streets, so all I did was imperil myself and a few other skilled bicyclists who maneuvered, muttering, out of my out-of-control way. It took about fifteen or twenty minutes for me to realize I was doing at least two things wrong. First, I was afraid to turn the handlebars to avoid a tree for fear I'd fall over, as I would have done on a bike if I had turned that sharply. Second, I tried to avoid going the wrong way by leaning in the other direction, which for some reason (that escapes me) only makes the trike obstinately go the wrong way, only more so. Finally, after hours of practice, I realized that the only way you can safely make a turn at slow or moderate speeds is to lean slightly *away* from the direction of turn, instead of, as on a two-wheeler, *into* the direction of turn. In other words, on a trike, to turn right, you lean left a bit, and to turn left, you lean right, so that your weight is *always* on the outer wheel that wants to lift off the ground. It's a bit more vital to lean on the left wheel, and somewhat more heavily when you turn right, because in most trikes, as in mine, that's the driving wheel, and you need traction when it's slippery.

One final note of caution. When you're learning to ride a trike, a particularly dangerous thing to do is to ride on the sidewalk over a driveway that's on an incline into the street, as are most driveways. As you ride across the incline, the trike will try to turn into the street, and if you are afraid to simply force the wheel back so that you go straight, for fear you'll fall over, you *will* go out into the street, right into traffic. It happened to me, and it has happened to several skilled cyclists I let try my trike. Now I advise anyone who wants a trike to bring the machine to a large vacant parking lot or school yard and, very slowly at first, ride around until you have trained yourself to lean *against* the direction of turn, retrained your sense of balance not to send danger signals when you make sharp turns to keep from going off in an unwanted direction, and learned how good your brakes are. Brakes, incidentally, are a problem on better trikes, and on the Higgins conversion job. There's no way to put a brake on the rear wheels. You can't even use a hub brake because you have to use the hubs that come with the conversion unit, as they are splined to fit on a special axle. However, you *can* do what I did and add a hub brake on the front wheel, which, together with my old Mafac caliper brake, gives me plenty of stopping power. This combination puts an awful lot of strain on the front fork, so I have the hub brake for emergency reserve. So far I have been able to stop quite well with the single caliper brake. But some of the heavy trikes, and trike conversion units made in this country, have totally inadequate braking systems.

A Tandem Trike

If you put a trike conversion unit on your tandem you can combine the features of tandem togetherness and comradely cycling, working in harmony close enough to hold a conversation, with the features of a tricycle —stability, no problems balancing, more relaxed cycling. I did (Fig. 57)

Fig. 57: This tandem was converted to a trike tandem by bolting a tricycle conversion unit to tandem rear dropouts and by lengthening chain and moving location of derailleur. The trike tandem plows through snow and is stable even on ice, so it makes a good winter out-of-doors exerciser.

and it makes tandeming, especially on wintry, snowy streets, much safer and, for me, more fun. One word of caution, though. Adding the Higgins trike adapter means, as noted, you have no brake on the rear wheel, and so braking must be done only on the front wheel, which cuts braking power in half. If you have enough fork clearance, and brakes with long enough caliper arms (they come in different lengths), you may be able to put a double set of caliper brakes on the front wheel, one set in front and one behind the fork. Or you can put a drum brake on the front wheel, plus the caliper brake that grips the rim. You'd better have a strong fork, though, because stresses in stopping with a hub brake plus a caliper brake can bend the fork. You can't put caliper brakes on the rear wheels because there's no place to attach them, and you can't substitute a drum brake because you can use only the hub that comes with the trike adapter unit, and drum brakes are integral with their own hub. The same applies to a disc brake, used on some of the kiddy "Chopper"-style bikes.

MOTORIZED BICYCLES

I have received many letters, mostly from older readers, asking about a small gasoline or electric motor that could be put on a bicycle. You can buy such a gasoline motor, but I don't recommend it, and so far as I know they're illegal in most states. I can understand the attraction of a small motor on a bike; the older person can pedal as long as he wishes, and when he gets tired, or has to climb a hill, he can start up the motor. But any younger person who would put a motor on a bike simply has no soul, in my opinion, and would put an outboard motor on a canoe.

The best compromise I have found as a motorized bike is the French Solex (Fig. 58), which has a 7/8 hp motor that, when pushed down with a lever, friction engages and drives the front wheel of a bike built for the motor. You get about 200 miles per gallon of gas. This is a machine that's reasonably easy to pedal, and which at this writing costs under $200.00 (Solex Bicycle Shop, see Appendix). Unfortunately, for no logical reason, few states will license this machine. It's quiet, uses very little gas, has a caliper brake front, drum brake rear, powerful head and tail lights and the switch to the taillight comes on when rear brake is applied. You can legally ride this machine in Michigan, Minnesota, and some other states. I would like to see every state permit this utility bike for oldsters; it sure would ease congested city traffic and auto exhaust fumes. Top speed is about 20 mph on the flat, it readily climbs hills, can

Fig. 58: So many older people have asked me about a bike with a motor on it that I feel something should be said about them. This French-made Solex is one inexpensive answer (about $200.00). It can be pedaled, or, with the ⅞ hp motor, it will zip up to 20 mph on the flat. With a pedal assist it can climb a fairly steep hill, too. There are about 7 million Solexes in Europe.

carry a reasonable load of groceries, etc., takes bumps with surprisingly little shock, and is light enough to be lifted into a car trunk by one person. This was France's answer to her postwar transportation problem, and the Solex has been steadily improved since then. It starts easily even in extreme cold, and there are about seven million of them zipping all over Europe. And it could be one inexpensive solution to this nation's growing fuel shortage crisis. Remember, you bike fans, I said this is fine for oldsters; you youngsters should use your legs.

Another version of a motorized bike is all electric. It's the Solo (no relation to the Solex) made in West Germany. The Solo gets around 25 miles to the battery charge, recharges from a 24-volt battery charger you plug into house current (110 VAC) and has a top speed of around 16 mph. The Solo uses two 12 volt batteries in series. It has no throttle; it's either taking off with really fast acceleration to top speed or coasting. Has two pedals, but the bike weighs around 400 pounds so you aren't going to get very far under muscle power. The Solo is electric motor quiet and totally non-polluting at the vehicle end. Starts instantly in any weather, comes with a rear large wire shopping basket, rear view mirror, bell. Licensability is so far limited to only a few states. Built-in front and rear lights are powerful, which you might expect from a 24 v. power source. Solo is available from the U.S. importer, Solo Electric Motors, Inc., P.O. Box 5030, Cope-land Industrial Park, Newport News, Virginia 23605.

UNICYCLES

Strictly in the gimmick and toy area is yet another cycling variation, the unicycle. This is a one-wheeled cycle with a banana seat, which children seem to be able to ride with great facility for short distances, and with a lot of fun and enjoyment. Personally, I'd rather try a delayed parachute fall—at least I'd have a chance for an easy landing.

But, if your child wants a unicycle, I'd recommend a Columbia or Schwinn unicycle. Columbia furnishes a four-page instruction manual on how to ride the thing, which may ease the pain of the learning process. The Columbia model also seems to be the best made and comes in a 20-inch or 24-inch wheel size, the choice of which depends on your child's age, or your own size, if you're the one who wants to learn this circus trick. The manufacturer calls this "A new fun fad . . . ," which I suppose it is.

ABOUT IMPORTING PARTS

If you're importing a complete bicycle, it will have to be cleared through U.S. Customs, either at the port of entry or at the nearest customs office to you. For example, if you live in Terre Haute, Indiana, you could have the bike shipped via surface transportation (ship) to an East Coast port of entry, such as New York or Newark, or to Chicago. You would then have a customs broker arrange for U.S. Customs clearance either in New York, Newark, or in Chicago. Once you have customs clearance (and your broker has paid applicable duty), the broker can arrange for shipment to you either by truck or by REA air express, the latter being much faster. You might specify to your European source that he use a reputable freight forwarder and custom-house broker, such as Schenkers International, Inc., which has offices in major cities throughout Europe and Great Britain, and who can handle the entire shipment for you. But be warned that customs clearance is costly, with the minimum charge around $35.00. So it pays to clear through customs yourself, if you live near a U.S. Customs office, such as Chicago. All you do is have the shipment sent from the port of entry to the customs office nearest you (via REA air freight) and upon arrival the forwarder (such as Schenkers) will tell you where to pick up your shipment. You can go to that location, pay whatever duty is owed, and pick up your package.

When you order a part or bike from an overseas source, check with your bank for the latest currency rate so you can send the correct amount with your order. A bank draft on a bank near your European source will get you faster service than a personal check, since the latter will have to be cleared back to your own bank before shipment can be made.

However, I do not recommend direct purchase of small parts such as gears and derailleurs from overseas, since these components are usually available from a U.S. supplier such as those listed in the Appendix on page 497. I'd try to keep my direct foreign orders to custom frames or bicycles. Or, if you're going abroad, you might order your bike for pick-up in Europe or Great Britain.

Duty on bikes and parts, as of 1972, from "Tariff Schedules of the United States Annotated (1972)" is as follows:

"*Bicycles:* Valued over $16.33⅔ each, having both wheels over 25 inches in diameter, weighing less than 36 pounds and not designed for use with tires having a cross-sectional diameter exceeding 1.625 inches, complete, without accessories, 5½%."

TABLE 11 · **Duty on Bicycle Parts**

PART	DUTY
FRAMES: Valued over $8.33⅓ each	7½%
SADDLES:	None
PEDALS:	None
CHAINS: Valued at over 40¢ per pound	6%
TIRES:	5%
TUBES:	15%
REAR GEAR CLUSTER (Freewheel):	15%
REAR DERAILLEUR, complete:	None
REAR DERAILLEUR PARTS:	15%
REAR DERAILLEUR CABLE:	9½%
FRONT DERAILLEUR:	15%
FRONT DERAILLEUR PARTS:	15%
HUB:	15%
RIM:	15%
HANDLEBARS:	15%

I could find nothing on the chainwheel, but assume the worst at 15 percent. From the table, it is obviously less expensive to import a complete bike, at 5½ percent duty, than individual parts at up to 15 percent duty.

4

FITTING YOUR BICYCLE TO YOU

Perhaps the most vital step in bicycle selection is proper frame size. As the bicycle comparison charts on pages 120–126 show, frames come in a variety of sizes, from nineteen to twenty-seven inches and custom-made bikes can be made with even bigger frames.

Frame size is measured from the seat lug (a.) at the top of the seat tube to the center of the bottom bracket at the bottom of the seat tube (b.) (Fig. 59).

It is vital that you select a frame size that permits you to straddle the top bar with comfort, so that you can mount and dismount without difficulty (or injury). In general, you should select a frame size that measures nine to ten inches less than your inseam, as measured in your stocking feet.

If you are buying a bicycle in a bicycle store, take off your shoes, straddle the top tube (the horizontal bar from head stay to seat tube), and make sure you can stand up comfortably. I made the mistake, many years ago, of buying a bicycle with a frame too large for me—it was a bit hazardous coming to stops in the city. I had to lean sidewise to get my foot on the ground. Riding that bicycle was not only dangerous but decidedly uncomfortable.

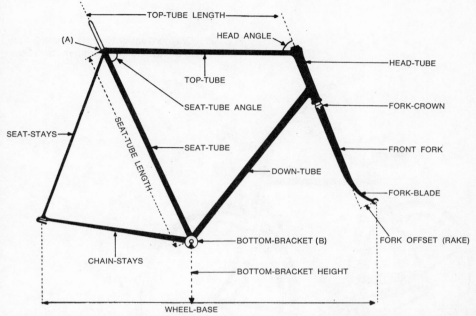

Fig. 59: An easy way to find the right size bike is by straddling the top tube, with both stockinged feet flat on the ground. You should have an inch clearance between crotch and top tube. To have less clearance is to invite injury on sudden dismount; to have more means saddle is at an awkward height or can't be raised high enough for pedaling comfort and efficiency. Saddle is approximately right height when knee is slightly bent with pedal near floor and crank in line with seat tube. For more precise saddle height adjustment, see page 162. Bikes come with frame sizes from 19 to 26 inches or their metric equivalent. Measure frame size with tape measure from centerline of bottom bracket to top of seat tube, as shown above.

HANDLEBARS

There are two basic types of handlebars, and a number of variations within each type, in use today. The more common are the upright or flat handlebars (Fig. 60) used with three-speed or coaster-brake bicycles. High-rise handlebars, a variation, force a child (no adult would use them) to ride with his hands at chin height, hardly a safe position or one which permits precise steering. Young children like to copy older children, though, so you do see many bikes with motorcycle-type high-rise handlebars on sixteen- and twenty-inch Sting-Ray bikes.

Fig. 60: On conventional "flat" handlebars, brake levers are located under handlebar grips.

Fig. 61: Here are the three basic types of turned-down handlebars: Left, Randonneur; center, Pista; and right, Maes. Randonneur is favored for cycle touring because it offers more hand positions.

The second kind of handlebars is the dropped or turned-down type (Fig. 61) used on good (and some not-so-good) ten-speed derailleur lightweights and on the one-speed fixed-gear track-racing bicycles.

Most adults who are interested in cycling express concern about dropped handlebars. They say that the crouch position (about forty-five degrees from upright position) must be uncomfortable, and that it must be difficult to see where one is going. But dropped handlebars have been preferred for over forty years by experienced cyclists in both this country and abroad for short- and long-distance touring. Flat handlebars are inefficient, uncomfortable, and tiring.

Dropped versus Flat Handlebars

There are so many reasons why dropped handlebars are better than flat bars for any kind of cycling that it would take ten pages to explain them fully. I hope this quick summary will sell you on the dropped bars, because I'm confident you'll be happier and more comfortable with them.

Obviously, you must crouch down at about a forty-five-degree angle with dropped bars (see racing photos in Chapter 8). This position is actually more effective and healthier. It cuts down wind resistance, which can save a lot of energy, particularly when you are pedaling into a fifteen- or twenty-knot wind. Also, with your back arched slightly, you can use more muscles, more effectively, for a longer period.

Try this demonstration to prove the muscle-using efficiency of dropped bars. Sit upright in a chair, with both feet flat on the floor in front of you. Try to stand up. Now sit back as before, and bend over about forty-five degrees and try to stand up. You have now positioned your body so that you can put some of those powerful back and thigh muscles to work.

A great deal of medical research has been done on the use of dropped handlebars and the human back, and the conclusions show that the bent-over position is better for the back than the sitting-up position.

An interesting article by Fred DeLong,[1] points out that

> at the small of the back the spine curves backward and the discs and vertebrae are pinched together at the rear. Upper body weight tends to further compress this region; excess weight accentuates the condition, and road impact compounds the problem. On the front of the spine, the ligaments which hold the spine from collapsing become strained.

[1] *American Cycling* (now *Bicycling!*), April, 1966, p. 16.

When leaning forward, however, the back relaxes and extends and the vertebrae separate, relieving the pinching, permitting absorption of impact without damage. If you will have someone measure with a tape you'll find that your spine will actually lengthen as much as two inches when you bend forward from the erect to the dropped bar position.

Riding is also a lot more comfortable with the dropped bars because body weight is more evenly divided between saddle and bars. This is particularly noticeable on long rides and bumpy roads. When the going gets rough, you can lean forward a bit, or even ease your weight off the saddle and onto the handlebars to reduce road shock. I recommend you do this when riding over railroad tracks, through intersections, or over very rough roads. This will spread the shock evenly over front and rear wheels and protect the wheels as well as yourself from the impact.

Types of Dropped Handlebars

As you browse through bicycle parts catalogs or watch other cyclists go by, you will see a great many shapes of dropped handlebars. The three most popular types (Fig. 61) are the Pista, the Maes and the Randonneur. The Pista have curves which bend quickly away from the main stem. This type may be fine for track racing, but they are no good for touring because there's no room to rest the hands at the top of the bars (the favorite position in distance cycling). The Maes offer just about the best combination of curvatures. They have a long, flat top bar section that permits the rider to ride gripping the top bar (a very comfortable position), yet bottom sections are readily available for dropping quickly to the low position for maximum energy exertion on hills, or for sprinting. Also, the curvature of the Maes bars permits plenty of variety in placing brake levers.

The Randonneur-type handlebars are best suited to persons with short arms, especially if the rider finds it consistently difficult, after a long trial period, to reach brake levers on Maes-type handlebars. French-type brake levers, located at the end of the stem just under the center section of the top bars, make it easier to grip brakes quickly from the top of the bar position (Fig. 62). The Randonneur are also well suited to women (or men) with short fingers.

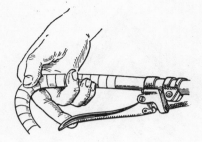

Fig. 62: Touring handlebars fitted with brake levers at top section of bars.

Fitting the Handlebars to You

A tiny off-adjustment in handlebars can make all the difference in the world to your cycling comfort, especially on a long trip. Therefore, handlebar adjustment is extremely important because no two persons have exactly the same arm and torso length. Handlebar height and stem length must be accurately selected for comfort.

The stem is the part of the frame that rises up from the steering head, to which handlebars are fastened. Stems come in various lengths (Fig. 63), the usual variation being 1¾ inches, 2 inches, 2¾ inches, 3½ inches, and 4 inches. You can see that there's plenty of variation to bring handlebars as close to you or move them as far away from you as necessary.

The problem is that you cannot always tell what stem length you need, and, you don't want to spend a lot of money trying out various stem lengths. If there are a number of people in your family who are planning to cycle seriously, it might be a good idea to invest in an adjustable stem, which can quickly adjust handlebars closer to and away from a rider.

The first rule of thumb for approximate or rough handlebar adjustment is to raise the bars until the top bar is level with the nose of the saddle. For safety, keep at least two inches of the stem, above the split part, inside the head tube.

The second handlebar adjustment is stem length. You cannot change stem length unless you have an adjustable stem (see Fig. 63), which must be purchased separately (or buy a new stem, as noted above). You can help make the handlebars come closer to you, however, by moving the saddle horizontally. Loosen the saddle clip nut and slide the saddle forward or backward. This adjustment is strictly limited, though, because if you move the saddle too far off the correct position (see pages 154–162),

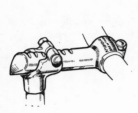

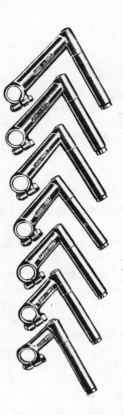

Fig. 63: Be sure to select the right handle-bar stem for your arm length. They come in lengths from 1¾ to 5½ inches. Or, unless you are competing, you can use an adjustable stem (upper left).

you will impair your pedaling efficiency. The saddle nose should be from ¾ to 1¾ inches behind the crank hanger, if you were to draw a vertical line from the saddle to the hanger. The variation will depend on your height and the wheel base of the bicycle. (A saddle position a bit to the rear will give you better "ankling" efficiency; see pages 167–168 for a description of ankling.)

A good way to find a correct stem length is to measure the distance from your elbow to your outstretched fingertips. This should be the distance from the very rear edge of the center part of the handlebars to the nose of the saddle.

Another way to check stem length is to sit on the bicycle, assume your usual riding position, and, with someone holding you, remove the left hand from the handlebars and rotate the arm freely, without stretching, until it comes back to the bars. If, as the hand comes back to the bar top it does not assume the same position as the right hand on the bars, you should adjust your stem length.

In fact, I would recommend that you use either or both of the horizontal fitting methods when you buy a new bicycle so that you will have at least approximately the correct stem length. Bicycles are fitted with stems for the *average* rider, so if you are a short woman with short arms, or a tall man with a long torso and long arms, the stem that comes automatically with the bicycle will probably never give you the correct horizontal handlebar adjustment. A good dealer, who specializes in high-quality machines, will have a selection of stem lengths in stock and will be able to fit your particular physique.

Once you have made these rough adjustments in the saddle and handlebars, do not make any further changes until you have given them a good trial (about fifty miles).

There is another handlebar adjustment, applying only to dropped handlebars, that has to do with the tilt of the dropped part of the bars (Fig. 64). You can alter tilt by loosening the stem nut and rotating the bars. For a first adjustment, which is the position that suits most people, tilt the lower section of the bars about ten degrees downward. Then, as you ride, drop your hands to this lower position to check how comfort-

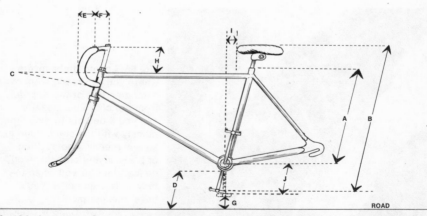

Fig. 64: Important frame measurements are (a) frame size, (b) saddle height, (c) handlebar angle, (d) bottom bracket road clearance, (e) handlebar throw, (f) stem length, (g) pedal-to-ground clearance, (h) handlebar height, (i) saddle position behind bottom bracket centerline, (j) crank length.

able it is for you. If it doesn't feel right, change the angle of the dropped section until it suits you. But do this only after you have made all other adjustments on the saddle and handlebars.

Position of Brake Levers Is Important

Chances are that when you buy a new ten-speed bicycle or some other type of bicycle, the dropped bars will already be taped and the brake levers will be tightened in position. This should not deter you from removing the tape and shifting the brake-lever position so you can reach the levers quickly from any riding position, no matter where your hands happen to be located on the bars. Quick stopping is vital in an emergency. Brake levers should be somewhere on the curve of the bars (Fig. 65), but the best position for you will depend on how easy it is for you to grab them.

Taping Handlebars

I always tape my handlebars, and I believe you will find taping a must on long trips. Taping gives you a better grip. Sweaty palms and light aluminum alloy are a slippery combination.

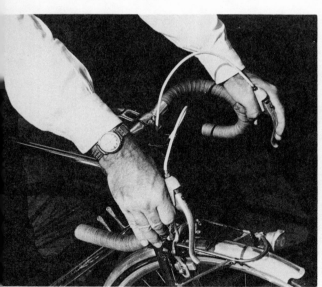

Fig. 65: Locate brake levers where you can reach them by extending one or two fingers from top of the bar position and you'll be able to grab them quickly with the entire hand in an emergency. The position of brake levers probably won't be just right for you when the bicycle is brand new. You'll have to experiment.

(Dr. Clifford Graves)

Before taping, be sure the brake levers are in the position that suits you best.

Most manual instructions call for beginning the taping job after leaving a space of about two inches between the stem and the top of the bar. I do a lot of riding in cold weather, so I prefer to tape right up to the stem. This provides a layer of tape between my gloves and the cold alloy of the bars.

In taping, first pull the tape taut then pass two or three layers over each other so that the first layer will hold in place. Tape the bars as you would a baseball bat, overlapping the tape by one-half. When you reach the brake levers, tape right down to where they are fastened to the bars, then pass behind the levers and continue taping. Leave two or three inches of tape beyond the end of the bars, and push this excess tape into the bars with your finger. Then plug the end of the bars with a bar plug (Fig. 66). Even if you don't tape your bars, you should use bar plugs as a safety measure. The open unplugged end of the bars could give you a nasty gash in a spill.

If you use the push-on kind of bar plug (the type without an expanding screw), you can cut a small hole in it and use it to hold spare light bulbs (the glass part of the bulb inside the plug).

To tape handlebars when handlebar gear-shift levers are installed, start at the lever end (Fig. 67) with the cable cover *under* the tape, so tape holds cable to handlebars, as shown. Tape over bars and cable cover to

Fig. 66: How to tape handlebars. (*Courtesy of Wheel Goods Corporation*)

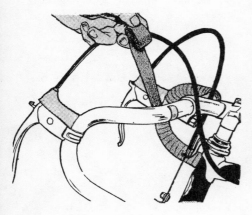

1. Both plastic and cloth tape have their advantages; which tape you use is entirely up to you. If the cloth is adhesive, start at the bottom and work upward; if not, it will have to be plugged into the end of the bars with a rubber or plastic bar plug; starting at the top of the bars is necessary.

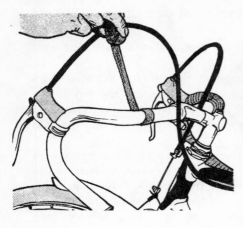

2. Leave about two inches of space on each side of the bar extension clip. Stick the end of the tape to the bars with a small piece of adhesive tape or paper. Then work downward toward the brake lever, making sure not to leave any unsightly gaps of metal between each twist of the tape.

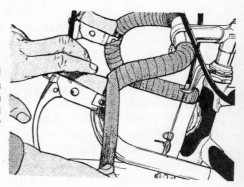

3. Tape over the lever (useful for added comfort if the lever is not fitted with a hood rubber) or (as illustrated) loosen the lever, tape the bars inside it and over the clip, then screw the lever tightly back.

4. When you reach the end of the bars, push about two or three inches of tape inside the end of the bars with your fingers. Then check to see that you have left no gaps through which metal is showing.

5. Finally, plug the end with a bar plug, which will secure the tape and complete a workmanlike job.

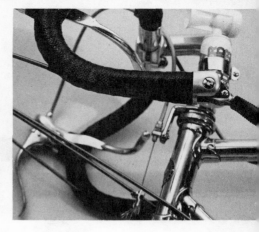

Fig. 67: When taping over handlebar end shift-lever cable, start at handlebar end just behind shift lever, tape over cable up to about two inches below brake lever, then tape over handlebar only, letting shift-lever cable stick out as shown. Finish up at top of handlebars. If tape is not the sticky kind, secure ends with contact cement.

about 1½ inches from brake-lever body and finish at this point by taping two or three turns of tape for reinforcement. Without cutting tape, continue on behind cable, with cable *not* being taped under, and up to and around brake-lever body as with standard taping, then finish the usual two inches or so from the stem. You should use gummed cloth tape, available in a variety of colors to match your bike finish, for this type of lacing. I prefer gummed cloth tape in any case. However, if you have really long fingers and the bars seem too skinny to hold well, you can build up the bars by using the inch-wide leather tape used on tennis rackets. This tape comes in only 2½ or 3 foot lengths, so you'll have to be careful in matching ends; you'll also have to use contact cement since the leather is only mildly gummed and won't hold as well on slick aluminum as it will on tennis racket wood.

The best thing to hit handlebars since handlebars were invented is, in my opinion, a totally new kind of tape, the Bailey III cushioned, beveled rubber tape. The tape is easy to apply, a lot easier than cloth tape, and goes a long way to avoid numbness, tingling, and "pins and needles" in hands. Numbness of this type comes from compression of the nerves connected to the fingers. Compression comes when the base of the palm of the hands is pushed against the handlebars. The new Bailey III not only cushions against numbness, but also against road shock. It also conforms far better to the natural contours of the hand than cloth or plastic tape. Although Bailey III tape is expensive, about $4.00 for a roll which will cover both sides of the handlebars, it lasts at least ten times as long as conventional tape, and it resists dirt. A box is long enough to tape over cables of handlebar end gear shifters. Taping with Bailey III is simple. Just stretch the tape to overlap the first two turns at handlebar end tips (Fig. 68), then ease off but still keep tension, and overlap at the beveled edges by about one-eighth inch. Finish up by securing the ends with the reflective sticky tape supplied. If you can't find Bailey III tape in your

Fig. 68: Here's a new and much improved handlebar tape that cushions against road shock and helps prevent numbness, tingling, and the "pins and needles" of hand so common to cyclists. It's rubber, beveled, immune to dirt, wears at least ten times longer than conventional tape, and is made by Bailey III. It can be washed clean with soap and water.

bike store, write the manufacturer, Bailey III, Inc., P. O. Box 6367, Surfside, Florida 33154. Don't plug this tape in bar ends with plug. You *must* start taping at bar bottom, finish at top. Do not stretch it when taping.

TOE CLIPS, A SAFETY FEATURE

Toe clips are both an important safety feature and a major contributor to cycling efficiency. Clips with straps will keep your feet from sliding off the pedals when you need to accelerate quickly, or keep them from sliding off accidentally at any time, causing you to lose control of the bicycle. Toe clips also permit you to pull back and up with one foot while you are pushing down and forward with the other. This can increase your cycling efficiency about 40 percent.

For the beginning cyclist, the major concern about toe clips that are tightened with straps is that he will not be able to pull his foot out fast enough if he has to stop quickly. Let me say that no cyclist should ride with straps tightened firmly in city traffic anyway, but you can pull your foot off the pedal, with or without straps, if you have to stop fast and support yourself.

It is important to get the right size toe clips. Toe clips come in three sizes—small, medium, and large. The toe of your shoe should not touch the inside edge of the clip; if it does, it could cause uncomfortable chafing, which could be troublesome, especially on a long trip. If toe clips are too long, the top edge will hit your shoe tongue and chafe the top part of your foot. In general, men who wear American shoe sizes from six to eight should use the small size toe clips; shoe sizes from eight and a half to ten, the medium size; and over ten, the large clips.

Because my feet are broad, I have found that conventional cycling shoes, even Belgian shoes, pinch just behind my toes, especially when I wear extra-heavy ski socks in cold weather. I solved this problem by wearing shoes a size larger, which moves my foot back away from the toe of the shoe, so I can wiggle my toes inside the shoe in comfort and pinching is eliminated. But then I found that to keep the ball of my foot in the proper position on the pedal, the toe of the larger shoe hit hard against the toe clip, and I was already using the large size clip. I then used a spacer of ½ inch wide by ⅜ inch thick aluminum, with holes drilled for toe clip bolts, longer bolts being required. This positions the ball of the foot correctly on the pedal.

SHOE CLEATS AND SHOES

I also recommend using shoe cleats (Fig. 69). Cleats give you more cycling efficiency because they fit firmly into the pedal and let you pull back and down without allowing your foot to slip out of the pedal. You should also consider investing in Italian or Belgian cycling shoes. They have long, built-in steel shanks, which keep the steel pedal and your innersole apart, allowing you to put more even pressure on the pedals.

Italian cycling shoes are fine if you have narrow feet, but if your feet are broad in the toe and the arch areas, by all means use Belgian shoes. They offer a wider last.

Fig. 69: Shoe cleats, for use only with road- or track-racing shoes made for this purpose. Cleats fit into rattrap pedals, permit you to pull pedals up and push them down, and keep feet from sliding off pedals. Shoe cleat at left is for cyclo-cross racing; next, a leather model used for touring; third, a track cleat, and on the right, a road cleat.

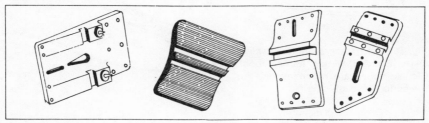

When you first buy cycling shoes, do not attach cleats to them until you have pedaled about a hundred miles. This amount of cycling on the bare pedals will make an imprint on the leather sole of the shoes, which will show you exactly where to mount the cleats. When you mount the cleats, the cleat tunnel should be exactly on top of and aligned with the mark made by the pedal on the shoe sole. Any shoemaker can tack the cleats onto the cycling shoes.

Cycling shoes (Fig. 70) cost anywhere from $8.50 to $15.00 and can be purchased from cycle shops specializing in the sale and repair of high-quality bicycles, or from any of the bicycle mail-order shops listed on page 497.

If you order shoes by mail, be sure to indicate your correct size (see conversion chart, page 159). You can do this by putting on a pair of light-weight socks and standing on a plain piece of paper and tracing the outline of your left foot, or your right, if it's larger. Send this outline to the mail-order shop. Cycling shoes should always be a little tight when new. They will loosen considerably with use.

Whatever you do, do not wear tennis shoes on a long cycling trip. Rubber shoes are no protection from rattrap pedals; after a few hours you will feel as if you were pedaling with bare feet. Ordinary shoes are not much better; they aren't flexible enough for efficient ankling. Cycling shoes are light, flexible, steel-shanked (as already noted), and very comfortable.

Oh yes, one final reason for wearing cycling shoes; when you're pedaling hard, say uphill, you can put as much as 1,500 pounds per square inch pressure on the metatarsal bones of your feet. Sneakers permit this

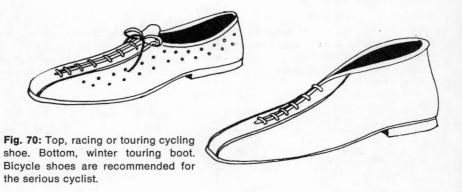

Fig. 70: Top, racing or touring cycling shoe. Bottom, winter touring boot. Bicycle shoes are recommended for the serious cyclist.

pressure to concentrate at one spot; bicycle shoes spread it around. Good shoes I recommend are the handmade ones by Peter Salisbury of England (from Holdsworth, see Appendix); Lambertini of Mexico (from BPDI, see Appendix); Detto Pietro (I saw a nifty pair of DP shoes at the Bike Show in Milan, Italy, in 1971, with attached cleats on a track, adjustable with an Allen wrench); and new fur-lined winter cycling bootees by Reynolds of Northampton, England (from Holdsworth) and Anquetil of France from Shaker Velo-Sport (see Appendix).

The best way to order shoes, as noted, is to send an outline of your foot to the dealer. You may also find the conversion table below of help.

TABLE 12 · **Conversion Chart for Shoes**

U.S.A. & Britain	6	6½	7	7½	8	8½	9	9½	10	10½	11	11½	12	12½	13
Mexico	4	4½	5	5½	6	6½	7	7½	8	8½	9	9½	10	10½	11
Italy & Spain	40		41		42		43		44		45		46		47
France	39		40		41		42		43		44		45		46

SADDLE ADJUSTMENT

Proper adjustment of the saddle (or seat) is very important to riding comfort. But first, let's review quickly the various types of saddles (Fig. 71).

Fig. 71: Typical road saddles. Left, mattress saddle; right, touring saddles. (For the racing cyclist, many different makes and styles of saddles are available.) Reprinted with the permission of the English Universities Press Limited from *Teach Yourself Cycling* by Reginald C. Shaw.

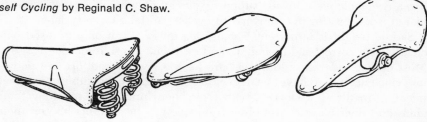

The mattress-spring, wide saddle, which is found on conventional three-speed bicycles, is fine for that type of machine. The three-speed bicycle has conventional handlebars, so most of the rider's weight is on the saddle.

The smaller, lighter, and more compact saddle found on better ten-speed derailleur bicycles may look uncomfortable at first. However, an experienced cyclist knows that with dropped handlebars, the body is bent forward and the hands are on the bars, so that his weight is distributed more or less evenly between the seat and the handlebars with a minimum on the bars. A wide saddle would interfere with thigh movement. Also, the mattress springs in the wide saddle absorb a great deal of energy that an experienced cyclist would much prefer to apply to the pedals.

Actually, the narrow, racing-type saddles can be very comfortable, particularly on long tours. The narrow saddles are made of either saddle leather or nylon. Nylon is lighter and fine for racing. For touring, however, I prefer leather because it will absorb moisture, so there is less sliding about, particularly in hot weather.

A Word About Nylon Saddles: The best thing I can say about nylon or other plastic saddles is that they are sheer murder on the posterior. Nylon, even soft-feeling, padded, quilted nylon saddles, will simply never conform to your natural contours, even after 10,000 miles of saddle-weary pedaling. A good leather saddle, on the other hand, if treated with Lexoil or neatsfoot oil, will eventually shape itself to the intricate contours of your nether extremities and be comfortable to ride. I strongly recommend you switch to a leather saddle if you're buying a new bike, or if you have an old one. I prefer the Brooks Professional leather saddle, which takes more time to break in, but once shaped to you is a joy to ride. The better leather saddles will eventually stretch, so they have an expansion bolt fitted at the nose of the saddle that can be taken up to remove the saddle stretch and prevent the saddle from becoming "sway-backed." Stay away from cheap leather saddles; they must be made partly of paper, because one exposure to rain and they collapse at the sides, leaving the top shaped like a ridgepole with no side support; you can imagine what that shape is like to ride—it's a form of torture no cyclist can take for very long.

Saddle height is important because leg muscles can only be used efficiently with correct saddle height, and everyone has different leg lengths. Most cyclists ride on saddles that are far too low for comfort and pedaling efficiency. You have seen cyclists on any city or suburban street pedaling madly (but slowly), with their knees practically touching their chins and their bicycles wobbling from side to side. Parents hop on their child's bike, and sometimes take it for a four- or five-mile ride without

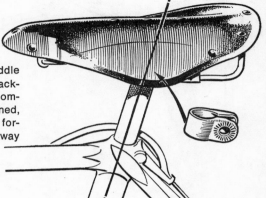

Fig. 72: Loosening the nut on the saddle clip enables you to move your seat backward and forward to find the most comfortable position. When clip is loosened, saddle can also be slid backward or forward to bring you closer to or further away from handlebars.

ever considering saddle height. Some bicycle dealers don't give this a thought either. A discount house or department store will offer you no choice; all adjustments are strictly do-it-yourself.

While sitting on the saddle, you should be able to just reach the pedals comfortably with the heels of your feet. At first, you might feel it a bit awkward when you raise the saddle to its proper height, but after about a mile of cycling you will find that pedaling is a great deal easier, and that you are actually balanced on the seat better. You will be able to turn around occasionally to check traffic without losing your balance.

Saddles can be adjusted by loosening the screw and nut located at the bottom of the seat pillar, and pulling the saddle and saddle pillar up or down as needed. *At least two inches of the seat post must remain inside the seat tube, for safety.*

A saddle can be repositioned toward or away from the handlebars by loosening the nut on the saddle clip (Fig. 72) and moving the saddle in either direction. While individual preferences vary according to arm length, the average rider is best fitted when the nose of the saddle is between two and three inches behind a vertical line drawn through the center of the bottom bracket (see Fig. 59). Or, for a rough fit, adjust the saddle so that its center bisects the center of the seat post. Make no further adjustments until you have ridden the bicycle for at least two miles, after which fine adjustments should be made to comply with individual differences in arm and body length.

When you loosen the saddle clip nut, you will also be able to tilt the saddle up or down. A saddle should have a very slight upward tilt—its

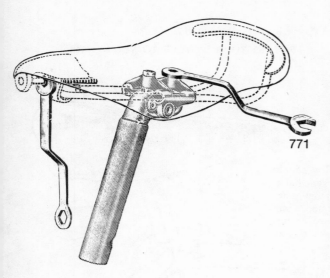

Fig. 73: Typical aluminum alloy micro-adjusting seat post, this Campagnolo post is adjustable by loosening the two top bolts with the special Campy No. 771 spanner (or a 10-mm. socket, which, with a ratchet wrench, is a lot easier to use). The other end of the Campy spanner is 13 mm., for taking up stretch from leather saddles. To move saddle forward or backward, loosen both bolts. To tilt saddle nose up, loosen front bolt two turns and tighten rear bolt two turns; repeat as necessary. To tilt saddle nose down, reverse sequence.

forward peak slightly higher than its rear—for best distribution of weight between legs and arms (Fig. 73).

All of the above instructions apply to both men and women.

Scientific Saddle Height Adjustment

Experiments conducted at Loughborough University, England, illustrate the importance of saddle height to cycling efficiency.[2]

The experiments, which used well-known racing cyclists and a bicycle ergometer (a stationary bicycle) with a harness to hold the rider in position, showed that cycling energy output varies signficantly with minor changes in saddle height. Tests proved that alterations in saddle height of 4 percent of inside leg measurement affected power output by about 5 percent. Experimenters also concluded that the most efficient saddle height is 109 percent of inside leg measurement.

These are average values, however, and it must be expected that some minor variations will be necessary for individual builds and preferences. But it is interesting to note that recent studies of racing cyclists reveal that the better racers tend to have their saddle height conform to this formula.

[2] Vaughn Thomas, "Scientific Setting of Saddle Position," *American Cycling* (now *Bicycling!*), June, 1967, p. 12.

How does one adjust saddle height to 109 percent of leg length? The method is easy:

First, measure the length of your leg *on the inside,* from the floor to the crotch bone, while standing erect and without shoes.

Then, multiply this length as measured in inches by 109 percent. Let's say, for example, that your leg measures 32 inches from floor to crotch. Multiply $32 \times 1.09 = 34.88$ inches (or approximately 34⅞ inches). With the crank parallel to the plane of the seat tube (Fig. 74), measure or adjust the saddle so that the top of the saddle is 34⅞ inches from the pedal spindle.

Some cyclists will not want to follow this formula because they feel more comfortable at some other saddle-to-leg length ratio. But you should bear in mind that saddle height is something one becomes accustomed to, and any particular saddle adjustment is not necessarily the most efficient because it is, at the moment, the most comfortable. The beginning cyclist who adjusts his saddle according to the formula above will, in my opinion, be more likely to wind up a more efficient cyclist than the experienced cyclist who departs from this formula.

Few people are more opinionated than racing cyclists, or more con-

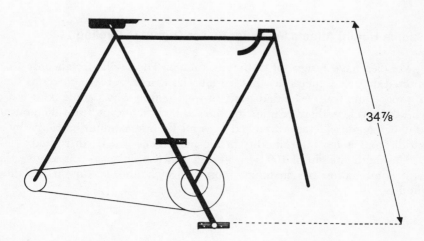

Fig. 74: A scientific method of adjusting saddle height is measuring leg height from floor to crotch, on inside of leg, and multiplying this measurement by 1.09. Result should equal length from top of saddle to pedal spindle, as shown above. If leg measures 32 inches, saddle height should be 34⅞ inches for example.

cerned with the minute details of technique and equipment. Yet, when this formula for saddle height adjustment was announced in 1967, a fierce controversy arose and many skeptics protested. The furor appears to have died down, and many professional cyclists, as well as their coaches and scientists who are interested in cycling, have adopted the formula.

Don't forget that this formula is the result of tests on 100 racing cyclists, ranging from beginners to the late world champion, Tommy Simpson. Four hundred readings were obtained at four different saddle heights—105, 109, 113, and 117 percent of inside leg measurements. These measurements were made from the top of the saddle to the pedal spindle at the bottom of the stroke, with the *crank* aligned with the seat tube.

If you find that there is a great difference between the formula height and the present height of your saddle, I would suggest that you make the adjustment gradually, in increments of one eighth of an inch, over a period of several months. This will give you time to adjust to the new setting, and give the formula a fair try. If you boost or lower the saddle height an inch or so to adjust to the formula at one time, you might find the new setting uncomfortable. Saddle height, as I said above, is something one must adjust to.

I have tried this formula on long trips. Once I had become used to the minor change I had to make, I found my cycling more efficient.

Saddle Height Affects Muscular Power Output in Cycling

Muscles have ranges of optimum stretch. They will stretch only to a limited degree. Experts say that leg muscles can exert more power as they approach the fully extended position—one reason why people who use a child's bicycle without readjusting the saddle huff and puff so ridiculously. But if leg muscles are stretched beyond their maximum capacity by a saddle that is too high, fluidity of leg movement will be disrupted.

The saddle height of 109 percent of leg measurement seems to give the best combination of maximum muscle stretch and maximum pedaling fluidity.

5

ANYONE CAN RIDE A
BICYCLE — HOW TO DO IT

If you don't know how to ride a bicycle at all, the best way to start is with a 26-inch-wheel, three-speed bicycle with seat and handlebars adjusted to fit, as discussed on pages 59 and 94–144 (see Fig. 15, page 73). Have someone hold you up as you sit on the bicycle until you get the feel of the machine and can balance a little. Most people have a pretty good sense of balance, and with an hour's practice you should be able to wobble around your block.

WHY A BIKE STAYS UP

Before I tell you a simple, quick way to teach anyone, even a child of five or six how to ride a bicycle let's review what makes a bicycle stay up in the first place. Gravity? Try stopping. Centrifugal force of the wheels? Rev the rear wheel up to 50 mph, hanging the bike from a centered piece of rope, and try to move the bike. Bike moves easily, so it's not centrifugal force. Micro-balancing act of rider, who moves to counteract forces tending to make the bike fall over? Maybe. Geometry of the front fork? Perhaps. Get the picture? Nobody knows for sure. Schwinn Bicycle Company has funded a study of what makes a bike stay up, by Cornell Aeronautical Research Laboratories, Buffalo, New York, and after a computerized study of some duration, the reason, at this writing, is not yet clear. Dr. David E. H. Jones, a British scientist, built a number of bicycles deliberately designed to be unrideable. He built three models, one with an extra front (third) wheel kept clear of the ground and spun opposite to the two wheels on the ground to neutralize gyro effect; the bike rode fine. His second bike put the wheel hub directly in line with the steering axis, eliminating curvature of the front fork and using a furniture caster as a front wheel. The one-inch wheel caused the bike to fall when it hit bumps as small as one-half inch and the wheel became red hot. A third model had the fork turned backwards, so the curved part was reversed from usual geometry. This bike rode fine, too. Dr. Jones fed all data from these bikes into a computer and came up with the suggestion (no more than that, mind you) that the most significant factor seemed to be the "trail distance," which is the difference between the point on the ground you would reach by following out the rake of the fork, and the point hit by a plumb bob suspended from the centerline of the front wheel axle. In most bicycles this is around two inches or so. According to Dr. Jones, the trail distance affects generation of a sideways force on the front wheel, which in turn produces a torque around the steering axis. In turn, this torque lowers the center of gravity of the bicycle. Perfectly clear? No? Well, forget it, and let's get on with learning how to ride your bicycle, which is why you're reading this section anyhow.

Okay. Hop up on your bike, with someone holding the bike by standing in front with the front wheel wedged between his legs and with both his arms holding the handlebars firm. Now you should be able to sit on the bike without falling over. Lean slightly to the left. The bicycle leans to the left. Lean slightly to the right. The bicycle leans to the right. That's all there is to it. All you need do now is practice learning *when* your bike starts to lean to one side, and train yourself to react instantly to lean to the other side just enough to counteract the forces tending to make the bike fall to the side to which it started to fall. Let me make this perfectly clear. Inside your skull, buried inside a small hunk of solid bone, is your balance mechanism, which I shall refrain from describing further. What you need to do to ride a bicycle is to make a lot of neural connections between your balance system, your brain, and your muscles so you can react instantly and just enough to counteract by your own weight those forces of gravity which are pushing the bicycle over to one side or the other. The bike leans one way, you lean the other. You learn to ride by realizing it's mostly a balancing act, with the bike one pendulum, and your body another, both neutralizing each other. The shifts in leaning or balance you need to do to stay up are very minute, perhaps an inch or two lean one way or the other to keep upright. I've seen trained racing cyclists·with fixed gear locking wheels immovable, balancing upright on their bikes, which is a lot harder to do than if you're moving forward. (Don't ask me why, ask the scientists at Cornell Aeronautical.) Of course, when you first step out on a bike, someone should run alongside for a couple of hours (ten minutes at a time) until you get the hang of it. This applies also to a child. I don't think "training" wheels help a child to learn how to ride as much as they keep him from having to learn how to ride. Training wheels are a poor excuse for a parent not taking the time to teach his child by offering him the moral and physical support he needs as he learns.

Even if you think you *know* how to ride a bicycle already, chances are that unless you've ridden a lot with experienced cyclists, you don't know the technique that will send you soaring over hilltops while others are struggling behind.

Let me tell you a story that Keith Kingbay, Cycling Activities Director of the Schwinn Company, likes to relate. Keith and his wife, Rosetta (a young-looking grandmother), were visiting friends in Florida, when a young man (let's call him Jack) dropped in, on his weekly sixteen- to twenty-mile bicycle trip into the country. Keith told Jack that he and Rosetta would like to go along, to which Jack replied that they were welcome, if they could keep up. Keith said he thought they could. Keith let Rosetta set the pace, and to Jack's surprise, after a few miles he was gasping for breath. By the time they reached their destination, some twenty miles away, Jack was virtually exhausted and suggested a lunch stop. Rosetta blandly said that she was just warming up and that if they turned right around, they'd be just in time for a late lunch at the home of one of their friends.

Obviously, there was quite a difference between the cycling techniques of the young, muscular rider and the older man and woman. (They all had the same type bicycle.)

Proper cycling technique is the secret to tireless long cycling trips and real bicycling enjoyment. Naturally, the bicycle itself makes a big difference; you can't pedal a fifty-pound, balloon-tired machine for as long as a precision-built, twenty-one-pound bicycle.

"ANKLING" TECHNIQUE

The most important first step in learning to cycle efficiently is to "ankle" correctly (Fig. 75). Ankling simply means efficient pedaling. If your

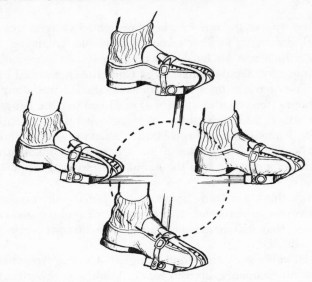

Fig. 75: The "ankling" technique taught to racing cyclists permits more efficient pedaling because muscles can be used more efficiently. At the beginning of the downward stroke, at twelve o'clock, the foot is flat and remains flat until the six o'clock position. As it passes six o'clock, the heel is pulled up slightly as leg and foot muscles pull the pedal upward to twelve o'clock, at which point the foot becomes flat again. If you don't use rattrap pedals, toe clips, cleats and straps, however, you can vary ankling by pushing down with the toe, the foot pointing slightly downward, on the down power stroke. The heel can be at more of an angle on the upward stroke, which, without cleats and straps, etc., won't go much beyond the eight o'clock position in any case.

bicycle is a conventional three-speed machine with rubber pedals, start by cycling *only* with the ball of your foot. *Never* place your arch on the pedals; you'll never be able to use your leg muscles effectively that way. When you use rattrap, all-steel pedals and toe clips, you have no choice; the toe clips keep the ball of the foot on the pedal correctly.

To learn how to ankle properly, ride your bicycle some place where you can watch your ankles as you ride, without having to beware of traffic or obstructions. A bicycle exerciser is an excellent way to practice ankling. Or a country road or school parking lot will do.

The foot should be flat at the top of the stroke and remain flat all the way down on the downward power stroke. At the bottom, or six o'clock position of the power stroke, the heel should be slightly downward. This permits, on the down power stroke, the use of leg and foot muscles more efficiently. The tendency is to pull the heel up on the downward power stroke, which leads to using the toe part of the foot during this stroke, which does not provide as much thrust as the flat position. Toes are weaker than leg muscles, and with toes down, leg muscles aren't used as effectively. As you pass six o'clock, a slight lift of the heel upward permits pulling the pedal up to the twelve o'clock position, at which point the foot resumes a flat position. This is the "ankling" technique taught to racing cyclists.

Ankling or stroking should not be jerky. You should apply a steady pressure from the top of the stroke all the way to the bottom of the forward stroke. Try ankling with one foot only. Racing cyclists wear shoe cleats that fit into the steel pedal and are held on by toe straps, and they ankle "around the clock." As the pedal passes the six o'clock position, the heel is up slightly, the toe down, and, with shoe cleats, toe clips, and straps, you can actually *pull* the pedal back around to the ten o'clock position.

Racing cyclists, wearing toe clips (Fig. 76), straps, and shoe cleats (see Fig. 69), can also continue ankling around the clock by pulling the foot straight upward from the six to the twelve o'clock position.

Practice ankling correctly until you do it automatically, and you will find cycling much easier and more enjoyable. A good way to practice is to put the gears in the lowest ratio so that the pedals move as quickly as possible to perfect your ankling technique. If you wear straps, keep them tight, but not fully strapped, so you can release them quickly, if necessary.

Fig. 76: Toe clips are essential for any kind of distance riding, particularly for cycle touring. Only with toe clips and rattrap pedals can you ankle efficiently through 360 degrees of the pedal movement. Keep toe straps tight when touring, but loose in city traffic so you can draw foot out quickly when stopping for any reason.

THE IMPORTANCE OF CADENCE

The next step in attaining cycling efficiency is pedaling "cadence." Cadence means pedaling at a relatively constant crank rotation speed, changing gears only when pedaling becomes too hard in one gear, or so easy that cadence cannot be maintained.

We all have different natural cadences, or pedaling revolutions per minute, at which we feel most comfortable. For most of us, from sixty-five to eighty-five pedal strokes per minute is the pace we can maintain most comfortably for the longest period. The reason for gear changes on a bicycle, then, is not only to help you climb hills or go down grades faster; they also help you maintain your natural pedaling cadence at all times.

The mistake most beginning cyclists make is to think of bicycle gears as being like automobile gears, with their bodies as the engine. The fault in this thinking is that whereas you can advance gears on a car and the engine will push the car faster, on a bicycle, you can advance gears without getting much speed at all. As an engine your body is severely limited. And if you are thinking that you can travel faster and longer in high than low gears, then you are wrong, at least if you are an average cyclist and not a trained racing champion.. You would actually penalize yourself by riding in high gears for long distances; although you might be able to maintain your natural cadence for a short time, you would find your pedal revolutions per minute slowing down bit by bit until you were literally forcing your feet around the pedaling arc and making your body wobble from side to side with the effort.

Cycling should be fun, not strenuous. Find your natural cadence and shift gears only to maintain it.

As soon as it becomes work to maintain good cadence, shift down. When you find your feet zipping around the arc without resistance, shift up. Beginning cyclists should stick to the lower gear range until they find their natural cadence. On a three-speed bicycle, stay in low or second gear. On a ten- or fifteen-speed bicycle, stay in the next to lowest gear ratio for the first 100 miles. This will establish and help you to get used to your natural cadence pedaling rpm. Then you can change gears when necessary, according to the vagaries of wind velocity, road grade, your current physical condition, or a load you may be carrying.

Do not change through the whole ten gears at once. Shift from one gear range to the next until you feel comfortable at your natural cadence.

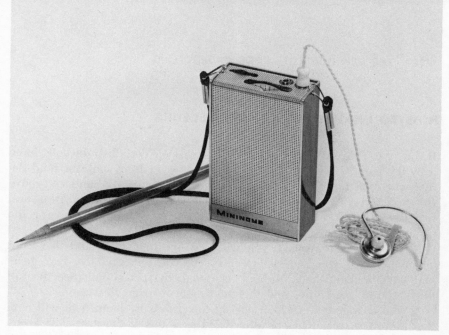

Fig. 77: A handy guide to training yourself to maintain a steady cadence, shifting gears so you can hold it comfortably, is a cigarette-pack-sized transistorized metronome, called the Mininome. It has a range of from 40 to 208 beats a minute, with adjustable volume, and weighs nine ounces.

An aid to maintaining steady cadence is an ingenious little transistorized metronome (Fig. 77), which costs about half the price of a good stop watch (under $25.00), and which you can carry in your breast pocket. It weighs only nine ounces, has a neck strap, and can be adjusted from 40 to 208 beats per minute. The click is audible enough to hear above normal street traffic even when the unit, called a Mininome, is in your breast pocket. The Mininome is available from the Touring Cyclist Shop (see Appendix).

HOW TO CHANGE GEARS—THREE-SPEED HUBS

To change gears on a three-speed internal rear hub, such as the Sturmey-Archer, ease off pedaling, pedal gently, and snap the gear quickly into the new gear. You can change gears at a stoplight, going to the lower gear for a quicker getaway. If you change gears when the bicycle is stopped, rest the weight of your foot on the higher pedal (at the two o'clock position) while you make the change. This will allow the internal gears to rotate and change easily.

HOW TO CHANGE GEARS—DERAILLEURS

Before you ride your new ten- or fifteen-speed derailleur bicycle, hang it by the handlebars and seat from the ceiling, or have someone hold the rear wheel off the ground while you turn the cranks by hand and move the gear levers from one position to another. Watch how the front and rear derailleurs work, as they change gears by derailing or moving the chain from one gear to the other.

If you have a ten-speed, you will find five rear gears and two front chainwheels, If you have a fifteen-speed, you will find five rear gears and a triple chainwheel. Never back-pedal; that's a no-no! (See the full discussion of gear ratios and their meaning on page 179).

As you change gears while moving the pedals by hand, you will note that there are no notches or other fixed positions of the gear-shift levers to tell you exactly what gear you're in, or when to stop the lever for a particular gear position. You will simply have to get used to shifting gears by the feel of it. Try changing gears. Watch how the chain moves from one gear to the next as you move the gear lever. You might note that the chain does not always go perfectly from one gear to the next, but seems to rub on an adjoining gear, and that sometimes you hear a grinding noise. This noise means that the gear-shift lever is not in the right position; you should readjust it in one direction or the other until you do not hear this noise. This is very important, for if you get into the habit of careless shifting, and ignore grinding noises, you will be in for trouble, such as a broken chain and marred gear teeth. If as you shift, the chain rubs against the spokes in the low-gear position or the seat stays (fork section holding wheel axle) in the high-gear position, readjust the derailleur mechanism as outlined on page 353.

Change gear before you have to. When approaching a steep hill, change down one gear as soon as you start to slow up. As you continue to slow or the hill gets steeper, change all the way down before you have to do so. If, at the same time that you're straining the pedals, you try to change all the way down to your lowest gear from your highest, the chain will be forced over at a steep angle and can "hang up" on gears at that angle and lock the rear wheel. Or, with some rear derailleurs, at that angle the chain can either bind in the derailleur cage and lock the wheel, or come out of the derailleur cage (on the Sun-Tour unit). This applies also to shifting up rapidly, as after cresting a steep hill and starting down the other side. The tendency is to shift suddenly from the very lowest to the very highest gear combination, which is an invitation to chain hang-up on gear cluster or in derailleur, or both, locking the rear wheel and in the process even possibly bending the dropout, wheel axle, or derailleur cage, body, or plate. I vividly remember one instance when I had just sweated up a steep hill in Austria's Packalpe district, with a fairly steep drop-off on the right side. I changed quickly all the way to my highest from my lowest gear, in order to get a good fast start down the hill, and to keep from having to bother with gear change once I got up to speed. The chain hung up, jamming between the gear cluster and seat stays, and locking my rear wheel so that I burned rubber for about ten feet, and caused the gal behind me to crash trying to avoid running into me. Now I change well in advance of when I think I will have to, and do it one gear at a time.

One further point about smooth shifting technique. If you shift down to the largest rear gear without changing position of the front derailleur, you will hear a metallic rubbing sound from the front derailleur. This sound is caused by the chain rubbing against the side of the front derailleur cage (the part the chain goes through and which "derails" the chain from one chainwheel to another). The chain rubs because as it approaches the largest rear gear it assumes an increasingly steep angle in relation to the front derailleur cage. So as you shift to a larger rear gear, you will also have to move the front derailleur so its cage moves to the left just enough to keep the chain from rubbing on the cage. As you continue to shift to a larger gear, you will have to continue to move the front derailleur cage to the left (in the direction of a smaller chainwheel). The opposite, of course, holds true when shifting from a large to a smaller rear gear. Get in the habit of automatically readjusting the front derailleur (minutely) every time you shift the rear gear. If the chainwheel is bent, you probably won't be able to keep the chain from rubbing; in this case, please see page 368 for a discussion on straightening the chainwheel. (Also check to make sure chainwheel pins are tight.)

Let me make one point perfectly clear. *You must never shift derailleur gears unless you are pedaling. The cranks must be moving when you shift.* If you stop pedaling, change gears, then start pedaling again, you might tear up the chain or the teeth and possibly damage the derailleur mechanism.

Good ten-speed derailleur-equipped bicycles are still enough of a novelty to tempt itchy-fingered young children (and some adults) to play with the gear-shift levers, if you park your bicycle where they can get at it. If someone has moved your gear-shift levers from the position they were in when you parked your bicycle, and you unsuspectingly climb on and start to ride, you may also damage gears and derailleur, just as if you shifted gears improperly without continuing to pedal. So, always, after you have left your bicycle unattended for a while, start riding very gingerly, applying very gentle pressure to the pedals. If the gear levers have been moved, very gentle pedaling will at least permit the derailleur to work without tearing up the works. Another technique is to hoist up the rear wheels by the seat with one hand and twirl the crank with the other. This will let the chain move to another position without damaging it. Then you can mount, ride, and return the chain to the gear combination you prefer. (For a full discussion of gearing, see Chapter 6.)

RIDING THE STRAIGHT AND NARROW

Part of correct riding is to be able to ride and steer accurately. With a little training and attention to correct riding technique, you should be able to steer right down a yellow dividing line (a path about four inches wide) and stay on it. This is important to safety, as we have already discussed.

Meanwhile, remember that good riding is easy riding. You should ride relatively relaxed, without your muscles being all knotted up.

TIPS FOR EASY CYCLING

There are six positions (Fig. 78–Fig. 84) for riding bikes with dropped handlebars; shifting from one to another will help you beat fatigue on a long trip. In particular, notice Fig. 84. Here hands are on the lowest part of the handlebars. This is the position that's safest on speedy downhill "slalom" runs, particularly where you have to steer around potholes or debris. I also strongly recommend that the inside of your wrists be locked tight against the handlebars, just above the brake levers, on the sides of the bars. In this position you can help prevent front wheel "shimmy" from starting; once shimmy starts it's almost impossible to stop it, and you should brake to a stop as soon as possible. (See page 57 for a discussion of front wheel shimmy and its causes.)

On tours, do not try to be the first in line, unless you're in top physical condition. If you stay behind the leader, or behind two or three other riders, they will "break the wind" for you, and you will be able to ride

Fig. 78: There are seven basic positions for placing hands on handlebars, which you can vary from time to time to change cycling position on long rides. In this position, hands are at top of handlebars, next to stem. This is also a good position to use when hill climbing with your bottom in the saddle; it permits you to brace against the effort put out by strong leg and back muscles.

Fig. 79: Hands at end of bars, just above brake levers. This is the usual position most riders seem to prefer.

Fig. 80: In the same position as in Figure 79, but with thumb and forefinger extended downward.

Fig. 81: Base of thumb and forefinger rest on brake levers, providing support for forward weight of upper torso. This is a particularly restful position to adopt on long downhill "coasts," with the added safety factor of allowing you to reach brake levers quickly and conveniently. This is also the position to use when "honking" uphill, climbing with bottom out of the saddle.

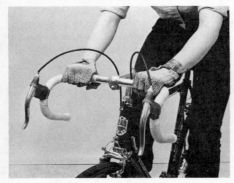

Fig. 82: An alternate position frequently used when "honking" uphill. Here the hands are grasping the top of the handlebars firmly; arm muscles are helping "honk" up a steep hill.

Fig. 83: This position is used frequently when the going is hard, as on an uphill climb. This is also a position which reduces wind resistance.

Fig. 84: On high-speed downhill runs, especially over a bumpy road, it is possible, for any of a number of reasons, for a bicycle to develop a front wheel wobble or shimmy which could lead to disastrous loss of control. In the position held here, front wheel shimmy possibility is minimized by the way the handlebars are locked into position between the inside of both forearms, as well as held firmly by the hands. This is the recommended position when riding a camping-gear-laden bike at high speed, downhill especially. *(Figures 78 through 84 by the author)*

farther before tiring. This technique is called "drafting," and to do it safely you should never get right behind and in line with the person in front, but rather stay behind and two or three inches to one side. Then if the rider in front suddenly brakes or slows, you can go by without running into him. I've had following riders run right into me, with their front wheel jamming between my right chain stay and derailleur, bending and ruining the derailleur. (If I seem more concerned about damage to the bike than to the rider, I am not. It's so obvious that chain hang-up and resulting wheel lock, or being run into from the rear, can cause you to lose control and hit a passing car or the curb, that I prefer to tell you what can happen to your bicycle. *Any* type of equipment failure is an invitation to an accident.)

Watch yourself as you ride. Make sure you do not wobble from side to side, or bend your back up and down as you pump. Learn to use your stomach, back, ankle, thigh, and leg muscles as a team to help you cycle smoothly, without tiring.

I have spent hours watching highly trained road and track cyclists riding their bicycles, trying to learn their technique. These cyclists are a symphony of effortless motion. They ride true as an arrow, with absolutely no side wobble, legs pumping like smooth-functioning pistons, and the ankles and feet like wrist pins. It looks so easy, until you mount your bicycle and try to fall in behind them. You discover that while the racing cyclist looks like he is just loafing along, he is actually pedaling away at about twenty to twenty-five miles per hour, and you will probably not be able to catch up to him, or, if you do, not for long.

I am not trying to make a racing cyclist out of every overweight adult American, though. I am just simply showing you how proper technique will make cycling more fun, even if to learn this technique takes practice. Once these good riding methods have become a habit, cycling will really be a joy for you, and perhaps someday you will surprise all your friends by doing the century (100-mile) tour in a single eight-hour day. There are hundreds of others—fathers, mothers, grandfathers, grandmothers— who do the century run regularly every year.

MOUNTING

I prefer cleated cycling shoes and toe clips because they increase pedaling efficiency about 30 to 40 percent, but you might not like them. Whatever you prefer, if you do use rattrap pedals with straps, you will have to learn how to mount the bicycle and how to insert one foot into the pedal quickly and safely. Once under way, you won't have time to fuss and look down, trying to fit your foot into the pedal; you must keep your eye on the road. You should practice slipping your free foot promptly into the pedal.

Try this mounting technique. Straddle the bicycle, put one foot in a toe-clip pedal, and pull the pedal up to the one o'clock position. One foot is in a pedal; the other is on the ground. Use the foot on the ground to shove you off and get you moving, while in one graceful, quick motion you pull yourself up into the saddle by pushing down on the other pedal and hoisting yourself up by pressure on the handlebars. The foot that pushes down the pedal should get you 90 percent of the way into the saddle and, at the same time, get you going forward quickly. Hold the pedals still a moment while you insert your toe and then your foot into the empty pedal. Practice this technique until it's as easy as rising from a chair to walk around the room. Mounting your bicycle this way will distinguish you as an experienced cyclist, at least to other experienced cyclists.

6

GEARS TO FIT THE RIDER
TO THE ROAD —
ALL ABOUT BICYCLE GEARING

The whole subject of gear ratios may seem complicated or even trivial to you. If your interest in cycling is confined to using a no-gear coaster-brake monster, or a three-speed hub utility bicycle, then you should skip this chapter.

But, if you have a ten- or fifteen-speed derailleur-equipped bicycle, and are interested in cycle touring as well as around-the-block jaunts, gear ratios are important because they can mean the difference between efficient or wasted use of the muscles you have with the wheels you push them with. If you want to become a road, track, or other type of racer, an avid and dedicated interest in gear ratios is a "must."

Let me explain why. Automobiles have engines of a fixed horsepower and wheels of a fixed size. Given these fixed factors, the car designer selects gears of specific ratios for maximum or at least relatively efficient performance. The gear ratios he selects are based on the horsepower available to him.

When you go into a bicycle store to buy one of the popular American-made, low-cost, ten-speed derailleur-equipped machines, you don't have to worry much about gear ratios, because manufacturers have long since learned that the average buyer is usually a long way from being as physically strong and as competent a cyclist as the really experienced bicycle enthusiast. You'll find that gears on the less expensive models

179

jump from high to low in fairly substantial increments, so that you have a pretty wide range of gears to shift from on the road.

If you spend a little extra money, however, and buy a really fine machine, you'll more likely than not get a bicycle with close gear ratios, so that the difference between the highest and the lowest gear selections is much smaller than on the lower-cost machines. The reason for this difference is that all the finer machines except the Schwinn Paramount are European-made and European manufacturers make bikes for the more dedicated and therefore, presumably, the more physically fit and competent cyclists, who will want closer gear ratios for maximum speed and performance. This should be a word of warning for you, because you might buy a higher-priced bicycle with ten-speed derailleur gears, and should not be too surprised to find that on steep hills the difference between the high and low gear ratios isn't as great as you might have imagined. In other words, if you want a good machine but aren't as experienced or as physically fit as you will be later on as you continue to cycle, you should specify gear ratios more in keeping with your needs. The dealer who sells you a good bicycle will most likely be among the rare few who knows how to change gears cogs on freewheels, and he will be able to select wider ratios for you very easily.

For example, the Schwinn P-15 Paramount, their top-line fifteen-speed model (just as good as the best European top-grade bicycles), comes with a range of gears specially selected for the touring cyclist. The rear gear cluster has teeth starting with the high gear of 14, 16, 19, 25, and 31 teeth, and the front triple chainwheel set has 36, 49, and 54 teeth. These gears give you a wide range of gears, from quite low for hill climbing to high for downhill speed runs or fast runs on the flats with the wind at your back. However, I changed the gearing on my P-15 by removing the rear gear cluster and substituting one of the new Shimano alternate-tooth freewheels with teeth of 14, 17, 22, 28, and 34, which gives an even greater range, in the low end, than the original gear cluster (Fig. 85). In tours over Vermont's Green Mountains, and in Germany, Belgium, Austria, Luxembourg, and France, I found the lower "Granny" gears indispensable for hill climbing with a loaded bike. I was cycling (slowly) up steep hills in the Austrian Alps while others (of my age) were shoving their bikes up on foot. Riding your bike uphill, no matter how slowly, is infinitely to be preferred to pushing it up on foot; the going is much easier on the saddle than it is by "shank's mare," especially if you are wearing cleated shoes. You can't walk comfortably with shoe cleats clanking on the pavement, although you can get by for a short distance if there's a grassy shoulder to walk on. This means you have to stop and

Fig. 85: Wide-range alternate-tooth freewheel, from 14 to 34 teeth, makes hill climbing easier (not easy, though). Alternate teeth on two biggest gears smooth shifting them.

change to loafers so you can walk up the hill, which is not terribly convenient.

We could stop here, secure in the knowledge that you have enough information about gears to select them intelligently. Unfortunately, this is only partially so, because you still need to know about gear ratios and gear ratios expressed in equivalent wheel inches and cadence to know how to use the gears you have efficiently; and how fast, at a given cadence in a given gear, you will be traveling.

ABOUT TRIPLE CHAINWHEELS

If you are planning to pack a thirty-pound load for cross-country distance touring, you will need a wide range of gears. I'd keep the wide-range rear freewheel cluster as described and change over to a three-speed triple front chainwheel. There are a number of makes of good triple chainwheels of lightweight dural metal (aluminum alloy) with cotterless cranks. Campagnolo triple chainwheels go down to 36 teeth on the small wheel. You can get an even lower gear ratio by using a 26-tooth T.A. chainwheel on a T.A. chainset or on a Stronglight chainset. The T.A. will fit the Stronglight, but you will need longer spacing washers, nuts, and bolts, as well as a longer axle to accommodate the third chainwheel, as noted. I like the combination of a 34-tooth big rear gear and a 26-tooth small chainwheel, which gives you a "Granny" gear that will take you over just about any hill you'll face.

Remember, though, to order the same make of triple chainwheel as the double chainwheel you now have. You will also need a longer axle (also of the same make) to accommodate the extra width of the third chainwheel, although you can use the cones and bearings you had on your double chainwheel. Before you do any changing over, be sure to review the instructions for chainwheel and axle maintenance, assembly, and disassembly, on page 420, including the tools required.

We mention this elsewhere, but it bears repeating. On a fifteen-speed bicycle, with five gears rear and three chainwheels up front, you must *never* use a gear combination that puts the chain on the biggest (most number of teeth) front and rear gears, because this means the chain is at an extreme angle, and will very likely bend the derailleur cage so future shifting will be difficult and erratic. A rule to remember, then, is always to use *only* the three largest (most teeth) rear gears with the smallest chainwheel, and never get the chain over at an extreme angle by putting it on either the biggest front and rear gears or the smallest front and rear gears. If you examine your gears, you will see that the biggest rear gear is on the far left and the biggest front gear is far right, and vice versa with the two small gears.

THE IMPORTANCE OF DERAILLEUR CAPACITY

Also, before you start changing freewheel and chainwheel gear ratios, remember that the ability of rear derailleurs to cope with wide variations in gear ratios is strictly limited. You may have to change your derailleur to one with more capacity. Rear derailleur capacity is measured by the maximum-minimum teeth it will handle. For example, let's say your large front chainwheel has 49 teeth and your small chainwheel 42 teeth. That's a pretty small range, and the 7-tooth difference falls well within the range of all derailleurs. But if you install a 36-tooth front third chainwheel and have a 34-tooth rear gear, you may have trouble using both lower gear ratios, unless you get a wide-range derailleur such as the Campagnolo Gran Turismo derailleur, or the Shimano GT Crane derailleur, which will accommodate even the new six-gear cluster freewheels. The major difference between a close and wide ratio rear derailleur is the length of the cage. A close ratio derailleur has a short cage; a wide ratio derailleur has a much longer cage so it can maintain chain tension correctly. This is especially important when the chain is on the smallest front and rear gears. And a close ratio derailleur that will maintain this correct chain tension won't permit use of a chain long enough so you can shift to bigger gears, which have more chain wraparound (uses more chain links).

A WORD ABOUT GEAR RATIOS

Gear ratio is simply the number of times the rear wheel will turn for every turn of the chainwheel up front. For example, my Paramount P-15 has, as stated, a low gear of 34 teeth on the rear freewheel gear cluster, and a low gear of 36 teeth on the front triple chainwheel. Gear ratio is found simply by dividing the number of teeth on the chainwheel by the number of teeth on the freewheel gear. In this case, the ratio in my lowest gear combination is $^{36}\!/_{34} = 1.06$ (eliminating additional decimal places). This ratio means that for every turn of the chainwheel, the rear 34-tooth gear (and thus the rear wheel it is driving) turns 1.06 times. This is a very low ratio indeed, although not the lowest obtainable, since I could switch my Campagnolo triple chainwheel to a T.A., or Stronglight with T.A. 26-tooth chainwheel, in which case my gear ratio would be $^{26}\!/_{34} = .76$, so the rear wheel turns .76 of a revolution for every turn of the 26 T chainwheel. Going to my highest gear combination, the rear 14 T and the front 54 T, this gives me $^{54}\!/_{14} = 3.86$, so for every turn of the chainwheel, the rear wheel turns 3.86 times.

EQUIVALENT WHEEL SIZE AND "GEARS"

If you will refer to the history of bicycling on page 263 of this book, you will note the bicycle evolved from a pedal-driven front wheel with both wheels of about the same size, to one with the rear wheel quite small and the pedal front wheel quite large, fifty-four inches or so. This means that you could increase the speed you can pedal either by making a pedal-driven front wheel bigger, or by gearing up a chain-driven rear wheel. The effect, so far as speed is concerned, is the same either way. As high-wheeler bicyclists of the 1880's soon realized, the larger the front wheel, the faster they could ride, up to a point beyond which the wheel became too big (i.e., the gear ratio too large and the pedals too far away) for them to pedal. The high-wheeler (Ordinary or Penny Farthing, as it was called) thus set the standard for gearing used today. You will hear modern cyclists on ten-speed bicycles talk about "the gear I'm in" or "what gear do you use to climb hills?" and if racing is involved, the "gear" the racer is using for a specific event. The "gear" shown in Table 13 on page 185 (computed by your author) is simply a conversion table which converts gear ratio to the equivalent high-wheeler front-wheel diameter in inches. This is something like converting the thrust of an aircraft jet engine into the horsepower of a piston engine to find out how much power the aircraft has . . . sort of roundabout, to say the least. But the gear chart is in wide use, cyclists use it to compare gear ratios, so there it is and we're stuck with it.

The Gear Chart is derived very simply by multiplying the gear ratio by the diameter in inches of the rear wheel, which then converts the rear-wheel diameter to the equivalent diameter of a "high-wheeler." Take the low gear of my P-15, for example; 34 teeth rear, 36 front: $^{36}\!/_{34} \times 27 = 28.6$, or, this gear is equal to riding a high-wheeler with a pedal-driven front wheel of 26 inches diameter. To find out how *far* one turn of the chain-wheel with this gear combination on the P-15 (or one turn of the front wheel on the "high-wheeler" equivalent) would take you, multiply the equivalent "gear" by pi, or 3.1416. In this case, one turn of a 36-tooth chainwheel connected to a 34-tooth rear gear ($^{36}\!/_{34} \times 27 \times 3.1416$) would cause the rear wheel to move forward 89.81 inches, or almost 7½ feet. The highest gears on my P-15 are $^{54}\!/_{14} \times 27 \times 3.1416$, 327 inches or about 27¼ feet forward for every turn of the crank. You can check the "Gear" for any combination of rear and front gear teeth by checking the chart on page 185. For example, find 14 teeth on the chart under "sprocket size" at left. Move along that line to the right to the 54 T column and you find 104.1, which multiplied by 3.1416 (*you'll* have to do it) tells that you will travel the 327 inches we came up with above (or $^{327}\!/_{12} = 27$¼ feet).

HOW TO TELL HOW FAST

All of these arithmetical shenanigans are fine, but they won't tell you how *fast* you are moving. We have to factor in another figure, which is the number of *times* you move the chainwheel one revolution in one minute. The formula to derive miles per hour at a given crank rpm (or chain-wheel, or rear wheel rpm, it's all the same) is gear ratio times crank rpm, 3.1416 × 60 divided by 63.360. All this work is saved for you, however, by the Cadence Chart (Fig. 86), which was kindly programmed on an IBM computer by Sam Rhoads of Boise, Idaho, who recognized the limitations of the conventional cadence chart.

TABLE 13 · **Gear Chart**

NUMBER OF TEETH
IN CHAINWHEEL

		24	25	26	27	28	29	30
NUMBER OF	12	54	56.2	58.5	60.8	63	65.2	67.5
TEETH IN REAR	13	49.8	51.9	54	56	58.2	60.2	62.3
SPROCKET	14	46.3	48.2	50.1	52.1	54	55.9	57.9
	15	43.2	45	46.8	48.6	50.4	52.2	54
	16	40.5	42.2	43.9	45.6	47.3	48.9	50.6
	17	38.1	39.7	41.3	42.9	44.5	46.1	47.6
	18	36	37.5	39	40.5	42	43.5	45
	19	34.1	35.5	36.9	38.4	39.8	41.2	42.6
	20	32.4	33.8	35.1	36.5	37.8	39.2	40.5
	21	30.9	32.1	33.4	34.7	36	37.3	38.6
	22	29.5	30.7	31.9	33.1	34.4	35.6	36.8
	23	28.2	29.3	30.5	31.7	32.9	34	35.2
	24	27	28.1	29.2	30.4	31.5	32.6	33.8
	25	25.9	27	28.1	29.2	30.3	31.3	32.4
	26	24.9	26	27	28.0	29.1	30.1	31.2
	27	23.9	24.9	25.9	27	27.9	28.9	29.9
	28	23.1	24.1	25.1	26	27	28	28.9
	29	22.3	23.3	24.2	25.1	26.1	27	27.9
	30	21.6	22.5	23.4	24.3	25.2	26.1	27
	31	20.9	21.8	22.6	23.5	24.4	25.3	26.1
	32	20.3	21.1	21.9	22.8	23.6	24.5	25.3
	33	19.6	20.5	21.3	22.1	22.9	23.7	24.5
	34	19.1	19.9	20.6	21.4	22.2	23	23.8

TABLE 13 · **Gear Chart** (continued)

NUMBER OF TEETH
IN CHAINWHEEL

		31	32	33	34	35	36	37	38	39	40
REAR	12	69.7	72	74.3	76.5	78.7	81	83.2	85.5	87.8	90
TEETH	13	64.4	66.5	68.5	70.6	72.7	74.8	76.8	78.9	81	83.1
	14	59.8	61.7	63.6	65.6	67.5	69.4	71.4	73.3	75.2	77.1
	15	55.8	57.6	59.4	61.2	63	64.8	66.6	68.4	70.2	72
	16	52.3	54	55.7	57.4	59.1	60.8	62.4	64.1	65.8	67.5
	17	49.2	50.8	52.4	54	55.6	57.2	58.8	60.4	61.9	63.5
	18	46.5	48	49.5	51	52.5	54	55.5	57	58.5	60
	19	44.1	45.5	46.9	48.3	49.7	51.2	52.6	54	55.4	56.8
	20	41.9	43.2	44.6	45.9	47.3	48.6	50	51.3	52.7	54
	21	39.9	41.1	42.4	43.7	45	46.3	47.6	48.9	50.1	51.4
	22	38	39.3	40.5	41.7	43	44.2	45.4	46.6	47.9	49.1
	23	36.4	37.6	38.7	39.9	41.1	42.3	43.4	44.6	45.8	47
	24	34.9	36	37.1	38.3	39.4	40.5	41.6	42.8	43.9	45
	25	33.5	34.6	35.6	36.7	37.8	38.9	40	41	42.1	43.2
	26	32.2	33.2	34.3	35.3	36.3	37.4	38.4	39.5	40.5	41.5
	27	30.9	31.9	32.9	33.9	34.9	35.9	36.9	37.9	38.9	40
	28	29.9	30.9	31.8	32.9	33.8	34.7	35.7	36.6	37.6	38.6
	29	28.9	29.8	30.7	31.7	32.6	33.5	34.4	35.4	36.3	37.2
	30	27.9	28.8	29.7	30.6	31.5	32.4	33.3	34.2	35.1	36
	31	27	27.9	28.7	29.6	30.5	31.4	32.2	33.1	34	34.8
	32	26.2	27	27.8	28.7	29.5	30.4	31.2	32.1	32.9	33.8
	33	25.4	26.2	27	27.8	28.6	29.5	30.3	31.1	31.9	32.7
	34	24.6	25.4	26.2	27	27.8	28.6	29.4	30.2	31	31.8

41	42	43	44	45	46	47	48	49	50
92.2	94.5	96.7	99	101.3	103.5	105.7	108	110.2	112.5
85.2	87.2	89.3	91.4	93.5	95.5	97.6	99.7	101.8	103.8
79.1	81	82.9	84.9	86.8	88.7	90.6	92.6	94.5	96.4
73.8	75.6	77.4	79.2	81	82.8	84.6	86.4	88.2	90
69.2	70.9	72.6	74.3	75.9	77.6	79.3	81	82.7	84.4
65.1	66.7	68.3	69.9	71.5	73.1	74.6	76.2	77.8	79.4
61.5	63	64.5	66.0	67.5	69	70.5	72	73.5	75
58.3	59.7	61.1	62.5	63.9	65.4	66.8	68.2	69.6	71.1
55.4	56.7	58.1	59.4	60.8	62.1	63.5	64.8	66.2	67.5
52.7	*54*	55.3	56.6	57.9	59.1	60.4	61.7	63	64.3
50.3	51.5	52.8	*54*	55.2	56.5	57.7	58.9	60.1	61.4
48.1	49.3	50.5	51.7	52.8	*54*	55.2	56.3	57.5	58.7
46.1	47.3	48.4	49.5	50.6	51.8	52.9	*54*	55.1	56.3
44.3	45.4	46.4	47.5	48.6	49.7	50.8	51.8	52.9	*54*
42.6	43.6	44.7	45.7	46.7	47.8	48.8	49.8	50.9	51.9
41	42	43	44	45	46	47	48	49	50
39.5	40.5	41.5	42.4	43.4	44.4	45.3	46.3	47.3	48.2
38.2	39.1	40	41	41.9	42.8	43.8	44.7	45.6	46.6
36.9	37.8	38.7	39.6	40.5	41.4	42.3	43.2	44.1	45
35.7	36.6	37.5	39.3	39.2	40.1	40.9	41.8	42.7	43.5
34.6	35.4	36.3	37.1	38	38.8	39.7	40.5	41.3	42.2
33.5	34.4	35.2	36	36.8	37.6	38.5	39.3	40.1	40.9
32.6	33.4	34.1	34.9	35.7	36.5	37.3	38.1	38.9	39.7

TABLE 13 · **Gear Chart** (continued)

NUMBER OF TEETH
IN CHAINWHEEL

		51	52	53	54	55	56	57	58	59	60
REAR	12	114.8	117	119.2	121.5	123.7	126	128.3	130.5	132.7	135
TEETH	13	105.9	108	110.1	112.2	114.2	116.3	118.4	120.5	122.5	124.6
	14	98.4	100.3	102.2	104.1	160.1	108	109.9	111.9	113.8	115.7
	15	91.8	93.6	95.4	97.2	99	100.8	102.6	104.4	106.2	108
	16	86.1	87.8	89.4	91.1	92.8	94.5	96.2	97.9	99.6	101.3
	17	81	82.6	84.2	85.8	87.4	88.9	90.5	92.1	93.7	95.3
	18	76.5	78	79.5	81	82.5	84	85.4	87	88.5	90
	19	72.5	73.9	75.3	76.7	78.2	79.6	81	82.4	83.8	85.3
	20	68.9	70.2	71.6	72.9	74.3	75.6	77	78.3	79.7	81
	21	65.6	66.9	68.1	69.4	70.7	72	73.3	74.6	75.9	77.1
	22	62.6	63.8	65	66.3	67.5	68.7	70	71.2	72.4	73.6
	23	59.9	61	62.2	63.4	64.6	65.7	66.9	68.1	69.3	70.4
	24	57.4	58.5	59.6	60.8	61.9	63	64.1	65.3	66.4	67.5
	25	55.1	56.2	57.2	58.3	59.4	60.5	61.6	62.6	63.7	64.8
	26	53	*54*	55	56.1	57.1	58.2	59.2	60.2	61.3	62.3
	27	51	52	53	*54*	55	56	57	58	59	60
	28	49.2	50.1	51.1	52.1	53	*54*	55	55.9	56.9	57.9
	29	47.5	48.4	49.3	50.3	51.2	52.1	53	*54*	54.9	55.9
	30	45.9	46.8	47.7	48.6	49.5	50.4	51.3	52.2	53.1	*54*
	31	44.4	45.3	46.2	47	47.9	48.8	49.6	50.5	51.4	52.3
	32	43	43.9	44.7	45.6	46.4	47.3	48.1	48.9	49.8	50.6
	33	41.7	42.5	43.4	44.2	45	45.8	46.6	47.5	48.3	49.1
	34	40.5	41.3	42.1	42.9	43.7	44.5	45.3	46.1	46.9	47.6

61	62	63	64	65	66	67	68	69	70
137.2	139.5	141.8	144	146.2	148.5	150.7	153	155.3	157.5
126.7	128.8	130.8	132.9	135	137.1	139.2	141.2	143.3	145.4
117.6	119.6	121.5	123.4	125.4	127.3	129.2	131.1	133.1	135
109.8	111.6	113.4	115.2	117	118.8	120.6	122.4	124.2	126
102.9	104.6	106.3	108	109.7	111.4	113.1	114.8	116.4	118.1
96.9	98.5	100.1	101.6	103.2	104.8	106.4	108	109.6	111.2
91.5	93	94.5	96	97.5	99	100.4	102	103.5	105
86.7	88.1	89.5	90.9	92.4	93.8	95.2	96.6	98.1	99.5
82.4	83.7	85.1	86.4	87.8	89.1	90.5	91.8	93.2	94.5
78.4	79.7	81	82.3	83.6	84.9	86.1	87.4	88.7	90
74.9	76.1	77.3	78.5	79.8	81	82.2	83.5	84.7	85.9
71.6	72.8	74	75.1	76.3	77.5	78.7	79.8	81	82.2
68.6	69.8	70.9	72	73.1	74.3	75.4	76.5	77.6	78.8
65.9	66.7	68	69.1	70.2	71.3	72.4	73.4	74.5	75.6
63.3	64.4	65.4	66.5	67.5	68.5	69.6	70.6	71.7	72.7
61	62	63	64	65	66	67	68	69	70
58.8	59.8	60.6	61.7	62.7	63.6	64.6	65.6	66.5	67.5
56.8	57.7	58.7	59.6	60.5	61.4	62.4	63.3	64.2	65.2
54.9	55.8	56.7	57.6	58.5	59.4	60.3	61.2	62.1	63
53.1	*54*	54.9	55.7	56.6	57.5	58.4	59.2	60.1	61
51.5	52.3	53.2	*54*	54.8	55.7	56.5	57.4	58.2	59.1
49.9	50.7	51.5	52.4	53.2	*54*	54.8	55.6	56.5	57.3
48.4	49.2	50	50.8	51.6	52.4	53.2	*54*	54.8	55.6

Fig. 86: To use this Cadence Chart, first find your "Gear" from Table 13 on page 185. Say you're in 14T rear and 54T front. Your *Gear* will be 104.1. Say further you're pedaling at 70 crank rpms. Find your *Gear* in gear column, left, and, following down the 70 crank rpm column above, you'll be moving your bicycle at 21.66 mph. (Congratulations!) (*Chart courtesy Sam Rhoads, Boise, Idaho, who programmed an IBM computer to come up with all these answers.*)

THE SPEED IN MPH EQUALS PI TIMES THE GEAR TIMES THE CRANK RPM TIMES 60 DIVIDED BY 63,

REVOLUTIONS PER MINUTE OF THE CRANK ARM

GEAR	60	70	80	90	100	110	120	130	140	150	160
26	4.64	5.41	6.19	6.96	7.73	8.51	9.28	10.06	10.83	11.60	12.38
27	4.82	5.62	6.43	7.23	8.03	8.84	9.64	10.44	11.25	12.05	12.85
28	5.00	5.83	6.66	7.50	8.33	9.16	10.00	10.83	11.66	12.49	13.33
29	5.18	6.04	6.90	7.76	8.63	9.49	10.35	11.22	12.08	12.94	13.80
30	5.35	6.25	7.14	8.03	8.92	9.82	10.71	11.60	12.49	13.39	14.28
31	5.53	6.46	7.38	8.30	9.22	10.14	11.07	11.99	12.91	13.83	14.76
32	5.71	6.66	7.62	8.57	9.52	10.47	11.42	12.38	13.33	14.28	15.23
33	5.89	6.87	7.85	8.84	9.82	10.80	11.78	12.76	13.74	14.73	15.71
34	6.07	7.08	8.09	9.10	10.11	11.13	12.14	13.15	14.16	15.17	16.18
35	6.25	7.29	8.33	9.37	10.41	11.45	12.49	13.54	14.58	15.62	16.66
36	6.43	7.50	8.57	9.64	10.71	11.78	12.85	13.92	14.99	16.06	17.14
37	6.60	7.71	8.81	9.91	11.01	12.11	13.21	14.31	15.41	16.51	17.61
38	6.78	7.91	9.04	10.17	11.30	12.44	13.57	14.70	15.83	16.96	18.09
39	6.96	8.12	9.28	10.44	11.60	12.76	13.92	15.08	16.24	17.40	18.56
40	7.14	8.33	9.52	10.71	11.90	13.09	14.28	15.47	16.66	17.85	19.04
41	7.32	8.54	9.76	10.98	12.20	13.42	14.64	15.86	17.08	18.30	19.52
42	7.50	8.75	10.00	11.25	12.49	13.74	14.99	16.24	17.49	18.74	19.99
43	7.68	8.95	10.23	11.51	12.79	14.07	15.35	16.63	17.91	19.19	20.47
44	7.85	9.16	10.47	11.78	13.09	14.40	15.71	17.02	18.33	19.63	20.94
45	8.03	9.37	10.71	12.05	13.39	14.73	16.06	17.40	18.74	20.08	21.42
46	8.21	9.58	10.95	12.32	13.68	15.05	16.42	17.79	19.16	20.53	21.90
47	8.39	9.79	11.19	12.58	13.98	15.38	16.78	18.18	19.58	20.97	22.37
48	8.57	10.00	11.42	12.85	14.28	15.71	17.14	18.56	19.99	21.42	22.85
49	8.75	10.20	11.66	13.12	14.58	16.04	17.49	18.95	20.41	21.87	23.32
50	8.92	10.41	11.90	13.39	14.87	16.36	17.85	19.34	20.82	22.31	23.80
51	9.10	10.62	12.14	13.66	15.17	16.69	18.21	19.72	21.24	22.76	24.28
52	9.28	10.83	12.38	13.92	15.47	17.02	18.56	20.11	21.66	23.20	24.75
53	9.46	11.04	12.61	14.19	15.77	17.34	18.92	20.50	22.07	23.65	25.23
54	9.64	11.25	12.85	14.46	16.06	17.67	19.28	20.88	22.49	24.10	25.70
55	9.82	11.45	13.09	14.73	16.36	18.00	19.63	21.27	22.91	24.54	26.18
56	10.00	11.66	13.33	14.99	16.66	18.33	19.99	21.66	23.32	24.99	26.66
57	10.17	11.87	13.57	15.26	16.96	18.65	20.35	22.04	23.74	25.44	27.13
58	10.35	12.08	13.80	15.53	17.25	18.98	20.71	22.43	24.16	25.88	27.61
59	10.53	12.29	14.04	15.80	17.55	19.31	21.06	22.82	24.57	26.33	28.08
60	10.71	12.49	14.28	16.06	17.85	19.63	21.42	23.20	24.99	26.77	28.56
61	10.89	12.70	14.52	16.33	18.15	19.96	21.78	23.59	25.41	27.22	29.04
62	11.07	12.91	14.76	16.60	18.44	20.29	22.13	23.98	25.82	27.67	29.51
63	11.25	13.12	14.99	16.87	18.74	20.62	22.49	24.37	26.24	28.11	29.99
64	11.42	13.33	15.23	17.14	19.04	20.94	22.85	24.75	26.66	28.56	30.46
65	11.60	13.54	15.47	17.40	19.34	21.27	23.20	25.14	27.07	29.01	30.94
66	11.78	13.74	15.71	17.67	19.63	21.60	23.56	25.53	27.49	29.45	31.42
67	11.96	13.95	15.95	17.94	19.93	21.93	23.92	25.91	27.91	29.90	31.89
68	12.14	14.16	16.18	18.21	20.23	22.25	24.28	26.30	28.32	30.34	32.37
69	12.32	14.37	16.42	18.47	20.53	22.58	24.63	26.69	28.74	30.79	32.84
70	12.49	14.58	16.66	18.74	20.82	22.91	24.99	27.07	29.15	31.24	33.32
71	12.67	14.79	16.90	19.01	21.12	23.23	25.35	27.46	29.57	31.68	33.80
72	12.85	14.99	17.14	19.28	21.42	23.56	25.70	27.85	29.99	32.13	34.27
73	13.03	15.20	17.37	19.55	21.72	23.89	26.06	28.23	30.40	32.58	34.75
74	13.21	15.41	17.61	19.81	22.01	24.22	26.42	28.62	30.82	33.02	35.22
75	13.39	15.62	17.85	20.08	22.31	24.54	26.77	29.01	31.24	33.47	35.70
76	13.57	15.83	18.09	20.35	22.61	24.87	27.13	29.39	31.65	33.91	36.18
77	13.74	16.04	18.33	20.62	22.91	25.20	27.49	29.78	32.07	34.36	36.65
78	13.92	16.24	18.56	20.88	23.20	25.53	27.85	30.17	32.49	34.81	37.13
79	14.10	16.45	18.80	21.15	23.50	25.85	28.20	30.55	32.90	35.25	37.60
80	14.28	16.66	19.04	21.42	23.80	26.18	28.56	30.94	33.32	35.70	38.00
81	14.46	16.87	19.28	21.69	24.10	26.51	28.92	31.33	33.74	36.15	38.56
82	14.64	17.08	19.52	21.96	24.39	26.83	29.27	31.71	34.15	36.59	39.00
83	14.82	17.28	19.75	22.22	24.69	27.16	29.63	32.10	34.57	37.04	39.51
84	14.99	17.49	19.99	22.49	24.99	27.49	29.99	32.49	34.99	37.48	39.98
85	15.17	17.70	20.23	22.76	25.29	27.82	30.34	32.87	35.40	37.93	40.46
86	15.35	17.91	20.47	23.03	25.58	28.14	30.70	33.26	35.82	38.38	40.94
87	15.53	18.12	20.71	23.29	25.88	28.47	31.06	33.65	36.24	38.82	41.41
88	15.71	18.33	20.94	23.56	26.18	28.80	31.42	34.03	36.65	39.27	41.89
89	15.89	18.53	21.18	23.83	26.48	29.13	31.77	34.42	37.07	39.72	42.3
90	16.06	18.74	21.42	24.10	26.77	29.45	32.13	34.81	37.48	40.16	42.8
91	16.24	18.95	21.66	24.37	27.07	29.78	32.49	35.19	37.90	40.61	43.3
92	16.42	19.16	21.90	24.63	27.37	30.11	32.84	35.58	38.32	41.05	43.7
93	16.60	19.37	22.13	24.90	27.67	30.43	33.20	35.97	38.73	41.50	44.2
94	16.78	19.58	22.37	25.17	27.96	30.76	33.56	36.35	39.15	41.95	44.7
95	16.96	19.78	22.61	25.44	28.26	31.09	33.91	36.74	39.57	42.39	45.2
96	17.14	19.99	22.85	25.70	28.56	31.42	34.27	37.13	39.98	42.84	45.7
97	17.31	20.20	23.09	25.97	28.86	31.74	34.63	37.51	40.40	43.29	46.1
98	17.49	20.41	23.32	26.24	29.15	32.07	34.99	37.90	40.82	43.73	46.6
99	17.67	20.62	23.56	26.51	29.45	32.40	35.34	38.29	41.23	44.18	47.1
100	17.85	20.82	23.80	26.77	29.75	32.72	35.70	38.67	41.65	44.62	47.6
101	18.03	21.03	24.04	27.04	30.05	33.05	36.06	39.06	42.07	45.07	48.0
102	18.21	21.24	24.28	27.31	30.34	33.38	36.41	39.45	42.48	45.52	48.5
103	18.39	21.45	24.51	27.58	30.64	33.71	36.77	39.84	42.90	45.96	49.0
104	18.56	21.66	24.75	27.85	30.94	34.03	37.13	40.22	43.32	46.41	49.5
105	18.74	21.87	24.99	28.11	31.24	34.36	37.48	40.61	43.73	46.86	49.9
106	18.92	22.07	25.23	28.38	31.53	34.69	37.84	41.00	44.15	47.30	50.4
107	19.10	22.28	25.47	28.65	31.83	35.02	38.20	41.38	44.57	47.75	50.9
108	19.28	22.49	25.70	28.92	32.13	35.34	38.56	41.77	44.98	48.19	51.4
109	19.46	22.70	25.94	29.18	32.43	35.67	38.91	42.16	45.40	48.64	51.8
110	19.63	22.91	26.18	29.45	32.72	36.00	39.27	42.54	45.81	49.09	52.3
111	19.81	23.12	26.42	29.72	33.02	36.32	39.63	42.93	46.23	49.53	52.8
112	19.99	23.32	26.66	29.99	33.32	36.65	39.98	43.32	46.65	49.98	53.3
113	20.17	23.53	26.89	30.26	33.62	36.98	40.34	43.70	47.06	50.43	53.7
114	20.35	23.74	27.13	30.52	33.91	37.31	40.70	44.09	47.48	50.87	54.2
115	20.53	23.95	27.37	30.79	34.21	37.63	41.05	44.48	47.90	51.32	54.7
116	20.71	24.16	27.61	31.06	34.51	37.96	41.41	44.86	48.31	51.76	55.2

CALIBRATED BY AN IBM 360 AND PROGRAMMED BY SAM RHOADS

Here's how to use this very convenient Cadence Chart. Let's say you're pedaling at 70 crank-revolutions per minute and your chain is on the small 14 T rear gear and the largest 54 T front gear. First, find your *Gear* from the Gear Chart on page 185, which will be 104.1. Then from the Cadence Chart, find 104 under the Gear Column (left) and, moving to the right under RPM of the crank arm of 70, you'll find you're moving at 21.66 miles per hour, which is a pretty good clip for anybody much over thirty. In the P-15's lowest gear combination of 34 T rear and 36 T front, we have a *Gear* of 28.6. From the Cadence Chart, at a *Gear* of 27 (we fudge a little) you will travel at 5.62 mph (which is not fast but better than walking up a steep hill).

An easy (but not quite as accurate) way to figure speed is to use the Speed Chart (Fig. 87). To find speed, first find your gear from the Gear chart on page 185 and, knowing your crank rpm, follow the gear line to its intersection with the crank rpm line. For example, you're in a 100 gear at 75 crank rpm. Reading to the right from 100 intersection with curve 75, and upward to the speed line, you will be doing almost 23 mph. This chart has limitations in crank rpm selections and jumps up in fairly large chunks, but it's handy to copy and take along on the road.

One more point. You can use a stopwatch fastened to your handlebars to keep tabs on crank rpms. But this means you have to take your eyes off the road momentarily to look at the stop watch, hardly a safe procedure. A better way is to use the small, light, shirt-pocket-size transistorized Mininome (see Fig. 77), which you can set at the crank rpm you wish to maintain. This unit has a clicking sound loud enough to hear over road traffic, and I find it an invaluable training aid in maintaining constant cadence or crank rpm.

THE MEANING OF CADENCE

First, let's establish what cadence means. Cadence is the pedaling or turning of the crank arm at more or less constant revolutions. It is important to understand this concept, because a regular cadence is necessary for smooth, long-distance cycling. You should try to pedal at the same rate of crank revolutions per minute all the time, varying your gear ratio to suit wind and road-grade conditions. For example, let's say you establish that a good cadence for you is between 60 and 75 turns of the crank per minute (for somebody with strong legs it may be 80 revolutions per minute and for a racing cyclist at high speed it may be 100 to 120, or more).

SPEED IN MILES PER HOUR

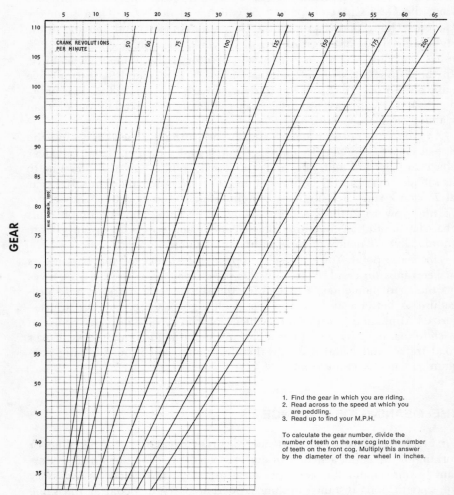

Fig. 87: Use this handy chart to figure how fast you go. From the Gear Table find your gear. Let's say your gear is 70, and you're pushing the crank around at 75 rpm. Following the line at 70 at left, move right till it intersects the 75 rpm line. Move up at this line to read 23 miles per hour at top. (*Chart courtesy of Mike Sackheim, Evanston, Illinois.*)

It's also a good idea to make up a Cadence Chart for your own particular combination of gears, so you always know how fast you are traveling at any crank rpm (see Table 14). This is one way to train yourself to work harder at pedaling, for better health. Also, since you can accurately predict how fast you can pedal (once you find your limitations), you can be quite accurate in estimating arrival times (however, consider hills).

TABLE 14 · **Sample Individualized Speed Chart ***

| | Number of Teeth In Rear Sprocket | | | | |
	14	17	22	28	34
Chainwheel T 54					
Gear (Inches Eq.)	104.1	85.8	66.3	52	42.9
MPH Speed	21.45	17.88	13.8	10.83	8.8
Chainwheel T 49					
Gear (Inches Eq.)	99.5	77.8	60.1	47.3	38.9
MPH Speed	19.35	16.8	12.5	9.8	8.0
Chainwheel T 36					
Gear (Inches Eq.)	69.4	57.1	44.2	34.7	28.6
MPH Speed	14.9	11.89	9.2	7.1	5.9

* Based on 72 rpm cadence. You'll probably be going a lot faster downhill, so you may want to gradually increase the cadence for fast runs downhill or before the wind. Or you can make up several charts, say one for a cadence of 72, one for 80, one for 85, etc., so you can pull out a 3 x 5 card for every road condition. And you may be pedaling a lot slower than 72 rpm up steep hills. Since the gear inches did not correspond exactly to the cadence chart, we made our own interpolations, which is why the speeds, or some of them, don't correspond exactly to speeds on the cadence chart.

7

CYCLE TOURING
AND CAMPING—
A FUN WAY
TO SEE THE WORLD

Sooner or later, if you have bought one of the better ten- or fifteen-speed derailleur bicycles described in Chapter 3, you'll want to do more than just pedal around the block. And you will never experience the real fun of cycling until you take weekend jaunts, or longer tours.

On an extended bicycle tour you almost have to be in intimate contact with nature and with the people you meet as you pedal by. On a bicycle, you are invigorated and alive, with the wind fresh in your face. Your heart, lungs, and circulatory system are at their peak . . . you just simply feel good to be alive. Contrast cycle touring with any other way—by car, bus, train, or plane. You're immobile, inhaling other people's stale cigarette smoke, sitting inside a metal and glass box, remote from the countryside, tired without knowing why . . . you'd be almost as well off viewing the country via a slide show or a movie travelogue. On a bike you can stop and admire a view, talk easily to local people, go up byways and pathways as your whim dictates, and yet have enough energy left over by evening for dining and dancing, or whatever.

I think this capsule description of a trip by bike I remember vividly, through Germany, Belgium, and that made-for-bicycle-touring country,

Holland, will illustrate the joys of cycle touring. I went to Cologne, Germany, in September, 1972 (after most of the tourists had left and the countryside was turning into autumn colors) to attend the International Bicycle Show. I brought my bicycle along so I could cycle later from Cologne to Amsterdam. After the show, I packed my panniers and put away my knit suit for a track suit more suitable for the chilly weather. I said goodbye to Cologne's ancient, magnificent cathedral and its modern city Centrum with miles of flower-laden pedestrian shopping malls, and cycled out of the city toward a country road that would take me to Euskirchen, about 50 miles away on the other side of a "Natur Park," with some small hills of about 500-feet elevation. Natur Parks are fine, deep, dark Valkyrian forests. Some of them are more scenic than hilly, and some are as hilly as scenic, with small mountains of about 1,500- to 2,000-feet elevation, a moderate hill climb. I remember the Natur Park between Nideggen and Gressenich, over the Hurten Wald. The *General-karte* map showed the twisting, snaky route with the words "Scenic View" in the legend, and it was all of that. Pine-fringed mountain tops parading in the distance, spectacular vistas of plunging valleys and mountain streams, and rural charm. One always begins a first trip through mountainous country with some misgiving, and it is a rewarding accomplishment to be able to climb mountains, or, as cyclists say, "storm" or "honk up" them. The secret to hill storming is seldom to look ahead or behind, but to keep your eyes glued to the few inches in front of your wheel, or glance to one side or the other, looking ahead only often enough to watch for turns in the road or an obstruction. If you look way up and see the 3,000 feet of mountain still looming before you, or behind to find you haven't really pedaled very far uphill, you can lose heart. I have made every hill so far except one short but steep monster, the 14 percent grade from Vermont's 100A up to Calvin Coolidge State Park, which rose 14 feet straight up for every 100 feet forward. Some AYH kids sweated past me on bikes, but I was not ashamed to get off and walk up that one.

Back to Germany: I noticed a lot of building walls pocked and chipped with the effluvia of various weaponry, and for the first time it came home to me that here, right here, in Nideggen and in Aachen and Heimbach, the wars had raged. It's hard for Americans to realize what it must have been like for parents with small children, with a war raging right up to their doorstep; the fear and insecurity and helplessness that prevailed when bombs dropped, shooting began, and great tanks rumbled past the front door. Somehow, as I cycled past these modest dwellings, the horror of war came home to me, who had spent World War II as a civilian in the U.S.A.

I cycled down the winding Moselle River Valley to the softly beautiful old Roman town of Trier, and across the Moselle back north again to Heimbach, on the Rhine. Here the Rhine was narrow and fast and deep, mysterious and black. My hotel was perched on the Rhine Valley just underneath an ancient and ruined castle, and dark woods filled the valley all around. I half expected a band of Nibelungen dwarfs to come storming out of the hills, and Siegfried and his warriors, dragging a slaughtered dragon, to meet and wage war with them.

In the small rural villages of Germany I had trouble paying for my noonday meal of wurst and beer, where, when curiosity overcame the natural reserve of the natives, they would crowd around my table to talk about me, my bike, my trip, and about America. More than once I staggered out of a noonday meal, replete with good food and much beer, an hour behind schedule but full of warmth and good cheer. How else can you get so close to these delightful folk; certainly not by driving through at 50 mph.

I did not look forward to unloading my panniers at border checkpoints, so it was with some dismay that I saw a long line of cars backed up at the Belgian border, just outside Aachen, Germany. But as I cycled past the string of cars up to the checkpoint, a Belgian customs official ran out into the road and waved me on, with a cheer I can only interpret as "Hooray, Eddy Merckx." Fortunately, I had stopped in a bike store that morning in Euskirchen, and bought a bicycle cap with Eddy Merckx's name on it. These are light, inexpensive cloth caps with a small visor, worn by racing cyclists. It just happened that Eddy Merckx is a national folk hero in Belgium, in Holland, and in Europe generally (professional racing cyclists can earn upward of $100,000 a year in Europe), who a few months earlier had for the fourth successive time won the grueling Tour de France, a several-thousand-mile bike race through the French Pyrenees, with climbs up 6,000-foot mountains a frequent occurrence. I was also cheered on past Customs into Holland, still wearing my Eddy Merckx cap, and wondering whether Customs thought I was Eddy's father, trainer, or perhaps a member of his team. Certainly my fifteen-speed, laden, chrome-gleaming touring bicycle could not be mistaken for a stripped racing machine, and the gray-haired rider would appear as anything but that.

Passing through small villages I was transported back to the Middle Ages, as I cycled down narrow cobblestone streets, past thatched roofed houses so old no one knew who built them, with farm animals sharing quarters with inhabitants, and definitely no fender clearance for Cadillacs.

Holland was a surprise. I had thought this tiny country to be jam packed, with little or no room for more housing. But Holland, as you enter it from the southeast corner, proved to be entirely rural, with gently rolling hills traversing forests and farm land. Most of the 12 million Hollanders seemed to be packed away in cities—in Rotterdam, The Hague, Amsterdam, Utrecht, and Eindhoven (home of Phillips Electronics). Beside every road, usually in a physically separated lane, there's a paved trail only for cyclists (Fig. 88). Even the main arteries, the four-lane separated superhighways, have bike trails that parallel them, but usually far enough away, and separated by a green barrier of trees and shrubs and lawn, for cars and trucks to be heard or seen only at rare intervals. Many of Holland's bike trails (marked on the map as are the roads) take you far from any roadway, through farmland, fields of tulips, avenues of tall waving corn, along canals (Fig. 89) laden with barges from which fly the day's wash for the family that lives on them. Cycle touring is, indeed, the best way to see a country, savoring the land and the people slowly and deeply, as you would a vintage wine. After a cycle tour, you'll find memories of the land and the people engraved in whatever portion of the mind pleasure resides.

Fig. 88: Typical lovely paved cycle trail in Holland. Numerous campgrounds are in this south section of the country.

Fig. 89: Author's loaded bike crossing a canal in Holland.

PLANNING YOUR BIKE TRIP

If you are thinking about taking a bicycle trip, and I urge you to do so, there are a few things you should know.

In the first place, your trip should be planned in meticulous detail with regard to route and equipment. If you plan to stop at motels, you can get by with a minimum of gear. But if you want to camp out, you will need a lightweight tent and sleeping bag, cooking gear, and other equipment that should be selected with careful attention to utility and portability.

Let's start with the trip itself. The American Youth Hostels regularly schedule bicycle trips of various distances and duration from most major cities. There are AYH chapters in most cities, which you may join even if you don't live in the particular city. Or you can be a member-at-large, and select the group you want to travel with. Don't let the word "youth" fool you. American Youth Hostels members are of all ages, although, naturally, the majority of cyclists are under thirty. The AYH maintain hostels all over the United States, and as a member, you will be entitled to a list of them. All you have to do to use the facilities is to bring either your own sheet (lightweight nylon is preferable) or a sleeping bag or both.

A big advantage of joining an AYH cycle-touring group is that you will be under the watchful eye of an experienced leader, who will make sure that the day's journey is within your physical capacity, and that you can handle the average speed of the group. Some AYH groups bring along a car-pulled "sag-wagon" for those whose ambitions are stronger than their legs. And there's usually someone in the group who is an expert in repairing broken chains, flat tires, busted spokes, and those problems which always seem to occur on long trips.

This reminds me to advise you strongly to overhaul your bike before you take off on a trip. (Review the chapter on maintenance in this book first.) Check brake blocks, all cables, tires, wheel alignment, and the condition of pedals and spokes. Your seat and handlebars should be properly adjusted for comfort and cycling efficiency.

About family touring: Many experienced European cyclists take small children on long trips in specially rigged child-carriers. But such families were raised on bicycles and carrying heavy burdens is second nature to them. I have children, and I have toured with children, but I would hesitate before taking a small child on a trip. On one trip our family took, my then-eleven-year-old youngster struggled manfully to stay with the group for a fifty-mile jaunt, strenuously resisting the ignominy of the sag-wagon. This was not one of my more successful trips. He was pretty tired and cranky for quite a while afterward. I don't think it is a good idea to take along youngsters under fifteen on a long trip; I prefer to keep the minimum age to around eighteen. There's a certain amount of individual responsibility and self-discipline involved in cycle touring that you cannot expect from youngsters.

I should also mention here that Asa Warren, Western Regional Director of the American Youth Hostels, has published a *North American Bicycle Atlas* which contains detailed routes and maps of bicycle tours throughout the United States and Canada. The tours are graded by length and difficulty. Easy trips are rated from eight to fifteen miles over fairly flat terrain, whereas rugged trips may contain hard mountain passes, unpaved roads, and go up to 100 miles a day. Mr. Warren's book is a handy and complete touring guide, and can be bought from your nearest AYH chapter.

The League of American Wheelmen is another old cycling club, whose members include some of America's most dedicated cyclists. The L.A.W. has chapters in most large and medium-sized American cities, and chapter members are usually quite willing to aid travelers and fellow L.A.W. members. The L.A.W. also has numerous tours prepared by local member groups. These are very well planned, with the routes worked out in painstaking detail by members who have local knowledge. You'll be with an older set than AYH and can be assured of enough bike enthusiasts on hand who can fix anything short of a busted frame. You should, in any case, support cycling by joining the L.A.W. *and* a local bicycle club (see list in Appendix). Local clubs are also a good way to participate in evening and week-end jaunts, and share cycling knowledge and experience. Many clubs have seminars on cycling safety and maintenance that can be of great help to you. As a League member you will receive the monthly L.A.W. *Bulletin,* which has dates and details on bicycle trips throughout the nation to keep you up to date on what's going on in local clubs. Of all the cycling publications, the L.A.W.'s is, to me, among the most valuable and it's free to members. You also receive a membership roster, which can be quite useful if you're stuck somewhere north of Boise, and need help.

Dr. Clifford Graves, a surgeon, President of the International Touring Society, and one of our most experienced cycle tourists, regularly heads up cycle tours in the United States and abroad. Many businessmen, housewives, and professional people join him on these tours, which are fairly deluxe trips, with most meals eaten in restaurants and with evening layovers in hotels.

Other cycle-touring groups that travel abroad are listed in the Appendix. The Cyclists' Touring Club of England, for example, conducts worldwide tours. I would urge you to join this club if you are interested in cycling in Europe. The club magazine *Cycle Touring* will come with your membership. Or I would recommend that you join a "Huff-'n-Puff" tour sponsored by the International Bicycle Touring Society.

The British publication *Cycling and Sporting Cyclist* is a biweekly magazine which contains many excellent articles on cycle touring in England, Wales, Scotland, Ireland, and the Continental countries. (Write to the publication at 161-166 Fleet Street, London, E.C.4, England 5011.) This publication caters to the racing cyclist as well as the tourist, which is about the only place I can think of that cycle racing and touring ever meet. Racing cyclists don't care for touring any more than a drag racer would care about auto touring. Racing is an arduous, highly competitive, complicated sport with a technique that has nothing in common with the leisurely pace and benign outlook of the average touring cyclist.

THE TOURING BICYCLE

As I mentioned at the beginning of this chapter, you will need a good bicycle if you want to take long trips. People do travel on three-speed English racers, but they pay a terrific penalty in the extra fifteen pounds or so of weight and the inefficient mechanism of these machines.

The ideal touring bicycle has downturned handlebars, a Reynolds tubular seamless butted steel frame throughout, high-quality fittings, and gears with ten- or fifteen-speed gear selections. Fifteen gears (using a triple chainwheel) are useful only if you plan to climb mountainous terrain. As I mention in the chapter on gears, any fifteen-speed gear selection is a compromise at best. For example, you won't be able to use the large chainwheel and the large rear gear. Which is to say that the only reason for fifteen gears is to let you use the small front chainwheel and the big rear gear together for steep grades. If you plan to climb the Rockies or do much touring around San Francisco, then a fifteen-speed combination is handy.

Elsewhere in this book I have reviewed wide-range gearing for touring bicycles (see page 179), and, again, I would recommend one of the new wide-range freewheel gear clusters, such as the Shimano, for the range of gears you need for all conditions of road grade, wind, and your physical state of being. These gear clusters have 14, 17, 22, 28, and 34 teeth. If you also have a Campagnolo triple chainwheel of 36, 49, and 54 teeth, you will have gears from a low of 28.6 to a high of 104.1. For an even wider range of gears, you can change to a T.A. triple chainwheel set with a low of 26 teeth, which, used with the 34-tooth rear gear, gives you a gear ratio of .764 to 1 (rear wheel turns .764 times to every turn of the front wheel) and a gear of 20.6, which will get you up anything but a brick wall.

Readers who are technically oriented might be interested in reading what Gene Portuesi says about fifteen-speed gears in his *Cyclo-Pedia* (see Appendix).

A fifteen-speed derailleur system utilizes a longer bottom bracket axle to accommodate the third chainwheel 3 mm. further to the right than on the normal ten-speed. Let us assume that the cycle has a triple chainwheel of 32 x 46 x 52 teeth or a similar combination, and the freewheel range is 13 to 30 teeth. When trying to run the chain from the 52-tooth front chainwheel to the 30-tooth rear cog, the angle of the chain is very acute. The tension is at a maximum, and so is friction. Chain also tends to hang on top of the 30-

tooth rear cog, and the front shifter cage has almost constant contact with the inside of the chain to keep it from coming off the outside chainwheel.

Conversely, when running on the 32-tooth inside chainwheel to the 13-tooth rear sprocket, the chain will have too much slack and might also rub on the inside of the 46-tooth chainwheel, or on the lower part of the front shifter cage.

HANDLEBARS

Although there are at least three distinct styles of handlebars (see pages 145–146), and the type you use should be that which gives you the most comfort over a long distance, you may want to consider one special type for touring. Most downturned handlebars are relatively flat on the top, so you have fewer places to hold onto. On a long trip, it helps if you can vary the position of your hands, because you space out the use of different muscles.

For women, in particular, Dr. Graves recommends a dropped handle-bar with a slight upswing, called a *randonneur*. A variation of this type of bar is sold by Cyclo-Pedia (see Appendix) for $8.50, complete with stem, levers, and rubber sleeves on the bars. The brake levers are positioned just under the top section of the bar, instead of on the foremost section, so that you can grasp the brake levers with the fingertips instead of having to lean forward.

Another good reason for using randonneur bars is that you have five or six places to rest your hands to relieve pressure on nerve endings in the base of the palms. Constant pressure at this point can eventually be painful. Next time you're out cycling, notice that you, as do we all, grip the bars so pressure is concentrated about where your "life line" starts, at the base of the palm. You brace yourself at that point against road shock as well. A clue on a long ride is to look at the palms of your hands. If you're having pain, chances are that area will be reddish. Shift hands around a lot, frequently, as you cycle; don't hold the same position on the bars for more than ten minutes or so. An important exception is when you're going full speed downhill, when hands should grip the curved part of the bars just under brake levers, with inside of wrists locked against side of bars at about the location of the brake levers, or just above them, so you keep a firm grip to prevent dangerous front-wheel "shimmy."

THE SADDLE

Your bicycle saddle, for a long trip, should be made of leather and be well broken-in to your particular contour. This means that the saddle should have been ridden for at least 500 miles for the required shaping and resilience. A hard new leather saddle is as unaccommodating as a new pair of leather shoes. One way to break in a saddle is to soak it overnight, or for a couple of days, in Lexoil or neat's-foot oil, then beat it with a baseball bat until the leather fibers have become more resilient. This of course applies only to leather saddles.

TIRES—TUBULARS OR CLINCHERS?

There are skilled cyclists who wouldn't think of touring on anything but tubular tires. (You might want to peruse the chapter on tires at this point.) There is no question that tubulars are more resilient and offer a livelier, more enjoyable ride and easier pedaling. But tubulars are more prone to puncture than the heavier-built clincher tires. Tubulars are also a good deal more difficult to repair because they are sewn up all the way around, inside, and a leak is sometimes difficult to find.

Therefore, if you are not a skilled cyclist or are not willing to spend extra time fixing flats, you should use clincher tires. I would especially recommend them if you intend to travel off the beaten path, on gravel roads, or other rough surfaces.

If you insist on using tubulars, be sure to ease your weight forward and rise up off the saddle as you pass over rough spots, to equalize the weight over both wheels. This is particularly important if you're carrying well-filled rear panniers, and is good advice even with clinchers.

Another advantage of clinchers is that replacement tires are more readily available; for example, you can buy them in most Sears Roebuck stores, whereas only special cycle shops carry tubulars.

FENDING OFF RAIN

You never know when you will be caught in a rain shower on a tour, so I recommend using lightweight plastic fenders. These are easy to attach and remove, and they will keep mud and water from splashing onto the brakes, panniers, and your legs. Some tourists carry clip-on spring-held "spats" which shield both sides of both wheels and keep water from splashing off the inside of the fenders onto the rider. You can't buy these in this country, to my knowledge, but you could make your own.

OTHER ACCOUTREMENTS

You'll get thirsty from time to time during the day, so I recommend that you carry at least one, preferably two, plastic bottles in carriers. Carriers can be mounted on the handlebars so that you can reach for a swig from the saddle. Or a single bottle can be affixed to the seat tube, which will not interfere with leg or thigh muscles, or the heel of your shoe as you reach the top of the pedal stroke.

Rattrap pedals and cleat-equipped shoes (see pages 156–157) are a "must" for cycle touring, in my opinion. If you learn to ankle properly (pages 167–168), you will find that on hills particularly, without shoe cleats your feet will slip off even rattrap pedals as you apply pressure, especially in the four- and seven-o'clock positions. Pedal straps should be tight enough to keep the shoe cleats in position. If you pedal in city traffic, or as you approach a reststop, you can bend over from the saddle and loosen the straps slightly so that you can lift your heel up and pull your feet out of the pedals quickly. Cycling shoes, built with steel shanks and shaped for this special use, are ideal for touring. You can carry a pair of slip-ons for off-bicycle use; cleat shoes aren't practical for walking about. I especially want to warn you against cycling with sneakers—they don't offer much protection against the surface of rattrap pedals. If you don't use cycling shoes, at least use flexible leather loafers. But cleats are preferable because they will keep your feet from sliding off the pedals.

Finally, if you want to get yourself in the picture, carry a miniature 35-millimeter camera with a time-delay shutter or attachment. You can also use a small "C" clamp to tie the camera down to a fence, sign, or tree limb.

WHERE TO TOUR

Whether East, West, North, or South, the United States offers much in the way of enjoyable scenery and terrain. For the most part, however, the Middle West is rather monotonous. Though parts of Wisconsin, Michigan, Indiana, and even Illinois are of interest to the cycle tourist, New England, the West Coast, and the South offer a good deal more variety. The Plains states, according to Dr. Graves, are best traversed by commercial carrier.

I won't go into a great deal of detail about specific tours, because Asa Warren's guide gives so much, but I will quote Dr. Graves with some general guidelines:

> If you want to tour in the East, you can choose almost any point along the Appalachians, between the Canadian border and northern Georgia. In the West, there is territory comparable to this along the coastal range as far south as Santa Barbara. Southern California is so overrun with freeways now that you have to pick and choose your areas there.
>
> In the vast region between the Great Plains and the Pacific coastal range there are magnificent mountains and canyons and beautiful valleys, but all are on a grand scale—not on the small scale a cyclist needs. Because he travels slowly, a cyclist has to have his scenery in a highly concentrated form. In the Great Plains area, most of the roads are high, wide and handsome instead of modest, gentle and intimate.

If you prefer to plan your own trip, or if you want to go no farther than a Sunday afternoon ride will take you, follow these tips: Use a local area map, preferably a county map. The Department of Interior publishes county maps at a scale of a quarter-inch to the mile. The United States Coast and Geodetic Survey publishes topographic maps that will give you an idea of how hilly a route is. For a specific route, select secondary paved roads that bisect as few main arteries as possible. Stick to county roads, if possible. Avoid state and federal highways at all costs. The back county roads generally go over more scenic, winding routes, while state and federal roads are designed for high-speed, straight-line travel. And, of course, superhighways and toll roads are not only dangerous but illegal for cycling use.

As for time of year, I recommend the spring and autumn. Try to avoid the hot season.

A WORD ABOUT TANDEMS

The ultimate in togetherness is a tandem. On a cycle tour, a husband-and-wife team can travel at a pace suitable to both, and chat about the scenery as they pedal. Many cycle tourists, including Dr. Graves, have found that tandems are easier to pedal because they are mechanically more efficient (provided the rear rider is not just a passenger).

Some people love to tour on tandem; other couples have tried them and prefer two separate bicycles. I can make no hard-and-fast rules except to suggest that if you and your partner have equable dispositions and matching physical endurance, perhaps a tandem is for you. But if you are considerably stronger than your mate, and tend to be a bit impatient, you might prefer to ride singly. If you can borrow a tandem for a short trip to try it out, by all means do so. Tandems are expensive; at least the good ones are. I recommend you review the sections on tandems. (I would also recommend the Jack Taylor tandem, mentioned in an earlier chapter, for touring. This is a first-class, high-quality machine).

CAMPING VERSUS TOURING

As I said earlier, cycle touring usually means a deluxe trip which involves restaurant meals and hotel accommodations. Personally, I prefer cycle camping, which permits you to stop where and when you want. A small folding rod and reel enables you to catch your own dinner, and with a bicycle, you can be more selective in the choice of campsite than if you are traveling by car.

WHERE TO PITCH CAMP

Try to plan your stops at public campsites. You will feel much happier camping with people around you and with the protection of a state or federal ranger than you will off alone in the woods or in a roadside park.

One young woman cyclist I heard about had a novel approach to camping. She had no trouble traveling alone coast to coast, although she made absolutely no plans for her nightly camp stops. She was a very personable young woman, yet no one ever bothered her. It seems she camped every night in the local graveyard, pitching her tent behind the largest mausoleum she could find, on the side away from the road!

If you carry your own foodstuffs, select a campsite about twenty-five miles away from the nearest small town or source of food and load up with what you will need for the next two or three meals at about 4:00 P.M.

EMERGENCY QUARTERS

If you can't find a youth hostel, camp ground, or motel for the evening, and it's getting dark, perhaps even raining, the flexibility of cycle camping and touring really comes to your aid. Cycle campers have found emergency quarters in jails (from kindly police), caves, under a Sherman tank in a small town park, barns (ask the farmer first and offer him your matches), and even under haystacks.

If it's raining, avoid the temptation to pitch a tent under a tree; you are more vulnerable to lightning under one than you would be out in the open.

RIDING A LOADED BICYCLE

If you've never ridden a bicycle loaded with camping gear (Fig. 90), take it easy the first day out until you get the feel of things. You'll find you can't bank steeply around sharp corners at high speed without risking a spill. Also, you must shift down sooner going uphill, and you must use brakes sooner to avoid speed build-up, unless the downgrade is straight, smooth, and relatively free of traffic.

A word of advice about downhill rides. We've talked about wheel

Fig. 90: The correct way to distribute load when cycle touring or camping. Note that bags are securely fastened, with carriers permanently fastened to frame.

(Dr. Clifford Graves)

shimmy, brake fade, tire roll-off, and other hazards of high-speed down-hill rides elsewhere in this book (page 57). There is one more point having to do with your comfort. On some very long hills, which can be five or ten miles or so of steady uphill pedaling, and another five or ten miles down the other side (if you're lucky), you will arrive at the crest of the hill in a sweat, with perspiration streaming from your brow, even though at the top of the hill the air temperature is only 50 or 60 degrees. Even if it's 70 or 80 degrees, remember that your body is bathed in sweat and your shirt may be wringing wet. If you go right on over the hill and start down, with a sigh of relief that you're about to cool off, you'll find you can cool off much too fast and arrive at the bottom quite chilled, so much so that you will be lacking the energy you may need to attack the next climb. On a fast run downhill, your body will lose heat very rapidly in two ways. First, the latent heat of evaporation as moisture dries will rob your body of heat. Second, heat will be lost by convection to the 40-mph rush of air passing over your body. That's why you'll see in races over mountain country, as in the Tour de France, spectators passing newspaper, magazines, anything the cyclist can stuff in his shirt front as he's about to go downhill to avoid debilitating excessive body heat loss.

I know it's tempting to go right down that hill, but I can assure you, one freezing, miserable ride following a sweat-filled mountain "storming" will see you stopping and spending the forty seconds it takes at the top of the next hill to pull out a light nylon windbreaker from your front bag to keep warm, and removing it when you start the next climb. Or you can simply wrap the windbreaker around your middle if you're facing a re-peated series of hills. You'll find, too, that cycling in hill country is mostly uphill; it may take an hour to climb a long, gradual incline to the top, and fifteen minutes to get down the other side; never long enough to rest up for the next climb, but long enough so you can make it, and make it, and make it, once you're in condition.

CYCLE TOURING GEAR

Cycle touring, as opposed to cycle camping, is by my definition a deluxe way to travel, and preferred by many people, especially those over thirty. (I like both, depending on the weather. Camping's great in summer, but warm motel beds and good restaurant meals are nice in cold weather.) Touring on a bicycle means, then, stopping at night in a good motel and eating all meals in a restaurant.

Touring with a large group, twenty or more, as with an International Bicycle Touring Society tour (page 200), permits all luggage to be carried in a "sag-wagon" so you need only carry the bare minimum of gear with you on your bicycle. You will want to carry along a set of rain clothes, tools, spare parts, and possibly a camera and mini-binocs, etc. The list of touring equipment below, less optional items, totals only 10.1 pounds, and with the optional items only 14.16 pounds. The bike lock in the list is flimsy but light, and will delay a theft (if you're where you can watch your bike from a restaurant) barely long enough for you to reach the front door and start yelling. Always take your bike up to your motel room at night; never leave it outside.

Reviewing some of the items in the list, you can add about one pound when you fill your water bottle. The can of "Halt" is for dogs, and the clip fits best on the top of the right fork blade (or left one if you're left-handed). You can reach it easily. The Schwinn rain suit isn't expensive, is totally waterproof, will keep you dry even in a downpour (total weight 1.625 pounds), and can be carried in the sag-wagon when you know it can't rain. The jacket part has a hood, and at night this jacket is particularly useful because it has reflectorized safety stripes, as do the pants. Of the choice of colors, I prefer the orange for visible safety. The jacket has a zipper plus a snap closing, and the pants roll up and snap into the hem of the jacket for a compact unit (see Fig. 6, page 91.)

The Cannondale front and rear bags (Fig. 91) are terrific! Best I've seen so far. The front bag straps into downturned handlebars, dispenses with cumbersome, heavy metal carrier other bar bags need, and can be fastened or removed in seconds. So when you go into a restaurant, it's easy to unsnap the front bag containing wallet, camera, and other valuables

Fig. 91: These Cannondale rear panniers are about the lightest on the market, but have only one large pocket each. Front and rear bags are the best I've seen, need no special supports.

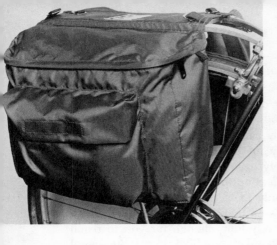

Fig. 92: Bellweather mini-pannier for short day trips or cycle touring when major luggage is carried on sag wagon. Plenty of heel clearance. Weighs only 16 ounces.

and take it with you. Front bag is 10.5 in. x 5.5 in. x 7 in., or 404 cu. in. Rear bag, snapped on rear of saddle and equally quick to remove or fasten, is 8.5 in. x 5 in. x 6.5 in. or 276.44 cu. in., plenty big enough to carry the tools, etc. If you want to carry more stuff (for souvenir shopping, for instance), I'd suggest the elegant little Bellweather panniers (saddlebags) (Fig. 92), instead of the Cannondale bags. You will, however, need a metal carrier (Fig. 93) over rear wheels. The Bellweather bags plus the carrier total three pounds, versus only three-quarters of a pound for both Cannondale bags. The Bellweather panniers will double the carrying capacity of the two smaller Cannondale bags, though.

In case it rains, save the plastic bags your shirts come back in from the laundry, and wrap wallet, camera, film, etc., in them. This also keeps these articles free of road dust. The map measure is a handy way to trace mileage for the day, and the compass is invaluable, if for no other reason than to reassure yourself that you are headed the right way (or that your fearless tour leader is).

If you're touring alone, or with a group too small to afford the luxury

Fig. 93: This steel carrier fastens to rear brake bridge with brake bolt, so it can't slide down to block brakes or mar seat stay finish. Loops on legs make it easy to tie down panniers. From your bike shop or Touring Cyclist Shop.

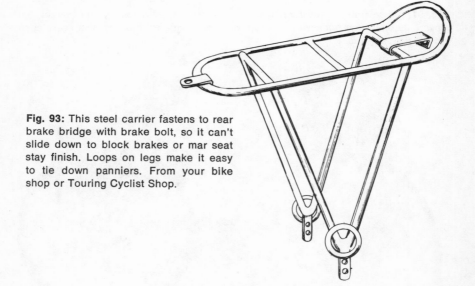

of a sag-wagon, you will either have to carry all your gear with you, or do as we did on one I.B.T.S. trip through the Lincoln country of Illinois and Indiana, and "stage"-advance all cars, or one car. Every morning we'd pack luggage, suitcases, etc., into one car. One of the trip members would then drive to the next motel stop, leaving late enough and driving slowly enough to be able to pick up any stragglers or riders with mechanical or physical trouble. (The latter can happen; one member of our tour began to have appendicitis pains on his bicycle, and wound up having an appendectomy in a local hospital.) An alternate approach was also used, in which the sag-wagon driver on this trip drove early and fast to the next stop, carrying his own bike, and spent the rest of the day cycling around the area, and phoning in to the motel from time to time during the day to check as to whether any of the group needed to be picked up. A third approach was also used. Since most of us drove to the starting point and did not want to cycle back the 350 miles or so to pick up our cars, and

TABLE 15 · **Touring Equipment** *

ITEM	MANUFACTURER	MODEL	WEIGHT (oz.)
WATER BOTTLE	T.A.	20	2.25
BOTTLE CAGE	T.A.		3.5
"HALT" WITH CLIP	Animal Repellents	3.5-oz. size	4
RAIN JACKET	Schwinn	Tuff-N-Dry	10
RAIN PANTS	Schwinn	Slac Jac	16
LOAFER SHOES			18
LEG LIGHT (WITH BATTERIES)	Schwinn		8
MAP MEASURE AND COMPASS	Cyclo-Pedia		1.5
FIRST AID KIT			12
COMBINATION LOCK AND CABLE	Schwinn		9
PUMP			5.5
TOOLS (SEE SEPARATE LIST)			48
HANDLEBAR BAG	Cannondale		7
SADDLE BAG	Cannondale		5
MISCELLANEOUS			12

Total weight; pounds: 10.1

With optional items (see Table 16): 14.16

* When you stop at motels and eat at restaurants.

there was no convenient public transport back to the start, we would have the day's sag-wagon driver drive us back the 50 to 90 miles to the day's starting point and we would drive our cars back to the evening's stop. I don't recommend this latter technique except in an emergency; after a day in the saddle, a 150-mile-plus round-trip car ride isn't the easiest way to spend an evening, or the most enjoyable. It's moot as to which is easier, though, and it seems strange that the prospect of a 350-mile seven-day bike ride is more enjoyable than a four- or five-hour car ride would be to go back to pick up your car; but that's cycle touring for you. Fun!

BICYCLE CAMPING EQUIPMENT

The equipment lists (see Tables 16 and 17, pages 213–216) have been very carefully selected to make you totally self-sufficient while bicycle camping. When you go on a camping trip on your bicycle, you will (or should) shun big cities, and so will need to be fairly well-equipped with tools and spare parts, and carry all cooking gear, stove, clothing, etc., on your bicycle.

The lists below are based on a bicycle camping trip by one person, alone, with no other cyclists. If you go with another person (I recommend you do) you can cut down the weight drastically. On a trip alone, the list totals 34½ pounds, and this assumes you will wash out clothing every other night, because there's only one change beyond what you start out wearing. You can cut off a few pounds by not taking *any* spare clothing except what you wear, and washing out every night. This isn't such a hardship because washing takes only a few minutes, and if clothes aren't dry you can wear them wet and count on them cooling you off as you travel. Or if the second set isn't dry, hang them flapping from panniers under shock cords (so they don't catch in spokes!) where they'll dry and also alert motorists. The above applies to summer trips, of course.

If two are cycle camping, you can cut the total load for each down to only 16¾ pounds and dispense with the Bellweather back pack used for food shopping. With two, you need only one tent, one set of basic tools (excluding parts), one set of cooking gear (except fork, knife and spoon set, and mug). Otherwise you need the Bellweather back pack because your panniers and bags will be full and you'll find no room to carry the

TABLE 16 · **Bicycle Camping Equipment**

	MANUFACTURER	MODEL	WEIGHT (oz.)
FASTENED TO THE BICYCLE			
WATER BOTTLE	T.A.	200	2.25
BOTTLE CAGE	T.A.		3.5
"HALT" WITH CLIP	Animal Repellents, Inc.	3.5 oz. size	4
PUMP			5.5
PANNIER BAGS	Touring Cyclist Shop	1721 cu. in.	35
METAL PANNIER CARRIER	Touring Cyclist Shop	Holdsworth	28
FRONT HANDLEBAR BAG	Cannondale		7
SADDLE BAG	Cannondale		5
		Subtotal, pounds:	5.64
SLEEPING GEAR			
DOWN-FILLED SLEEPING BAG	Comfy Div. Olin Mfg.	Mt. Vista (25°F)	40
HALF-LENGTH FOAM PAD	Gerry	Shortie	14
TENT	Gerry	Pioneer	27
		Subtotal, pounds:	5.06
COOKING GEAR			
BACK PACK (FOR SHOPPING)	Bellweather	Back Pack 400 BP	9
BRILLO PADS			2
PAPER TOWELS			4
BOWIE KNIFE			4
PLASTIC WATER BOTTLE, 2 GAL.	Gerry or L. L. Bean		1.5
LIQUID SOAP			6
COOK STOVE	Gerry or L. L. Bean	SVEA	9
FUEL BOTTLE, ALUM.	" "		4
NESTING POTS & PANS, ALUM.	" "		26
FORK, KNIFE, SPOON SET	" "		1.5
FOUR 6 x 12-IN. POLY BAGS	" "		8 (all)
TWO 9 x 18-IN. POLY BAGS	" "		4 (all)
ONE 18 x 30-IN. POLY BAG	" "		2
POT LIFTER	" "		3
PLASTIC MUG	" "		1.4
FOUR PLASTIC SQUEEZE BOTTLES	Gerry		8 (all)
		Subtotal, pounds:	5.83

TABLE 16 · **Bicycle Camping Equipment** (continued)

STAPLES	WEIGHT (oz.)	STAPLES	WEIGHT (oz.)
MATCHES	2	MUSTARD	3
SALT (SMALL CONTAINERS)	2	COFFEE	4
SUGAR (SMALL CONTAINERS)	3	MARGARINE	6
PEPPER (SMALL CONTAINERS)	1		
		Subtotal, pounds:	1.62

CLOTHING	MANUFACTURER	MODEL	WEIGHT (oz.)
(besides what you wear)			
KNIT JEANS			17
SHOES, LOAFERS (OR SNEAKERS)			20
SOCKS, ONE PAIR			1.6
UNDERWEAR, ONE PAIR (TOP & BOTTOM)			6
SHIRT, POLYESTER & COTTON, ONE			4
SHORTS, CYCLING, ONE PAIR			5
LIGHT SWEATER OR SWEATSHIRT			5
RAIN JACKET	Schwinn	Tuff-N-Dry	10
		Subtotal, pounds:	4.29

PERSONAL ARTICLES	WEIGHT (oz.)	PERSONAL ARTICLES	WEIGHT (oz.)
TOOTHPASTE	4	RAZOR	2
TOOTHBRUSH	1	COMB	½
SOAP AND SOAP BOX	3		
		Subtotal, pounds:	.656

MISCELLANEOUS	WEIGHT (oz.)	MISCELLANEOUS	WEIGHT (oz.)
FLASHLIGHT (GERRY A900)	19	WALLET, WATCH, ETC.	12
BATTERIES FOR ABOVE	2	FIRST AID KIT	14
BUG SPRAY	4	COMBINATION LOCK & CABLE	9
CARBIDE LAMP, JUSTRITE 4-IN. ROUND	12	SHOCK CORDS (FOUR)	10
CARBIDE	32	25-FT. NYLON CORD	5
		TOOLS	48
		Subtotal, pounds:	10.44

TABLE 16 · **Bicycle Camping Equipment** (continued)

OPTIONAL ITEMS	WEIGHT (oz.)	OPTIONAL ITEMS	WEIGHT (oz.)
SMALL AM-FM RADIO	12	PLAYING CARDS	5
35-MM CAMERA		POCKETBOOK	5
(OLYMPUS ECR)	12	FLY-FISHING OUTFIT	
FILM, 35 MM, FOUR ROLLS	4	(L. L. BEAN)	16
MINI-BINOCULARS		EXTRA EYEGLASSES	2
(KERN ALPICA)	9		
		Subtotal, pounds:	4.06

COLD WEATHER CLOTHING	MANUFACTURER	MODEL	WEIGHT (oz.)
DOWN COAT, WITH OUTER DETACHABLE SHELL	"Comfy" Div. Olin	Game Coat	44
KNIT WARM-UP SUIT	L. L. Bean	K & K	32
THERMAL SOCKS, TWO PAIR			14 (all)
EAR FLAPS			1.5
CYCLING BOOTEES, FLEECE-LINED	Detto Pietro	Ankle	30
DOWN SLEEPING BAG, 15° TO 25°	Gerry	Olympic	56
		Subtotal, pounds:	11.09
		less Mt. Vista bag	− 2.50
			8.59

TOTALS	POUNDS
BASIC EQUIPMENT FOR CAMPING	33.5
BASIC WITH OPTIONAL ITEMS	37.6
BASIC WITH COLD-WEATHER ITEMS	46

TABLE 17 · **Recommended Tools and Spare Parts for Touring and Camping**

DESCRIPTION	QUANTITY	WEIGHT (oz.)
DUMBELL WRENCH	1	4
SPOKE WRENCH	1	½
SPOKES	4	½
CHAIN RIVET REMOVER	1	6
CHAIN LINKS	4	½
4-IN. ADJUSTABLE WRENCH	1	4
3-IN. SCREWDRIVER	1	3
BRAKE BLOCKS	2	1½
BRAKE CABLE (REAR)	1	½
DERAILLEUR CABLE (REAR)	1	½
CHAINLUBE, CAN	1	4
GREASE, LUBRIPLATE	4 oz.	3
FREEWHEEL REMOVER	1	3
INNER TUBE (CLINCHER) *	1	4
TIRE IRONS *	2	1
TUBULAR TIRES (NEW) **	2	22 (pair)
RIM TAPE **		2
PATCH KIT, TUBULAR OR CLINCHER	1	2.5

* Total weight with clincher items: 2.4 lbs.
** Total weight with tubular items: 3.6 lbs.

groceries you'll want to buy at the first town before your camp site for dinner and breakfast. This pack (Fig. 94) is light and folds into a small ball.

Alternates to List

If you want a bit larger, roomier tent, use the Gerry Lodgepole (Fig. 95), which has a double roof to prevent moisture condensation inside the tent, a floor, sleeps two comfortably, and weighs 4 pounds. Another excellent tent for two is Winchester's Trailblazer at 2 pounds, or their Back Packer at 3.75 pounds. The Camel twosome tent is also good, and weighs about 4 pounds. All the tents are waterproof nylon. But if you zip them up tight, except for the Gerry Lodgepole, you'll find body moisture condensing on inside surfaces during the night. If you fold the tent up without drying it out, this condensed moisture develops a pretty hor-

Fig. 94: This Bellweather backpack is very handy for grocery shopping on a camping trip, when your panniers are loaded with other gear. It weighs only ounces, holds dinner and breakfast for two or even four, and folds up to practically nothing.

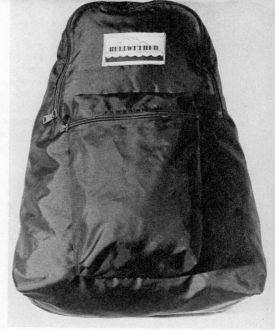

Fig. 95: Gerry Lodgepole tent sleeps two with plenty of room. It uses the "Rainvent" concept with a double roof to reduce condensation when it rains. If you've ever slept in a condensation-filled nylon tent, you'll appreciate this one. Weighs four pounds, is 4' x 7' x 3' high, with zippered waterproof window and door with nylon mosquito netting, and sewn-in waterproof floor.

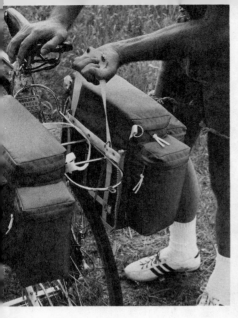

Fig. 96: The Touring Cyclist Shop (see Appendix) pannier is the best one checked. It's expensive, but well worth the money. It has 1,720 cu. in. of space in six compartments, but, best of all, it is water-proof and can be instantly attached or removed from bicycle. Zipped together, it has a handle and shoulder strap. Removed, it can also be fastened to back-pack frame.

Fig. 97: This is the Touring Cyclist Shop pannier as it appears loaded on the bicycle. Notice ample heel clearance.

rendous odor by the next night. So first thing on awakening, turn the tent inside out, shake off moisture, hang it to dry. Or rinse in clear water and allow to dry, or dry during the evening while you're cooking and eating.

I like the Touring Cyclist Shop's rear pannier set because it has six pockets, making it easier to find stuff; it can be clipped on to or removed from carrier in ten seconds or less; and, once removed and zipped to-gether, has a carrying handle and shoulder strap (Figs. 96 and 97). So if you tour without a sag-wagon, it's very convenient to be able to remove the TCS bag quickly at night. Ditto for carrying bike on plane, train, bus, or car. The TCS bag costs a bit more than the Gerry bag (Fig. 98). The TCS bag totals 1,720 cu. in. and is of waterproof eight-ounce nylon, very sturdily made. My TCS panniers have been through two trips to Europe on extensive tours there as well as in the U.S.A., and so far have held up well.

An inexpensive alternate to the TCS panniers which also have quick remove and attach capability are Cannondale panniers (see Fig. 91), with one pocket per side but extremely light. They weigh 1.63 pounds a pair, total 1,782 cu. in. You can use small plastic bags (such as shirt bags) to obtain waterproofness and compartmentalization. And they cost less than half the TCS or Gerry bags. The Gerry bags have five pockets, weigh 1.9 pounds, and hold the most of all the bags used, 3,100 cu. in., which per-

Fig. 98: Gerry (Colorado Outdoor Sports) bicycle pannier on rear of bike. With 3,100 cu. in. capacity in five pockets, it's the roomiest of all panniers, with room even to take a sleeping bag and tent, and keep them dry when it's wet outside.

mits you to put your sleeping bag in one of the pockets (there's *nothing* soggier or harder to dry out than a wet, down-filled sleeping bag). The Gerry pannier is not quick to remove, and needs to be held back with shock cords for heel clearance, though it is waterproof, or at least highly water resistant, and is well made, as are all Gerry products. The larger Bellweather set of rear panniers is intermediate in price to the Gerry and TCS panniers, has four pockets, weighs 2½ pounds and has about 2,200 cu. in. of space. A new carrier offers light weight plus scratch resistance and stays firmly in place (Fig. 99).

Fig. 99: The "Whirling Dervish" carrier, made of aluminum alloy, is heavily coated with vinyl. It has a ball-carrying ring, in case you want to carry a basket or beach ball. Designed to use elastic hold-down (Sandow) straps, it weighs about the same as a Pletcher (Swiss) alloy carrier. It has "anti-torque" mounting hardware with slip prevention. From California Leisure Industries, Inc., 2201 Filbert Street, San Francisco, California 94123 or your bike shop.

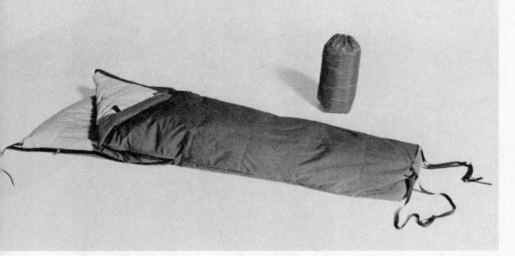

Fig. 100: Mt. Vista mummy bag by "Comfy" Seattle Quilt Division of Olin Manufacturing Company is, at 2½ pounds total weight, the lightest your author has used. It's goose-down insulated, good to 25°F, with water-repellent cotton-polyester outer shell, nylon quilting, tapered shape with box boot, and Delrin half zipper with insulated weatherstrip and stuff sack.

Product Review

Going over the list of items to take on a camping trip, besides those we have already mentioned, the poly bags are especially useful for storing coffee, breakfast cereal, flour, etc., so you can dispense with the heavy, bulky cans and boxes they come in, and for protecting camera, film, clothing and sleeping bag from dirt, dust, and heavy downpours of rain.

The knit cap is useful for keeping warm on cold nights. You will find that without head protection, even a good sleeping bag (Fig. 100) won't keep you warm enough. Save more weight by eliminating heavy canned items such as shaving soap (use wash soap for shaving, you'll get used to it). Avoid loose razor blades, use a razor that takes a "ribbon" blade good for thirty to forty shaves.

The carbide lamp (Fig. 101) with four-inch reflector throws a bright

Fig. 101: The Justrite carbide lamp can be fastened to front axle under quick-release skewer or axle nut, and quickly removed for general camp lighting. It throws a wide beam, and uses no batteries, only carbide and water. A two-pound can of carbide should last for two or three weeks of cycling.

beam and can be fastened to front wheel axle with quick-release skewer with a simple "L" clamp you can make. It can be removed at camp site for general lighting. The optional FM-AM radio should be a Sony, which is not cheap but the best I have used; it's useful to obtain needed advance weather information. If a real blast of a downpour is imminent, you may want to stay put in your camp site till the storm has passed, especially if you're in a wooden lean-to such as those in Vermont State Parks.

The Olympus ECR is a full-frame 35-mm camera with automatic exposure. All you do is focus and shoot; I've taken some fine shots on the run from the saddle. The camera can fit in a breast pocket (but have a strap around your neck, too). The mini-binoculars are very compact; the Alpica model is 8 x 18 power, remarkable for such a small pair. Bean's fly-fishing outfit is a Fenwick Spin-Fly kit with a four-piece fiberglas rod, fly and spinning reels, and floating and spinning lines. Be sure you have the correct state fishing license.

I like the "Comfy" down-filled coat, which can be used alone or with the canvas coat into which the inner coat snaps and which acts as a windbreaker. Another fine coat is L. L. Bean's Down-Jac shirt, which costs less than the Comfy Game Coat, is lighter, and can double as a pillow (as can the Game Coat's inner jacket).

The twenty-five feet of thin nylon line will be invaluable in pitching tent, tying down loose stuff, hanging out laundry, and mailing stuff home you shouldn't have taken and which weighs you down.

If you're a fishing enthusiast as well as a bicycle camper, you can get out on the lake where the big ones are with a compact, light, folding rubber two-man boat that, with aluminum oars and volume pump, weighs only 6.8 pounds (Fig. 102). I have used this little gem, and it's always fun to watch the faces of my fellow cyclists as a 72 x 43-inch boat unfolds from a small 8 x 20-inch tube. The boat has oarlocks, two inflatable seats, and a flared bow for dry rowing over rough water. Actually, the Pack-Raft weighs little more than a good full-size air mattress, for which it can double at night. And the inflatable seats make dandy pillows (they're removable). The Pack-Raft also holds water *inside* so you can use it as a bathtub. If two are traveling, you can eliminate two air mattresses because the Pack-Raft is big enough for two to sleep on . . . and cut the weight by your partner carrying the pump, patch kit, oars, and inflatable seats. Leaned against a tree, it offers emergency shelter. From sporting goods stores, or write to American Safety Recreation Products Group, 16055 Ventura Blvd., Encino, California 91316.

Fig. 102: Lightweight (6.8 pounds complete) rubber inflatable raft can get you out where the big ones are. Doubles as sleeping air mattress or emergency shelter.

Cooking Gear

The ardent cycle camper will pitch in for the evening not too far from a source of provisions and will take care to stock up at that time with the food items he will consume for dinner and the following day's breakfast and possibly lunch. To cook provisions (a hot meal is always desirable), I recommend the Hiker camp stove made in Sweden, the SVEA No. 123 (Fig. 103) which burns for forty-five minutes on one fueling of a third of a pint of white or leaded gasoline, boils one and a half pints of water in five to six minutes. Size: 5 in. high x 3¾ in. From L. L. Bean (see Appendix).

Fig. 103: By stacking, you can even cook a three-course meal with this compact, gasoline-burning Swedish stove. Your author has cooked hundreds of meals with his stove and it's still going strong. Be sure to buy the fitted nesting pots and pans and fuel bottle to go with the stove.

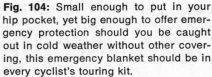

Fig. 104: Small enough to put in your hip pocket, yet big enough to offer emergency protection should you be caught out in cold weather without other covering, this emergency blanket should be in every cyclist's touring kit.

Rescue Blanket

An emergency blanket (Fig. 104) that comes in a plastic container small enough to fit in your shirt pocket, yet unfolds to 56 in. x 84 in. and reflects more than 90 percent of your body heat—if you might be stranded by cold weather on tour, and you are not equipped for camping-out, carry this blanket. Orange on one side for high visibility, silver on the inside for maximum reflectivity. Weight: 2 oz. Cost: $3.00. From L. L. Bean (see Appendix).

Tool Review

The list of tools is self-explanatory. You'll need the freewheel remover because if you break a spoke on the freewheel side, you must remove the freewheel to replace it. And the freewheel may get clogged with dust which can hold its pawls open so the freewheel won't operate. You pedal but nothing happens. If you can't clean it on the wheel it will have to be removed and soaked in a solvent such as kerosene. Chainlube (by Lubriplate, see Appendix) is very useful for chain lubrication, since it flushes out dirt which it replaces with lubricant. If you visit state parks you'll ride on dusty dirt roads. You should remove the chain, agitate it in kerosene, and relube with Chainlube as often as every three or four days, depending on how much grit gets into the chain. The small dab of grease is for the emergency that sometimes crops up when enough dust gets into pedal or wheel bearings to cause a grinding sound as you ride, or a sensation of grinding which works its way up from your toes to your consciousness. Don't pedal far when your bike is protesting that way. Either stop and take the hub apart, clean and regrease, or make that your first priority at the campsite. You don't need both a clincher tube and tubular spares, of course, so cut the tool- and parts-list weight by the appropriate amount if you don't use tubulars; you also won't need the rim tape. The dumbell wrench (Fig. 105) is very useful for adjusting saddle, bars, brakes, etc. The rivet remover is an absolute must because if you break a chain, it is very, very difficult to remove the broken link and replace it with a new link, or even simply to remove the link and bring the chain closer and rivet it back together. In an emergency you may, if skillful (or lucky enough), remove a rivet with a nail and a rock, and pound it back the same way. And if you get a tubular tire flat, be *sure* the spare is put on straight and with cement or rim tape. Happy cycle touring!

AIRLINE AND RAILROAD BICYCLE SHIPMENT

You may want to start your tour hundreds of miles from home, and you *can* take your bicycle with you on a plane or train. But common carriers differ as to handling and have certain regulations and restrictions which you should know about.

My usual procedure when taking a plane is to simply wheel my bike

Fig. 105: Use this dumbbell wrench on a trip instead of a handful of individual wrenches.

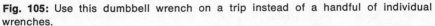

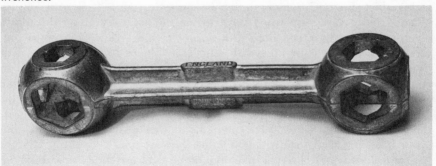

up to the ticket desk, get a luggage tag put on, then wheel it down to the baggage room where I hand it over to a baggage handler. The bicycle will not fit down a luggage chute, which is why you yourself should always take it to the baggage room. The luggage checker will show you where the room is.

Nowadays, though, with bicycle touring and camping all over the world on a steep increase, airlines are facing the problem of more and more people asking them to carry more and more bikes. This is a sticky one for the airlines, because bicycles require special handling and so slow up plane loading; they have sharp parts that can damage others' luggage or even the plane's fuselage; they take up a lot of room for their bulk; and they can themselves be easily damaged—derailleur and brake levers bent, fenders dented, lights broken off, finish scratched, and, worst of all, fork blades and chainstays bent if wheels are removed (it happened to me).

The airlines are approaching this problem in much the same way, with minor variations. American Airlines will sell you a plastic bag (Fig. 106) for around $3.00 into which you can stuff your bike, after first removing and reversing pedals, tying front wheel in place by loosening handlebar stem bolt, moving bars parallel to top tube, tightening stem bolt, and tying bars to top tube or tying wheel to down tube. This way chain stays and fork blades won't be bent because wheel axles will be in place, but you won't have any guarantee a baggage handler won't toss your bike around, or throw some heavy luggage on top of it; although I must praise the baggage men I have seen so far for their careful handling of my bicycle. You can reuse the American Airlines bag until it's too badly ripped to do so (which is inevitable). And this bag is light enough to fold up and tie to your carrier at the arrival end, so you'll have it when you need it at departure. It also makes a dandy "garage" for your bike if you camp and it should rain on your beloved machine. Other airlines will accept the American Airlines bike bag. United Airlines has come up with a bike box (Fig. 107) which, unlike AA's plastic bag, is free, so if you use United both ways, you won't have to pay for or carry along the plastic bag, and the box offers more protection for your bike. The box is long enough to accept your bike with wheels in place; all you do is turn the handlebars parallel to top tube, remove pedals, and stuff the bike in the box. United will also accept your bicycle if you simply wrap styrofoam or some similar padding around handlebars, pedals, and rear derailleur, but that's risking damage to your bicycle and I'd use the box as long as it's free. You'll spend a few extra moments at the ticket counter packaging your bike, but it's worth it if you value the machine.

Yet a third way to carry a bike on a plane is to use the Nishiki bike bag

Fig. 106: American Airlines' answer to carrying a bicycle on a plane is this heavy-gauge plastic bag. It sells for under $3.00, can be reused, is light, and doubles as a "garage" for your bicycle on a camping-trip wet night. All you do is remove pedals, tie front wheel so it stays straight, turn handlebars parallel to top tube by loosening stem bolt, and off you go. AA says there will be an excess baggage charge.

Fig. 107: Here's United Airlines' solution to carrying a bicycle on a plane. It's a heavy-duty cardboard box, which is free, so if you take United both ways you won't have to worry about a bike bag, or carry one. Just remove pedals and turn handlebars; leave wheels on. To turn bars, loosen stem bolt.

Fig. 108: A heavy canvas bike tote bag with inner compartments for wheels, with zipper outside all around, and with carrying handles is the Nishiki bike bag. Roomy enough for the biggest frame and for your pannier bags to boot. But use wood blocks or old axles to keep fork blades and stays from being bent. Ideal to protect good bike frame finish when carrying in car trunk.

(Fig. 108). This bag is of heavy black canvas, and says "Bicycle" on the side under a wheel emblem, so baggage handlers know what's inside. Advantages of this carrier are: good protection of finish; wheels go into special inner pockets, one on each side; bag is big enough to accept a pannier and other gear, as well as the complete bike. You should remove handlebars, as shown in photo, *and block fork blades and rear stay dropouts with wood or an old axle and nuts to avoid damage.* A disadvantage is that the bag is heavy and bulky, and unless you can find a place to store it on arrival to go back the same way, you have to carry it around on your bike till you return. However, the bag can pay for itself in one or two overseas trips because it will take a filled TCS bag with all your gear. You should be able to travel extensively abroad with no more than you can carry in one set of TCS panniers. I attended the Cologne, Germany, bike show, and carried a knit sports jacket, two pair of knit slacks, loafer shoes, two sets of underwear, drip-dry shirts and a tie, plus a wool track suit, a pair of cycling shorts, cleated cycling shoes, knit wool cap, camera, mini-binoculars, tools and spare parts (fortunately, because I broke a derailleur cable and I use a hard-to-find extra-long cable for handlebar shifters), and rain suit. Everything went into the Nishiki bag except toilet gear for the flight to Cologne, and since my total weight was very little over forty-four pounds, and the Nishiki bag relatively so compact, I paid no excess baggage charge. The airlines say you should pay excess baggage charge, even on domestic flights, using the American or United bags, but so far I haven't been asked to. On the return trip I was fairly heavily laden with purchased gifts and other items bought abroad, but I returned from Amsterdam on the Dutch KLM airline and again paid no excess baggage (I cycled from Cologne to Amsterdam, in case you're wondering). With the Dutch cycling is a way of life, and the baggage man calmly took my bike without my having to take it apart, just as it was as I rode it up to the ticket counter at Schiphol Airport, fourteen miles (by my roundabout route) from Amsterdam. I was asked to use cord to tie the panniers and assorted packages hanging from the bike, and to let some air out of the tires, but otherwise the bike went as was. I did remove the pump and water bottle because they can fall off easily, especially the pump. Security people always look askance at the pump if I carry it aboard, so if you do, be prepared to explain.

About Customs

If you take a foreign-made item from the U.S.A. overseas, such as a bicycle, camera, watch, or whatever, and don't declare it *before* you leave the country, you may have a tough time convincing customs officers on your return that you didn't buy it overseas. You can avoid this hassle by declaring in advance everything foreign-made you are taking out of the country on Customs Form 4457, revised as of March 1971 (Fig. 109). Fill in the items, with serial numbers if they have them, on the form, take it to the U.S. Customs office at the airport, and have a customs officer sign the form under your own signature. He will probably want to see the items you are registering, so wheel your bike, camera, etc., up to his office before you pack everything up and put it on the plane.

On the way back, about an hour or two before arrival, a stewardess will hand you a U.S. Customs form on which you are to list *everything* you have bought overseas. If your total purchases amount to less than $100 you won't have to itemize the list. But you may be subject to baggage check if you don't itemize. I keep a running record of everything I buy, no matter how trivial, if I take it home. The longer the list (with U.S. prices) you have, the less likely you'll be to have your bags checked at the airport back home. Maybe I'm just lucky, but I have yet to have had my luggage opened at a U.S. Customs checkpoint. I think customs officers really appreciate a long, detailed, itemized, and honestly priced list, because they know that with such a list in their hand you have no ex-

THE DEPARTMENT OF THE TREASURY **CERTIFICATE OF REGISTRATION** BUREAU OF CUSTOMS	Form Approved O.M.B. 48–R0394 Number
Name of Owner	Address of Owner

Description of Articles

I certify that the information shown hereon is true and correct to the best of my knowledge and belief.	Signature of Owner
Port Date	Signature of Customs Official

Customs Form 4457 (3/71)

Fig. 109: Register foreign-made articles such as bikes, watches, and cameras *before* you leave the U.S.A. so you don't have to pay duty when you return, by using this Bureau of Customs form 4457. Have a customs officer sign it before you leave, but have registered items on hand to show him.

cuse if a luggage check reveals something not on the list, and the chances are dim that they will find anything. That is, if you look like a solid citizen, and all cyclists do, don't they? If you're carrying a lot of stuff, and your bike is crated so you have to carry that, too, you should quickly grab one of the wire carts (like supermarket carts) that are in the customs area for tourists to use free, go get your luggage, load it on the cart, look for a short line at a customs counter and get in line. If you have a choice of counters, look for a youngish customs officer, preferably with a beard; he'll be more understanding about your bicycle, although by now all customs people have seen them on tour and should be used to them.

About Railroads

American railroads are hopeless. They have no good provision for carrying bicycles, and I think AMTRAK is going out of its way to discourage passenger traffic. If you *must* travel by train, make sure you check personally how your bike is put in the baggage car; be sure it is tied to something so it won't bang around or have heavy things fall on it. You can't rely on railroad people in the U.S.A. to be at all solicitous about anything having to do with passenger traffic.

In Europe it's different; a cyclist's delight. In Holland every through passenger train has a baggage car for bicycles (Fig. 110) and although you have to hoist it up yourself, the porter will give you a lift, and show you where to tie it down. A rubber shock cord will secure your bike to a rail. You can then walk from the baggage car to the nearest passenger car and forget about your bike till arrival, although it would be a good idea to lock the bike to the stanchion as well as tie it down. Other European railroads also have baggage cars for bikes and other things. And the trains are fast, clean, comfortable and usually uncrowded, except in Italy, and at rush hours. If the train is crowded, buy a first-class ticket so you will get a seat. You will need a ticket for the bike, which you usually get at the baggage counter. It's also a good idea to put your name tag on the bike, and keep it on.

Fig. 110: The author's bicycle in a railway baggage car on a touring trip through Holland. Note that one shock cord holds bike upright.

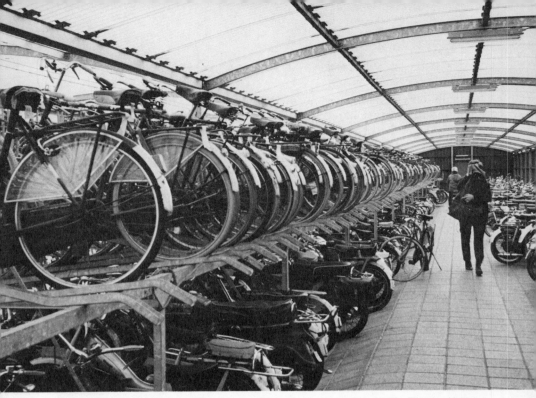

Fig. 111: Here's how bicycles are parked in the train station at Eindhoven, Holland, for about 50¢ a day. Area is enclosed and guarded.

IN CONCLUSION

I consider this chapter on cycle touring and camping the most important section of this book, because, until you start using your bicycle on trips, you will never really know how much fun cycling can be.

My objective in writing this chapter was to help you with planning details, using my own and the experience of others, so that when you step off on your own, your trip will be as enjoyable as possible, with minimum problems caused by unsuitable and insufficient gear and lack of route planning.

The data in this chapter are complete enough to permit you to do any kind of cycle touring or camping that appeals to you. You can select gear and equipment for short weekend trips, a more complete lash-up for extended trips, or cut gear to the bone and go deluxe by stopping at restaurants and motels.

How you go is up to you. But do go, and enjoy yourself!

8

BICYCLE RACING – A NEW
LOOK AT AN OLD SPORT

This chapter is about all aspects of bicycle racing. It will acquaint you with the types of races, and help you follow and understand, and therefore enjoy, bicycle races. If, after reading this chapter, you want to race, you should get in touch with the national headquarters of the Amateur Bicycle League of America (see Appendix for address), which is the governing body of racing in the United States. The ABL will be happy to refer you to the ABL official nearest you, and he, in turn, will help you get started in racing, if you meet the League's basic qualifications of health, stamina, and equipment.

I find bicycle racing a fascinating sport, which combines courage, speed, physical stamina, and skill with the mental agility and bluffing ability of a poker champion. Let me tell you why. In my opinion, as far as auto racing goes, I feel that after the first fifteen minutes, the Indianapolis 500 and similar races are just so much noisy, automaton-like movement around an oval track. You can't see the drivers, and the cars zoom past so fast that they make you dizzy or practically put you to sleep.

A bicycle race, on the other hand, takes place right in front of you. The riders are easy to see, and the physical agility and ability that goes into planning a race to outfox the other fellow is plain for all to see. Then, on the last lap, when the cyclists sprint, at thirty miles an hour or more, the excitement at the track is tremendous.

In France, Belgium, Italy, Holland, and England, where bicycle racing is understood and avidly followed as a national sport, winners of famous races, such as the Tour de France, are truly international heroes. They are covered with glory by the press, their national governments, and if they are professionals, with a good deal of money.

An interesting fact about bicycle racing is that, as a rule, the dedicated racing cyclist has almost no interest in cycle touring, any more than you'd expect auto racers to be interested in automobile touring. However, if you're far from home and something goes wrong with your bicycle, and you can't find a good bicycle shop, you'll find any ABL member in the area willing and able to help you. Incidentally, because the bicycle is so important in racing, the best bicycle stores are run by former champion racers. For example, Al Stiller, a champion and descendant of a family of Belgian racers, runs a store on Chicago's northwest side. Gene Portuesi, a Midwest champ and former United States Olympic Cycling Team coach runs a bicycle store and bicycle mail-order business in Cadillac, Michigan. And Tom Avenia, of New York City, one of the best bicycle mechanics in the East, still races on weekends.

In the limited space that we have to devote to racing in this book, it is not practical to do any more than discuss the various types of races. For tips and hints on racing techniques, I recommend the book *Cycle Racing* by Bowden and Matthews (see Bibliography). Incidentally, each racing champion has his own techniques, methods, and particular way of physical training, all of which, in most cases, he'd rather keep to himself.

TIME TRIAL RACING

In general, a time trial race is a race against time. A rider starts out alone, with a minute's space between him and the next man, so that no matter how many participate in any given race, the man with the best elapsed time wins. Because time trials need open roads, you'll find them starting very early in the morning, such as at 7:00 A.M. on a Sunday.

There are four types of time trials:

· 10, 25, and 30 miles
· 50 and 100 miles
· 12 and 24 hours
· Hill climbs, between 300 yards and 3 miles, depending on hill gradient

At the time of writing, the record for a 25-mile time trial is near 50 minutes, which means an average sustained speed of around 27 miles an hour for one l.our!

Fig. 112: Here's a typical road race. Notice how the group is "bunched up." In particular, you will see that the man in the foreground, at left, is closely followed by another cyclist. In this way the cyclist to the rear forces the front rider to "break the wind" for him. This technique saves the rear rider's strength until a strategic moment arrives when he can "jump" the pack at high speed and take off to win. *(Ray Boldt)*

A professional time trial track record for one hour was made in October, 1972, by Eddy Merckx of Belgium. Riding the track in the rarefied air of Mexico City, his hour record was 49.408.68 kilometers, or 30.7 miles for the one hour. Earlier, at the same track, the world record for 5 kilometers (3.1 miles) was set by Jorn Lund, an amateur cyclist, with an average speed of 50.5 kilometers (31.379 mph) per hour.

The world record for most miles cycled in one year was broken in 1972 by Ken Webb of Great Britain, who has at this writing cycled well over the previous world record in one year of 75,065 miles. To make this record, Mr. Webb spends every spare second away from his full-time job on his bicycle. He sleeps only four hours a day, and on one freezing winter weekend recounts finger-thick ice on his spokes, a derailleur frozen in a 72-inch gear, ice under fenders that had to be chipped away.

He wore out a pair of chamois-lined tights every 12,000 miles or so. On one day he was scheduled for an ear operation, so he rode the 40 miles to the doctor's office, had the operation, and rode home! That's single-minded dedication for you! Mr. Webb states that he's going on, at year end, to try for the 100,000 mile record.

A few more records: The 1972 professional road race of 272 kilometers (169.01 miles) was won by Marino Basso of Italy in 7 hours, 5 minutes and 59 seconds (7.5.59).

The tricycle world record for women in 1971 was 100 kilometers (62.13 miles), set by Jenny Noad of England with a time of 2.58.15; she also beat a twenty-year record in 1971 by doing 100 miles in 4.50.18 on a trike, or better than 25 miles an hour average.

The *official* coast-to-coast Los Angeles to New York City record was made by Pete Duker of Great Britain in 1972, with an elapsed time for the 3,000 miles of 18 days, 2½ hours, or an average of about 166 miles per day.

Last but not least, as every racing cyclist, amateur and pro, knows, Eddy Merckx won the 1972 Tour de France for the fourth consecutive time.

The women's Olympic 60 kilometer (36.682 miles) race was won by Genevieve Gambillon, a twenty-one-year-old Parisian nurse, in 1.30.41.

Okay, you tourists, if trained athletes can zip off 169 miles in little better than 7 hours, you (including me) should be able to do a good 75 miles a day with a camping-gear-laden bike, or 100 miles if the sag-wagon carries everything. Of course, when touring the word "day" in my vocabulary is pretty elastic, and it can, and has, meant anything from an 8 A.M. to 5 P.M. ride, or a 9 A.M. to a staggering-in-late 10 PM tour (otherwise known as a Tour de Force).

MASSED-START RACING

A massed-start race is one in which riders start together, with the first man over the finish line declared the winner. As compared with time-trialing, mass-start racing pits one rider against the other in a personal contest of strength, technique, and skill.

Massed-start racing may be held on a public highway (at daybreak), in which case it is called a "road race," or on a circular park road, which is closed off to traffic for the duration of the race.

The famous Tour de France is a massed-start race. It takes the riders 2,600 miles in 22 days, over some of the most grueling ground in the world, including the Pyrenees Mountains, from Lille to Paris.

CYCLO-CROSS RACING

A variation of massed-start racing is real he-man stuff—cyclo-cross racing. Cyclo-cross is a combination of road racing and cross-country running, using special bicycles with high brackets, chainwheel guards to keep the mud out, and special knobbed tires for high traction.

Most events are one or two miles long, but some are as long as eight miles, over open fields and streams, through bogs of mud and sand and even wooded areas. Part of the time the cyclist is riding, other times he is running, and sometimes he is carrying his bicycle.

If you like to wallow in mud, slither through grass, grope your way through dense woods, ford streams, climb cliffs, and do all this with a bicycle on your back at maximum physical effort, then cyclo-cross racing is for you.

TRACK RACING

Tracks for bicycle racing are built to very rigid specifications, and few cities have them because they are so costly. There are fine tracks in the United States, however, in Encino, California (near Los Angeles); San Jose, California; Portland, Oregon; Northbrook, Illinois (near Chicago); St. Louis, Missouri; New York City, at the old World's Fair Grounds; and Kenosha and Milwaukee, Wisconsin.

Track racing is unquestionably the most complex of all the forms of bicycle racing; to understand it takes some study and real dedication on the part of the spectator. But it is an exciting sport and well worth learning. There are various types of track racing.

Handicaps

These are short distance races, from a quarter-mile to a half-mile. Riders are handicapped by ability, with space between riders at the start according to the handicap.

Fig. 113: At the track in Northbrook, Illinois, the three leaders in a 1968 ten-mile track race are, left to right, Eddie Van Guyse, Dennis Ellerton, and John Van De Velde. The three are in the middle of a sprint. (*Ray Boldt*)

Fig. 114: In high-speed cycling, racers sometimes stay absolutely still. "Jockeying" is the technical term for this maneuver. In Denmark, in 1966, from left to right, Preston Handy, Gordon Johnson, and John Chapman at the start of a heat in the Grand Prix of Arhus.

Sprint

One of the most exciting types of racing, the sprint, takes two forms. Match-racing, used in the Olympic Games, involves only two or three racers per race. Usually sprint races are over 800 or 1,000 meter courses, or two or three lengths of a specific track. The last 220 yards or 200 meters only are timed, with the rest of the race used for tactical maneuvering.

In major championship races, most of the riders will be evenly matched physically, so that the only way to win is by outsmarting the opponent. One tactic is to jump to speed before the other rider is aware that you are sprinting to speed and before he can ready himself to keep up.

Another method is for one rider to give the impression that he is going all out, when actually he has considerable reserve power. This involves going around the track at a fast but comfortable pace, luring the opponent into following you closely and, at the last stretch, jumping to speed before the rearward rider can recover and try to catch up.

Another tactic is the attack from the rear. The attacker comes from behind and reaches the last banked turn before his opponent. Then he boxes him in until, in desperation, the trapped man eases back to try to pass, at which point the leading rider jumps to sprint speed.

Pursuit Track Racing

A pursuit track race is one in which two riders start on opposites sides of the track and try to catch each other over a standard distance, usually 4,000 meters. Because riders are usually evenly matched, they rarely do catch each other, so the race is decided on time, with the winner having covered the distance in the least amount of time.

Team pursuit races involve teams of four men, starting on opposite sides of the track. Each rider takes a turn at the lead, sheltering the others behind him. Smooth change of pace is essential to keep the pace and avoid breaking the chain of closely spaced riders. Time is called on the third member of each team as he passes the finish line.

An Australian pursuit involves teams of up to eight riders spaced out at equal distances, with any riders who are caught eliminated. An Italian pursuit involves two or more teams of three, four, or five riders, in which teams are equally spaced around the track and each team drops off one rider from the race each lap of the track. The last man in each team with the best time wins the race.

Fig. 115: The West German tandem team of Juergen Barth and Rainer Mueller, left, skid to a fall on the Olympic track at Munich, Germany, during the 1972 Olympic Games. On a collision course with the German team is the Polish tandem team of Androej Bek and Benedykt Kocot. Major injury was avoided as the Polish team managed to glance off the German tandem team. (*United Press International*)

OTHER TYPES OF TRACK RACES

Scratch races are any races where all competitors start together, usually over a three-, five-, or ten-mile course.

Miss-and-out eliminates the last rider over each lap until at the last lap the remaining racers sprint to the finish line.

Unknown distance is a race in which the riders go on until a gong signals the last lap, at which point they sprint to the finish. If the field is solidly packed, the best attacker will usually win.

Point-to-point involves any number of competitors up to the capacity of the track for a specific distance or number of laps, with sprints at each lap or half-lap for points. Points are given to the first man over the line, or to the first two or three men over the line. The winner is the racer with the most points at the end of the race.

Madison takes its name from the old Madison Square Garden (New York City) six-day bicycle races. The original version was a fairly bloody, barbarous event, in which riders staggered around the track for six days, frequently falling. Although the race was finally banned, a version of it, in which teams of two riders pair up in a race, one rider racing while the other rests, is popular today. In Europe, the Madison is a very popular six-day race, although it can be any length, from thirty minutes to six days, or any distance. An exciting aspect of this race is the entry of a relieving rider into the melee, in which he is thrown by a grasp of the hand and a push on the bottom as a tired rider leaves the group. Variations of Madisons are point-to-point competitions, where the disadvantage for the spectator is that in order to make sense out of the race, he has to keep count on all points made by all riders as they are accumulated.

Fig. 116: A sprint during the ten-mile point race at a National Championship match in St. Louis, 1967. At far left is six-time U.S. Champion Jim Rossi, who, at the time this photo was taken, was at the point of coming from twelfth to second place. Leading the pack at far right is Allen Bell, who won, and immediately behind him is the one-time Junior National Champ, Perry Metzler. *Bicycling!* (formerly *American Cycling*)

Fig. 117: A scene from the 1972 Milan to San Remo race, on the Italian Riviera, which takes the racing cyclist over some fairly rugged country. As usual, this famous annual racing event draws spectators to line the roads all along the route. (*United Press International*)

Paced riding is usually done behind a motorcycle, attaining speeds of fifty miles an hour tearing around a small track, with the cyclist staying glued behind the motorcycle as it breaks the wind. This type of racing is rarely seen in the United States, because it requires a specially made track that is properly banked and very smooth. The motorcycles used for these events have a small roller projecting from the rear to make sure the cyclist behind can't touch the motorcycle wheel and cause a wreck. If he catches up and contacts the motorcycle, the cyclist's front wheel merely spins against the roller without effect. The idea is to permit the cyclist to obtain a uniform "shield" from the motorcycle he's following by maintaining distance behind it.

A *"repechage"* literally means a "second chance". This is a race in which riders who are eliminated in a heat get a second chance in the form of another heat, usually with four or five other riders (only one or perhaps two who finally qualify), to qualify for the quarter- or semi-finals of one event.

TIPS FOR ASPIRING RACERS

The following tips for would-be racers were taken from a tape recording made by Gene Portuesi of Cadillac, Michigan, some years ago, which he sent to members of his team before the Olympic Games in Tokyo:

If you're in training, keep a day-to-day record of track and wind conditions, how you feel, your times, hours of sleep per night, everything and anything that bears on your performance. At the end of the year you'll have a vivid picture of your performance and what affected it.

Proper rest and diet are extremely important. Use general good sense and stick to a basic diet of good meat, lots of vegetables, and milk.

In selecting gears, the mistake most novices make is to find out what the champions are using, and then strain on these gears. This makes about as much sense as to enter a weight-lifting contest and strain to lift a weight just because this is what the champ can lift. To select your gears, use a stopwatch and a little arithmetic. Trial and error will teach you what is possible with different gear ratios in terms of your own physical conditioning, and how to apply these ratios to a race of any kind, be it a hill-climb, sprint, time trial, or break-away. For example, a top-notch sprinter who covers the last 200 meters of a race in 12 seconds, using a 24 x 7 or a 92.6 gear [see page 179 for a complete explanation of gear ratios], would spin his cranks an average of 135 revolutions per minute.

Fig. 118: Professional road racer Michele Dancelli shows power at the top of a hill climb as he's cheered on his way. (*United Press International*)

Check your own cadence at the gear you can sprint best. For example, if you ride a 25 x 8 gear, in the last 200 meters of a race your crank revolutions per minute will revolve 31 times; with 23 x 7 gears, cranks will revolve 29.5 times; with 24 x 7, 28.2 times and 25 x 7, 27 revolutions. The factor determining gear selection, as stated before, has to involve a combination of your physical condition with the mechanical factors of gear selections. It makes no sense to ride a big gear like the champions, if you're not ready for it. [Note: Mr. Portuesi refers to one-inch pitch racing chains and gears instead of the usual one-half inch standard pitch. To relate the gears he's quoting to road or touring gears, multiply his figures by two.]

About Training

Many cyclists start their training in the spring, but for those of us who live in cold northern climates, this is not soon enough. The power you can get into your muscles is directly related to your heart and respiratory system. To begin training in April after a four-month lay-off and expect to get in championship condition in ten to twelve weeks is not practical. A winter program is essential. Many cyclists take up speed skating, or some indoor athletic program. Anything that makes the heart and lungs work hard will keep these organs in superior condition and permit you to enter racing training in reasonably good condition.

Weight lifting is a good winter training activity. Weight lifting, or weight training, keeps the heart and lungs in top condition, and increases muscle power, in particular, conditioning the muscles of the upper torso to a far greater degree than is possible by cycling alone.

Let me give you an example of the importance of winter training. When Nancy Neimann of Detroit was National Women's Champion, and rode for the first time on the famous Herne Hill Track in London, England, she used a gear that had won her the national championship. [Mr. Portuesi was Nancy's coach.] In what was then the fastest field of girl track riders, she spun her gear wide open. In trying to use the bigger ratios, Nancy found that she was not able to open up to top speed because the power required from her back and shoulder muscles to equalize the thrust from her legs simply wasn't there.

We instituted a winter training program for Nancy designed to improve the muscles in her upper torso, and as a result, she was able to improve her time by a half-second in the critical last 200 meters, and was able to beat the top women sprinters of England and Europe, and officially equal the then women's world record. The following year she beat the world record many times in the flats while training at home. What I am saying is that powerful legs will not give full thrust into the pedals unaided by equally powerful back, arm, and shoulder muscles.

What do I mean by weight lifting? For women, try 10 repetitions of fifty pounds in arm exercises and 100 pounds in squats. For men, some variation is permissible according to build. For example, a man of 150 pounds should stay to a maximum of 100 pounds in arm exercises and 160 to 180 pounds for squats, ten repetitions of each. Do all exercises quickly, with rapid motion and deep breathing. Work out every third day or twice weekly. Start the program in the late fall and gradually build up the weights lifted. Put emphasis on the areas of your greatest weakness, then as soon as the good weather rolls around, forget the indoor training and hop on your bicycle.

Spring Training

For your first ride in the spring, go about 25 miles, and keep in low gear (23 x 10 will do). Dress warmly, keep your legs covered with skating tights and seat pants, and use light layers of warm clothing for your upper torso. Put a sheet of newspaper between your last two outer garments to keep your chest warm against the cold wind.

Don't loaf along in low gear. Once you get warmed up, try to keep your cadence up over 100 revolutions per minute. Use your stopwatch and count your pedal action over a 30-second period. In other words, do something with

your miles and time besides sitting in the saddle and just pedaling.

After you are well warmed up, try a couple of one-mile time trials, with a slight rest in between. Then try a few jumps from almost a dead stop. First take off with the right foot, next take off with the left foot, and so on. Keep your action smooth. You will find this is very hard with a low gear, but the better you can coordinate yourself with a low gear, the more you will get out of a big one.

After about two weeks or 300 miles of low-gear riding, move up about 7 or 8 points on your gear. Pick a 5-mile course and see how much faster you are with the 69 than with a 62. Keep practicing your jumps from almost a dead stop. The gear is too small to go into it from a rolling start. Concentrate on using your straps. The top of your arch should hurt from having pulled up after a good workout. Stay smooth. Stay in a 69 for about 200 miles, then move up, just like your weight-training program. Keep a record of how fast you time-trial with each gear before you move up. Put it in the book. It will be something for you to improve next year. After the girls get into a 76 and

Fig. 119: Cyclists in the Tour of Sardinia wheel past the impressive backdrop of the Colosseum at the beginning of the first lap of the event. (*United Press International*)

the men into an 80 gear, go back to using your 62 a couple of times a week for a 25-mile workout. It's a good idea to work out on your low gears the day after a specially hard ride. Get at least two days of rest per week. Try to vary your riding so it's hard, but not fatiguing. Work out hard, but don't run yourself into the ground.

Now, with girls on a 76 and men on an 80, start timing yourself over a 200-meter, marked flying start. Try for five or six good times over a period of a week. Then move up two points on your gear and repeat. This is one reason I prefer the use of a half-inch pitch chain. You'll find that fewer changes in sprockets are required, and gears can be moved up in smaller graduations.

When the men and boys start getting into the 86 and 88 gears, some will find that a 4-point jump is too much. As you can see, this system allows you to feel your way up into your racing ratios as your physical condition improves. And, as the gears get higher, the graduations are smaller. Also, you will find that when you start using those speeds on your road-racing bike, you will know what to expect from every ratio on your bicycle.

Keep a weekly check on your body weight. Loss of weight can mean not enough rest, improper diet, or too many hard miles. Use a little common sense and try to correct what you think is wrong. If you must make changes in your routine, don't make too many at a time, because then you will not be able to attribute any change in performance to that which was directly responsible.

Gene Portuesi should know what he's talking about. Twice Michigan state champion himself, he coached Doris Travani, four times national champion woman cyclist; Robert Travani, formerly on America's Olympic team; Nancy Neimann, four times national champion, who tied the world's record; and Joanni Specken, national champion. He served as coach of the 1964 United States Olympic Cycling Team, and runs a national bicycle and parts business from his Cadillac, Michigan, headquarters (Cyclo-Pedia, see Appendix, page 497).

TRACK VERSUS ROAD-TRAINING TECHNIQUES

Bill Kund, a racing cyclist, offers some practical advice to track and racing cyclists as to the different types and methods of conditioning each should engage in.[1]

I have found that the best way to gain endurance is to ride. I spend from two and a half to three hours on the road daily, usually riding in a small gear, 62 to 70 inches (46 x 20 to 47 x 18), at a fairly comfortable pace. If I am feeling good I will include some hills in the ride, or go into higher gear, 88 to 94 inches, and ride hard for five to ten miles. If I am feeling especially weak or stiff I will still ride for three hours, but at an easy pace in a small gear.

I also do speed work three times a week, and on Tuesday evenings, I go to the track and do interval training. This consists of about ten repetitions of 500-meter sprints at seven-eighths speed, with a one-mile rest between each one. The whole work-out, including fifteen minutes of pacing to warm up, lasts about an hour. This is a very tiring work-out, and I would not advise doing it more than once a week. On Thursday evenings I do four to six 300-meter sprints with long rests between. The emphasis on these sprints is speed, not fatigue. I usually get together with one or two other riders when doing this, and we take turns leading out the sprints. On Fridays, I incorporate at least one hour of hard motor pacing (30 to 35 miles per hour) into my three-hour stint on the road.

[1] Bill Kund, "Speed + Endurance = Victory," *American Cycling* (now *Bicycling!*), April, 1966. Page 17.

Fig. 120: At the 1972 Olympic track, Munich, Germany, the U.S. Olympic track team trains behind Coach Jerry Rimoldi from San Diego, California. To the right of Rimoldi, in order, are Mike Hiltner, Chicago, James Rich, Chicago, James Ochowitz, Milwaukee, Jim Mensching, Chicago, Dave Chauner, Rosemont, Pa., and John Van De Velde, Chicago. (*United Press International*)

It is only through balanced training of this type that a rider can develop to his fullest capacity. Races are won with both speed and endurance, not with only one or the other. A sprinter who is unable to sustain his speed to the line is as worthless as a roadman in a bunch sprint who is consistently last.

ABOUT THE RACING BICYCLE

Track-racing bicycles are very special machines indeed. The wheelbase is shorter, the fork rake is fairly straight, and rear dropouts are open to the rear so wheels can be bolted in place and can't come out under the stress of powerful racing cyclists. The track bike has fixed gear and no brakes, and weighs at most 18 pounds. Special design bicycles are built for specific types of track races. Chain-stay diameter varies according to preferences of track racers, the heavier cyclists preferring stays as thick as ⅝ inch, with ½ inch for lighter racers. The idea is to minimize power-wasting "frame whip" and arrive at a stiff frame. For pursuit racing, the very lightest Columbus tubing can be used, but for track sprints or road

Fig. 121: Danish cycling ace Ole Ritter puts the power on during the fourth stage of the fifty-second Tour of Italy cycle race in May, 1969. This photograph illustrates how some racers drill out their brake levers, and the side-pull brake itself, for lightness. Notice also the small flange hubs on this bicycle; these make wheels more flexible and comfortable on bumpy Continental roads. Note also radially spoked wheels, which save weight by cutting down spoke length. (*United Press International*)

racing, heavier tubing is needed to withstand greater stress. Professional cyclists in Europe have several bicycles designed specially for each type of race.

For races involving steep banks or turns, a racing bicycle can have a 75-degree head angle, 73-degree seat angle, fork blades with almost no rake, extra-short wheelbase and thicker rear stays.

Road-racing machines and better touring bicycles have 72-degree parallel head and seat tubes. Taller bicyclists, if having a custom frame built, can order a 73-degree head and 71-degree seat tube.

DIET AND GENERAL HINTS

Every champion bike racer has his own favorite dietary rules which he firmly believes constitute one of the main ingredients of his success. Champs usually are loath to part with these secrets, which is understandable; but with some persuasion, we were able to pry some general rules, at least, out of a few of them.

Jim Rossi of Chicago, a United States national champion (from 1959 to 1963, and winner of the United States ten-mile race in 1965), a silver medal winner in the 1963 Pan American games in Brazil, and a gold medal winner in the 1959 Pan American games, began his dissertation on diet and training by pointing out that as far as he is concerned diet is very much an individual matter, depending on physical and emotional makeup. He pointed out that trainers often use placebo psychology, when they prescribe for a racer a prerace conditioning diet in which a sugar pill is included. Near-magical powers can be attributed to the sugar pill, and with this mental boost the racer can often win. The rider, of course, does not know what is in the pill. Incidentally, American bicycle racers are strictly forbidden to take dope, although barbiturates and stronger drugs are regularly, though surreptitiously, used by European cyclists. More about the drug problem later in this chapter.

To continue about diet: Cycle champs, including Jim Rossi, start off the spring training season by abstaining from all greasy fried foods and high-starch foods such as potatoes. Diet for a racing cyclist is very much a matter of meat and vegetables, with steak a favorite, accompanied by fresh vegetables cooked with a minimum of water to preserve the natural vitamin content. He drinks lots of fresh fruit juices (without sugar) and keeps on this diet until winter-accumulated body fat is replaced by muscle tissue, and he is down to his racing weight. Bread, if eaten, is either rye or whole wheat.

Although physicians say that additional vitamins are not needed with a proper diet, many racing cyclists take them anyway. Any good daily vitamin tablet or pill will do, such as Upjohn's Unicaps.

Whether you are setting off on a tour of a couple of hundred miles or getting into shape for the bicycle-racing season, you must remember that cycling, more than most other sports, uses most of the muscles of the body and works them hard. Therefore, to keep in shape, a simple diet of fresh vegetables and meat, with a salad and lots of milk, is the best energy source you can provide your body.

Much about cycle training and racing diet is applicable also to other forms of athletic activity. For example, you should never gulp down large quantities of cold water right after a hard ride. If you do, you court stomach cramps that can slow you up. Instead, drink warm water laced with sugar, until your body temperature returns to normal.

Although personal habits differ, and some cyclists do not eat anything the morning of their race, Jim Rossi takes aboard a hearty breakfast consisting of steak and eggs, with coffee or tea, one hour before setting off

Fig. 122: Felice Gimondi gives a drink of water to Belgium's cycling champ Eddy Merckx during the twelfth stage of the 1969 Tour of Italy. (*United Press International*)

for a long ride or race. Rossi also recommends raw eggs as an easily digested source of quick energy just before a race.

Diet in road racing, particularly a century (100-mile) run, is a little complicated, because no feeding stops are allowed for the first 50 miles. Yet Rossi and other champs assert that it's very important to replace energy lost through exertion *at the time* it's lost, rather than to wait until hunger signals appear. For by the time your stomach tells you when to eat, the time has passed when immediate muscle energy demands can be satisfied. This is why long-distance racers carry a small feedbag slung over their chest or back, filled with such sources of quick energy as sliced oranges, grapes, peaches, bananas, and meat sandwiches. If you watch these cyclists, you'll see that they eat small amounts of these foods frequently. And they take small sips, *not* huge gulps, of water, weak tea, or water laced with a sugar cube or two from feeder bottles mounted on their handlebars.

Cycle tourists would do well to take a tip from racing champions and instead of waiting for the conventional three meals on a long trip, avoid starving their muscle tissue by snacking once or twice an hour. The best schedule would be to eat a hearty breakfast one hour before departure (cycling right after a *full* meal is not recommended), snack during the morning ride, eat a light lunch, snack during the afternoon, then settle down to a nutritious dinner in the evening. Tea and coffee are not recommended with the evening meal because the stimulants they contain tend to keep you awake, when you should be resting up for the next day's ride. Besides fruits and sandwiches for snacks en route, Rossi suggests candy bars that won't melt or stick to your throat and gag you. Fresh figs or fig bars and dextrose tablets are also excellent. Stay away from honey and similar sticky liquids because they can clog your throat.

Following these general rules, you can alter what you eat to suit your own tastes and preferences. If you don't like fresh calf's liver, for example, try steak, chops, or broiled (not fried) chicken. For sandwiches, try roast beef, sliced chicken, or turkey on rye or whole wheat bread. Stay away from sandwiches that come apart easily, make a mess, and are hard to hold onto, such as salad ingredients (chicken or egg salad, for example), unless you are prepared to stop while you snack. Most racers eat on the go, or at least snack while they ride.

THE QUESTION OF DRUGS

As I have already stated, it is virtually unheard of for anyone on the United States cycle-racing teams to take drugs. In the first place, in this country the sport comes under rules governing amateur athletics. There are no professional bicycle racers. In Europe, however, where bicycle racing is a national obsession akin to baseball or football here, professional bicycle racers can earn from $50,000 to $100,000 a year. Pro racing competition is keen, and most racing athletes are fairly evenly matched physically, thus leaving only technique or drugs to decide who wins. The taking of drugs, either by injection into the bloodstream or orally, has long been a real problem in bicycle-racing circles abroad. Authorities prohibited all forms of stimulants long ago, and athletes are tested for drugs either by a spot check or by a careful physical checkup.

Taking drugs is a dangerous practice for athletes because it masks true symptoms of fatigue that, when ignored, can cause heart failure. Drugs have killed more than one racing cyclist, and have "burned out" many more athletes before their time. In fact, during a recent Tour de France road race, a world-famous cycling champion died shortly after toppling off his bicycle. At first, death was attributed to sunstroke, but a later examination showed that he had taken a stimulant which permitted exertion to the point of heart failure.

European cycling pros who take drugs follow a typical cycle of racing success, says Rossi. Generally, a cyclist who takes drugs can remain in peak form and condition from eighteen to twenty-four years of age, but during this period he will build up a tolerance for the drug, which will require progressively larger doses. After the age of twenty-four, he cannot continue taking drugs without becoming addicted and endangering his life. A racer will drop out of active competition for from two to four years until his body throws off the effects of the drugs he has been taking. And, at twenty-six or twenty-eight, he will be found again in the championship ranks until, after an even shorter period of drug-stimulated racing, he either drops out for good, goes through another "cure," or becomes permanently addicted.

I asked Rossi why cyclists don't carry small containers of pressurized oxygen which they could sniff from time to time to make up the oxygen deficiency caused by physical stress. His answer was that pure oxygen isn't much help because racing cyclists undergo physical stress that is sustained longer than in most other sports, and their training is rigorous enough that they should be able to oxygenize blood by means of normal respiration. Also, says Rossi, the few times a racing cyclist would be able to inhale a fractional cubic foot of oxygen during the heat and intense mental and physical strain of a race makes oxygen-sniffing impractical.

A WORD ABOUT CONDITIONING

There are a few special rules that apply to a cyclist who wants to keep in shape all year round that may not apply to other sports.

For example, swimming and bicycling simply don't mix, because leg muscles are stretched in different ways by these activities. Don't be surprised if, after a long, hard, and hot ride, your leg muscles cramp up if you jump in the lake for a swim. For safety's sake, if you tour, wait until you have at least cooled down before going in for a swim. For the cycle-racing enthusiast, swimming is strictly taboo, according to Rossi, who at one point in his career had to choose between water polo and cycle racing for this very reason.

At the beginning of this chapter, I pointed out that bicycle racers are strictly uninterested in touring. The major reason for this, Jim Rossi points cut, is that a racer is not interested in anything that will not contribute to his physical conditioning, and touring is useless in this respect. Most tourists, even those who are in prime condition, go far too slowly to permit a racing cyclist to stay in peak shape. Racing cyclists on hard training rides frequently roll up 100 miles in well under 5½ hours, which is impractical, to say the least, for a touring cyclist riding a heavy touring or road bicycle laden with gear. I know of at least one racer turned tourist, though. At the age of fifty-five he went 600 miles in three days, from Chicago to his lakeside cabin in upper Minnesota. One hundred miles a day is plenty for me; for the average tourist, fifty to seventy-five miles daily is enough. This amount of mileage is child's play to the racing cyclist. Rossi says that he would rather run around the block a hundred times than go on a cycling tour, at least where physical

Fig. 123: Start of the 1972 Milan to San Remo race, which began in Milan's famous Piazza del Duomo and involved hundreds of racing teams over an up and down course for about 350 miles. (*United Press International*)

conditioning is concerned. Rossi is in the air-conditioning business, and on his trips to office buildings he spurns the elevator and *runs* up and down stairs, carrying his tools. I don't recommend this strenuous an activity for the average desk jockey, although I do feel that it is a good idea for anyone to climb at least the first twenty-five flights slowly, with pauses for rest every five or six flights. Certainly there's no excuse for taking an elevator *down* any number of flights. Exercise works the body to its maximum capacity in terms of output and time, and your heart should be forced to work up to 120 beats per minute, assuming you're in good shape.

An athlete in prime condition typically has a heartbeat that is rather low at rest, but one that goes to top cardiac output quickly under stress and returns quickly to the rest beat when stress stops. For example, Rossi's heartbeat when he was twenty-eight years old and in training was from sixty-five to sixty-eight per minute. After two minutes of squats, his beat would rise to 128 and after two minutes of rest return to sixty-five. If you can establish this, consider yourself ready for the Olympics.

IMPORTANCE OF WARM-UP

Your body cannot be expected to perform at maximum work output from a cold start, any more than the motor of your car can. Not, at least, without damage. In the case of the body, it's nearly physiologically impossible. When the body is at rest, the blood vessels are not dilated, which means that they will handle a minimum amount of blood volume flow. This is why the first two or three miles of cycling, from a resting state start, is a strain for most of us. Once the muscles begin to demand more oxygen and nutrients, the blood vessels dilate wide open, the heart speeds up, and the muscles' needs are satisfied. The body performs more smoothly and you feel much more comfortable and ready to go a hundred miles. But until the muscles get fed, the first couple of miles are tough.

WINTER TRAINING

Few racing cyclists make much of an effort to ride outdoors during very cold weather. Roads are frequently clogged with ice and snow, so that the regular riding mileage at the speed demanded by effective training techniques is not possible.

Instead, cyclists turn to other forms of *regular* exercise, such as basketball, speed skating, handball, weight lifting, or simply running around the block. The importance of frequent regular (at least three times a week) exercise cannot be stressed enough, because, as Gene Portuesi stated earlier in this chapter, once out of condition an athlete cannot be expected to get back in shape soon enough during the spring to compete in major cycling events. As for the rest of us, we too need regular winter exercise. If you can't fit into last summer's clothes, and if a ten-mile bike ride exhausts you, your winter exercise program needs a closer look.

Winter or summer, at least eight hours of sleep is indicated, and cycle champs in training often go to bed around 10:00 P.M. This makes for a dull life, as far as parties are concerned, but that's the stuff champions are made of. Speaking of parties, a champion in training should not drink alcoholic beverages, certainly nothing stronger than beer and not much of that. Alcohol is fattening, and there is also a strong temptation to snack while drinking.

If you do ride in cold weather, remember that it's best to dress for the weather as though you were not exercising, and peel off layers of clothing as your body warms up. I cycle to work frequently during the winter months, and on cold days I start out with thermal underwear, pants, thermal socks, a heavy long-sleeved shirt, a sweater or two, and a thermal nylon jacket. After three miles or so I stop, take off the jacket, peel off the sweater and possibly the shirt, put the jacket back on, and continue cycling.

I must admit that I have never raced myself, although I thoroughly enjoy the sport as a spectator. I hope that, along with the increased popularity of cycling as a healthful hobby, we will see the spread of cycle-racing tracks to all parts of the country, and that this truly exciting spectator sport will get the audience it deserves.

GLOSSARY OF RACING TERMS

Road Races

- *Criterium*—A road race held over a fairly short closed circuit, closed off to traffic. Known in Europe as a Kermesse.
- *Australian Pursuit*—Slowest groups of riders start first, spaced at intervals, with faster riders up to the very fastest starting last.

Fig. 124: Competitors in the 1972 Tour of Sardinia cycle race make their way around a hairpin curve on the mountainous island as the race nears Sassari. Cycle racers from Italy, Belgium, France, Holland, and Switzerland are competing in the race, which is the opening event of the Italian bicycle racing season. The favorite is Belgium's veteran champion, Rick Van Looy, who has won three of the four laps completed so far on the Mediterranean Island. (*United Press International*)

- *Stage Race*—A long-distance race, staged over a number of days, such as the Tour de France. Rider with the best time per day is the winner.
- *Individual Time Trial*—Based on a predetermined distance, winner is the rider completing that distance in the shortest time.

Track Races

- *Course des Primes*—Involves a large number of riders, over a distance of three to five miles, with the winner amassing the most points on sprints held every other lap.
- *Paced*—Riders follow a small motorcycle called a "Derny" which "breaks the wind."
- *Miss and Out*—Each lap eliminates a last rider and narrows the field down to three, after which a sprint for the finish determines the winner.
- *Handicap*—Slow riders start a predetermined distance ahead of faster riders.
- *Madison*—Two-man teams compete over a fixed distance, usually 100 kilometers (62.14 miles). While one man rides, his partner circles slowly around the track and, at fixed intervals, takes the active partner's place. Winners of sprints that take place during the race amass points, determining the ultimate winning team.
- *Motor Paced*—Racers ride behind a specially built motorcycle on a specially designed bicycle with the front wheel smaller than the rear wheel, mounted on a reversed fork to enable the rider to keep close behind the motorcycle. See *Paced*.
- *Omnium*—Omnium means "all" in Latin, and this is a race of all types, with the winner the rider who has the most points gained from each type of race.
- *Italian Pursuit*—A team race, involving teams of four to six cyclists who start across from each other, one team on either side of the track. Slowest rider drops out each lap; the number of riders starting determine the number of laps.
- *Team Pursuit*—This is the same as an individual pursuit race but involving teams of four riders.
- *Scratch*—A handicap sprint race in which the slowest rider starts first, the fastest, last.
- *Time Trial*—A 1,000-meter (3,280.3 feet, or .62 mile) race, in which the rider attempts to cover this distance in the shortest possible time.

BICYCLE POLO, ANYONE?

Yes, bicycle polo. It's fairly new in the U.S., although of long standing in Great Britain. If you think bicycle racing is a little known, exotic sport in this country, you haven't seen anything quite as rarefied as bicycle polo.

Fig. 125: Bicycle polo, played like horse polo with variations, is a growing sport in the U.S. Object is to hit ball through goal posts in background (no, the girl is not the goalee). In the photo, Buenos Aires team member Gene Bierhorst attempts an offside forehand, while Wisteria Country Club team captain, Russell Corey, stops dead to avoid crossing the line of the ball, which would have caused a foul to have been called against him. (*Photo courtesy United States Bicycle Polo Association*)

At this writing bicycle polo is beginning to come alive, though, and if you're interested, you might write the U.S. Bicycle Polo Association, P. O. Box 565, FDR Station, New York, New York 10022.

Bicycle polo is played something like horse polo (Fig. 125). You need a bicycle, preferably with small wheels for maneuverability, a mallet with a 30-inch shaft, a dozen or so polo balls, and some like-minded friends, also with mallets and bikes. The sport is limited to two teams of four players in an outdoor field, and for points you shoot a ball through goal post several feet apart at opposite ends of a 110-yard-long field (60 yards wide).

Rules of bicycle polo vary from horse polo, and the U.S. BPA will be happy to send you a set of them along with all the information you need to set up a couple of teams. Sounds like fun, but wear a hard hat, play on soft grass, and don't take any wooden mallets on your shin bone.

BICYCLE SAILING, YET!

Sailing on a bicycle is not particularly new; I've seen drawings of attempts at this combination of two sports as far back as 1898 issues of *Outing* Magazine. Still, cycle sailing offers a lot of promise as a fun thing to do, and a new sail, made specially for bicycles, seems to make it practical! Unfortunately, the new sail came on the market just as we were going to press with this revised edition, so your author has not had time to test and report on it. Since he is an experienced sailor as well as a cyclist, however, he can tell you that what he has seen of the sail (in the press release) would make this sport something you can do with a little practice. The sail is made of clear plastic, which is vital so you can see where you are going, because it can only be used *before* the wind (the wind is coming from behind you), which in sailing parlance is called "running" or "sailing before the wind." You can't very well sail with the wind coming from one side or the other, since you would be knocked over. From my sailing experience, I would judge you'd need a good 8 or 10 mph breeze, and 20 mph would be better, to get up any speed at all on the bike with this sail. I could have used the sail in Holland, since the wind blows pretty steadily from the northwest at 18 mph and on some days, on tour, when I wanted to stretch the trip for the day out to 125 miles to make a good hotel for the night, the sail would have helped, since I was running (pedaling) before the wind. The press release says the sail has 16 square feet and fits on an aluminum mast with a tiller (which substitutes for a main sheet on a regular sailboat), so you can turn the sail to "spill" the wind out of it when you want to stop or make a turn. I would imagine, without having used the sail, you'd want to stop and take the sail down if you're going to turn or do anything but sail-cycle in a straight line. The mast steps into a bracket permanently attached to your handlebars. When not in use, the press release says, the sail, mast, and supports fold into a compact package secured to your top tube. Sail and accessories sell, at this writing, for about $20.00 and are available from Viking Bicycle Sail, P. O. Box 603, Oregon City, Oregon 97045. Better try

Fig. 126: Cycle sailing is possible with this sailing rig. If you try it out just for fun, be sure to wear a hard crash helmet, select a traffic-free country road and have the wind at your back. Don't try to tack, which would involve weaving from one side of the road to the other. A dry lake surface would be ideal.

this sail out first on a lonely paved road with about five miles of clear sailing. In use, the sail is stepped on the mast directly over the handlebars, and is stretched across the handlebars to about 30 inches above them (Fig. 126). I'd suggest a crash helmet, at least until you get the hang of the sail.

9

THE FAD THAT LASTED —
A SHORT HISTORY
OF BICYCLING

When Baron Karl von Drais introduced his "Hobby-Horse" to the citizens of Karlsruhe, Germany, in 1816, he started a love affair with man-propelled wheels that has persisted to this day.

The Hobby-Horse, or "Draisene," (Fig. 127) was a monstrously heavy affair, consisting of a wooden frame, wooden wheels, and a most uncomfortable-looking saddle. The rider straddled the Draisene and propelled himself forward by pushing with his feet—the result was something like riding a kiddie-car.

Costly and cumbersome though it was, the Draisene was immediately

Fig. 127: The original Hobby-Horse, invented by Baron von Drais, in the Museum at Breslau. (*The Bettmann Archive*)

accepted by the wealthy and the more enterprising middle class of the day. Within a few years, playboys of western Europe were pushing their way up and down the boulevards of major cities on the hobby-horse. Draisene owners formed clubs and held races and sporting events.

Obviously, the Draisene was only suitable for the young and sturdy. Also, since it was so heavy and cumbersome, it could not be pushed very far or fast. Therefore, there was great incentive to find a way to make this form of propulsion more efficient.

One of the earliest attempts at mechanizing the hobby-horse was made by an Englishman, Lewis Gompertz, who in 1821 devised a rack-and-pinion arrangement that enabled the rider to pull the handlebars back and forth. By pushing with his feet and pulling with his arms, he could presumably go faster and farther. How he steered this contraption at the same time has not been recorded, but most likely it was inaccurate.

Bicycling really began to take over the streets and countryside when an enterprising Englishman named Kirkpatrick MacMillan put foot pedals on the front wheel of the hobby-horse in 1835. By the mid-1800s, it was truly the fad of the century. Young people found bicycling a good way to get out from under the stern eye of their parents; society saw the bicycle as an expensive and exclusive toy and pastime; and sporting enthusiasts of all ages adopted one of the thousands of variations of the two-wheeler for their activities.

As the bicycle improved, more and more people began to ride and even to go on picnics in the country and take short tours. At last man was free from the horse and wagon. A bicycle never needed daily cleaning and currying; it didn't eat, and it did not use an expensive harness that took time to put on and take off. One could jump on his bicycle and quickly be away from his house. The impact of the bicycle was almost as great, in fact, as the advent of the Model T Ford. Much to the indignation and consternation of their elders and the ministers of the day, young boys and girls could ride out into the country together. Women's fashions changed to suit the bicycle. Clothes became less confining; the Gibson Girl on her bicycle, with her voluminous bloomers and leg-of-mutton sleeves, set a new style (Fig. 128).

Just as with the automobile, the first bicycles were costly, so in the beginning, they were the playthings of the wealthy only. Between 1890 and 1896, over $100 million was spent on bicycles. If you consider $250 too high a price for the best modern bicycle, what would you think about paying $800? The $100 price for bikes in 1896 is the equivalent of $800 today. There was a cheaper model available for $80. The earliest bicycles

Fig. 128: This old photograph shows an early female bike enthusiast in the clothing fashion of the day. (*The Bettmann Archive*)

—those sold in the 1860s—cost upward of $300 (which would be $2,400 today). Complicated machines, such as tandems and two- and even three-seat side-by-side rigs, cost even more.

The exhilarating new freedom of mobility which the bicycle brought to the common man was undoubtedly the cause of what was truly a bicycle mania in the 1800s. An early form of this velocipede was introduced to the United States from England in 1869. This machine had iron-rimmed wooden wheels, for which it was nicknamed the "boneshaker." The front wheel was equipped with pedals.

The velocipede became so popular that riding academies with indoor rinks were established where would-be cyclists were taught, and where feats of riding skill were performed before enthralled audiences. Cycling clubs were formed in large cities across the nation by social sets, and were soon very exclusive indeed. The Michaux Cycle Club of New York

Fig. 129: The bicycle fad at its peak. New York's Michaux Cycle Club. (*The Bettmann Archive*)

(Fig. 129), for example, was housed in an elegant three-story brownstone mansion. Its riding rink was well lighted, and ladies and gentlemen could watch riders drill from balconies, while waiters brought them food and drinks.

The five-foot-high "Penny-Farthing," which emerged in England in 1872 (Fig. 131), was an outgrowth of the boneshaker, and an attempt at achieving more speed. It wasn't long before an enterprising engineer figured out that the bigger the wheel with the pedals, the faster the bicycle would go (up to a point, that is). Eventually, the wheel diameter became too big for even the strongest human to push. It would seem that

Fig. 130: View of Oldreive's tricycle, or the new iron horse, with a lady inside. (*The Bettmann Archive*)

bicycles developed backward for a while, until the Penny-Farthing or "ordinary," as it was called in the United States, eventually became a dangerous thing to ride, with its sixty-inch-diameter front wheel and tiny rear wheel. The ordinary was very unstable—if the rider hit a pothole, he could easily be thrown over the front wheel from a height of more than five feet, and possibly at a speed of six to ten miles an hour. There were a good many fatalities and cracked heads associated with it. Only the novelty of cycling and the freedom of movement it gave to riders accounted for the continued growth of the sport when this machine was in its heyday.

In 1876, Colonel Albert A. Pope of Massachusetts began to import these high-wheelers from England, and in 1878, he began to manufacture them in Boston. At this time the ordinary weighed around sixty pounds and cost $150, which would be about $1,200 today.

Prominent men of the day—one might call them the forerunners of our "jet set"—biked around the country on ordinarys. Well-known social fig-

Fig. 131: American wheelmen reposing in the woods, ca. 1890. (*The Bettmann Archive*)

ures made headlines by touring from coast to coast, from Chicago to New York, and New York to Boston. British nobility in the 1880s rode bikes around their estates, and even the Prince of Wales attended the bicycle races of the day. Bicycle clubs grew and became ritualized and institutionalized as the bicycle became improved mechanically.

In 1885 the high-wheeled ordinary gave way to the "safety bicycle," invented by an Englishman, J. K. Starley. This bicycle had a chain-driven rear wheel, and wheels about thirty inches in diameter, with solid rubber tires. Three years later, an Irish veterinary surgeon produced an invention without which the automobile could never have flourished. Dr. J. B. Dunlop of Belfast, Ireland, gave a hard-tired tricycle to his son, Johnny, who reported that his new present was quite uncomfortable and very hard to pedal. Dr. Dunlop liked to tinker in his spare time, and one of his hobbies was fabricating his own gloves out of canvas and rubber From these he devised a set of "gloves" that could be filled with air for his son's tricycle. From rubber sheeting and strips of linen from one of his wife's old dresses, he built an air-filled tire, thus the first pneumatic bicycle tire.

Dr. Dunlop continued to make improvements on his tire until one day his friend, William Hume, president of the Belfast Cruiser's Cycling Club, persuaded him to make up a pair of tires for his racing machine. With his new tires, Mr. Hume easily beat the crack cyclists of the area in a race on May 18, 1889. After this, Dr. Dunlop was in business, and soon pneumatic tires were being manufactured by a number of firms in the United States. By 1891, the pneumatic tire was an accepted bicycle feature. The fad continued to flourish and spread.

During the 1890s, the bicycle population grew by leaps and bounds—by 1896, there were over 400 bicycle manufacturers in the United States alone. The bicycle craze even alarmed businessmen in major cities for a while. They thought the bicycle would bring the nation to economic collapse, and there were a number of compelling statistics to bear them out. The bicycle was not only a status symbol of major importance; it was the only way the average person could move about, unless he owned a horse and carriage. By 1896, the watch and jewelry business had fallen almost to zero, piano sales had been cut in half, and book sales had dropped disastrously. Apparently, no one stayed home and played the piano or read, and instead of buying jewelry, people bought bicycles.

Also, most people must have been too tired or too broke at night to go to the theatre, because attendance at theatrical performances also fell off drastically during the 1890s. The song that would have reached the top of the hit parade, had there been one in 1896, was about a girl named Daisy and her "bicycle built for two."

There were also plays written about bicycling. *The Bicyclers,* by John Kendrick Bangs, was a farce published by Harper & Brothers in 1896. It opens in the drawing room of Mr. and Mrs. Thaddeus Perkins, at their home in New York's Gramercy Square. It is early evening.

The bell rings and Mr. Perkins, attired in a cycling costume of knickers and socks, answers the door. His friend, Ed Barlow, is at the door, attired in evening dress. There follows much good-humored banter, during which Ed asks Thad if he might speak to his father. It seems that up until the bicycle craze only children wore knickers. Ed's wife, it is revealed, is en route by bicycle from the Barlow home in the upper Seventies, a distance of some eight miles from Gramercy Square.

While waiting for the arrival of Mrs. Barlow, Thad Perkins brags about his new "Czar" bicycle. He says, in answer to Ed Barlow's question about whether he's had any riding lessons:

"None yet. Fact is, just got my wheel. That's it, over by the door—pneumatic tires, tool-chest, cyclometer, lamp—all for a hun. The only thing they gave me extra was a Ki-Yi gun; it's filled with ammonia and it shoots dogs. You shoot it into the dog's face; it doesn't hurt him, but it gives him something to think of."

While Mr. and Mrs. Perkins and Ed Barlow await the arrival of Mrs. Barlow, the phone rings. It is Mrs. Barlow, in great agitation, phoning from a police station. She has been arrested for riding without a light. Ed Barlow, in his concern about his wife, forgets that he's had no riding experience, and jumps on Thad's bicycle. The play ends with Barlow's voice, off-stage, louder at times, then fainter, as he circles around and around the block, not knowing how to steer properly, or how to stop.

Much of the dialogue in the play is devoted to the merits and shortcomings of various makes of bicycles. Certainly, bicyclists of the 1890s had a good many machines to talk about, just as car owners do today.

Among the bicycle manufacturers of the era were many famous names —Henry Ford, Wilbur and Orville Wright, Glenn Curtiss, and Charles Duryea. United States manufacturers alone produced and sold 2,000,000 bicycles in 1897, when the population was 72,189,000—that is, 27.7 bicycles were sold per 1,000 people. It wasn't until 1947 that bicycle sales exceeded 2,000,000 and by that time the population was 146,093,000, so the 2.8 million bicycles sold in 1947 amounted only to 19.17 bikes per 1,000 population. By contrast, in 1972 an estimated 13.5 million bicycles were sold in the U.S., when the population was 208 million, so bicycle sales amounted to 64.9 per thousand, a new all-time high, and an increase of 419% over 1968. Sales in 1973 were around 14 million.

The following description of the bicycle business in the February, 1896, issue of *Outing* Magazine resembles an article in today's *Business Week*. Cycling in those days was a sport of the wealthy. *Outing* was devoted to the leisure time of the moneyed class, somewhat like today's *Holiday*.

> The cycle trade is now one of the chief industries of the world. Its ramifications are beyond ordinary comprehension. Its prosperity contributes in no small degree to that of the steel, wire, rubber, and leather markets. Time was when the spider web monsters, now nearly extinct, were built in one story annexes to English and American machine shops; now a single patented type of a jointless wood rim, one of the minor parts of a modern bicycle, is the sole product of an English factory covering over two acres of ground. A decade ago the American steel tube industry was unprofitable. The production of this most essential part of cycle construction has, during the past two years, been unequal to the demand, and even now every high-grade tube mill in this country is working night and day on orders that will keep them busy throughout the year. Nearly every season since 1890 has witnessed a doubling of the number of our factories and a multiplication of the product of a large proportion of the older ones. Yet the supply from the opening of last season to mid-summer was unequal to the demand, and although preparations of astounding proportions have been and are being made to meet with a multiplicity of models of the most approved designs and best workmanship, the demands of '96, the prospects are that the field offers reasonable prosperity to all makers of high-grade products. The present prices are quite reasonable, considering the quality of material and workmanship involved. Prices will be very generally maintained, and the number of riders, of both sexes, will be at least doubled.

It might interest some of our readers to review the specifications of a few of the safety bicycles of the 1890s. For example, the new 1898 line of Columbia bicycles, made by Pope Manufacturing Company, had a split crank shaft. Model 40 Columbia "light roadsters," selling for $100, had a "23-inch frame, 10-inch steering head, 28-inch wheels, 1⅝ pneumatic 'Hartford' tires, detachable sprockets, improved self-oiling chain, 6¾-inch patent round cranks, 5-inch tread, 3⅝-inch pedals, reversible handlebars, tubular seat rod, 66-inch gear and weighed 24 lbs."

Reviewing the specifications of these early bicycles points up the fact that gearing was low, which was necessary because there were no gearshift mechanisms in popular use at the time. In addition, the metallurgy of the bicycle frame and parts was far inferior to that of today's higher-quality bicycles. Gene Portuesi has told me that racing cyclists of the day could reach fantastic crank speeds. Zimmerman, a racing champion of the 1890s, could wind up to 140 crank revolutions per minute, which he had to do to get any speed out of the low gear ratios used even on the best racing bicycles of the day, A powerful modern racing cyclist would literally tear apart a racing bicycle of the 1890s, according to Portuesi.

Reviewing the names of the bicycle manufacturers of the 1890s, which seemed to be located in every major city, made me somewhat nostalgic. The Columbia line was popular up until the late 1920s or early 1930s. Some readers will remember the Spalding, Iver Johnson, Rambler, Remington, Waltham, and Singer bicycles.

Most of the better bicycles produced during this period had turned-down handlebars. One bicycle of 1896 even had an all-aluminum frame. It was manufactured by the Lu-mi-num Company of St. Louis, Missouri, and was successful enough to be licensed for production in England. You can buy all aluminum bicycles today, much improved, of course, over those of yesteryear, made by Hi-E Engineering Co., Nashville, Tennessee, and a new bike introduced at the 1973 Paris Bicycle Exposition, the tubing for which is provided by Super-Vitus of France.

The introduction of the "safety" bicycle, complete with chain drive and twenty-eight-inch wheels and brakes, did not guarantee safe cycling, however. A review of early cycling hazards makes cycling today seem safe, despite the density of urban motor vehicle traffic.

There may have been no automobiles back in the 1890s, but the roads were full of potholes, except for main arteries in and near major cities. And dogs attacked cyclists just as they do now. In those days, they were not restrained as they are today in cities.

Also, the general populace resented cyclists, just as many people were against the early automobiles. Farmers took personal delight in blocking the narrow roads of the day with their wagons, and they went as slowly as possible just to aggravate cyclists behind them. Country bumpkins took great delight in thrusting sticks between the spokes of cyclists' wheels to knock them off their seats. When people were riding the "penny-farthing" in the early days of cycling, a stick between the spokes of the high wheel brought disaster to the cyclist and guffaws from pranksters. One of the reasons the early cycling clubs were formed, aside from social purposes, was to provide protection against wanton attacks on cyclists. Horse-drawn vehicles, in addition to blocking the roads, were often deliberately sent careening into groups of cyclists, which injured the riders as well as harmed their machines.

In England, at this time, restaurant and tea-shop owners refused to serve cyclists, particularly female riders who wore what the owner of one restaurant described as "outlandish and shocking costumes."

The world's first nationwide cycling club, the British Touring Club, organized for political as well as for social reasons, was formed in England in 1878. It was an amalgamation of a number of small regional cycling organizations, and soon began publishing its own magazine, *The Bicycling Times*. In 1883, the BTC's name was changed to its present title, the Cyclists' Touring Club. The publication became known as *The Gazette* and is now *Cycle Touring*.

The Gazette was an outspoken and fearless defender of cyclists and cycling in England. In fact, its early pronouncements must have been fairly vitriolic, because in 1898 the editor was denounced for his outspokenness at one of the Club's national meetings by some of the members, some of whom were the representatives of bicycle manufacturers. At the same meeting, George Bernard Shaw, who was an ardent cyclist and lifetime member of the Club, arose to defend *The Gazette:* "Do you want it to contain fact or fiction?" he said. "You already have plenty of fiction in the advertising pages . . . I want to raise a strong protest against what has been said as to raising the tone of *The Gazette*. What we want above all things is an abusive *Gazette*. If I wish to read a nice complimentary cycling paper, one that has a good word for everybody, for every dealer and seller, and every sort of kind of invention—I can easily buy one for a penny at any news shop. But we want something quite in the opposite direction and we get it in our *Gazette,* even if that publication does sometimes refer to a lady's article as piffle." (Roars of laughter.) "In my view the gentlemen who object to ladies having to stand the same treatment as is meted out to men are the same people who object to ladies cycling altogether, and therefore I do not think they need be taken very seriously."

The hostility of the noncycling public seemed to be universal, so throughout the Western world, Europe and America, cyclists banded together into clubs such as the CTC to protect their status. In England, the Highway and Railway (Amendment) Act of 1878 referred specifically to bicycles, and gave county authorities power to regulate their use. Many of the laws passed by local authorities were unreasonably restrictive. In some instances, cyclists were forbidden to use public highways, or had to pull over and stop whenever a horse-drawn vehicle appeared on the horizon. Within ten years, however, the CTC had grown enough in size and importance so that it was able to push through Parliament what became known as the Magna Carta of Bicyclists. The Local Government Act abolished the power given by the Highway and Railway Act to local county governments to regulate bicycling. This signaled further successes for the Club, which was able to push through other laws that provided for the improvement of highways, the safe carrying of bicycles on railroad baggage cars, and recourse against the antagonisms of the general public against cycling.

A landmark case occurred in 1899 in Surrey, England, when Lady Harbeton, an influential member of the CTC, was refused service in the coffee room of the Hautboy Hotel. They offered to serve her in the bar parlor instead. The Club jumped to Lady Harbeton's defense, and the hotel's owner was indicted for "wilfully and unlawfully neglecting and refusing to supply a traveller with victuals." Lady Harbeton showed the court a picture of herself, which was described as portraying "an elderly lady, wearing a pair of exceedingly baggy knickerbockers reaching below the knee, and a jacket which came well over the hips and opened sufficiently to reveal the silk blouse underneath."

In the summer of 1880, a group of American cyclists visited the CTC's headquarters in Liverpool, and returned to the United States to form the League of American Wheelmen, in Newport, Rhode Island. By 1898, membership in the League of American Wheelmen had soared to its all-time high of 102,636. But thanks to the horseless carriage, it dwindled to 8,629 by 1902.

In 1964, the League was reactivated, this time in Chicago, under the leadership of Joe Hart. With its membership exceeding 12,000, the L.A.W. today, as it was before the turn of the century, is dedicated to the needs and interests of the ardent cyclist. To the tourist traveling across the land, an L.A.W. membership roster is a sure guarantee of welcome in every community where the League has a chapter.

In the days before road maps, the L.A.W. published its own maps, lists of accommodations, condition of roads, and other vital information which was otherwise unobtainable. To embark on an extended tour without an L.A.W. touring bureau itinerary was unthinkable in those days. By 1890, the L.A.W. had a chapter in virtually every town big enough to have a hotel.

During its heyday, many famous men and women were L.A.W. members, among them Orville and Wilbur Wright, Commodore Vanderbilt, and even Diamond Jim Brady. The organization was a political force to be reckoned with, more because of the influence of its wealthy members than for the size of its membership. During the early days of its existence, the League faced many of the same problems as did its counterpart in Great Britain. Cyclists were denied the right of way in America, excluded from public parks, and horsemen and, later, early motorists deliberately crowded them off the highways. The L.A.W. first flexed its political muscle around 1884, when it dealt with the Haddonfield (N.J.) Turnpike case.[1] The turnpike authorities refused to permit cyclists on the turnpike. At that time, turnpikes were simply cross-state roads used by horse-drawn vehicles. There were no automobiles yet. The turnpike's ruling caused a furor among cyclists. If this was allowed it would set a precedent, which could restrict cyclists to cowpaths, or worse. With the backing of the League, the Philadelphia chapter brought a test case, which resulted in the turnpike authority's rescinding its no-cycling stricture.

Before this landmark decision in 1879, the New York Board of Commissioners had decided that bicycles in New York City's Central Park were an eyesore and a menace to the citizenry. Shortly after the League was formed, it took this case to the courts and, after an eight-year fight, was successful in getting the governor of New York to revoke all restrictions against bicycles. After this ruling, cyclists were free to ride on any public roadway in the state of New York, which set a precedent in other states which granted cyclists the same privileges. Today, New York's Central Park is the exclusive province of cyclists on weekends, weekdays from 10–4 P.M. and Tuesday evenings during the summer, when no automobiles are allowed in the park at all.

Under joint backing of the L.A.W. and the Bicycle Institute of America (an organization formed by United States bicycle manufacturers to promote cycling generally), bicycle paths are now being laid down by a number of cities and states throughout the country. Today there are a number of fine bicycle paths and trails. Chicago, for instance, has a cycle path that extends nearly the entire 20-mile length of the city, along Lake Michigan. Wisconsin has a trail across the state from LaCrosse to Kenosha (a distance of 350 miles). It traverses much of the state's most scenic spots. Fifty miles of it is over an abandoned, cinder-tracked railway that is restricted to bicycles, and far from any road. Milwaukee, Wisconsin; Clearwater, Florida; Arlington, Virginia; and many other cities also have good trails and paths now. There are also, or will be soon, bikeways in many of our national and state parks, including the Indiana Dunes National Lakeshore, Sleeping Bear Dunes National Park in Michigan, Cape Cod (Mass.) National Sea Shore, and Fire Island National Seashore in New York. I should point out that cross-state bicycle trails are also used by automobiles for much of the way, at least. However, these trails are carefully chosen back roads, which traverse scenic areas that bear little traffic and have a good black-top or concrete surface. Efforts are now being made to link cross-state trails so that cyclists can ride all the way across the nation.

[1] *American Cycling* (now *Bicycling!*), August, 1965.

These wonderful new bikeways might, and should, tempt you to take extended touring and cycle camping trips, but long-distance touring was a far different situation back before the automobile. The first man to cross the United States by bicycle was Thomas Stevens, who in 1884 rode a high-wheel "ordinary" from Oakland, California, to Boston. "Rode" is hardly accurate—Mr. Stevens carried, pushed, shoved, and dragged his seventy-five-pound steed across mountains, deserts, streams, and fields. His journey took him 103½ days. In comparison, in 1954, Richard Berg of Northbrook, Illinois, cycled from Santa Monica, California, to New York City in just over 14 days.

Mr. Stevens had a horrendous task. He rode an ungainly high-wheeler over roads that were largely uncharted (where they existed at all), and public accommodations were chancy all the way. Also, the attitudes of the people he met ranged from scornful indifference to downright hostility.

Let's take a look at the kind of bicycle Stevens rode. It had a high front wheel, about fifty inches in diameter, and a small rear wheel, about seventeen inches in diameter. The frame was like a curved backbone, topped by a saddle just aft of a pair of flat handlebars. The machine weighed about seventy-five pounds.

The high wheel was not very maneuverable. Stevens was wedged right up against the handlebars, so steering way was limited and sharp turns nearly impossible to make. He had to sit almost over the centerline of the front wheel, which made even slight uphill runs a matter of hard pedaling. Coasting downhill was precarious, for a small chuckhole in the road, or even a pebble, could upset the delicate balance of the rider and send him toppling headfirst toward an unyielding roadway. In fact, Stevens used to practice taking headers, and his skill at it probably contributed as much to his survival as did his cycling proficiency.

It was quite an eventful trip. Much happened to Tom Stevens, including being made to perform for a bunch of rowdy cowpokes who shot bullets around him as he rode in and around pool tables, being pursued by packs of coyotes, crossing a railroad trestle in the Rockies and discovering halfway across that a train was coming (he hung onto the side of the trestle, seventy-five-pound bicycle and all), fording rivers swollen to flood stage, riding down the Rockies at breakneck speed, with his metal brake spoons heated red hot, and being cursed at by boatmen on the Erie Canal, whose mules reared and balked at the sight of him. He was feted from Chicago on, and in Boston received the magnificent reception he deserved.

If you are interested in reading the complete account of this unusual trip, you might try to find a copy of the two-volume story of his adventure, *First Across America by Bicycle,* which was published in 1887. Original copies are rather hard to come by, according to Dr. Irving Leonard, who has published an excellent shorter version of his book which you may obtain for around $5.95 from Bear Camp Press, South Tamworth, New Hampshire. Copies of the original book are currently going for $50.00 or more!

Fine collections of old bicycles have been made by private collectors, such as Roger Johnson of Hadley, Massachusetts; and excellent museum collections are at the Smithsonian Institution, Washington, D.C.; Museum of Science and Industry, Chicago; Greenfield Village (Ford), Dearborn, Michigan; Carillon Park Museum, Dayton, Ohio; Franklin Institute, Philadelphia; New York Historical Society, New York; Ponderosa Museum, Quarryville, Pennsylvania; Pioneer Village, Minden, Nebraska; and the Technical Museums of London, England, Milan, Italy, and Vienna, Austria.

There have been other cross-country and even around-the-world trips by bicycle, many of which make fascinating reading to the experienced cycle tourist who has been through similar adventures. In 1894, a young American girl named Annie Londonberry set out one July morning to tour the world, which she succeeded in doing. She left without a penny, and earned over $2,000 en route from publicizing her cycling exploits. Another famous woman traveler was Fannie Bullock Workman, who spent ten years touring the world, accompanied by her husband William. Mrs. Workman was the wealthy daughter of a governor of Massachusetts, and her husband was a physician. Old photographs show Mrs. Workman mounted on her trusty Rover safety bicycle, clad always in a high-necked blouse, a voluminous skirt, and a pith helmet.

The Workmans made an unforgettable trip over the Atlas Mountains to the Sahara, in 1895. One can only marvel at their fortitude. They published at least three lengthy volumes of their trips, which, if you are lucky, you might find in your public library or an old bookstore.

Mr. Richard Berg's record-breaking fourteen-day trip across the United States in 1954, which we mentioned earlier, was not without incident. Berg, an experienced, twenty-three-year-old racing cyclist, rode a bicycle stripped down to the essentials, an eight-speed machine with tubular sew-up racing tires. He carried no luggage, not even a toothbrush or shaving kit. He made concessions to safety and comfort only; a rear light for night travel and a water bottle.

Berg left Santa Monica's City Hall, bound for New York, with speed his main concern. He crossed the Mohave Desert at night, as he had planned, and rode twenty-four hours a day more than once during this trip. Coming down the eastern slopes of the Rockies he often hit better than sixty miles per hour, as he was told by incredulous motorists after he passed them.

Berg stayed at any motel he came to, when he was tired from the day's exertions. If he could not find a motel, he would pull off into the nearest field for the night. His biggest problem was flat tires. It seems that out West, where the cactus grows, there are two-sided pronged thorns waiting in ambush on all roads. He used to spend his evenings repairing his sew-ups, and reports having had as many as thirteen flats in one day until he hit the plains of Kansas. Incidentally, he told me he would still use tubular sew-ups if he were to make the trip again, because he believes that thorns will pierce any tire, and tubulars make cycling much easier.

RACING BEGAN AT ONCE

Starting with the Draisene, and as each improved version of the bicycle became popular, stripped-down models were used in racing events. The first bicycle race in America—at least the first officially sanctioned race—was held in 1878, over a one-mile course. It was won by Will R. Pitman in three minutes and fifty-seven seconds of what must have been arduous exertion indeed. His machine was heavy, crude, and even more cumbersome than the racing bicycles of the 1890s. In 1895, the fastest racing cyclist beat the fastest race horse for the first time, when E. F. Leonert pedaled one mile in one minute and thirty-five seconds. At this time, also, cycle racing turned professional. Six-day bicycle races held at Madison Square Garden in New York drew thousands to view this murderous and bloody spectacle. The first six-day race, held in 1891 at the Garden, was won by William "Plugger" Martin, who pedaled 1,466 miles and four laps during the six days. The non-stop six-day race has been discontinued; however, a less gory version called the "Madison" is still run in Europe.

Perhaps the greatest bicycle racer of all time was A. A. Zimmerman. Zimmerman, a professional racer, was king of the wheel in both the United States and Europe, and is still talked about by racing cyclists today. In 1891, Zimmerman pedaled to a new world record for the half-mile—on the seventy-pound high-wheel "ordinary"—in one minute, 10¾ seconds.

Zimmerman violated all the laws and rules of training, going out with the boys and drinking and carousing, while his teammates slept. In one notable instance, he climbed on his trusty safety bicycle, after having

attended an all-night party and pedaled a paced mile in one minute, 57⅘ seconds at the annual L.A.W. meet in Asbury Park, New Jersey. But what seemed to gain Zimmerman the most notoriety was the fact that he never attempted to beat a record or win a race by any more effort or speed than was necessary. There is no record of how long he lived.

Until the advent of the automobile turned America's interest from bicycle to auto racing, many professional bicycle racers became wealthy from their winnings. In 1895, there were over 600 professional racing cyclists in the United States alone, and more than that in Europe. Today there are *no* professional racing cyclists in this country, although there are hundreds in Europe who have earned a lot of money from the sport. In Europe, bicycle racing has always been the principal national sport of many countries, such as Italy, France, Spain, and Belgium. The average low income of the European worker, plus the high price of gasoline, helped keep the bicycle popular, although, with the rising standard of living of the past few years, bicycling has decreased somewhat there. In the meantime, the sport has grown in popularity in America.

Early track records are mighty impressive today, when one considers the crude bicycles on which they were made. In 1895, the long-distance track record (made in Paris on September 8 and 9 by Constance Huret) was 529 miles, 585 yards, in 24 hours. This was a sustained average of about 22 miles per hour. By contrast, in 1968, Beryl Burton, England's current top female racer, made 100 miles in three hours and fifty-five minutes and five seconds, at an average speed of 25.4 miles per hour. In 1899, Charles "Mile-a-Minute" Murphy pedaled a record mile in 57.8 seconds, following a train over a boarded-over section of the Long Island Railroad. It wasn't until 1905 that a car beat this record, when Barney Oldfield did a mile in 55.8 seconds in Henry Ford's "999."

Fig. 132: Bicycle racing in the 1890s —an unusual action shot. (*The Bettmann Archive*)

Things got really fast later on. On May 17, 1941, Alfred Letourner zipped to 108.92 miles per hour behind a racing car at Bakersfield, California. Letourner rode a gear of 256.5, combining a microscopic six-tooth rear gear with a fifty-seven-tooth chainwheel which equals $^{12}\!/_{114}$ ½-inch pitchgear (one-inch pitch). On July 19, 1962, Jose Meiffret of France reached a fantastic 128 miles per hour behind a car on Germany's Autobahn.

ANSWERING THE COUNTRY'S CALL

There is one development on the history of bicycles we haven't mentioned so far. At one time, bicycling was threatened with incorporation into the army. The military mind of the 1890s clearly visualized the bicycle as an invaluable tool in advance scouting, for outpost duties, for patrols, and for convoys, and to enable officers to make quick observations.

Harper's Weekly's special bicycle issue of April 11, 1896, carried this notice: "It is in rapidly moving considerable bodies of infantry that the bicycle will find its highest function in time of war. Fancy a force of infantry, independent of roads and railroads moving in any direction, forty or fifty miles in one morning, and appearing on a field not weary and exhausted as after a two-day's march, but fresh and prepared to fight . . ."

The Italian army was the first to adopt the bicycle. In 1870, four bicycles were furnished to each regiment of infantry, "grenadiers, sappers and miners, engineers and cavalry. The machines are provided with a brake, lantern, knapsack, rifle support and a leather pouch for orders." I suppose the first folding bicycle was made with a soldier in mind, for,

Fig. 133: The use of bicycles by the military. In this photograph, two soldiers carry early collapsible bikes on their backs. (*The Bettmann Archive*)

in 1896, the French army had one with a hinged frame. This machine weighed only twenty-three pounds and could be carried slung over a soldier's back. In 1885, Austrian soldiers, carrying full field kit, made 100 miles per day with bicycles during field maneuvers, outdoing what the cavalry could do on horseback.

In America, the first branch of the military to use bicycles was the National Guard of Connecticut. Eventually, the U.S. Army Signal Corps and other divisions of the military used the bicycle as a direct weapon of war. The army bolted two bicycles side by side and mounted a "mountain-cannon" between them. A military tandem was equipped with rifles and revolvers as well as a field pack, and a duplex (tricycle) was rigged with a machine-gun. Another tricycle was equipped with a Colt rapid-firing machine-gun mounted on the headstay and handlebars.

Between 1890 and 1900, large numbers of soldiers learned how to ride, drill, and deploy on bicycles. New methods of using the bicycle were continually studied by an organization formed for this specific purpose.

The United States Military Wheelmen, a volunteer auxiliary adjunct to the National Guard, trained soldiers in the use of the bicycle. Lieutenant Whitney, of this association, stated in 1896: "The balance of power is so nicely adjusted that the chances in the coming conflict will be governed by efficiency in detailed preparation. The bicycle will weigh in the scale. We are told somewhere that for want of a horseshoe nail a battle was lost. In the next war, for want of a bicycle the independence of a nation may be forfeited."

Over the past 150 years, we have seen the bicycle evolve from a wealthy man's toy to a vehicle of precision and beauty, with an infinite variety of uses. There are faster ways of getting places but few more enjoyable than this ever-growing sport.

Fig. 134: Police in city and suburbs use bikes for patrol. This officer uses a bicycle in Hennepin County, Minneapolis. Bicycle mounties also patrol New York's Central Park, Fire Island off Long Island, New York, and a number of California cities. Though this photo shows a heavy "clunker," officers in other cities use faster, lighter 10-speed bikes, which make them far more mobile than officers on foot patrol. (*United Press International*)

Fig: 135: Bicycling is an ever-growing sport! New York City's Central Park is closed to automobiles during summer months on weekends and from 10:00 AM to 4:00 PM Monday through Friday, and on Tuesday and Wednesday evenings from 7:00 PM to 10:30 PM (subject to change), to allow cyclists to pedal freely without worry about traffic. Above, New Yorkers prepare for a "pedal-in" at Bethesda Fountain in the park. (*United Press International*)

10

ACCESSORIES,
PLAIN AND FANCY

The gadgets that are available to be hung on bicycles and weigh them down number in the hundreds. The accessories you will find really useful, however, are fairly few. Unless you look long and hard, most of the accessories you will see will be of poor quality. The truth of the matter is that many bicycle accessory equipment manufacturers persist in thinking of a bicycle as a toy, rather than the serious hobby it is for many thousands of adults.

LIGHTS

If you do any night cycling at all, good front and rear lights are a life-saving necessity. You will seldom need a front light to see where you are going, particularly on moonlit nights or lighted city streets, but both front and rear light *will* let the motorist see *you*, and are therefore vital to your safety.

A good rear light *must* be visible from both sides as well as from the rear. British Standard BS3648 specifies that rear lights shall have a re-flector, a feature I find makes for a highly visible light, one the motorist can see for several blocks. One light that has a reflector and which, unlike other bike lights, has a reliable switch and battery contacts, is the Sturmey Archer Rear Lamp and Battery Case. It has a separate case

Fig. 136: This Sturmey Archer rear light has reflector for brightness. Case fits on seat stays, light on left seat stay.

Fig. 137: Left, single-cell mini-lite fits on handlebar stem, is very light-weight, and throws enough of a beam so motorists can see you. Right, Raleigh Rearguard light has reflector, throws excellent ruby light, but so far is made only for right-hand seat stay mounting.

which takes two standard "D" cells, and a rear light visible from the rear and both sides, with a reflector (Fig. 136). The case is locked with a screw so batteries can't fall out under rough road vibration, a problem you'll find with other flimsy lights made to toy specifications. Another good rear light is EverReady's Rearguard (Fig. 137 right). This light is more brilliant than the Sturmey Archer unit, but unfortunately so far is made only to fit right-hand seat stays. Raleigh may, by the time this new revised issue is off the press, have left-hand Rearguards available, so keep after them.

A good front light, which won't show you where you're going but will show you to cars, is very light, takes a "D" cell, and mounts on handlebar stem left (Fig. 137 left), is available from Holdsworth (see Appendix).

Dynamo Lights

If you want to see where you're going, you'll have to use a dynamo light, or a carbide lamp. Dynamo lights are really no heavier than battery lamps, when you add weight of batteries versus generator, but they do

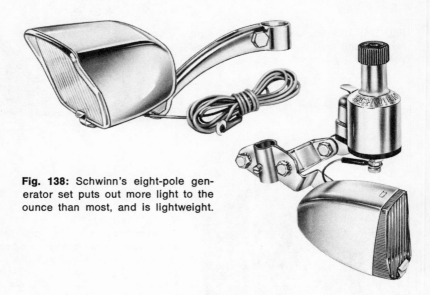

Fig. 138: Schwinn's eight-pole generator set puts out more light to the ounce than most, and is lightweight.

add drag, and when you stop so does the light. There's a wide quality variation in dynamo generator sets. The better sets have eight-pole generators, instead of six-pole, and so put out more power and light for their weight. Schwinn stores sell a dandy, powerful 8-pole generator-light set (Fig. 138) with front and rear lights that weighs only 12 ounces. This unit, model 04-200, puts out more light to the ounce than any generator set I've tested.

Carbide Lamps

You can step right back to the 1880s with Justrite's model 3-204 carbide lamp (see Fig. 101, page 220). It throws a powerful white beam, and can be quickly attached to and removed from front wheel quick-release hub. The light has a slight flicker which makes it an eye-stopper for motorists and pedestrians; truly an unusual light in this day and age. The four-inch reflector model is the best. A two-pound can of carbide comes with the light. One filling should last six to seven hours; all you need is carbide and water. If your hardware store can't supply you, write to Justrite Manufacturing Company, 2061 N. Southport Ave., Chicago, Illinois 60614. The lamp, empty, weighs about 12 ounces. (You'll still need a battery rear lamp.)

Justrite also makes a very powerful focusable battery light, model

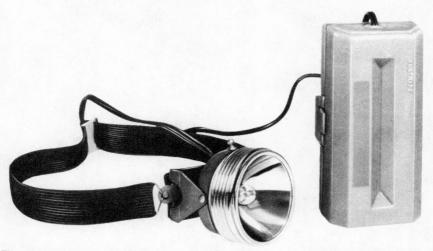

Fig. 139: Justrite headlamp throws powerful adjustable beam that can be aimed at motorists coming at you from the side by simply looking at the car. Can be spot or broad beam.

1904-0, with separate battery case good for seven hours, using four "D" cells, which can be mounted on your head so you can point at motorists coming at you at night from side streets, or make yourself highly visible to oncoming motorists by waving your head from side to side (Fig. 139).

Remember, you don't need to see where you're going on brightly lighted city streets, but you do need to light yourself up so motorists can see where you're going.

The so-called Dynahub used on Raleigh bicycles, usually on the front wheel, reduces generator drag considerably but, like the generator itself, it is heavy and will not work when the bicycle isn't moving.

There is one other light I recommend. This is a French-made light (Fig. 140) that can be strapped on an arm or leg. It costs only $2.50, without batteries, uses two "C" size flashlight cells, and weighs only five ounces with batteries. This light has a red light to the rear and a white light to the front, and, when strapped to a leg, the up-and-down motion of the leg adds extra visibility to it. On long night trips this light is an excellent back-up to main lights, if they fail. Detached, it can also be used to read maps, to signal with, and to make repairs by. These lamps are made by a number of companies. I've had trouble with some of them; the plastic neck was weak and so it was easy to strip threads. The ones Schwinn sells are the best, in my opinion, because they are very strong, and the head is more translucent.

Fig. 140: Here's a real attention-getter. This French-made light can be strapped on arm or, better yet, leg, where it throws a red light to rear and white light to front. Can also be used to read maps and the like.

NAIL PULLERS

Nail pullers are available but can be used only in tubular tires of the smooth tread type. They attach to the front and rear handbrake center post and ride lightly on the tire. If a nail, piece of glass, or other foreign body becomes embedded in the tread (which can cause a flat if not removed), the nail-puller accessory will scrape it away automatically. Nail pullers cost about $1.00 a pair and weigh about a half-ounce. They can be ordered from Cyclo-Pedia (see Appendix).

LOCKS AND CHAINS

The bike boom has brought a boom in bike thefts. Hundreds of thousands of bikes are being ripped off all over the country today, with a retail value in the millions. Organized gangs have factories that strip, sand-blast, and repaint stolen bicycles. Thieves use sophisticated techniques such as freezing hardened-steel lock shackles and chain links to −42° with Freon 22, so a sharp blow with a hammer will shatter hardened metal. And if F-22 won't work, liquid nitrogen with temperatures of −100° or colder will. I remember a police officer in Cambridge, Massachusetts, ruefully showing me all that was left of his own bike, a sawed-off lock shackle. Thieves are adept at concealing a pair of 18-inch bolt cutters in a paper sack with a hole at the end, snapping bike chains as they walk past, and coming back a few minutes later to pick up the bicycle. Thieves also use acid to weaken case-hardened chains. Case hardening means a microinch of the chain is hardened; soft steel is underneath. Acid etches away the case-hardened surface to let a hacksaw chew through the rest in seconds.

The moral of this sad tale is: Don't lock your bike to anything that can be stolen. I'd go one step further and say for 100% protection, keep your bike next to you at all times. Good bikes should be kept locked in your basement, *not* in the garage. If you take the bike to your office, chain it to your desk. When you eat out, chain the bicycle to a telephone post, *not* to a parking meter where it can be lifted off and put in a car trunk, lock and chain and all. In the restaurant, sit near the door with one eye on the bike all the time; be ready to run out at a moment's notice.

Other steps you can take to make it slower for a thief to make off with your bike are okay if you are able to run to the bike if someone starts working on it, but are no good as positive theft protection. I'm convinced there is no such thing as 100% protection; you may have a good lock, but the chain can always be cut. Some chains are harder to cut than others, not all padlocks offer good protection, and we'll review these in a moment. Let's sum up, first, methods of bike protection:

- *Don't lock a FINE bicycle to anything.* Keep your Cinelli, Masi, Paramount locked up at home when not out riding, and use a clunker for commuting. Fine bikes will be stripped down to the frame very quickly, if not stolen outright.
- *Lock less costly bikes to a tree,* telephone post, steel bike rack. Lock *both* wheels through frame to whatever you're locking it to. Remember, wheels can be easily removed and they are expensive. You'll have to risk your saddle.
- *Use a ⅜ in. x 5 ft. through-hardened* (not case-hardened) alloy steel chain, and a pin-tumbler padlock with pick-resistant, hardened shackle and body. The chain will weigh about 8 pounds (*with* the lock about 10 pounds). You can keep them both where you lock up, i.e., on campus, at the office,

Fig. 141: This American padlock and twisted cable is also a good combination deterrent to having your bike ripped off. But remember to lock the bike to something unrippable, such as a telephone post or concrete-embedded bike rack. Don't lock expensive bikes, though; keep these where you can eyeball them at all times, or locked in your basement. (Bolt basement windows, too.)

Fig. 142: In my opinion this is the best padlock on the market. An Ideal Security "Boss" model, it has a unique 16-pin tumbler that's highly pick-resistant, and a hardened shackle that dead-bolts at both sides. But any padlock is no better than its chain or cable, or what you tie it to. If you use a chain, use two or three padlocks to make things tougher for thieves.

etc., so you don't have to lug them around. I like the twisted wire cable with "eyes" at each end (Fig. 141), which *can* be hacksawed or cut with a bolt cutter, but not quickly or easily. The best moderately priced lock I've seen, and I've seen most, is the 16-pin tumbler "Boss" padlock by Ideal Security, available in hardware and lock stores (Fig. 142). The 16-pin brass tumbler has 16^{16} (millions) of combinations, is virtually pick-proof, has a solid brass body and shackle deadbolts at both heel and toe sides. The four-sided keys can't be duplicated except by a locksmith with special equipment. The 2-inch pin tumbler model DB-9626 should fit a ⅜-inch chain, since two sections of ⅜-inch chain equal ¾ inch.

· *Register bike serial number with local police.* Register also with International Cycling Association, which has a three-year registration program tied into local police organizations, with computer registration for quick, nationwide identification. As the ICA's program expands, more bikes will be recovered. Recovery rate is still dismally low. ICA is at Suite 405 Maritime Building, Seattle, Washington 98104.
· *With an electric engraving pencil, engrave your Social Security number* on small parts of bike, rims, hubs, stem (part that fits inside headset), seat post, bottom bracket, handlebars under tape.
· *Make sure your bicycle is covered by your renter's or home owner's comprehensive insurance policy.*
· *Keep a color photo of your bike on hand.*
· *Expedients to slow up anyone trying to ride off* with your bike include jamming a washer or coin into brake levers to hold brakes locked, throwing chain off freewheel, or tangling rubber shock cord in rear wheel spokes.

There are three or four motion-actuated alarm-type locks on the market. These use a sensitive wand that when in motion sets off a loud electric buzzer (the same buzzer that comes in kid bike horns). Given the state of public morality these days, I question whether a bike alarm lock will alarm a thief *or* the general public. It will alarm *you*, if you hear it, of course, so alarm locks do have their limited value, especially when you're in a tent at night and the bike is outside (Fig. 143).

Fig. 143: There are a number of alarm-type bike locks on the market. This one howls when the cable is cut; with fresh alkaline batteries it will howl for an hour. Other types don't have a cable, but have a motion-sensitive wand which sets off an alarm if the bicycle is moved. Best use for these alarms is on bike camping trips; they are lightweight, and when you're in a tent no one can make off with the bike without waking up the entire camp. (Raccoons can also knock into the bike and set off the alarm, which is a chance you'll have to take.) The alarm shown is by RYCO, One First Street, Los Altos, California. 94022. It weights about one pound.

Fig. 144: One of my favorite locks is this "Kryptonite" bicycle lock designed by a couple of bright young M.I.T. types. Made by KBL Corp., 20 E. Concord St., Boston, it's available in bike stores. It's made of heavy-gauge stainless steel, and is designed so the lock shackle is recessed into jaws of the lock so it cannot be reached by a cutter. The KBL people say they left a bike locked with the Kryptonite where it could be stolen. After two weeks the bike was still there, and there were cutter and hacksaw blade marks all over the lock. Lock weighs 2½ pounds with padlock.

Fig. 145: Another view of the Kryptonite lock, showing how the front wheel, removed, is locked together with the rear wheel to a tree. I prefer to lock the rear wheel and the frame to a tree, and take the front wheel along with me to wherever I am going.

Don't use cheap combination locks such as are used on school lockers. The shackle is hardened, but you can cut through the sheet metal casing in seconds and pry shackles out. Stranded aircraft cable, twisted and with a total diameter of ½ inch, is also hard to cut, lighter and easier to carry than an 8-pound chain, but I still prefer the chain for maximum security. Another good lock is the American (see Fig. 141). The ultimate in padlock security is expensive: Sargent & Greenleaf's "Impregnable" padlock. Shackle resists 8,000 pounds pull pressure, is of high carbon steel, deadbolts at heel and toe. Body is hardened laminated steel. These are the kind of padlocks you see on fences protecting high security areas. Remember, you can't *buy* 100% security, but you *can* make your bike tough to steal (Figs. 144 and 145).

KICKSTANDS

I think a kickstand is an utterly unnecessary piece of equipment. In the first place, it is unreliable. A good breeze or a slight shove from a passer-by can knock the bicycle over, and in doing so, damage the derailleur. It is much better, in my opinion, to lean the bicycle against a tree, store-front, or telephone post, where you can also put a chain around it. Kick-stands are heavy; they add at least a pound of dead weight. They can actually damage the chain stays, too, because it's easy to overtighten the kickstand when it becomes loose, as it will, and in so doing, you can bend and weaken the chains stays behind the bottom bracket.

ODOMETERS AND SPEEDOMETERS

An odometer is a good idea if you like to keep accurate track of your cycling mileage. The Lucas cyclometer, available to fit twenty-four-, twenty-six-, twenty-seven-, and twenty-eight-inch wheels, costs $2.50 and fits on the front fork. However, I find the tick of the cyclometer, as the metal striker on the spoke hits the counter wheel, annoying. I prefer the more natural sounds of the countryside.

As for speedometers, these are strictly in the gadget and toy category. They all have a habit of going bad and causing trouble on trips, the most common complaint being jammed cables. There is considerable drag on the wheel striker—try moving the striker by hand and imagine this working against your pedaling. And the speedometer adds another unnecessary pound or so to your bicycle, which makes pedaling still more difficult. Since most of us who tour seldom, if ever, at least on a flat road, get above fifteen miles an hour for very long, the idea of carrying around a toy to check speed is ridiculous. A speedometer is fine for a child, who still equates a bicycle with a scaled-down automobile.

TIRE PUMPS

For tubular tires, the best bicycle-mounted pump you can buy is the "Silca" with a Campagnolo head. This pump comes in various lengths to fit your top or down tube. It can also be mounted on the seat tube. A Japanese version of this pump has a good head, but the pump shaft is weak and easy to snap or bend if you strain it hard, so I don't recommend this pump.

Until its introduction at the 1973 Paris Bicycle Exposition, there was no decent pump for clincher tires with Schraeder valve tubes. The pumps for these valves were made to toy standards, easy to break, hard to pump and almost useless. Finally a new pump has been introduced that, by the time this revision is published, should be available through better bicycle shops, for Schraeder valve tubes. It's the new Zefal HP pump, which also has a wing fitting to lock the pump on the valve so you can pump without having to hold the pump firmly on the valve. This is a pump made to highest standards; I have used it and can recommend it highly. Zefal also has a similar pump, but for Presta valves, the skinnier kind that come on tubular tires and some European clincher tubes. For your home pump you can have a Presta or a Schraeder valve head, as noted below.

Bigger hand pumps are great, but of course too heavy to carry on a bike. A number of firms make adapters to fit these large hand pumps so you can pump up your Presta valve tubular tires at home, with about half the strokes and twice as fast as with the Silca bike-mounted pump. Groaning experience tells me it takes about 55 to 60 hard pumps with a Silca but only 20 to 25 pumps with a big hand pump to bring tubulars up to 90 psi. The best tubular-tire hand pump I can find has a U.S.-made Presta valve head that really works. Trouble with other press-on tubular Presta valve-head adapters is that they tend to slip off under pressure as you pump. All of these heads have a hard rubber core that's supposed to keep the head on the Presta valve. The only one that really works for me is made by Eco-Cyclery, and if you can't find one in a bike shop (Fig.

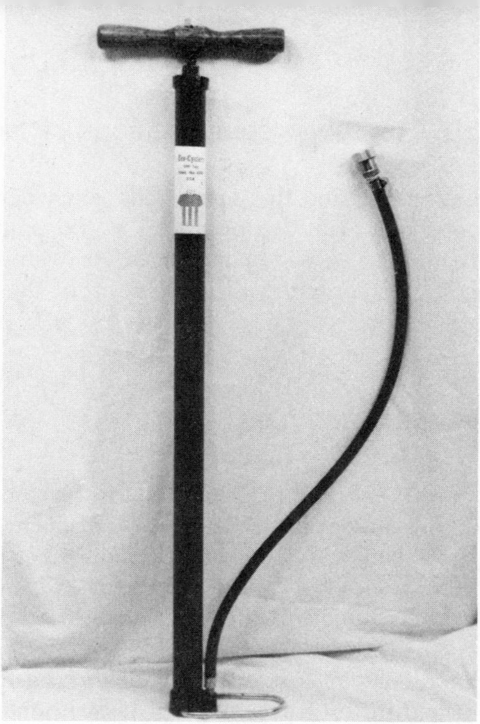

Fig. 146: For Presta valves (as on tubular and some clincher tire tubes) this hand pump has a press-on head that really works, makes inflating by hand quick and easy. From Eco-Cyclery, 5907 Todd, Oxford, Ohio 45056, or your bike shop.

146) write this firm at 5907 Todd, Oxford, Ohio 45056. If you already have a big pump, you can buy the head only. The firm also has replacement rubber cores for this head.

The best clincher-tire large hand pump is sold by Schwinn, (Fig. 147). It has an air chamber and a pressure gauge. This is the easiest pump I

Fig. 147: For clincher tires or Presta, if you change heads to the Eco-Cyclery model (see text), the best hand pump I have used is this air-chamber model with pressure gauge, that you can buy in any Schwinn store.

have used, and the gauge tells you when you have reached the pressure you want. You can pump up to 150 pounds with ease. As you withdraw the hose, you will hear a lot of air escaping; don't worry, it's not your tire going flat, only the air coming out of the air chamber on the pump.

FEEDER BOTTLES

Feeder bottles, to carry liquids for long tours, are available in either aluminum or plastic. They are kept in cages mounted on either the handlebars, seat, or down tube. Aluminum bottles are more elegant, but I prefer plastic ones for lightness. A plastic feeder bottle, with its cage, weighs only six ounces. A thermos feeder bottle is also available, if you like to keep drinkables hot or cold. I would recommend mounting bottles on handlebar or seat tube. On downtube they quickly get messy from dirt kicked up by front wheel (if it's without fenders).

HORNS

The loudest horn you can buy is a light, miniature Freon horn, a small brother to Freon boat horns. It comes with a clip for stem mounting, and makes quite a blast. After using such a horn for a year, I can report that it serves only to frighten motorists and to reduce one's own feeling of anger and frustration. This horn never saved me from an accident. I find that if I have to warn a pedestrian that I am approaching, a shout serves just as well, and it also prevents him from suffering a heart attack as a result of the sudden blast of the Freon.

There *was* one occasion when my Freon horn came in very handy. I was in immediate danger of being jumped by hoodlums in a park one night. When the youngsters suddenly appeared from the bushes in my path, I waited until I was almost upon them before blasting my horn. They fled with satisfying alacrity. The lesson of this story, however, is not to buy this horn but to avoid riding in lonely places at night.

For sidewalk riding, for children, a simple handlebar, bell-type, lever-actuated tinkle horn is pleasant sounding and unmistakably warns a pedestrian that a bicycle is approaching. All other horns are either junk that soon stops working, such as the bulb-bugle horn, or too heavy, too expensive, or easily damaged. There's nothing, in my opinion, like one's own vocal cords to sound an alarm. They're free, automatically installed, and add no extra weight.

BICYCLE CARRIERS

Most of us live in big cities or major metropolitan areas, where opportunities for enjoyable, leisurely, and scenic cycling are almost nonexistent. For this reason, many cyclists prefer to get a head start on a weekend of cycling by carrying their bicycles on cars the fifteen to twenty-five miles necessary to get out into the country.

The problem is that even disassembled bicycles are ungainly things that take up a lot of room in a car. Without some sort of carrier, transporting more than two assembled bicycles at a time is well beyond the space capacity of the average car. A good deal of attention has been given to the problem of car bicycle carriers. The best results have been the homemade contraptions. All the commercially made carriers are limited to two bicycles, some are junky, all are costly. You would be much better off making your own.

How to Make Your Own Carrier

Anyone can easily make his own rooftop bicycle carrier with a little ingenuity and effort. Start with any ordinary pair of metal bar roof carriers, the kind that clamp to rain gutters or bolt to the roof, *not* the suction cup type, which can come loose.

L. L. Bean (see Appendix) carries an aluminum alloy load bracket with drip eave clamps and carriage bolts for your own wood crossbar, costing $12.60 for a set of four (Fig. 148). These are made by Quik-n-Easy Products, Monrovia, California.

"Chick" Mead, a bicycle dealer in Marion, Massachusetts, has designed a fine homemade carrier. His instructions, which follow, are simple (Fig. 149). They call for:

1. One set of brackets, L. L. Bean "Quick-N-Easy," or Sears Roebuck rain-gutter type.
2. Two 9-foot two-by-fours.
3. One quart wood preservative.
4. 12 carriage bolts ¼ in.x 1⅝ in.

Fig. 148: You can carry up to five or even six bicycles on the roof of even the smallest European car with the "Chick" Mead carrier illustrated in Figures 149 to 151. These cast aluminum brackets are sturdy, reliable, and inexpensive. From L. L. Bean (see Appendix).

5. 12 feet of ⅜- or ⁷⁄₁₆-inch aluminum round (stock) for pegs.
6. 64 one-inch-wide rubber bands, made from old tire tubes.
7. Two pieces of ⅛ x 1 x 32-inch aluminum flat or ¾-inch angle stock for adjustable struts (total 62 inches).
8. One pint weatherstrip adhesive to glue on padding
9. Scrap ends of thick felt or carpeting for padding
10. One quart exterior-grade preservative finish paint, such as Rustoleum.
11. One quart liquid Neoprene for waterproofing top of pad.

If you can't scrounge old inner tubes from a gas station, try a foreign car dealer, such as a Peugeot garage, where inner tubes are used with radial tires.

Plans should be self-explanatory. An unexpected side benefit was the fact that after about a thousand miles of driving, the slight bouncing up and down movement thoroughly broke in all our saddles! Note that the adjustable struts of aluminum flats or angles permit saddle position to be changed to conform to wheelbase of bicycle.

The nine-inch dowels of the aluminum rod should stick out about two inches from the two-by-fours.

Allowing thirteen inches apart for each bicycle, you will be able to carry up to four bicycles on this carrier. Be sure to pad the two-by-fours liberally with old hose or other soft but durable material, to avoid marring the handlebar finish.

When ready to tie down the bicycle, use the rubber holders (or leather straps) to tie both sides of the handlebars and the seat to the carrier.

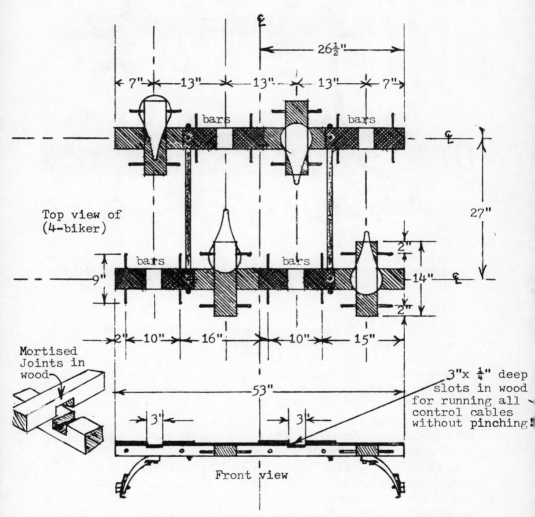

Fig. 149: This "Chick" Mead car-top bike carrier will hold four bicycles and you can make it for about $15.00 even if you have ten thumbs.

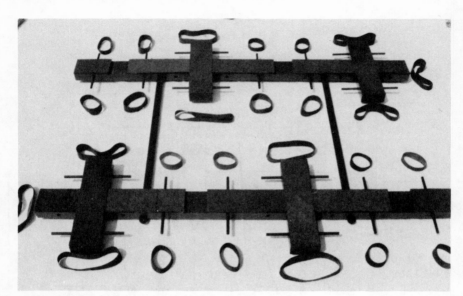

Fig. 150: Photo shows "Chick" Mead carrier ready to mount on roof-top carrier fixture. Note staggered arrangement so bikes can be mounted front and rear alternately.

Stagger bicycles on the carrier, as shown in Fig. 150. And make sure the carrier is securely fastened to the car roof!

I made one of these "Chick" Mead carriers myself, and I am able to carry four bikes on my Volkswagen (Fig. 151). My expenses totaled about $15.00 for everything, and the result is a very useful and practical carrier indeed.

With any bike carrier, remember that you must unload the bicycles before driving into the garage. This seems obvious, but some people have been known to forget it with disastrous results.

Incidentally, the "Chick" Mead bike carrier is also very handy for transporting luggage and other miscellany. The aluminum rod tiedowns are very convenient for securing almost anything. My carrier is always fitted to my car, though it could be removed quickly and easily.

Fig. 151: This is how the "Chick" Mead carrier looks on a Volkswagen square-back Elastic bands made from an old tire tube hold the bicycles firmly, even at high car speeds. (*Chick Mead*)

BABY SEATS

This popular accessory can be used to safely carry a small child up to three or four years of age (Fig. 152). However, only the *rear* baby seat is safe. Balancing a child weighing up to thirty or forty pounds on a carrier mounted over the front wheel makes for a very unbalanced situation and is dangerous.

After examining and using a number of these carriers, I recommend a child-carrier design that is suitable for either 26-inch or 27-inch wheels and which has leg shields to keep the child's feet out of the spokes. A

Fig. 152: Safe way to carry children is with bike-trailer baby-seat combination, made by Cannondale Corporation. Trailer helps balance bicycle; with seat removed it doubles as grocery or camping-gear toter, and as a yard cart.

child of two or three can easily get his foot tangled up in the spokes, and, if this happens, you are in for a nasty spill, at best, and, at worst. for both a spill and an injured foot for your child.

The seat should have an adjustable foot rest and a safety strap to tie the child in. One such design costs about $9.00, weighs two pounds, eight ounces, and is obtainable from your bicycle store or from Cyclo-Pedia. There are a number of other seats on the market, but this is the only one I have found with leg shields.

The safest way to carry a child or even two or three, if they're small enough, is in a trailer made specially for bicycles. Such a trailer, made by Cannondale Corporation, 35 Pulaski Street, Stamford, Connecticut 06902, should be available from your local bicycle shop. It has as an accessory a molded plastic seat with safety strap that will hold two or three small children safely in place. The seat is easily removed so the trailer can be used for shopping or for bicycle touring and camping. The trailer also comes with a zippered nylon cover for completely enclosing a week's load of groceries for a family of four, or camping gear. The child seat can be installed on top of the nylon bag when zippered wide open. The trailer hitches onto the seat post quickly, has an additional wire cable safety hitch. My Cannondale trailer also serves double duty as a yard carryall for leaves, plants and anything else I used to use the heavier wheelbarrow for. And children consider riding in this trailer about as much fun as going to an amusement park. First time I took it out into the street I saw every kid on the block from three to ten begging for rides. I should also point out that the trailer actually adds very little side space; you can zip through street traffic about as well with it as without it, but you should be careful about cornering and slow down for all turns. Remember, too, you have added weight, especially if you carry kids, so brake sooner than usual. And keep the trailer seat safety belt fastened!

11

YOUR TIRES
AND HOW TO CARE FOR THEM

There is a lot more to bicycle tires than first meets the eye. With proper care they can last a lot longer than you think they can, and they need not go flat so often. But you should know that not even the knobby, balloon-tired monsters are immune to abuse. You simply cannot ride up and down curbs as though they weren't there, or ride on tires half-inflated, and not expect a bruised tire and a punctured tube, not to mention a ruined rim.

On the other hand, you can cross the continent on flimsy road-racing tires that weigh less than sixteen ounces including tire, tube, and valve, if you know how to take care of the tire, and ride properly.

All this is to introduce one of the least understood aspects of bicycle maintenance and use—tires and tubing.

With a little care in use and maintenance, bicycle tires can last for thousands of miles. The scrap pile of cut and bruised tires that you can see in any bicycle store, however, is sad testimony to the fact that young cyclists, and some adults, need to learn more about tire care. Proper care will yield many more miles of life from tires than most cyclists seem to get today. When it comes to the more costly tubular-type tires used for touring and racing, careful maintenance is essential.

There are many different kinds of tires—tires for everyday use; for road, track, and cross-country racing; for rain and mud; for high speed; for touring; and for carrying loads (Table 18 and Fig. 153). But the tire is only part of the story; the entire bicycle must be considered in the light of the kind of riding you plan to do.

TABLE 18 · **Tubular Tire Applications**

There are literally dozens of different types of tubular (sewn-up) tires. Table 18 lists most of the popular applications and the tires available for these uses, ranging from racing of all kinds to touring. The "Clement Elvezia" is recommended for cycle touring.

MAKE	RECOMMENDED FOR	TREAD PATTERN	WEIGHT (oz.)
Vittoria—			
201B Butyl	Training & Touring	Mixed	13
Gran Turismo	Training & Touring	Mixed	12
Super Sport	24-hour Time Trial & Touring, Short, medium and long	Mixed	10½
Competizione	Time Trials & Massed Starts	Ribbed	10
Pistard Silk	Concrete Track	Smooth	4½
Pistard Cotton	Wood Track	Smooth	5
Clement—			
No. 1 Silk	Smooth Tracks	Matt	4
Super 10	Track, short distance road	Fine rib	8
No. 50 Silk	Road, medium	Fine rib	11
No. 48 Silk	Massed Start Training	Rough file	12
Gran Sport	Massed Start	Fine rib/File	14
Elvezia	Training	Fine rib	14
Freebairn—			
Track	All tracks	Matt	8
Road	General Road	Rib	11
D'Allesandro—			
Imperforabile	Road	File or matt	9¾
Primo	Track/Short Road	Matt	7¼
Criterium	Distance Road	Matt	8¾
Imperial	Road		12½
Leone	Massed Start	File	13¼
Sport	Rough Road surfaces	File	14
Worthy	Training, Grass tracks	File	16
Constrictor—			
Viper	Road	File	12
Fifty	Road	File	11
Supalatti	Path/Short Distance Road	Centre File	10

   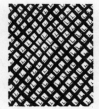 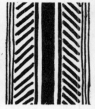

| Multirib | Diagonal or herringbone | File (lot of little pyramids) | Mesh (lot of little pits) | Mixed . . . here consisting of rib, diagonal and rib |

1. Everyday or training 12/ 15 ozs. Mesh or file treads are common

2. Vulcanized road racing 7/11 ozs. Tread according to taste. Multirib shown here

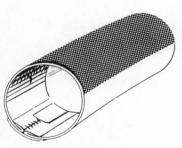 

3. Handmade road racing shown here with matt tread. Range between 6 and 10 ozs.

4. Cyclo Cross. Very specialized tread to operate on loose or muddy surfaces. Weight 10/16 ozs.

Fig. 153: Just a few of the tire patterns of tubular tires. Note how these tires are sewn up all around, so that the tire and tube become virtually one unit. The heavier tires, shown at top left, used for training and weighing from 12 to 15 ounces, are also ideal for cycle touring.

TIRE PRESSURE

Probably the most neglected aspect of tire care is air pressure. Use this tire chart as a guide to correct minimum tire pressure, increasing pressure according to the weight of the rider and any extra load carried.

TABLE 19 · **Air Pressure**

In general, these are the air pressures you should use with various types of tires. Remember that if you are a bit heavier than average, you should add about five pounds more pressure. If tire bulges markedly, you are too heavy for the pressure used. Tire should not bulge, or at most, bulge very slightly when ridden.

TIRE SIZE	AIR PRESSURE (in lbs. per sq. in.)
12 in. x 1⅜ in.	30–40
16 in. x 1⅜ in.	30–40
18 in. x 1⅜ in.	35–45
20 in. x 1⅜ in.	45–50
24 in. x 2⅛ in.	35–45
26 in. x 1¼ in.	45–50
26 in. x 1⅜ in.	45–50
26 in. x 1¾ in.	30–35
26 in. x 2⅛ in.	35–45
27 in. x 1¼ in.	75–85
27-in. tubular tires	Tracks with very smooth surfaces: rear wheels, 100–130; front tires, 90–110
	Tracks with uneven surfaces: rear tires, 90–100; front tires, 90
	Road racing: rear tires, 90–100; front tires, 90, depending on road conditions
	Touring: rear tires, 85–100, depending on load and road conditions; front tires, 85–90

For tires used on tandem bicycles, increase above pressures from 10 to 20 pounds per square inch to handle the extra load safely.

NOTE: On cool days one can inflate tires to maximum pressures safely. However, on very hot days, with temperatures in the eighties and higher, it is safer to reduce pressures by 3 to 5 pounds under the maximum to avoid heat buildup. Air expands as it heats, and on a hot day, you could experience a blow-out if your bike stands exposed to the sun.

HOW TO INFLATE

Most tires are inflated at gasoline service stations. Many tires are also overinflated and blown out at service stations. Bicycle tires take so little air that with the automatic pressure gauges that provide air at upward of 200 pounds per square inch, it takes just seconds to fill a tire and a split second more to blow it out. Tire gauges on hoses at service stations can be off as much as 10 pounds either way, because (among other reasons) the volume of air in bike tires is so low it's hard to get an accurate reading when the gauge is upward of twenty-five feet of hose away from the tire valve. I recommend using a hand pump. Best hand pump I've used is sold by Schwinn (see Fig. 147), their model 60-685 "Deluxe foot pump with air reservoir and color-coded pressure gauge." The gauge is quite accurate, and you can pump your tires up easily and fast with this pump without risk of blow-out or inaccurate pressure readings. Adapters are available to fit Presta valves, since the Schwinn pump comes with a Schraeder valve connector. You can take this connector off the hose and replace it with a Presta connector. If you don't have near you a service station with an air pump that you can dial to set the pressure you want, and not have to worry about overinflation, you should be very careful about using an air hose. The best procedure to follow is to push the air hose firmly down onto the tire valve for a second and release it immediately, then squeeze the tire between thumb and forefinger, continuing this process until the tire feels hard. This process won't guarantee your tire against a blow-out, however, so if you can, use a dial-type air outlet, a tire gauge, or a hand-operated tire pump, preferably with a built-in gauge.

Do not let a service station attendant fill your tires. If you're a good-looking woman, he'll probably rush to help you, and is likely to blow your tire off the rim. He's used to car tires, which need a lot of air.

Tubular tires (27 inches) come with Presta (Fig. 154) or Woods Continental-type valves. For service station air filling, you'll need to convert the Presta valve to an American Schraeder valve connection. The adapter that you buy for this screws right down over the valve. Presta valve cores must be screwed open (counterclockwise) before you can fill the tire with air, and screwed closed after filling to prevent leakage.

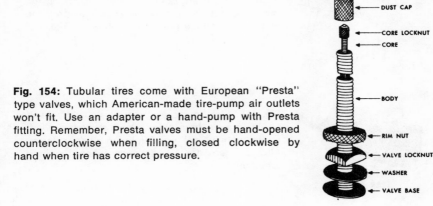

Fig. 154: Tubular tires come with European "Presta" type valves, which American-made tire-pump air outlets won't fit. Use an adapter or a hand-pump with Presta fitting. Remember, Presta valves must be hand-opened counterclockwise when filling, closed clockwise by hand when tire has correct pressure.

UNDERINFLATION DAMAGE

Underinflated tires put more tire tread on the road and use up more energy by flexing and creating heat, which makes the bicycle considerably harder to pedal.

An underinflated tire cannot take bumps and stones, and ordinary contact with pavement roughness can be sufficient to force the tire casing inward far enough to pinch the tube against the metal wheel rim. This can cause a blow-out and might even bruise the tire casing beyond repair, causing a flat spot on the rim that cannot be pulled out. Here are some common types of tire damage and how to avoid them.

Glass damage causes knife-like cuts on the tread or the sidewall. To avoid running over glass and similar sharp objects. watch the road just in front of you as you ride. If you ride at night, ride only on roads with which you are familiar and know are not likely to have glass, and use a good light to detect glass as far in advance as possible to give you time to swing out of the way. (Watch out for passing cars—swing right instead of left if you can to avoid glass.)

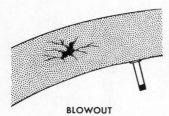

BLOWOUT

Fig. 155: Tube blow-outs are often caused by overinflation. If tire is not seated properly on the rim, tube may also blow out because pressure can force the tube out between tire and rim.

STAR BREAK

Fig. 156: Star breaks on tires are usually caused by riding over sharp objects such as stones. Such an injury may not be visible on tire's exterior. Always check for tire damage when repairing tube puncture.

RUPTURE

Fig. 157: Jumping curbs and riding over sharp objects such as stones cause this type of tire rupture. Stop, dismount, and ease bike gently over curbs, if you ride on sidewalks.

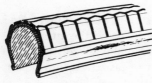

RIM CUT

Fig. 158: Rim cuts like this one are caused by riding on underinflated tires, overloading the bicycle, or rusty rims.

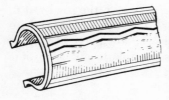

UNEVEN TREAD WEAR

Fig. 159: Uneven tire wear can be caused by improperly adjusted brakes that grab or lock the wheel, skidding stops (all too popular with youngsters), or crooked rims. (*Figures 157 through 159 courtesy Schwinn Bicycle Company.*)

Blow-outs can be caused by overinflation (Fig. 155), underinflation, and tire-casing damage such as glass cuts. A glass wound (Fig. 156) will open and close as the tire casing flexes and will eventually pinch a hole in the tire tube. This is why you should always look for the *cause* of a flat after a patch has been applied to the tube.

Nails and other sharp objects such as fine pieces of wire will cause a flat by piercing both tire and tube. Be sure to remove the nail before reinstalling the tire and tube. If the nail is still in the tire when you go to repair it, it will be a good guide to the location of the leak in the tube.

Ruptures (Fig. 157) are *always* a sign of abuse, barring accidents. Riding up and down curbs, into sharp stones and curbs, is a sure invitation to ruptures and a very short tire life.

Rim cuts (Fig. 158) are long, thin-looking cuts in the sidewalls and are caused by riding an underinflated tire, rusty rims, or an overloaded bicycle.

Uneven tread wear (Fig. 159) can be due to crooked rims, quick stops that grab and lock the wheel (otherwise known as skidding to a stop for kicks), or out-of-adjustment caliper brakes that grab the rim. Out-of-true rims also cause excessive tire wear because the caliper brake will grab at the out-of-true spot. It is a good idea to look far enough ahead to be able to avoid sudden stops, for your own as well as for your tires' longevity.

HOW TO REPAIR TUBULAR TIRES

Tubular tires (Fig. 160) are the kind used by track- and road-racing cyclists. They come on the more expensive European bicycles and the one high-grade American-made racing bicycle (Schwinn Paramount). These tires come in a variety of weights, ranging from the very lightest track-racing types, which weigh in at three and one-half ounces, to heavier road-racing and touring tubulars at twelve to sixteen ounces or more. (These weights include tube and valve.) Tubulars give great strength with extreme lightness. The heavier types are quite suitable for even extended touring, although they are somewhat more prone to punctures than conventional wired-on types of tires, and considerably more difficult to mend. Personally, I prefer tubulars to more conventional tires, except for city cycling, where streets are more likely to be littered with glass shards and other puncture-causing debris (Fig. 161). A plus for tubular tires is the fact that you can carry one or two complete tires and

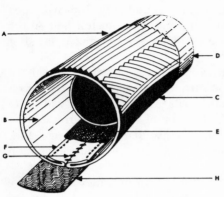

A. Tread.

B. Casing, made of fabric.

C. Outside of casing, between bottom of tread and base tape, is called the "wall."

D. Inner tube.

E. Chafing tape, to prevent inner tube from puncture by rubbing on tire stitching.

F. Hems of casing are made by gluing back the edges of fabric to the inside. In some tires, hems are folded to the outside.

G. Stitching. When repairing, use a simple hand-over-hand stitch.

H. Base tape protects stitching and provides seating for entire tire.

Fig. 160: If you use tubular tires, you should know how they are made and the names of each part. This drawing dissects tubular tires, naming the parts.

tubes rolled up and fastened to the seat strut on the back underside of the saddle. (A special strap can be bought for this purpose, or you can use an old toe strap.) In the event of a puncture, you can change these tires far more easily and quickly than you can the conventional wired-on types, without any tools. The tube is sewn in place, so you don't have to worry about pinching it when you fit the tire to the rim.

However, because the tube is sewn in, these tires, as mentioned, are considerably more difficult to repair punctures on than conventional tires.

To repair tubular tires, you will have to cut a few stitches in the area where the puncture is located, repair the puncture, and restitch the tire. To repair tubulars, follow this procedure:

Fig. 161: If you use tubular tires, you will need double-palm gloves so you can reach over and brush off any piece of glass, etc., you think you have run over before it gets deep enough to puncture the tube. These are from Eco-Cyclery (See Fig. 146, page 295) but good bike stores carry them. Best kind are from Italy and Spain. Avoid plastic gloves; leather is best. Tab button on back will hold glove on your hand, but Velcro fastener is quicker and easier to use.

STEP ONE: You will need a patch set (Fig. 162) consisting of:

a. Special thin tube patches (such as the ones made by Dunlop)
b. A triangular-pointed hand-sewing needle
c. Tubular tire linen thread
d. Rubber cement
e. A small tube of talc powder
f. A small piece of yellow chalk
g. A small screwdriver
h. A sharp knife or razor blade
i. A small square of fine sandpaper

Most of the bicycle mail-order houses (page 497) sell a tubular tire repair kit with most of the above items. The reason for the extra-thin tube patches is that tubular tires have a very thin tube. An ordinary bicycle tire patch is far too thick for this tube and would cause a lump inside the tire which would thump as you ride. Thin patches are especially needed for the six-ounce track-racing tires, which are generally handmade from silk cord and rubber latex. An old piece of tubular tube will do in an emergency.

STEP TWO: If you have an old rim, mount the tire on the rim, inflate it to sixty or seventy pounds of air pressure, and set the tire and rim in a half-

Fig. 162: Tubular tire repair kit has everything you need to repair these tires.

Fig. 163: Step Three

filled washtub. Or simply remove the tire from the wheel, inflate as above, and put it, a bit at a time, into the washtub. If you can see no puncture, you could have a loose or torn valve or a puncture at the valve area (Fig. 163).

STEP THREE: As you insert the tubular tire into the tub of water, you will notice that a lot of air seems to be bubbling up from around the valve stem first (Fig. 164). The tire is sewn and has a rubber-cemented strip over the sewing, so this is about the only place air *can* escape, except through the puncture itself.

Rotate the tire slowly until you come to the spot where air is seeping out through a small puncture in the tire casing. With a piece of yellow chalk, mark this area; it is also the location of the tube puncture. Deflate the tire and remove it from the rim.

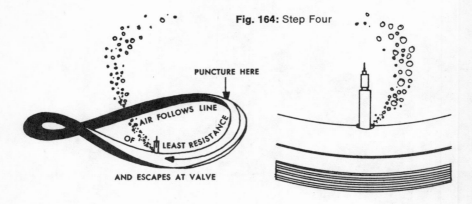

Fig. 164: Step Four

PUNCTURE HERE

AIR FOLLOWS LINE OF LEAST RESISTANCE

AND ESCAPES AT VALVE

STEP FOUR: With the small screwdriver or another flat (but not sharp!) tool, carefully pry about two-and-a-half inches of the tape on both sides of the puncture away from the inner circumference of the tire (Fig. 165).

STEP FIVE: With the razor or small sharp knife, carefully cut the stitching about two inches on either side of the puncture. Do not cut down *into* the tire, but insert the knife edge under the stitching and cut upward to avoid cutting into the tube, which lies just under the stitching (Figs. 166 and 167).

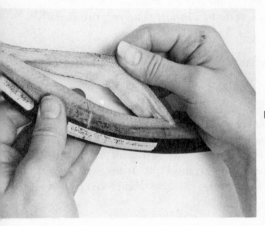

Fig. 165: Step Four

Fig. 166: Step Five

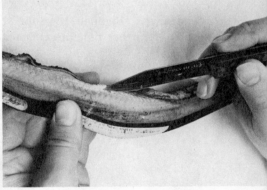

Fig. 167: Step Five

STEP SIX: Pull about four inches of the tube out gently and, with a hand pump, inflate the tube enough to find the puncture (Fig. 168). With the yellow chalk, outline the puncture, centering it in a chalked circle about the size of a quarter. A simple way to find the puncture is to hold the tube near your lips and rotate it slowly. You should be able to feel the flow of air from the puncture. If you can't find the puncture this way, put a drop of liquid soap in a glass, fill it with warm water, and place this mixture on the tube until you find a bubble marking the location of the puncture.

STEP SEVEN: Dry the tube thoroughly, if you have wet it. With the sandpaper, abrade lightly the area you have marked off around the puncture, putting a small, solid object under the tube to support it as you rub it with the sandpaper (Fig. 169).

STEP EIGHT: Apply several light coatings of rubber cement to the area abraded. Let each coating dry to a hard glaze (Fig. 170).

STEP NINE: Apply a patch of finest grade thin rubber to the tube over the puncture. Dust with talcum powder to prevent the tube from sticking to the casing. Note that two patches have been applied to this tube. This is because whatever caused the flat often goes through *both sides* of the tube, so you should check the other side of the tube from where you found the first puncture to make sure *that* side also hasn't been penetrated (Figs. 171 and 172).

STEP TEN: Reinflate the tube slightly with the hand pump. Check the area for further punctures. Deflate the tube.

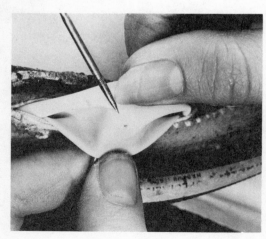

Fig. 168: Step Six

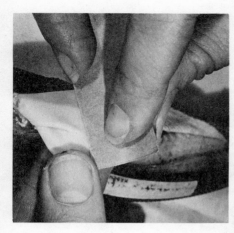

Fig. 169: Step Seven

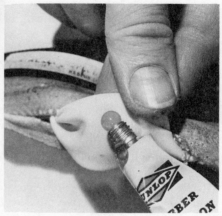

Fig. 170: Step Eight

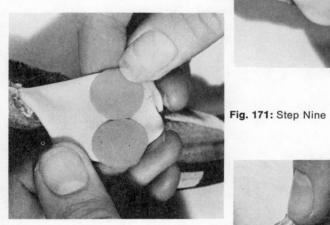

Fig. 171: Step Nine

Fig. 172: Step Nine

STEP ELEVEN: Inspect the tire casing for damage, such as bruises, gouges, rips, tears, and the rare manufacturing defect (Figs. 173 and 174). If the tire casing itself is damaged, I recommend relegating the tire to the spare-use-only category, because while the casing damage can be patched with a thin piece of canvas applied with rubber cement, if the bruise or hole is small, even this patch will bulge and cause the tire to "thump" annoyingly, especially at high speeds. Tubular tire repair kits do come with a special piece of canvas for this purpose, but I recommend its use for emergency situations only. Patched tires can, of course, serve ideally as spares.

STEP TWELVE: Sew up the tire, using the triangular-pointed needle and doubled thread. In an emergency, a twelve-pound-test linen thread or double thread *silk* fishing line will do. Nylon line won't serve the purpose; it cuts into the tire. Start by sewing back about a half-inch over the cut stitching. Use a simple overhand stitch to finish the stitching, running the thread about a half-inch through *existing* holes left from the manufacturer's original stitching. Don't make new holes. Pull stitches firm, but don't overdo it or you'll cut the tire casing (Fig. 175).

STEP THIRTEEN: Apply rubber cement over the area revealed when you peeled back the protective tape over the stitching and on the tape itself (Fig. 176). Let dry. Carefully lay tape back in position.

STEP FOURTEEN: Mount the tire, inflate to riding pressure, and check again for leaks. Leave inflated so rubber cement has a chance to dry thoroughly.

STEP FIFTEEN: Fill in any cuts in the tread with black rubber cement (*not* patch cement) that comes with your patch kit, or with black plastic rubber cement you can buy in a hardware store (Fig. 177).

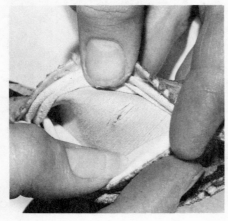

Fig. 173: Step Eleven

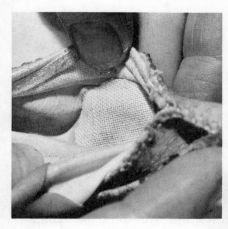

Fig. 174: Step Eleven

Fig. 175: Step Twelve

Fig. 176: Step Thirteen

Fig. 177: Step Fourteen

A CLINCHER ANSWER TO TUBULARS

There are two new clincher tires on the market that offer a real challenge to all the heretofore exclusive benefits offered by tubular tires.

Clincher or wired-on tires have long been known to be much heavier, harder to pedal, and to offer less "feel of the road" than tubular tires. This is because the 27 × 1¼-inch dimension of the clincher gives greater rolling resistance than the narrower 27 × 1⅛-inch tubulars. In addition, clinchers are heavier than tubulars and bulkier, so they add to the work a cyclist has to do. A conventional clincher tire with tube, for example, weighs 26 ounces. The heavier touring tubular tire, such as the Clement "Elvezia" (see Table 18, page 305), weighs 14 ounces, or almost half as much as the clincher.

Now there's a new clincher that weighs, with tube, only 18½ ounces and that's no bigger than a tubular. In fact, at 27 × 1⅛-inch, the new clincher is the same size as a tubular. Best of all, it can fit on your regular clincher rims. You will need a 27 × 1⅛-inch tube, although in a pinch you can get by with the 1¼-inch standard clincher tube. The new clincher tire offers about the same rolling resistance as a tubular, although it does not give the same feel of the road a tubular does, and it is a bit heavier. But the new clincher is so much like a tubular and is, of course, so much easier to repair, that it may well put tubulars out of business so far as the touring cyclist is concerned, since the relative merits of both are now so narrow. I foresee only the finickiest cyclist sticking to tubulars, now that the new clinchers are available. The 18½-ounce (with tube) new clincher is distributed by Raleigh through their dealers, is called the Raleigh Special Lightweight, and comes from Japan.

Another even lighter and more responsive clincher, made in Italy, should also be on the market by the time you read this edition. Distributed by Raleigh, it is called the Raleigh "Corsa Strada." This new clincher weighs only 17 ounces with tube, or only 3 ounces more than the Clement "Elvezia" training and touring tubular. It's lightweight and can be rolled up and carried just like a tubular, but it must be seated on the rim perfectly or it will blow off at its recommended pressure of 90 pounds per square inch. The best way to seat both this tire, and the Special Lightweight, is to make sure the bead is firmly in place all the way around, and then inflate it very slowly, no more than 20 psi at a time, and between inflations, make sure the bead is seated well into the rim all the way around.

I toured about 1200 miles in France in 1973 with these tires, and had only one flat, which I quickly repaired on the spot. They do give excellent ride, good "feel-of-the-road" and, so far as I am concerned, will replace tubulars for touring. Now the only time I will use tubular tires is for local tours and rides when it is possible for me to repair them at home, at my leisure. These new tires are also known as "cheaters" because they are wired-on, but look like tubulars.

A NEW WAY TO REPAIR TUBULAR TIRES

The hassle of unstitching, patching, and restitching tubular tires may well be a thing of the past if a new method of tubular tire repair proves practical (just introduced at this writing). The new way is a latex foam in a Freon base in a power tube, which, when squirted into a tubular tire, simultaneously inflates the tire and repairs the puncture. The entire job takes seconds and is done without removing the tire from the rim. All you do is find the puncture, pick out whatever caused it, such as a sliver of glass or a nailhole, back off the valve (unscrew it), screw on a Schraeder valve adapter (you can buy one from most bike stores), shake the can of tire repair stuff for 15 seconds, put the can over the valve and press it down. Instantly the tire is inflated, and you should see a tiny froth of white stuff coming out of the puncture. The bike should be upside down, so that as soon as the tire is inflated you can rotate the wheel rapidly for about two or three minutes to get the sealant distributed evenly inside the tube. There's enough sealant to repair two tubular tires, according to the supplier.

I recently watched a demonstration of this sealant, during which a tubular tire was punctured and sealed about 100 times and could still be ridden off. Of course nothing will seal a big blow-out, but for the ordinary puncture caused by slivers of glass or a nail this stuff works fine, so far as I can tell. The propellant gas in this sealant is a "locked-in" mixture of Freon and Propane gasses, which the manufacturer states will permit the user to apply the sealant from temperatures of $-4°F$ to $+212°F$. I was a bit worried about the propellant because Freon's coefficient of expansion relates directly to temperature, and people who have used Freon have blown out tires as air temperature went up or as the tire was exposed to the sun. However, the manufacturer says the Freon/Propane propellant has about the same expansion characteristics as air. However, be warned that repairs made with this stuff are not permanent, but will get you home or last around 200 miles or so. At least it did so for me twice. The sealant is called "Instant Seal 'N' Air," is distributed nationally by D & N Enterprises, Inc., Faribault, Minnesota 55021, and by the time you read this should be available from bike stores. Oh, yes, it works fine for most clincher tube punctures, too. It should be a blessing for the weighed-down touring cyclist who would otherwise have a problem fixing a flat. This stuff won't close the leak forever, but it will get you another couple of hundred miles down the road and let you fix the flat at your leisure.

TUBULAR VERSUS TUBE TIRES

Many experienced cyclists prefer tubular tires because they are much easier to change than conventional tires. The advantage of tubulars for touring is that you can carry four or five complete tires and tubes rolled up with you. They are light, very flexible, and extremely compact, and, with care, they'll last 4,000 miles or more. However, if you are going to tour with tubulars buy only the heaviest weight, the twelve- to sixteen-ounce type. I prefer the Clement "Elvezia," but if you can't find the Clement line, the Vittoria 201-B with butyl tube is excellent. The butyl tube is a good idea, because it will hold tire pressure for weeks. Tubulars without butyl tubes need some air added daily because tube walls are so thin that they "exhale" air. Remember, if you go the tubular route, buy a few valve adapters (twenty-five cents each) so you can use American service station air hose outlets.

If most of your cycling is going to be back and forth from work, touring in a big city or on rough country roads, however, I recommend you use conventional "wired-on" tube tires (Fig. 178). These are much more resistant to punctures than tubulars. City streets have on them a good deal of broken glass, bits of sharp metal, and assorted other tire-

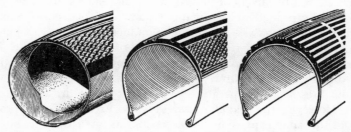

Fig. 178: Tubular and wired-on tube tires compared. Tubular tire is at left. Center tire is suitable for touring, as is the heavier wired-on tire at right. Reprinted with the permission of Temple Press Ltd. from "The Cycling Book of Maintenance."

puncturing junk that is always located where you must cycle for safety. The problem is that you usually don't have room to maneuver away from or around such hazards, because of the flow of motor vehicles around you; so, while city cycling can be quite safe if you know how to cope with it (see page 28), you are often forced to run into areas where you can get punctures. If you cycle at night in the city, you can't always see puncture hazards in time to get away from them.

I have two complete sets of wheels—one set with tubulars for local or short-distance cycling, and one set with wired-on "cheaters" for touring. When you change wheels, you might also have to readjust the brake shoes because the rim diameter might be slightly different from a touring clincher wheel to a racing tubular rim. Make sure the brake blocks contact the rim properly. You cannot interchange tubular and wired-on tires on the same rim. Each type of tire requires its own rim design, although you can get home with a tubular mounted on a clincher rim, if you ride carefully.

FITTING TUBULAR TIRES TO RIMS

Although tubular tires are quick and easy to change, there is a best way, as follows:

STEP ONE: Make sure there are no spoke heads protruding from the rim. If there are, file them down flush with the spoke nipple, so they won't puncture the tire and tube.

STEP TWO: Apply a very thin layer of tire cement (shellac for track racing, road-tire cement for road racing and touring) to the rim and tire base tape and allow it to dry to a tacky state (Figs. 179 and 180). The

Fig. 179: Step Two

Fig. 180: Step Two

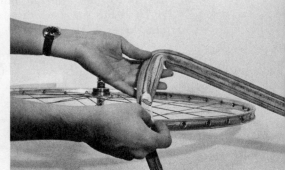

Fig. 181: If tubular tire is not cemented on rim firmly, the forces of "roll" or "creep" can force tire off rim, causing an accident often at high speed or when cornering. If you're racing, or touring in hilly country, use of rim cement can be a lifesaver.

cement is essential for safe cycling, because tubulars can be pushed off the wheel rim under the stress of cornering and other maneuvers, which at high speed can be embarrassing, if not downright unsafe. Also, if rim cement is not used, tubular tires tend to "creep" around the rim and bulge up around the valve, causing a thumping effect and eventually tearing the valve from the tube (Fig. 181).

A handy alternative to rim cement is double-sided sticky rim tape. A roll of French Jantex rim tape No. T-80 should be enough for a couple of wheels. Rim tape is a lot handier than rim cement, especially on a tour. But it's not very sticky in wet weather, so beware!

If you are on the road and you wish to change a tire quickly, you can get by without adding more cement to the rim, and just use the tacky effect of the old cement until you get home. It is a good idea to remove all old cement before applying fresh cement, to prevent cement buildup and bulge spots on the rim. Any good shellac solvent, or even paint remover liquid (be careful not to get this on the bicycle frame!) will do.

STEP THREE: Deflate tire almost completely, leaving just enough air to give the tire a little body. Hold wheel in an upright position and insert valve through the valve hole in the rim (Fig. 182).

STEP FOUR: With the valve at the top of the wheel and the wheel on a soft pad on the floor, stand behind the wheel and with both hands push the tire downward onto the rim, finishing on the side opposite the valve (Fig. 183). Hold the rim away from your body while you're doing this— or wear old clothes.

STEP FIVE: With the tire on the rim as far as possible, force the remainder of the tire onto the rim with both thumbs (Fig. 184).

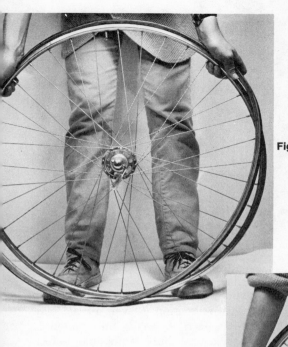

Fig. 182: Step Three

Fig. 183: Step Four

Fig. 184: Step Five

Fig. 185: Step Six

STEP SIX: True up the tire with your fingers (Fig. 185) so that it sits evenly all the way around the rim and tire tension is even all the way around. Inflate the tire partially and inspect it to make sure that it is seated evenly. Leave the tire inflated for a few hours, if possible, before using it, to give the rim cement time to dry and become fixed.

TIPS ON TUBULARS

Buy your season's supply of tubulars in December, mount them on old rims, inflate to about fifteen pounds, and let them "age." It takes time to make factory-fresh tubulars tough and strong.

Never let globs of rim cement build up on rims. If you've had a flat and had to add more rim cement, as soon as you get home remove all cement with solvent or paint thinner, wash off in warm water and soap, then dry and apply fresh rim cement or rim tape.

As tubulars age, you'll notice that the thin rubber coating on the side walls disappears (actually, it evaporates), leaving fabric exposed. Replace this thin coating with a very thin solution of latex rubber which you can buy from a rubber supply house. First inflate tire lightly, then wash with soap and water, dry, and apply latex suds with a small brush.

Store tubulars in a dark, cool, well-ventilated place. In off-season, never leave bicycle with tubulars on the ground; hang the bike from the ceiling so tubulars won't take a "set." Never put a bike away for a long period without letting out most of the air from tubulars so they won't stretch. Lighter tubulars should be deflated between use (every day if necessary).

If you're riding clinchers and have no spare tube or patch kit, you can use a borrowed tubular for long enough to get home. First build up the clincher rim with tape from your handlebars.

Never let oil, grease, kerosene, gasoline, rubber cement or any other kind of solvent touch your tubulars. Solvents will eventually eat right through your tubular.

When you're car-carrying tubulars, partially deflate them so the hot sun won't heat the air inside the tube, causing a blow-out. Keep tires from rubbing anything; preferably use a tire cover. You can make a tire cover out of an old 27 × 1¼-inch tire casing by removing its wire bead.

Don't fill tubulars with CO_2 because it leaks out even faster than air. If you use a pressure cartridge, use nitrogen.

On the road, protect spare tubulars against road dirt with plastic cloth. *And before you leave on a long trip, check rim cement to make sure it hasn't dried out.* Try to pry the tire off with fingers. If it lifts easily, the cement is dry. Remove tire, old cement, and recement. Do try to keep rim cement off side walls; that makes for a fast, skidding stop every time, and it's messy, besides.

TUBULAR TIRE CARE

The hints and tips that follow will greatly prolong the useful life of your expensive tubular tires (the sew-up types).

Do not leave spares folded on bicycles longer than two weeks. Remove the spare, inflate lightly, let it stand overnight, deflate, and reroll. This prevents spares from taking a "set" on the folds. In refolding, fold the opposite way so that the part that was on the inside is now on the outside. However, always fold so that the tread is on the outside. When folded, mount the spare so that it cannot rub or chafe anywhere. Ideally, you should carry it in a plastic bag.

Valves should be protected against dirt with a light plastic dust cap. Remember to close the valve on the spare. Open, it can be easily bent.

Extra spares should always be stored lightly inflated, in a warm, dry place. Be very careful not to store tubulars that have become wet, unless you inflate them so they can dry out.

For safety, particularly if you do a lot of riding, check rim cement frequently. If you are on a tour, check rim cement at least weekly, because this cement can dry out and flake off. Rim cement is absolutely essential to keep tires from creeping and crawling.

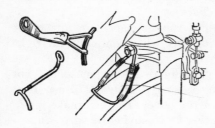

Fig. 186: Nail catchers, installed on brake pinion bolt and adjusted to ride lightly over tire, can save many a flat by pulling out nails, pieces of glass, or bits of stone before they can cause a puncture. Three types of nail catchers are shown here. The Reg type, lower left, is most popular in the United States. Other types shown: Pelissier, upper left; Carlton, right.

Prevent punctures by using a "thorn puller" or "nail puller" (Fig. 186), a tire accessory that weighs only a half-ounce and that can be fitted to the caliper-brake center bolt over the tire to scrape off nails, thorns, and other impedimenta stuck to the tire, before they can puncture the tube. Check treads regularly and pull out foreign material embedded in the tire.

If you realign your rim, remember that retensioning spokes can cause spoke heads to protrude and puncture the tire. Remove the tire, and check and file off any protruding spoke heads.

If you carry your bicycle, be careful not to let the tires rub on any metal or wooden parts. Check the placement of wheels against car seats, carrying racks, toe straps, and tie-down straps.

On an airplane trip, if you bring your bicycle, remember to half-deflate your tires, because if your bicycle is stored in an unpressurized or partly pressurized baggage compartment, the low pressures at high altitudes may permit the high pressures inside the tire to cause a blow-out.

Add a little air every day to tubular tires. Walls of tubes are so thin that they "breathe" a little air, so make up for the loss by adding air daily. Five or ten strokes of the pump should do. Use a gauge to find the correct pressure.

Use the pump correctly. Do not push it on from side to side, or pull it off slowly and erratically. You do not need adapters to convert European valve stems to American stems if you use the press-on type of bicycle pump. I prefer Silca or Zefal pumps (Fig. 187), which can be carried on the bicycle. Be sure to knock off this press-on pump from the valve by a sharp blow with the side of your hand (Figs. 188 and 189).

Keep oil from the tire. Do not oil the tire pump; use light grease. Oil can be blown into the tire, grease cannot. And oil will eat away and ruin the tire tube, making it necessary to junk the tire (on sew-ups).

Fig. 187: When inflating tire with "Presta" valve, first open valve stem by turning it counterclockwise, push valve stem up for a second to free it, then apply pump firmly. Hold pump onto valve with thumb and forefingers.

Fig. 188: When finished pumping tubular tire, knock pump off valve by quick, firm downward jab with side of fist. Don't try to wiggle or pull pump off valve.

Fig. 189: Here's what can happen if you don't push on or pull off a tubular tire pump straight. The Presta valve stem is broken off so it can't be threaded down. Tire is usable as a spare, but tends to leak a bit.

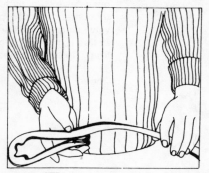
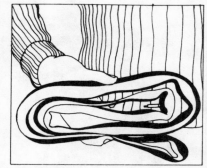

Fig. 190: Spare tire can be folded as shown for carrying under saddle or elsewhere. Be sure valve is in position shown, where it can't chafe tire.

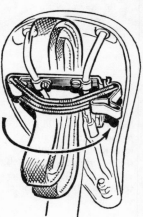

Fig. 191: Here's how to carry spare tire under saddle, secured by rubber bands. Tire carrier is made by Vittoria. If you can't find this carrier, use old pedal strap.

HOW TO CARRY TUBULAR SPARES

Because tubulars do take time to repair, you should always carry at least one spare on any trip. A convenient way to carry the spare is to fold the tire so that the tread is on the outside and not folded back on itself (Fig. 190). Wrap the tire under the seat, behind the seat post, with a strap (Fig. 191).

HOW TO REPAIR TUBE TIRES

In the bicycle trade, conventional tires are called "wired-on" tires because they depend on metal wire beads around the two lips of the tire for rim adhesion. These tires are open inside, and the tube is removed easily from the tire for repair.

STEP ONE: If the tire goes flat overnight, you may have either a tiny puncture or a slow leak through the valve. You can check for a valve core leak by removing the valve cap (Figs. 192 and 193), inflating the tire to normal pressure, and putting a bit of soapy water in the valve. If the valve leaks, you will see bubbles. In this case, all you need to do is tighten the valve core. If the valve still leaks, replace the valve core with a new one. You will need an old-fashioned metal valve cap to tighten or remove the core. This is available from any bicycle shop and most service stations.

STEP TWO: To repair a tube puncture you will need two flat-end tire levers, or two dull-edge, broad-blade screwdrivers, to pry the tire off and put it on. First, remove the valve core from the valve, with a valve cap. If there is a locknut on the valve stem, remove it from the stem.

STEP THREE: Although you don't need to remove the wheel, it is usually easier to do so. However, if you're on the road and touring, with saddle-bags or carriers in the way, you can attack the repair by removing the tire in the vicinity of the puncture, pulling out the tube, and patching it as described below. Otherwise, remove the wheel and, with the two tire levers, pry one side of the tire away from the rim until one side is loose

Fig. 192: Remove and reinstall valve core from clincher tire tube with valve cover.

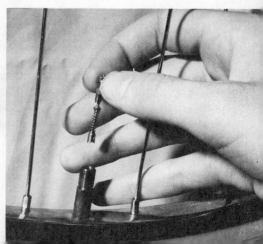

Fig. 193: When valve core is screwed out, lift out of valve core barrel. Valve cores do go bad, and after you screw it back in, test with bit of soapy water at valve barrel head to make sure it doesn't leak. If it does leak, replace it.

enough to pull all the way off. Remove the tire by hand from the other side of the rim.

STEP FOUR: Inflate the tube and rotate it near your ear until you find the location of the puncture by hearing the hiss of escaping air. Draw a circle around the puncture with a piece of chalk. If you can't find it by listening for escaping air, immerse the tube in a tub of water and watch for bubbles as you rotate the tube in the water. Hold your finger in the puncture area while you dry the tube off thoroughly. Mark the puncture with a piece of chalk.

STEP FIVE: With a piece of sandpaper or the metal abrader that comes with tire repair kits, scrape the tube around the puncture and put a thin layer of rubber cement around it, extending outward about a half-inch in all directions. Let the rubber cement get tacky, pull the paper backing off the appropriate-sized tube patch, and press the patch firmly down onto the coated area over the puncture. Be careful, in handling the tube patch, not to finger the patch over the coated area where you have removed the paper covering. Hold the patch carefully by the edges until you have pressed it into place over the puncture.

STEP SIX: While the rubber under the patch is drying, check the outside of the tire carefully and pry out any embedded glass, nails, and the like. Remember, *something* caused that tire to go flat, and that something is most likely still embedded in the tire. Then, spreading the tire apart as you go, check the inside walls for any breaks. Breaks, if not too bad, can be patched with a tire patch. However, if the tire has bad cuts or bruises, discard it and buy a new one. Check for loose spokes, and tighten them. Remove the rubber strip inside the wheel and check to make sure all spokes are flush with the spoke nipples. File down any protruding spokes to prevent a later puncture, and replace the rubber strip. Realign the rim, if necessary, as discussed on page 449.

STEP SEVEN: Install the tire on the wheel. First, make sure most but not all the air is out of the tube. Tuck the tube carefully back into the tire. Put the valve into the valve hole in the rim. Next, starting at the valve, with hands on either side of the wheel, push the beaded edge of the tire all the way around until one side of the tire is on the rim. Then push the other side of the tire on the rim in the same manner. You should not need to use the tire levers to install the tire. But if you do use them, make sure that when you have the lever pushed up under the tire, you do not pinch

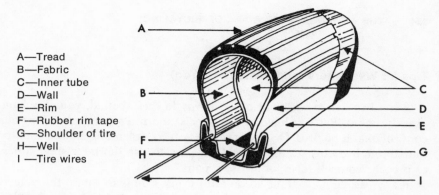

A—Tread
B—Fabric
C—Inner tube
D—Wall
E—Rim
F—Rubber rim tape
G—Shoulder of tire
H—Well
I —Tire wires

Fig. 194: How a wired-on tube-type tire fits on rim.

the tube between the lever and the rim and cause a puncture. Inflate the tire and check for leaks before remounting the wheel.

Due to the narrowness of the 27 × 1¼-inch wired-on tires, you will sometimes have trouble getting the bead of the tire to seat properly on the rim, particularly around the valve. If the bead isn't seated correctly, you can blow out the tube on inflation. To make sure the bead is set, before inflating, shove down on the valve stem so it will seat over the tire edges. Then inflate to around twenty pounds. Remove the pump and rotate the wheel to make sure clincher is seated all the way around. Any bulges should be removed by deflating tire and reseated by pushing bead in.

On page 320 I mentioned the new ultra-lightweight "cheater" tires that offer almost all the advantages of tubulars but are actually wired-on tires that can be repaired as easily as conventional wired-on tires. I said these are available through Raleigh dealers. However, at the 1973 Paris Bicycle Exposition I talked to several firms who make these tires. They tell me they are in quite limited production, and one firm only makes around 100 of them a day. If you can't find the new "cheaters" at a bike shop you might try writing the manufacturers for the name of the United States importer to track down which local bike store handles them. The "cheaters" are made by Atalanta Gomma, S.P.A., 24030 Terno Isola, Bergamo, Italy, for Raleigh under the "Corsa Strada" label. Gomma's company name for the same tire is "Record Copertura"; they also make it for Milremo under the "Bertin" label. The "cheater" is also made by ETS Dourdoigne, 15 Rue de la Dr. Passardiere, 50350 Donville-les-Bains, France.

Note: *New tubular tire equipped bicycles often do not come from the factory with rim cement applied. Double check to make sure dealer has glued these tires on before you leave the store!*

Tips for Westerners (and Easterners, Too)

If you live where cactus or other thorny bushes abound, you may have already found that you have to buy special thorn-resisting tubes for your conventional tube tires. Or, if you're an Easterner planning a cross-country tour through cactus states, you should plan to use thorn-resisting tubes, or prepare yourself for a lot of tire repairs.

In any case, a good thing to do after every ride is to rotate the wheels slowly and check for thorns and other puncture-causing debris embedded in the tire casing. This is a good procedure for any cyclist, by the way.

12

PREVENTIVE MEDICINE FOR BICYCLES – A COMPLETE MAINTENANCE GUIDE

Until just recently, before we grown-ups caught on to what wonderful fun, relaxation, and healthy exercise bicycling is, bikes were mostly for kids. But, even the cheapest bicycles need maintenance and repair. The more costly and complicated (as well as the more pleasurable) machines are really worth your tender loving care.

Given proper attention, the better bicycles will last you a lifetime, with just a few of the running gear parts having to be replaced from time to time.

WHO SHOULD DO THE MAINTENANCE

Unless you are absolutely all thumbs and your mind boggles at the slightest thing mechanical, you should do much of your own bicycle maintenance, for at least three reasons.

In the first place, good bicycle mechanics are very scarce. About all some bicycle stores can do competently are fix flats (on wired-on tires only, not on sewn tires), repair coaster brakes, and do other minor nut-and-bolt-type work. When it comes to aligning precision ten-speed derailleur mechanisms, and doing other work on foreign, high-quality, more expensive bicycles, or even on the less expensive, lower grade ten-speed models, finding a good mechanic can be a real problem.

I have found, and everyone I know who has had a lot of cycling experience confirms the fact, that bicycle mechanics today, good ones, are in short supply. The bicycle boom has brought a deluge of bicycle stores throughout the country, so what good mechanics there were in 1970 are today spread pretty thin. Good bicycle mechanics may be born, but the gestation period is long—about three years' full-time experience under the tutelage of a trained mechanic—to get really good.

If you have a good bicycle with a ten-speed derailleur, but you are absolutely all thumbs with tools, you can generally find a good enough mechanic by looking in the classified telephone directory for a bicycle store that advertises foreign-made bicycles such as Raleigh, Frejus, Gitane, Peugeot, and the like. Also, the larger Schwinn dealers can usually be counted on to have good mechanics, because Schwinn has an aggressive full-time training program for bicycle mechanics, with factory- and field-training schools. In general, you should avoid the smaller family-type bike shops, especially if they are involved in other businesses, such as lawnmower repairing.

Another good way to find a qualified bicycle mechanic is to check with a bicycle club in your area. For a list of the bicycle organizations of America, see page 443. Also, check with your local AYH chapter.

Since the bike boom, many young men have found their way into the bike business and have become really excellent mechanics. So don't be put off by the kids in the backroom; many of them really know what they're doing. But they are often overloaded in season and you may have to wait quite a while to get your bike back. And in a small town you will very likely have no choice but to do your own repair work.

In the second place, bicycle stores today charge $8.50 or more an hour, plus parts, for repairs. You will save a lot of money by fixing your own bicycle, especially if there is more than one bike in the family. For example, a new ten-speed derailleur mechanism can be bought for as little as $9.50 and installed in less than a half-hour. A bicycle store would charge you at least $18.00 for the job.

Also, while bicycles are easy to maintain and repair, with the better machines, fine adjustment and tuning of the various parts can be an art—an art you will want to learn in order to get the most out of your bicycle. With a little practice you can do your own work faster and at least as well as bicycle mechanics in bike stores. And if you go in for touring, long trips, youth hosteling, and the like, you should at least know how to make emergency repairs.

TOOLS YOU WILL NEED

Most foreign-made bicycles, as well as American-made bicycles using foreign-made parts such as derailleur gears (all derailleurs are foreign-made), caliper brakes, and the like, use metric nuts and bolts and therefore require metric tools.

A Plea for the Metric System

If you're at all serious about bicycling, you'll have a good bicycle, and maybe two or three of them, for yourself, not counting your wife's and children's machines. Real bike freaks are always tinkering with their machines, changing chainwheels, freewheels, rims, hubs, and what not. As you get into cycling, you'll find a need to measure parts to make sure you get an accurate replacement—ball bearings, axles, nuts and bolts, seat posts and stems, spokes and rims. If you're working on a good bike, most of these parts are metric, as stated. Let me give you an example of what happens when you try to convert metric, or even when you try to start with and stick to U.S. inches. When you lace a new rim on a hub (page 433), you need to measure the distance from axle locknut to axle locknut, the width of the rim, and subtract rim width from total axle-locknut-to-locknut width and multiply by two. Never mind why, you have to, and you'll find out in the wheel-lacing section. To do it in inches, either fractions or decimals, is a nightmare. In millimeters it's simple and very accurate. A typical locknut-to-locknut distance is 120.3 millimeters—or in decimal inches, 4.72779, or in fractions, 4¾ inches, which isn't *quite* accurate. Typical rim width is 19.4 mm.—or .76242 inches or 49/64 inches. Just dandy. Subtracting the two gives 100.9 mm. or 3.96537 inches or 3¹²⁴⁄₁₂₈ inches. Metric is a *lot* simpler to work with. So as basic measuring tools, I suggest you buy three inexpensive items: a plastic vernier caliper which measures inside, outside, and depth in inches and millimeters (Fig. 195), an inch-metric tape measure, and a set of metric screw gauges (Fig. 196) so you can find an accurate replacement for every nut and bolt on your bicycle. I'm not trying to turn you into a machinist, but you will need to know these simple measurement methods. And the inch-millimeter measuring devices are a handy way to convert to metric and back. Metric measuring instruments are available from Ametric Supply Co., 2309 W. Leland Ave., Chicago, Illinois 60625, or Metric & Multistandard Com-

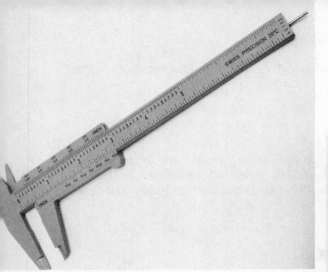

Fig. 195: This vernier caliper inside, outside, and depth gauge measures both inches and millimeters, is very accurate. Metric measurements are easier and more accurate to work with. This gauge costs only around $3.50.

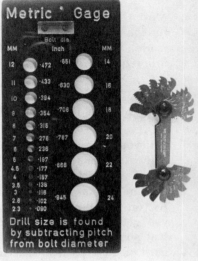

Fig. 196: Metric thread gauges and drill gauge are useful when working on bicycles imported from Europe, to find exact replacement parts.

ponents Corp.. 198 Saw Mill River Road. Elmsford, New York. M & M also has a warehouse full of metric nuts and bolts.

Below is a list of tools and their uses. If you think they are expensive, remember that most bike repair shops charge $8.50 an hour and up for repairs, and some do a fairly poor job, especially on the more expensive foreign-made bicycles where precise adjustment and alignment are vital to get the performance you have paid for. A good bicycle is truly a lifetime investment, and the right tools will help you keep your investment in tip-top shape. Most of the tools listed here are light enough to go along with you on extended tours, so for all but the most serious problems, you can be mechanically self-sufficient, no matter where you go.

DERAILLEURS, FRONT AND REAR: For Campagnolo derailleurs, a combination Allen and Socket Campagnolo "T" wrench, costing $1.75. For all other derailleurs, a Mafac ultralight (7½-ounce) tool kit, containing spanners and wrenches that also fit all brake nuts and many other smaller metric parts. Cost: $3.00 (Fig. 197). (I consider the Mafac kit in its plastic bag a must for road trips.)

Fig. 197: This Mafac metric tool kit fits most parts on most European bicycles, as well as American-made bicycles using European components. Includes kit of tire patches for tubular or wired-on tires.

CHAIN RIVET REMOVER: On the ³⁄₃₂-inch-wide chains used on derailleur-equipped bicycles, you cannot use a master locking link as you can on the ⅛-inch-wide chains used on coaster-brake and three-speed hub bicycles such as the Raleigh Sturmey-Archer hub and Schwinn Bendix two- and three-speed hubs and coaster brakes. The ³⁄₃₂-inch chain must fit between the closely spaced cogs on the five-speed freewheel, and the extra width of a master link would cause the chain to hang up on one of the cogs, with resulting considerable damage to the derailleur and, if you've been going fast, possibly to you.

So, to remove the ³⁄₃₂-inch-wide chains on derailleur-equipped bicycles, you'll need a combination rivet extractor and rivet-installing tool, for $2.75 (Fig. 198). Buy a replacement pin and screw for this tool.

NOTE: All the tools mentioned here can be bought from any good bicycle dealer or one of the specialty mail-order houses. such as Cyclo-Pedia in Cadillac, Michigan (see Appendix). I use them for most of my foreign bike parts, because their prices are considerably lower. However, they do not carry everything; for a list of specialty bike-part and tool mail-order houses, see page 497.

FREEWHEEL REMOVER: You will need the type of freewheel-removing tool that fits your freewheel. There are at least two types of internally

Fig. 198: You must have this tool to remove or replace chains in derailleur equipped bicycles. The tool is used to press out chain rivet so you can take chain apart and to press the rivet back to reinstall the chain. Handle and pin are replaceable. Never take an extended bike trip without this tool, because if the chain breaks you must have it to remove the broken link and pull the chain up to the next link, so you can keep going.

Fig. 199: Types of freewheel-removing tools. Left and right, splined types for Schwinn, Shimano, Atom, and some Sun Tour freewheels. Center, pronged type for Regina, Milremo, and some Sun Tour freewheels.

splined freewheels, and several types that take a pronged tool (Fig. 199). Splined freewheels are much easier to remove. Simply remove the quick-release skewer from the hollow axle, put the tool in a vise, set freewheel and two centering springs off skewer (on wheel) on tool, and twist the wheel counterclockwise. Reinstall the same way, twisting the wheel clockwise. To use the pronged tool, remove the quick-release skewer, insert tool, reinstall skewer snugly and back it away two turns. Use adjustable wrench on tool, counterclockwise, to break the freewheel loose from threads. Then remove the skewer and unscrew freewheel with wrench the rest of the way. Reinstall the same way, only clockwise.

METRIC ALLEN WRENCH SET: A set of metric Allen wrenches is invaluable. Sears sells such a set as a "Metric Hex Key Set" in a plastic pouch that will fit anything you'll find on a bike using Allen nuts and screws. This includes most derailleurs. At this writing, though, this set is missing a 7 mm wrench.

WHEEL HUBS: Two Campagnolo offset thin wrenches for adjusting the hub cones of standard and racing wheels are very handy. A set of 13 × 14 and 15 × 16 millimeters will fit most hubs, and you can buy 17 × 18 hub-cone wrenches to fit some of the Japanese hubs (Fig. 200).

PEDALS: Good pedals should be dismantled, cleaned, and regreased several times a year. You'll save time by using a special wing-nut pedal wrench to fit the small nut holding the pedal on its axle, or use a metric socket wrench.

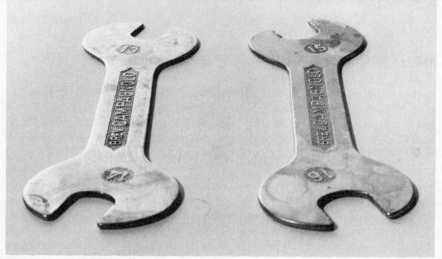

Fig. 200: To disassemble and adjust cone play in hubs requires special thin cone wrenches, such as the two Campagnolo hub wrenches shown here. Wrench at left is 13 and 14 mm., the wrench at right is 15 and 16 mm.

A Word About Interchangeability

American, French, English, and Italian manufacturers often have little that's interchangeable, either between bicycles or components. And even component manufacturers, such as Campagnolo, who have had over thirty years experience, seem to go out of their way to insure that none of their parts are interchangeable with similar parts made by even other Italian manufacturers.

The problem lies in fitting parts such as pedals, chainwheels, bottom bracket sets, cranks, headsets, seat posts, stems, handlebars and forks to bicycles. For example, you may well wish to change your double Campagnolo chainwheel to a triple chainwheel to obain a lower gear ratio for hill-climbing on tours. (A double chainwheel with 49 and 54 teeth, even with a wide-range rear-freewheel gear cluster, isn't going to give you what I would consider a truly wide range of gears that will take the heart-pounding work out of long uphill climbs, say from sea level to 5,000 feet.) And if you bend a pedal axle on tour, you should know what thread diameter and threads-per-inch (T.P.I.) pedal axle will replace it, or you may strip a crank.

Campagnolo, Stronglight, and T.A. make excellent triple alloy cotter-less chainwheels and bottom bracket sets. Campy's smallest chainwheel on the triple ring set is 36 teeth; Stronglight goes down to 36 (and says it will have a 26-tooth chainwheel); and T.A. goes down to a super-low, low 26 teeth. Campagnolo parts are not interchangeable with any other make, so if you want to add the small 36-tooth Campy chainwheel to your double Campy chainset, you will have to stick with Campy. If you have a Stronglight chainset and want to go down to the 26 range, T.A. will fit onto your existing Stronglight chainwheels, unless they're Stronglight type 57 or 63. To add the T.A. 26-tooth chainwheel, you'll also need a longer bottom bracket axle so you can move the chainwheels further away from the chain stay and seat tube for the necessary clearances for the extra chainwheel. You will also need longer pins and nuts for the T.A. chainwheel. You may even want to switch to a T.A. or Stronglight bottom bracket to take advantage of the smaller T.A. 26-tooth chainwheel. If you do, make sure you know what size set of hangar cups (the parts that screw into the bottom bracket hangar and around which the bearings rotate) to order, and which way they turn, because they differ between bicycles made in different countries, as the table below indicates:

TABLE 20 · Bottom-Bracket Hangar-Cup Thread Dimensions

TYPE	THREAD DIAMETER (inches)	THREADS PER INCH	THREAD DIRECTION (handed)	
			RIGHT CUP (fixed)	LEFT CUP (adjustable)
English & Japanese	1.370 (34.798 mm.)	24	Left	Right
French & Spanish	1.378 (35 mm.)	25.4 (1.0 pitch)	Right	Right
Italian	1.417 (36 mm.)	24	Right	Right
Swiss	1.378 (35 mm.)	25.4 (1.0 pitch)	Left	Right

BOTTOM BRACKETS

It would take another fifty pages in this book to give you detailed dimensional specifications for every combination of chainwheel, bottom bracket set, and bottom bracket hangars on the market. You should know, however, about the dimensional problems, as illustrated in the bottom-bracket hangar-cup dimension table (Fig. 201). In addition, you can't convert a double to a triple chainwheel without buying another, longer bottom bracket axle, as noted, which will move the chainwheels out to the right so the third chainwheel will have the necessary clearances between R.H. stays and chainwheel. Obviously, a triple chainwheel is wider than a

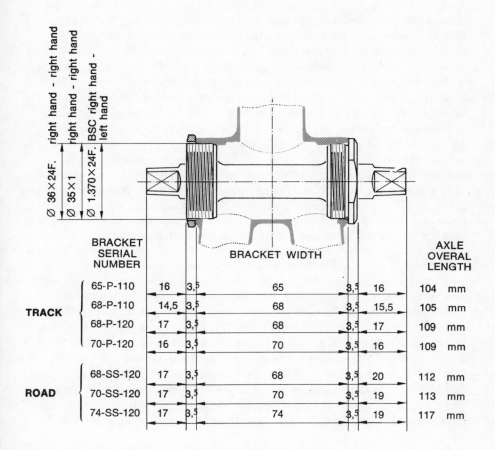

BRACKET SERIAL NUMBER			BRACKET WIDTH			AXLE OVERALL LENGTH	
TRACK 65-P-110	16	3,5	65	3,5	16	104	mm
68-P-110	14,5	3,5	68	3,5	15,5	105	mm
68-P-120	17	3,5	68	3,5	17	109	mm
70-P-120	16	3,5	70	3,5	16	109	mm
ROAD 68-SS-120	17	3,5	68	3,5	20	112	mm
70-SS-120	17	3,5	70	3,5	19	113	mm
74-SS-120	17	3,5	74	3,5	19	117	mm

Details of the bracket serial number (ex.: 65-P-110)

— The number (65) indicates the bracket width
— (P) indicates track
— (SS) indicate road
— The number (110) indicates the suggested width of the rear hub for a perfect chain line

Fig. 201: If you change bottom-bracket assemblies, you will need to know bottom-bracket hangar width (from 65 to 74 mm.), over-all length of axle (single, double, or triple chainwheel), whether cups are threaded metric, BSC (British) or ASA (U.S.), and whether right-hand fixed cup is left- or right-hand thread.

double. How *far* you should move to the right (i.e., how wide an axle you should buy) is a problem you can only solve by measuring the clearance you now have with your double chainwheel (use Vernier caliper shown in Fig. 195), and adding the clearance you would need for a triple chainwheel. An additional chainwheel adds around 4½ to 5 mm., depending on the chainwheel. For example, the Stronglight double chainwheel takes a 120-mm. axle, and the same make triple chainwheel a 125.5-mm. axle, a difference of 5.5 mm. in over-all length to allow for the third chainwheel.

Remember also that bottom bracket hangars vary in width, from 65 to 74 mm., the most popular being 68, 69, and 70 mm. If you use the wrong axle for the width of the hangar cup, you may not be able to take up the left adjustable cup enough to prevent axle side play, or you may not be able to screw the cup in far enough to avoid it rubbing on the left-hand crank. Fig. 201 shows typical Campagnolo bottom-bracket dimensions for track and road. Note that Campagnolo also recommends width of the rear hub for "a perfect chainline." We'll get back to the subject of chainline alignment later on in this section.

Summing up, to add a third chainwheel to a compatible chainset, you will need a longer axle to provide clearance between chainwheel and stay. If you install a longer axle, you will need to know the width of your bike's bottom bracket hangars in order to order an exact replacement axle with the longer right-hand dimension for triple chainwheel clearance. If you change to a different make bottom bracket assembly, you will need to order all the above correct dimensions, with hangar cups of the diameter and threads per inch to fit your bottom bracket hangar, and these dimensions vary depending on whether your bicycle was made in France, England, Italy, Spain, or Japan. Hangar cups are not safe to interchange between makes. If you change bottom bracket makes, change cups to the same make.

PEDALS

As noted, pedal threading differs between countries where bikes are made. As the table below shows, there is a slight difference in size between pedal threading of English and European bicycles. If you're stuck with a bent pedal or crank in England with a French bike, for example, and can't find a .55 (14 mm.) replacement, it will thread into an English crank; but if it's an alloy crank the threads will be force-changed, and I don't recommend it. Better to stagger along to the nearest bike shop that can supply you properly. Bicycling is still a way of life in Europe, and this way of life does not, at this writing, ordinarily encompass ten-speed bicycles, but rather the garden-variety utility one-speed or three-speed machines used strictly to get from here to there, at most four or five miles to a trip. Bike shops in England and throughout Europe cater to the major business, the utility trade. In Bonn, Germany, and, of all places, Amsterdam, Holland, I had to go to four or five bike shops before I found a tubular tire patch kit, rim cement, and a chain rivet remover. In fact, I was told by other bike stores that only one shop in Bonn catered to the ten-speed trade, and when I found it, this shop was devoted to the racing cyclist; I felt the proprietor took a fairly dim view of my pannier-loaded, ultra-wide-range-geared fifteen-speed Paramount. You can tell a ten-speed specialist bike shop in Europe, if not by the window display of parts, certainly by the photos of racing cyclists proudly displayed from every available inch of wall space.

TABLE 21 · **Crank Pedal Threading**

COUNTRY	DIAMETER		THREADS PER INCH
	Inches	Millimeters	
U.S.A. Std. (Heavier Bikes)	.50	12.7	20
U.S.A., British, Japanese	.5625	14.3	20
European	.55	14	20.4

HEADSETS

Thread dimensions on fork stems vary between the U.S.A., Britain, and the Continent, and the fixed cups (parts-drive fitted on top and bottom of the steering head and bottom of the fork stem) vary as to size. Head-tube dimensions vary, so races aren't necessarily interchangeable. For example, British, U.S., and Japanese standard fork-stem threading is 1 inch and 24 threads per inch, and Continental (European) stem threading is .98 inches and 25.4 threads per inch. I have found cracked bottom races and had to use an inside vernier caliper and metric thread gauge to make sure I had specified the correct size replacement.

HANDLEBARS AND STEMS

As noted above, steering heads and fork-stem diameters can vary, so if you wish to buy a different stem to move handlebars farther away or

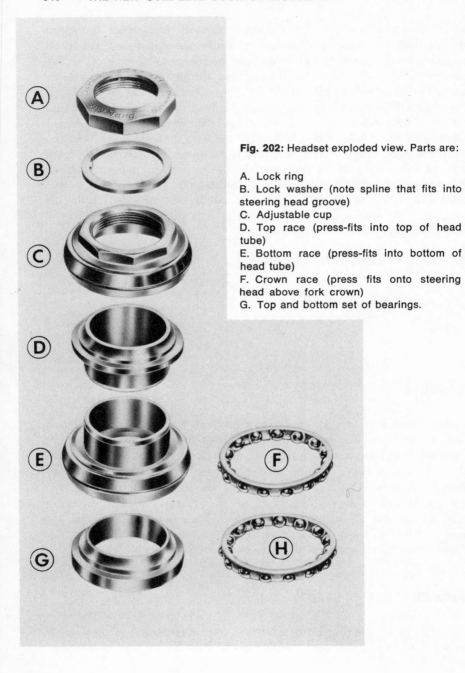

Fig. 202: Headset exploded view. Parts are:

A. Lock ring
B. Lock washer (note spline that fits into steering head groove)
C. Adjustable cup
D. Top race (press-fits into top of head tube)
E. Bottom race (press-fits into bottom of head tube)
F. Crown race (press fits onto steering head above fork crown)
G. Top and bottom set of bearings.

closer to the saddle, you need to know which size stem diameter to order. On standard heavyweight bicycles made in this country, stem diameters are either ⅞ or .813 inches. British fork-stem inside diameter is .873246 inches (22.22 mm.) and requires a stem with that outside diameter. French fork stem I.D. is .8646 inches (22 mm.) and takes a fork stem with a 22 mm. O.D.

As you will find, if you try to switch handlebars between stems, the ferruled space on the handlebar that fits into the stem opening can vary as to O.D. You can use a copper shim when the stem is too large, but this is makeshift and you should use the correct size stem (or handlebars). Use the vernier caliper to measure stem and bar diameters accurately (see Fig. 195).

SEAT TUBES AND POSTS

Seat tube (the tube on the bicycle frame that extends from the seat-post opening to the bottom bracket hangar) inside diameters also vary, both because of the O.D. of the tubing and the gauge of the tubing. The same O.D. tubing can have different I.D.'s if the tubing gauge changes; the heavier gauge tubing will have a smaller I.D. You may want to change seat posts to upgrade from a standard steel "wire gripper" post to a Campagnolo micro-adjust alloy post (or one of the good Japanese or Zeus equivalents), or to a longer post to get your saddle up higher (you probably need a larger frame, if so).

TABLE 22 · **Standard Seat-Post Diameters**

METRIC	INCHES (decimal)	INCHES FRACTION (approx.)
25	.98437	63/64
25.8	1.01562	1 1/64
26	1.03125	1 1/32
26.2	1.03911	1 1/32
26.4	1.04687	1 3/64
26.6	1.05473	1 3/64
26.8	1.06250	1 1/16
27	1.07036	1 1/16
27.2	1.07812	1 5/64
27.4	1.08598	1 5/64

Alloy seat posts, such as made by Campagnolo, Zeus, and T.A., are fairly limited in length. The shortest is 130 mm. (5.1090 or 5¹⁄₆₄ inches) and the longest is 180 mm. (7.0740 or 7⁵⁄₆₄ inches). You *must* have at least *2½ inches* of seat post inside the seat tube for safety (see Fig. 13). If the 180-mm. length still doesn't get you high enough, you should change to a larger frame size. If you can't change frames, a compromise would be to use a steel seat post (you will need a saddle clip), which comes only in O.D. diameter of 1⅛ inch (1.1250 inches or 28.58 mm.) in lengths of 7, 9, 12, and 15 inches, and in 1-inch diameter (25.4 mm.) in lengths of 7, 10, 12 and 14 inches. You should be able to adjust the saddle as per instructions on page 163 and still have at least 2½ inches of seat post in the seat tube. If not you need a larger frame. Otherwise, if you're perched 10 or 15 inches above the seat post, you look awkward and will feel the same way, as if you were wearing a suit two sizes too small. The reason for getting the right size bike in the first place is to permit proper placement of arms, legs and torso for maximum cycling efficiency and comfort. If the frame is too small you will also need a longer stem unless you have unusually short arms for your height. This is why a custom-made frame may be necessary if your arms, legs or torso are unusually short or long for the rest of you. I know six-footers who have such short legs they need a 21-inch frame but such a long torso and arms they need a long top tube and longer (3½ to 4 inches) stem.

One more point. You might have trouble fitting your saddle to a micro-adjusting seat post, such as is made by Campagnolo, Unica-Nitor or Zeus, if your saddle cradle wires are wider or narrower than usual. Campagnolo's micro-adjusting alloy seat post comes in either wide or narrow widths. You can tell which seat post to order by measuring your saddle where the cradle wires are straight (Fig. 203). Some saddles are narrow

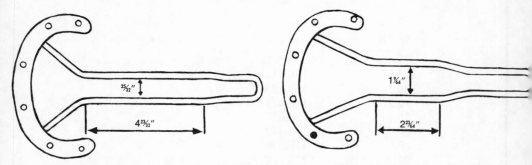

Fig. 203: Section of saddle-wire cage that fits into seat-post slots varies as to dimension, so if you change to a saddle with a different cage size you will have to change seat posts; and vice versa. As shown above, common saddle-wire slot area dimensions are: top, 25/32 inches wide (20 mm.) and 4 23/32 long (120 mm.), and bottom, 1 9/64 inches wide (36 mm.) and 2 23/64 inches long (60 mm.).

and long, others wider and shorter, even of the "narrow" racing variety. Narrow and long saddles are $^{25}/_{32}$ inches wide and $4^{23}/_{32}$ inches long at this point, and short and wide saddles are $1^{61}/_{64}$ inches wide and $2^{23}/_{64}$ inches long at the straight section of the wire cradle.

RIMS

Rims, for tubular tires in particular and also for clinchers, come in a wide variety of shapes and sizes. However, since clincher rims of a given size are for all practical purposes interchangeable, we will concentrate on tubular rim applications here. First, though, I think the strongest clincher $27 \times 1\frac{1}{4}$-inch rim on the market is the Milremo Super Champion which has deep section sidewalls for improved braking, and reinforcing ferrules which are pressed into spoke holes to give a watertight fit to tires. At 30 ounces this rim isn't light, but it will take a lot of cobblestones, pot holes, and rough abuse. Clincher rims are generally available in 32, 36, and 40-spoke hole drillings, tubulars from 24 to 40 in multiples of four, depending on the rim (lighter rims such as Milremo Weltmeister go down to 24 holes).

A well-made tubular rim is characterized by a high polish on the inside diameter, ferruled spoke holes with a watertight fit that keeps water from the tire (and from rotting it), a joint that's very close fitting, and serrations on the outside diameter surface to help grip the tire on the rim. For road and touring tires, wide brake flats (sides) with serrations provide improved braking. Wood-filled rims give elasticity and permit setting spoke holes closer to rim edge to retain trueness, once aligned. The disadvantage of the wood rim is that it is very light, and suitable primarily for track and time trials (*not* for touring), and spoke nipple heads fit into rim alloy only and not into reinforced ferrules or washers, which makes it easier for spoke nipple to pull through the wood-filled rim under pedaling stress.

TUBULAR TIRE RIM SELECTION TABLE

The rims in the table below are only a small sampling of the dozens of makes of rims available (Fig. 204). Since space forbids mentioning them all, I have selected a few to give you a rough idea of the various types and applications of rims on the market. Outstanding rim makers are Mavic, A.V.A., Grunert, and Araya (Japanese).

TABLE 23 · Tubular Tire Rim Applications

APPLICATION	MANUFACTURER	MODEL	FERRULED	NON-FERRULED	WOOD FILLED	HOLES DRILLED	WEIGHT (oz. each)
TOURING	Milremo	Corsa		X		32,36,40	12
	Milremo	Super Champion	X			28,32,36,40	9½
	Weinmann	294	X			36,40	12½
MASSED START, LONG-DISTANCE	Mavic	Piste	X			32,36,40	13
	Milremo	Giro	X			28,32,36,40	12½
TIME TRIALS	Mavic	Piste		X		28,32,36,40	13
SHORT TIME TRIALS AND PURSUITS	Milremo	Weltmeister			X	24,28,32,40	7
MEDIUM-DISTANCE TIME TRIALS AND CRITERIUMS	Mavic	Monthlery	X			28,32,36,40	11¼
	Milremo	Giro	X			28,32,36,40	12½
SPRINTS	Milremo	Super Record		X		36 (only)	11
	Mavic	Sport		X		28,32,36,40	14½

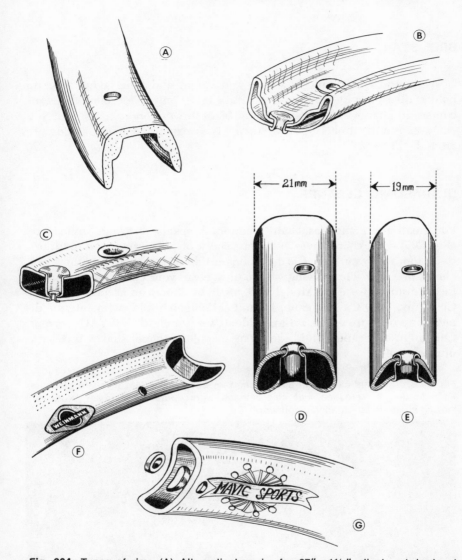

Fig. 204: Types of rims (A) Alloy clincher rim for 27″ x 1¼″ clincher (wired on) tires. (B) Rim for French size 700C 27″ x 1⅝″ clincher tires. (If you buy a bike in Europe make sure you specify it comes with 27 x 1¼ tires; French 700C tires are not easily available in the U.S.) (C) Typical ferruled rim for tubular tires. (D) Road-racing rim for tubular tires. (E) Track-racing rim for tubular tires (note narrower width). (F) Wood-filled tubular tire rim. (G) Nonferruled rim, using washers.

BIKE STAND

Costs around $85.00, and is a very convenient and time-saving ways to hold a bike upright while you work on it. A "must" for bike shops, of course, and handy if you have a lot of bikes to work on at home, or if you enjoy constantly tinkering with them. Less expensive home stands are around $15 to $20.

ULTRASONIC CLEANER

For small parts such as chains, bottom brackets, bearings, hubs, etc. (Fig. 205). Quickly removes every last speck of grit, grime, and old lubricant from every surface. Cleans chains inside and out, so that they look almost like new. Time-saving way to ultra-clean your parts; recommended for bike stores. I use the Model 5-50, made by American Electrical Heater Company, 6110 Cass Avenue, Detroit, Michigan 48212, with interior dimensions of 5 in. x 9 in. x 4-in. wide. Uses standard 110-VAC current. Cavitation of cleaning fluid (kerosene or chloroethane) shakes dirt loose ultrasonically.

Fig. 205: Ultrasonic cleaner in action, showing cavitation effect in chain cleaning. Fluid in unit is kerosene, but chloroethane works better and faster. Note dirt leaving chain under ultrasonic agitation.

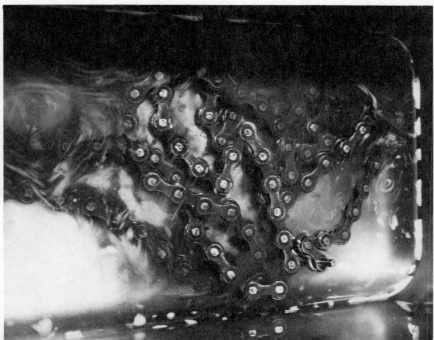

A WORD ABOUT LUBRICANTS

Elsewhere in this book I have recommended Lubriplate Type A or Lubriplate Marinelube grease (both are the same), which are available from auto- or marine-supply stores. However, if you plan to do cold-weather cycling, I recommend Lubriplate Snowmobile grease, which maintains its low viscosity (does not thicken and harden and make pedaling harder) down to −65°F and is, in addition, quite resistant to being washed off bearings should you ride in the rain, snow or slush. Use any of these lubricants for hubs, bottom brackets, pedals and headset bearings. Phil Wood also distributes a good bearing grease that resists washing away by water, available from bike stores.

For chains I recommend Lubriplate's Chainlube, which you can buy in motorcycle stores. This is a low viscosity lubricant in a spray can for easy application. *Don't get it on tires or brake blocks!* It tends to wash dirt off chain as you spray; was formulated for motorcycle chains but works well on bike chains too in my experience.

For freewheels I also use Chainlube since it is a thin liquid and won't gum up and so hold open freewheel pawls, a problem more fully discussed in the section under freewheel maintenance on page 369.

DERAILLEURS: MAINTENANCE AND ADJUSTMENT

Derailleurs are simple and easy to keep in efficient operating condition. But they are not toys. The better makes are as finely constructed and as precision-machined as the parts of the finest automobiles, and they are just as deserving of your care and attention.

A properly aligned, adjusted, and lubricated derailleur reduces drag, wear and tear on gears and chain, and makes the bicycle far easier to pedal. If you go on trips, you should at least know how to make the basic adjustments on derailleurs yourself.

Derailleur Gear Changers

The derailleur type of gear-changing mechanism has been developed over the past fifty years or so until today it is just about the most efficient and foolproof gear switcher made for bicycles.

However, the mechanism is exposed, and people, particularly young people, damage even the sturdiest of the derailleur breed by careless handling or improper use. (See page 172, for instructions on how to change derailleur gears quickly, safely, and without damaging the mechanism.)

Derailleur is a French word meaning, literally, to "derail," or to push a bicycle chain from one gear to the next larger or smaller gear. While we're at it, let's get acquainted with more derailleur terminology—the various parts of front and rear derailleurs and how they work. All of the popular makes of derailleurs—French, Italian, Spanish, and Japanese—operate on the same basic principle.

A rear derailleur transmission (Fig. 206) consists of the gear-shifter mechanism, and four, five, or six gears. The gears are mounted on a freewheel unit, which means the cyclist can stop pedaling without stopping the bicycle (coasting). The freewheel unit with its gears threads

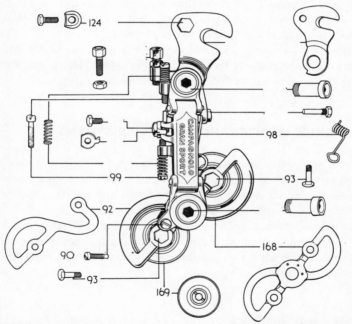

Fig. 206: Typical derailleur mechanism, in this case the Campagnolo "Gran Sport" unit. Parts are as follows (major ones only): 90-peg stop; 92-inner roller plate; 93-bolt to jockey roller; 98-traverse spring; 99-limit stop adjuster bolts (top bolt is for low or larger gear limit travel, lower bolt is for high or smaller gear limit travel); 124-chainstay bolt; 168-outer roller plate; 169-tension roller.

onto the rear wheel hub. The gear derailleur is mounted on a threaded "ear" or adapter bracket on the rear dropout and can be removed with only a metric socket or Allen wrench.

Since derailleurs are exposed to the elements, they can easily get knocked out of alignment or adjustment if the bicycle falls on the derailleur side, or if too much dirt and dust get into the mechanism. I have had derailleurs shoved out of whack by so simple a thing as an inexperienced cyclist running into my derailleur from behind. (After this happened, I decided to ride behind novice cyclists.) Also, if your quick-release lever is pointing straight backwards and a rider hits you there from the rear, your lever could be unsnapped, resulting in your rear wheel coming off, or jamming sideways between chainstays.

How Derailleurs Work

To see how the derailleur mechanism works, hang your bicycle from two ceiling hooks, or turn it upside down. Then, turn the pedals and move the rear derailleur gear-shift lever up and down. Look at the mechanism. You'll see that while a four-sided cage moves from side to side, its sides always remain parallel. This is known as the parallelogram-changer principle, and its purpose is to keep the two small wheels in the derailleur and the chain parallel to the vertical plane of the freewheel gears. (Note: The terms "gears," "cogs," and "sprockets" refer to the same thing; we'll use "gears" because it's more familiar.)

The top wheel in the derailleur gear shifter is called the "jockey" wheel because it "jockeys" the chain from one freewheel gear to the other. The lower wheel is called the "tension" wheel because it keeps the chain under constant tension even though different lengths of chain are required, depending on what combination of rear and front derailleur gears and chainwheel you are using. Obviously the lowest (largest) rear gear and the highest (largest) front chainwheel will use up more chain than the opposite combination. The derailleur mechanism must therefore not only derail or move the chain from one rear gear to another of larger or smaller diameter, but it must also maintain constant tension on the chain. The derailleur keeps the chain taut by spring-loaded shafts which keep the jockey and tension wheels under constant pull toward the rear of the bicycle. This tension is adjustable (Figs. 207 and 208).

Figure 206 shows a typical rear derailleur mechanism. Study this photo to learn the names of the parts. Figure 209 shows a typical front derailleur.

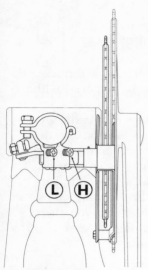

Fig. 207: Typical front derailleur, showing location of low gear "L" and high gear "H" adjustable stop bolts, which limit left and right movement of derailleur body so chain won't shift off high or low gear.

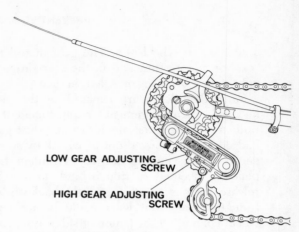

LOW GEAR ADJUSTING SCREW

HIGH GEAR ADJUSTING SCREW

Fig. 208: Shimano Eagle derailleur showing location of high and low gear adjustment stops. Location of these stops varies from make to make of derailleur. To find which of yours is which, shift to high gear and check which stop bolt rests on or is closest to derailleur cage or body.

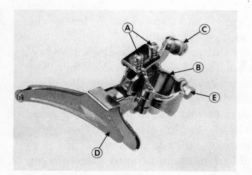

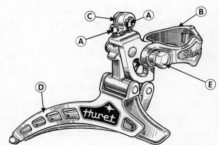

Fig. 209: Two modern front derailleurs, for shifting chain from one chainwheel to another. Will handle two or three chainwheels. Left, Shimano "Thunderbird" derailleur; right, Huret derailleur. On both: (A) Stop limit adjustments, to keep chain from going too far to left and right and coming off chainwheels. (B) Ring to hold derailleur on down tube. (C) Cable locknut, holds shift cable on derailleur mechanism. (D) Cage through which passes chain, and which derails or moves chain from one chainwheel to another. (E) Locknut holding derailleur on down tube. Loosen to move derailleur up or down so cage is about ⅛ inch above largest chainwheel, and from side to side so cage is parallel to chainwheels.

Derailleurs, front and rear, have two things in common besides their function. Both have derailleur adjustable travel "stops" which limit derailleur body travel, so the chain won't jump off high or low gears. There are too many makes and models of derailleurs on the market to cover them all; all you need know is that one adjusting screw is for the high-gear travel limit and one for the low-gear travel limit. Which adjusting screw is which varies from make to make, but you can tell one from the other by shifting to the highest gear and looking to see which adjustment bolt is hitting or is closest to the derailleur body. Obviously, the other bolt is for the low-gear travel limit. Look at Fig. 208, for example. The low-gear adjustment keeps the derailleur from moving too far to the left and moving the chain so that it overrides the big gear and gets jammed between that gear and the spokes, causing the wheel to lock and resulting in a possible accident. The high-gear adjusting screw keeps the derailleur body from moving too far to the right, which would cause the chain to override the little gear and possibly jam between that gear and the right seat stay, again locking the rear wheel. (The cable has not been installed on the derailleur in this drawing.)

Now look at Fig. 207. This is the front derailleur. The "L" shows the low-gear stop and the "H" the high-gear stop. The low-gear chainwheel is the small gear at the left. To adjust rear or front derailleur, shift so the chain rides on the highest gear without making grinding noises or coming off to the right. Move the high-gear stop bolt so it is snug against derailleur body. Shift to low gear, so the chain does not come off or grind, and adjust the stop bolt against the derailleur body.

Derailleur Troubles and Their Solutions

Derailleurs can behave badly not only because of their own malfunction, but also because of trouble in the parts associated with them. In this section, therefore, we will also treat maintenance of the chain, the freewheel, and the chainwheel. The freewheel is the four- or five-geared widget on the rear wheel hub. The chainwheel is the big sprocket up front next to the right pedal crank.

1. PROBLEM: Gear changes while riding.
   CAUSE: Gear-shift control lever too loose.
   SOLUTION: Tighten gear-control-lever thumbscrew (wing nut), or use a screwdriver on nut type (Fig 210). Caution: Tighten just enough so lever feels slightly tight. Do not tighten so hard that shifting becomes difficult.

Fig. 210: Derailleur will move and cause gears to skip if gear shift lever nut gets loose. This nut will always eventually work loose, which is why it has a handy wing ("A") so you can tighten it by hand from time to time. If front or rear gears jump from a higher to a lower (big to small) gear, first check to make sure gearshift lever axle nut is tight.

On Schwinn children's bicycles using a "Stik-Shift," and other similar machines with this shift, tighten the lever-adjusting nut under the shift cover somewhat. Do not overtighten or the shift will not operate smoothly.

2. PROBLEM: Gear changes erratically, slowly, and noisily.
   CAUSE: Derailleur jockey and tension sprockets are not lined up in the same plane as rear gears.
   SOLUTION: Turn bike upside down. (Note: I prefer to hang the bicycle from the ceiling by hooks attached to the saddle [seat] and handlebars, which puts all parts at eye level or close to it or use a bike stand.) Sight along a vertical line to check that tension and jockey wheels are parallel to rear hub gears, as shown in Fig. 211.

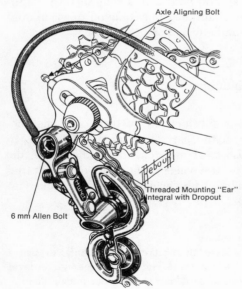

Axle Aligning Bolt

Threaded Mounting "Ear"
Integral with Dropout

6 mm Allen Bolt

Fig. 211: There are two ways of mounting derailleurs. On better bicycles, the derailleur is mounted on a threaded "ear" which is part of the forged steel dropout. A Campagnolo "T" wrench, or 6 mm. Allen wrench, will fit into Allen socket (arrow) on most of these derailleurs. If you are fitting a new derailleur into a dropout ear, discard any mounting plate that comes with it. Less expensive bicycles do not have the threaded dropout ear to accept a derailleur. Instead, a mounting bracket is used. Mounting bracket is held in place with screw and nut, and by pressure of axle nut for quick-release skewer.

Another indication of misalignment is chain rub marks on the inside of the derailleur cage. If derailleur wheels do not line up with rear hub gears, check first to make sure the derailleur itself is positioned correctly. Some derailleurs' top shafts are screwed into a threaded opening in the rear dropout, or the top shaft can be fitted into a threaded opening in a mounting bracket that fits into the rear dropout and is held on by a mounting screw and the wheel axle bolt or quick-release skewer. In any case, do not attempt a manhandling cure by hitting the side of the derailleur chain cage with a hammer. If the chain cage is badly bent due to abuse (such as dropping the bicycle on the derailleur side), it can be replaced by a new chain cage, which you can order from one of the mail-order shops listed on page 497. If the cage is only slightly bent, gripping it with an adjustable open-end wrench and twisting it gently can often bring the chain cage back into alignment. Use a steady "levering" action.

On Campagnolo derailleurs, use an adjustable wrench over the outside of the heavy casting (the part that has "Campagnolo" stamped on it), and gently twist it back into alignment.

On Huret Allvit derailleurs, and many others, if the derailleur arm is out of alignment, the jockey wheel will not track down the center of the chain but may, instead, press on the side of the chain and cause a grinding noise. To remedy this, give a slight twist of the derailleur arm with an adjustable wrench, first putting the derailleur in the low-gear (large-gear) position. Remember, in this case the derailleur "arm" (see Fig. 206) is *not* the derailleur main body we mentioned above. On the Huret Allvit, it is the arm that comes out from the bottom of the derailleur body next to the low-gear adjusting screw (see Fig. 206). This arm is bent out of alignment relatively easily, particularly when the bike is used carelessly.

A good reason for having everything in correct alignment on derailleur mechanisms, aside from the noise and extra wear and tear caused by misalignment, is that a good deal of energy-wasting friction can also result from such misalignment.

Shimano derailleurs (Japanese-made, used on many American bicycles), five-speed derailleur mechanisms, are very similar to better European makes, and have low- and high-gear stops that may need adjustment from time to time (Fig. 212 and 213). The Shimano "Crane" alloy unit is an excellent mechanism, easy to adjust and sturdy.

3. PROBLEM: Chain keeps riding up on the rear low-gear sprocket (the largest rear gear). This can cause the chain to bind in the spokes, with disastrous results.

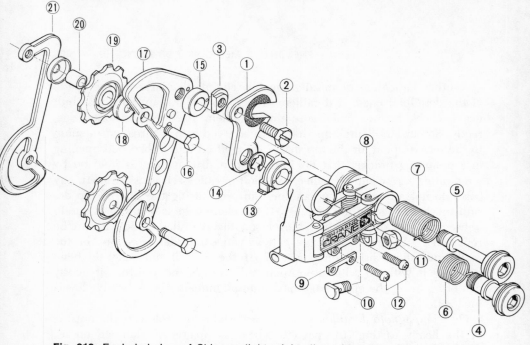

Fig. 212: Exploded view of Shimano lightweight-alloy wide-range Crane GS derailleur. (1) Adapter bracket (not needed if dropout has threaded "ear" to accept part 4); (2) Adapter screw; (3) Adapter nut; (4) Adapter mounting bolt; (5) Plate mounting bolt; (6) B-tension spring; (7) P-tension spring; (8) Mechanism assembly; (9) Adjusting plate; (10) Cable fixing bolt; (11) Cable fixing nut; (12) Adjusting screw; (13) Adapter bushing assembly; (14) Stop ring; (15) Plate bushing; (16) Pulley bolt; (17) Inner cage plate; (18) Pulley cap; (19) Pulley; (20) Pulley bushing; (21) Outer cage plate.

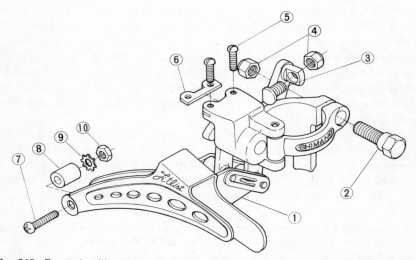

Fig. 213: Front derailleur exploded view. This is Shimano's alloy Titlist derailleur. Drawing gives an idea as to how this type of derailleur is constructed. Parts are: (1) Mechanism assembly, lower inlet type (1⅛"); (2) Clamp bolt; (3) Cable fixing bolt; (4) Cable fixing nut; (5) Adjusting bolt (M4 x 12); (6) Adjusting plate; (7) Bolt (M4 x 16); (8) Bushing; (9) Toothed lock washer; (10) Nut (M4).

Fig. 214: If chain jumps off big rear gear and gets jammed between that gear and chain, or jumps off small rear gear and jams between it and *chainstay,* the derailleur high- or low-limit stop screws need adjustment. There are far too many derailleurs now on the market to tell you where each screw is. Usually the high-gear (small-gear) screw is at the bottom of the derailleur, as shown on this Shimano Crane GS wide-range derailleur above. Check where yours is by shifting chain and derailleur to low (big) gear; the screw whose end is closest to a machined stop inside the derailleur cage is the low-gear adjustment. Of course, the other screw is for the high-gear limit. To adjust, shift to big gear and screw adjustment screw till it hits stop. Repeat for small gear. Check by shifting from big to small gears and up again and make sure chain does not jump off either gear.

CAUSE: The low-gear derailleur adjustment screw needs readjustment (Fig. 214).

SOLUTION: Make this adjustment. On Huret Allvit and Sprint derailleurs used with most Schwinn and other American-made bicycles, the low-gear (large-sprocket) adjustment screw is located at the bottom of the derailleur, next to the cable pivot bolt and nut. On Simplex "Prestige" and "Raid" derailleurs, the low-gear adjustment is the top of the two thumbscrews in the center of the derailleur body. On Campagnolo derailleurs, the low-gear adjusting screw is at the top of the derailleur, as it is also on the Cycle Benelux P.2 derailleur (English). This takes care of the popular makes of derailleurs. The low-gear adjuster keeps the derailleur from moving too far inward and derailing the chain beyond the largest gear into the spokes. Adjust so the chain will not climb beyond the large gear.

4. PROBLEM: Chain runs off high-gear (small) sprocket.

CAUSE: High-gear adjusting screw is moved out of place because of vibration.

SOLUTION: Readjust the high-gear adjusting screw (Fig. 214). Turn wheel so that the chain is on the large front chainwheel and small rear gear. If the chain has jammed between seat stay and gear, be careful that in pulling it out you don't bend it or the derailleur. If necessary, loosen the quick-release skewer or axle nuts and push the wheel forward, or rotate it gently backward. Turn the high-gear adjusting screw until the chain will not slip off high gear. On Huret Allvit derailleurs, the high-gear adjusting screw is the small screw about two-thirds of the way down the outside face of the main housing bracket, recessed into a small hole in the bracket. On Campagnolo derailleurs, the high-gear adjusting screw is located about halfway down, at the rear of the main housing casting, and points toward the bottom. On Benelux derailleurs, the high-gear stop is at the bottom of the unit, pointing toward the ground, and on the Shimano "Skylark," it is at the bottom of the two Phillips-head screws at the center rear of the derailleur.

Note: Every time your bicycle is knocked over on the derailleur side, you should check high- and low-gear stops on the rear derailleur. If you've parked (and locked) your bicycle where people can get at it, curious passersby may have played with the gear shifters. If this is the case, look at the position of the gear-shift handle, move it back about where it was when you parked, and start off by pedaling very gently, while, at the same time, adjusting the gear-shift levers. Otherwise, if you take off with the chain on one and the lever in position for another gear, you can catch the chain between gears and damage the derailleur. This goes for the front (chainwheel) derailleur too.

If you've had your bicycle for some time (six months or so), or you've ridden on sandy or dusty roads, sand or dirt can get into the derailleur linkage arms and clog the derailleur up. It is a good idea to clean the mechanism about every hundred miles, and relubricate pivot points and linkage with light oil.

5. PROBLEM: Chain skips while pedaling, usually in high gear.
   CAUSE: Insufficient chain tension.
   SOLUTION: Varies with type of derailleur.

   HURET ALLVIT DERAILLEUR: Move the chain tension spring back a notch.

   SIMPLEX DERAILLEUR: For more spring tension on a Simplex derailleur, remove the screw and dust cap from the bottom pivot bolt, and insert a metric Allen wrench in the hole you'll now see. Then, while you hold the locknut between the pivot bolt and the cage (the bracket with two half-moons holding the two small derailleur wheels), with a wrench (metric), turn the Allen wrench toward the rear of the bicycle for more chain tension, or toward the front for less tension. (Note: Use as little tension as possible to reduce drag, wear and tear, and make pedaling easier. This applies to all derailleurs.)

   CAMPAGNOLO DERAILLEUR: To increase chain tension on a Campagnolo rear derailleur, remove the chain cage stop-bolt (the thin bolt with a small round head that looks like a water tower lying on the ground, and that keeps the cage from rotating too far clockwise). Let the cage unwind until no more spring tension can be felt. Then, with an Allen wrench, remove the cage pivot bolt (the bolt that holds cage to derailleur), located at the bottom of the derailleur, and remove the cage from the spring end. Turn the cage slightly forward until the end of the spring fits into the next of the three holes. Replace the pivot bolt and cage assembly and tighten the pivot bolt. Wind the cage assembly counterclockwise one-half to one-and-a-half turns, hold it in this position, and reinstall the cage stop-bolt. (Make sure the cage assembly is right side up by checking that the top roller is the one that has the inner side exposed. The bottom roller has the cage on both sides of the wheel, the top wheel has the cage on the outer side only.)

Replace the chain (with rear wheel in place) and check the shifting while pedaling. (Always check the bicycle on the road, not hanging from the ceiling.) Be sure to check high- and low-gear adjustment screws.

SHIMANO SKYLARK DERAILLEUR: Increase chain tension by removing the chain cage stop-bolt and by winding the cage assembly forward one turn and replacing the stop-bolt.

BENELUX DERAILLEUR: Cable tension adjustment is similar to the Campagnolo.

CAUSE: Burrs on teeth of freewheel gear.
SOLUTION: File or grind burrs off.

CAUSE: A chain link too tight or binding.
SOLUTION: If you've removed and reinstalled the chain, check the link involved. Or check *all* the chain links. If a link binds or is tight (when you move it up and down), twist the chain gently from side to side. Of course, if your chain is rusty, don't bother with this procedure; simply install a new chain.

CAUSE: Excessive wear in chain or gears.
SOLUTION: Chains and gears do wear, and old chains stretch as a result of wear. Always replace worn loose chains (an old chain always breaks when you're miles from a bike shop). Do not replace an old chain and leave worn gears. Replace both at the same time. Old gears are identifiable by a slight hook on the inner lip of the gear teeth, which can catch the chain and make it "skip." Check the most used gears first, using your fingernail. Hooks can be filed or ground off. Removing a gear from the freewheel is not difficult, but you will need a special tool. Therefore, I will not describe this procedure here.

CHECK CHAINWHEEL TEETH: Chainwheel teeth can also wear. They show this wear on the "lands" of the teeth; that is, by wearing away the face of the curvature of the gear teeth on the side toward the rear of the bicycle, away from the direction of rotation of the chainwheel. If the chainwheel is worn this much, it should be discarded and replaced with a new one, to avoid rough pedaling and erratic drive. Also, a worn chainwheel will soon wear out a new chain. If you're in doubt about chainwheel wear, check the chainwheel as follows: wrap a chain around the chainwheel and pull the chain down into the teeth by holding the ends of the chain snugly together. If the chain links fit tightly into the chainwheel teeth and cannot be picked away from the wheel at any gear, the wheel is in good shape. But if the chain climbs up on the teeth without being lifted up by you, mark this point of climb. Then try a new chain and repeat the procedure. If the new chain comes up at the same point, the gear is worn and should be replaced. However, if the new chain fits nicely, the old chain is shot and should be replaced.

Remember that a chain doesn't actually "stretch," but because the parts wear and "give," it acts as though it *has* stretched. It takes only a few thousandths of an inch of wear on each of the rivets to make the chain stretch a half-inch. (This is why frequent cleaning and lubrication are important in chain maintenance.)

Another check for the chainwheel and chain fit is to put the chain you intend to use on the chainwheel, already installed on the bicycle, and watch how the chain flows over the chainwheel teeth. There should be no "lifting" or sticking of the chain to the chainwheel teeth.

See page 420 on crank axle maintenance for instructions on replacing the chainwheel.

CAUSE: Chain is too long.

SOLUTION: Remove extra links. See page 372 for correct chain length adjustment.

6. PROBLEM: Gear won't shift all the way into low (onto rear, large sprocket).
   CAUSE: Low-gear adjusting screw is out of adjustment.
   SOLUTION: Readjust as per instructions above.

   CAUSE: Cable has stretched, or has slipped in the cable pivot bolt (where it is fastened to derailleur).
   SOLUTION: Shift derailleur into high gear while turning pedals. Cable should have small amount of slack. If too loose, take up slack by turning the adjusting barrel on the derailleur, or, if there is no barrel on your machine (many good bicycles don't have one), put shift lever in high-gear position, all the way toward the front of the bicycle, loosen the cable pivot bolt-nut, pull some of the cable slack through, and retighten. Be sure to leave a little slack in the cable.

If the gear-shift cable breaks while you are on a trip, you can at least avoid having to pedal all the way home in high gear by screwing the high-gear adjustment to keep the chain on the first or second gear up from the highest (small-sprocket) gear.

7. PROBLEM: Chain slips off small front chainwheel sprocket.
   CAUSE: Low-gear limit screw is out of adjustment.

Fig. 215: Arrow shows location of high- and low-limit stops on front derailleur. One adjustment screw keeps derailleur from moving too far to the left so chain can't jump off small chainwheel; the other keeps derailleur from moving too far to the right, so chain can't jump off big chainwheel.

SOLUTION: Turn pedals and shift front derailleur to small chainwheel. Re-adjust low-gear limit screw (Fig. 215). On Huret Allvit front derailleurs, this screw is on the body of the derailleur, just under the righthand (chain-side) clamp bolt, facing toward the chain guide. On Campagnolo front derailleurs, the low-gear adjusting screw is the inner (closest to seat tube) screw, just forward of the cable anchor screw. Remember, the function of the chain guard is to derail or move the chain from one chainwheel sprocket to the other. There is no tension adjustment to the front derailleur; this is taken care of by the rear derailleur. To avoid confusion, I must also point out that on rear derailleur freewheel gear clusters, the smaller the gear the higher the gear ratio (for high speeds) and the larger the gear the lower the gear ratio (for climbing steep hills). Gear sizes and ratios are the other way around for front derailleurs; the small chainwheel is for low speed (hills) and the big chainwheel is for high speed.

8. PROBLEM: Chain won't stay on large chainwheel (front derailleur).
   CAUSE: High-gear adjusting screw is out of adjustment.
   SOLUTION: Since there are only two adjusting screws on front derailleurs (chainwheels), and we have already told you where the low-gear adjustment screw is on all popular front derailleurs, all you need do is shift the front derailleur lever to the high position (toward the rear of the bicycle), while turning the pedals, and adjust the chain guide over the large chainwheel with the high-gear adjusting screw. If shifting from small to large chainwheel after this adjustment is hard, bend the upper front corner of the inner part of the chain guide (cage) slightly inward, toward the chainwheel. If, however, the chain tends to jump off the chainwheel toward the outside (away from the bicycle), bend the upper front corner of the outer chain guide slightly toward the chainwheel. To find the exact spot where you bend the chainwheel guide, turn the pedals (cranks) by hand while

the bicycle is off the ground and move the front shift lever until the chain just starts to lift off the chainwheel teeth. The part of the chain guide (cage) to be bent is touching the chain at this point.

9. PROBLEM: Chain won't shift onto large front chainwheel.
CAUSE: High-gear adjusting screw is out of adjustment.
SOLUTION: Readjust screw (see Fig. 214) so chain guide will push chain up onto large front chainwheel.

CAUSE: Cable has stretched.
SOLUTION: Push front derailleur control lever all the way forward while turning pedals (cranks). Cable should be nearly tight. If it is loose, move shift lever all the way forward, unscrew cable bolt (the bolt that holds the cable to the front derailleur shifting mechanism), pull cable through, and retighten cable bolt (Fig. 216 and 217).

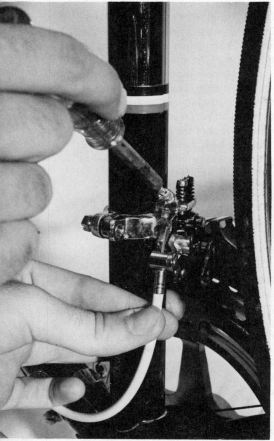

Fig. 216: If chain won't shift to big chainwheel, and you have loosened the derailleur adjustment screw to permit the derailleur to move to the right (Fig. 213), then cable has stretched. Take out excess cable slack by loosening cable locknut (see above), pulling through excess cable, and retightening locknut. Check to make sure chain will now shift to the big chainwheel. If not, readjust right-hand stop nut.

Fig. 217: When replacing the chain, it is sometimes confusing, if you haven't done it many times, to know how to fit the chain back on the bike. The best way is to install the rear wheel, if it is off, and start the chain with the protruding link toward front of bike and facing you on left side of bike (so you can use rivet remover to press it back in from left side of bike); then put the chain end without the protruding link through front derailleur cage first, then around *top* of rear gear (see above), then down on *front* of top derailleur pulley (jockey wheel), then around *back* of bottom pulley (tension wheel). It will be easier if, during this process, you leave the chain off all the front chainwheels (you can pull it back on when you're finished with the chain). Now join the two chain ends together. If you've left about 1/64 inch of the rivet *inside* the link, you can force both links together until you feel a slight "pop" as the ends fit together and the inside link pops into the other link. Now just use the rivet tool (Fig. 198) to push the rivet back the way it was. Watch the adjoining rivet so you know when to stop pushing. Remove rivet tool, twist the link you were working on back and forth to remove stiffness, put chain back on front chainwheel, and you're finished!

10. PROBLEM: Front derailleur chain cage rubs on chain. Chain rattles.
CAUSE: Low- or high-gear adjustment screws have vibrated out of adjustment.
SOLUTION: Readjust screws.

CAUSE: Front derailleur mechanism not aligned so chain cage is parallel with chainwheel.
SOLUTION: Loosen the two bolts that hold the front derailleur mechanism to seat tube (frame) and turn the derailleur mechanism left or right to align the chain cage parallel to the chainwheel. While you've got the mechanism loose, make sure it is as close (low) to the chainwheel as possible, so that the outer plate of the chain cage just clears the teeth of the large chainwheel (Fig. 218).

CAUSE: Crooked or wavy chainwheel. Chain rattles.
SOLUTION: Straighten chainwheel by prying it back into position with a long, square-shanked screwdriver. To avoid bending the chainwheel more than you want to, use as fulcrum (levering) points the bottom bracket cup (holding chainwheel axle in frame bottom), inside the right crank and chain-ring mounting bolts, with chain on large chainwheel. To judge which way to bend the chainwheel, sight through the front derailleur chain cage, and use the inside plane of the chain cage as a guide.

Another good way to straighten a chainwheel is to use the rear stay as a guide, turn the chainwheel, and mark the high and low spots (near and far distances from chain stay) on the chainwheel with a china-marking pencil or a piece of chalk. If a high and low spot are opposite each other (directly across the chainwheel), using adjustable wrenches and pulling on the low point and pushing on the high point will usually bring the chainwheel back into true.

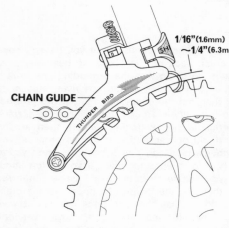

1/16"(1.6mm)
~1/4"(6.3mm)

CHAIN GUIDE

Fig. 218: Front derailleur cage should be no closer than ⅟₁₆ inch to, or ¼ inch away from biggest chainwheel. Loosen derailleur body ring bolt and slide entire derailleur up or down seat tube as needed to align. Move from side to side to align parallel to chainwheel.

To protect chrome plating or finish on the chainwheel, use a piece of rag between the paws of the wrench. Take it easy as you push—don't overdo it. It is far better to make too slight a push than to give it all you've got and shove the chainwheel out of true in the other direction.

If, however, there are two high points opposite each other, and two low points opposite each other, all you need do is push the two high points inward toward the frame simultaneously.

If the chainwheel is wavy, the straightening job is going to be tougher. Use an adjustable wrench at the point where the wave peaks or bottoms out and press gently in the required direction. Move around the wheel and adjust all waves or bends in this manner. If you can't bring the wheel back into true, you'd better buy and install a new chainwheel. Find out what rough treatment bent the chainwheel in the first place so this won't happen again. (If you have to replace it with a new chainwheel, see page 420 for instructions on removing and installing chainwheels.)

11. PROBLEM: Pedals turn, crank turns, chain turns, freewheel turns, but the wheel doesn't turn.

   CAUSE: Pawls inside the freewheel mechanism are stuck open by a piece of dirt or by the use of too heavy a lubricating oil in the freewheel.

   SOLUTION: Remove the freewheel and soak it in kerosene to remove dirt and/or heavy oil. Oil again with a light oil such as No. 5 SAE.

NOTE: If the spacing washers in the rear wheel on the freewheel side are too narrow or too wide, the freewheel gears will not be aligned correctly with the chainwheel and you will have chain rub front or rear, as well as loss of power due to rub. Please see section on alignment, page 412, for this alignment check and solution.

It is also important to know that if the chain is on the small front chainwheel and on the large rear gear, as you start to shift the chain down from the largest to the smallest rear gear the chain will assume a sharp angle. Try it—put the chain on the small front chainwheel and on the small rear gear and notice that the chain is at an extreme angle and, in fact, is rubbing on the inside of the front derailleur cage. You can avoid this type of rub if you will shift the front cage slightly to the left as you shift up, and slightly to the right as you shift down to the small gear.

12. PROBLEM: Chain won't shift to combination of largest front chainwheel and next to largest and largest rear gears.

   CAUSE: Chain is too short.

   SOLUTION: Add one or two links. See page 372 for instructions in finding correct chain length.

13. PROBLEM: Chain won't shift to small rear gear, or rubs on chainstay when in this position.

   CAUSE: Too little clearance between small gear and chainstay.

SOLUTION: Add clearance by removing washer from left side of axle and adding one or two washers to right side of axle under lock nut. This will move freewheel far enough to left to allow chain clearance.

CAUSE: You have too long a bolt head holding carrier onto frame. Replace with shorter bolt or file bolt head flat so it projects as little as possible on inside of seat stays, and clears chain.

14. PROBLEM: Chain rubs on spokes when in largest rear gear, and rubbing cannot be removed by adjusting derailleur stop nut.
CAUSE: You, or someone, has either laced a new wheel and trued it wrong, or aligned wheel wrong. Either way, you need to "dish" the wheel more to the right. See page 449 for wheel-truing instructions. This will pull rim and spokes to the right away from chain path.

How to Remove the Freewheel

There are two basic types of freewheels, each requiring its own special tool (see Fig. 199, page 340). If you have an "Atom," Milremo, or Sun Tour, you will need the two-prong type; if you have Shimano, Regina, and other splined types, you will need a matching splined removing tool. The splined freewheels are *much* easier to remove than the pronged type.

To remove pronged types, remove wheel. Remove quick-release skewer, put pronged tool in place so prongs fit into freewheel, reinstall skewer and tighten snug, then back off a half turn. With wrench, turn freewheel tool counterclockwise one quarter turn. Loosen skewer a few turns, turn freewheel tool a few turns. By now you should be able to remove the freewheel by hand, or by holding the tool in place and turning it with a wrench. Remove skewer entirely and back off the freewheel. When reinstalling, be careful to thread on accurately so you don't strip threads on hub, especially on aluminum hubs. Light oil on hub threads will make reinstalling the freewheel easier.

To remove splined freewheels, put tool in bench vise, lay freewheel on it so tool splines fit into freewheel splines, and twist wheel counterclockwise.

Routine Derailleur Maintenance: Lubrication

CHAIN: If you've been out riding in the rain, wipe water off chain (and the rest of bicycle too), and spray Lubriplate Chainlube (available from motorcycle stores or your bike shop) on chain to replace lubricant washed away and to prevent rust. Chainlube penetrates to chain roller bearings, and tends to wash dirt out of links as it is sprayed on. Every 200 miles or so (oftener if you've been riding on dusty, dirty country roads), remove the chain and agitate it in a pan of kerosene. With an old toothbrush, scrub off dirt that sticks to links. Remove from pan, letting excess kerosene drip into pan; wipe chain with rag. Lay chain out flat on a piece of paper and spray with Lubriplate Chainlube (available from motorcycle shops) on *both* sides. Wipe off excess oil; reinstall chain. If chain hasn't accumulated dirt, relube chain without removing it from bicycle, being careful not to spray Chainlube on tire or brake blocks. Wipe off excess Chainlube with rag so bike and you don't get sprayed as you ride.

In order to remove the chain, you'll need a rivet-remover tool (see Fig. 198, page 339). When pressing the chain rivet out with the tool, be careful not to press the rivet out all the way. Stop when the rivet is part way out, remove the tool, and see if you can complete the job by prying the chain apart with a small screwdriver or by twisting the chain away from the rivet. Ideally, you should leave just a bit of the rivet end showing inside the chain link, so that when you reinstall the chain, the small section of rivet can be popped back into the link hole. The job can be completed by pushing the rivet home with the same tool you used to push it out. If you should push a rivet all the way out of the hole by accident, remove chain, hold rivet with needle nose pliers, put mating link in place, tap rivet in chain plate with small hammer, or press in with vise. Do not remove an entire link, chain length is critical.

Incidentally, if you're installing a new derailleur ³⁄₃₂-inch-wide chain, remember that some new chains (I have never been able to figure out why) come with a master link, just like the ⅛-inch-wide chains used on three-speed and coaster-brake bicycles. You should remove this master (or spring-connecting) link by prying it off, and discard it along with the link it was supposed to hold. If you use the master link, it will rub on the gears.

DERAILLEUR: Lubricate pivot points every thirty days or every 200 miles. Every month, clean off dirt and grease from the derailleur with a brush dipped in kerosene (remove the wheel first so you don't drip kerosene on tires, and keep kerosene from brake pads), and relubricate the derailleur wheels with a light oil. Better yet, and this is best if you're finicky about performance, remove the entire derailleur mechanism from the bicycle and soak it in kerosene. Remove the small wheels from the cage (place them on a rag on the bench so as not to lose the small ball-bearings). Use Lubriplate grease inside the small wheel cones and stick the ball-bearings back in place. Reassemble derailleur.

NOTE: Some rear derailleurs have bronze or nylon sleeves in jockey and tension wheels, instead of ball bearings. For these derailleurs, simply squirt a bit of light oil on pulley bearings from time to time; they will not require disassembly.

If the derailleur wheels have worn smooth, replace them with new wheels, which you can order from one of the mail-order stores (see Appendix, page 497).

Selecting Correct Chain Length

New chains usually have 112, 116, or 120 links (two links per inch) and may be too long for your bicycle. Chain lengths vary according to bicycle wheelbase, whether you are using low, medium, or high ratio gears, and by type of rear derailleur (medium or wide range). If the chain is too long, you'll have too much slack when the chain is on the small rear gear and small or intermediate front chainwheel; as a result, the chain will tend to jump off gear, rub on front derailleur cage, and in general shift erratically. If the chain is too short, the rear derailleur will be pulled forward when chain is on biggest rear gear. Then the chain either will not shift into biggest rear gear, or will tend to jump back off it onto next higher (smaller) gear.

Narrow-range gears are defined as a freewheel with 13 to 22, medium-range 14 to 28 teeth. Wide-range gears are freewheels with 14 to 34 teeth. Before adjusting chain length, bicycle should be upright and parallel to floor.

We can ignore whether gear ratio is narrow or wide-range when checking chain length on ten- or fifteen-speed bicycles. On these bikes, put chain on largest front and rear gears. Bring the chain together by squeezing links until the rear changer pulleys are flat, parallel to the chain (Fig. 219). Add or remove links to maintain this chain length, when chain is on biggest front and rear gears. If installing a new chain, remember that if it comes with a master link, this link must be discarded because it will be too wide to use with five-sprocket freewheels. Use chain rivet tool instead.

On five-speed bicycles with narrow- or medium-gear range, put chain on smallest (highest) rear gear. Derailleur pulleys and pulley cage should be vertical, perpendicular to ground (Fig. 220). If not, add or remove links as necessary.

On five-speed bicycles with wide gear range, put chain on lowest (biggest) gear. Derailleur pulley cage and wheels should be flat, parallel

Fig. 219: For correct chain length on a ten-speed bicycle, put chain on biggest (most teeth) front and rear gears and add or remove chain links until rear derailleur wheels and cage are flat, parallel to chain, as shown above. These instructions apply also to five-speed bicycles with wide-range gears (14-34 T), with chain on biggest rear gear.

Fig. 220: For correct chain length on five-speed, medium-gear bicycles (1-22, 14-26, 14-28-teeth rear gear), put chain on smallest (least number of teeth) rear gear. Add or remove chain links as necessary so rear derailleur wheels and cage are about vertical, perpendicular to ground, as shown.

to chain and chainstay (Fig. 220). If not, add or remove links as necessary.

If pulley on any of the bicycles above is too far to the rear, the chain is too long. For example, on a ten-speed bicycle, with chain on biggest front and rear gears, if the front (tension wheel) end of the cage is tilted toward the ground, the chain is too long. If on a five-speed bike, with chain on highest (small) gear, the derailleur pulley cage is tilted toward the rear of the bicycle, the chain is too long.

How to Change to Handlebar Shifters

Ordinarily, ten-speed-derailleur gear-shift levers are mounted on the down tube. Or they may be mounted on the stem, behind the handlebars. In my opinion this is an unsafe location, because any accident that propels you over the handlebars may bring you into contact with these levers, which project up over the stem. Damage to the groin area may result.

You may wish to change gear-shift levers to a more convenient loca-

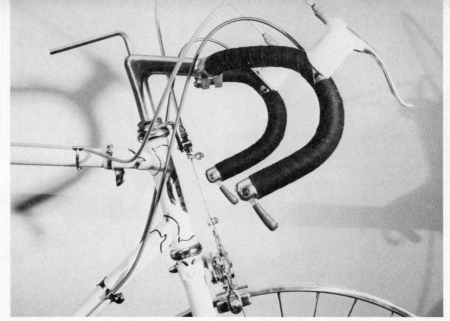

Fig. 221: Handlebar gear-shift levers for derailleur bicycles are easy to reach, and easy to install. Follow steps in text for simple installation. (Allen wrench in stem bolt illustrates recessed stem bolt.)

tion on the ends of the handlebars (Fig. 221). Here you can change gears without having to lean down and unbalance yourself; you can shift both levers quickly without losing steering control; and for short-armed riders this is altogether the most convenient location for shifters.

Here is a pictorial step-by-step method for changing to handlebar shift levers. First, though, a word about which lever system to change to. Handlebar shifters are made by Campagnolo, Shimano, Sun Tour, Huret, and Simplex, among others. I prefer the Shimano (Fig. 222) levers because

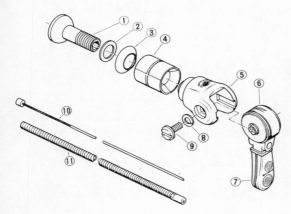

Fig. 222: Exploded view of Shimano bar-end controls. (1) Anchor bolt; (2) Plastic washer; (3) Tapered washer; (4) Segment assembly with spring; (5) Body; (6) Lever assembly with lever cap; (7) Lever cap; (8) Spring washer; (9) Lever fixing bolt; (10) Front inner cable, rear inner cable; (11) Lever-end outer casing, front derailleur outer casing, rear derailleur outer casing.

they have internal spring tension, which compensates for derailleur spring tension, making shifting easier. Next I prefer the Sun Tour, which has a ratchet mechanism which holds the gear where you shifted. I don't like the Campagnolo bar levers because they are hard to shift and won't stay in place; it's easy for the rear gear to shift by itself. Construction details among the various makes of handlebar shifters vary slightly, but basic principles are the same. If you can master one, you can install any of them. Tools and materials you will need are: Campagnolo "T" wrench or 6-mm. Allen wrench; medium-size screwdriver; new handlebar tape, preferably the cloth type; extra-long derailleur cables for handlebar-end shifters (if yours did not come with them); ⅛-inch or ³⁄₁₆-inch inside-diameter clear plastic tubing (from a chemical supply or hobby store, to keep cable tubing from rubbing on head tube); 6- or 8-mm. socket wrench or adjustable wrench to remove old cable and install new cable on derailleurs.

STEP ONE: Become acquainted with the basic parts of handlebar shifters. (A) shift lever-axle bolt; (B) housing barrel; (C) lever housing; (D) cable (extra long); (E) lever; (F) lever-axle nut; (G) lever-axle locknut. (H) is not a part of the shifters; it is the 6-mm. Allen wrench you will need to tighten barrel in handlebar end (Fig. 223).

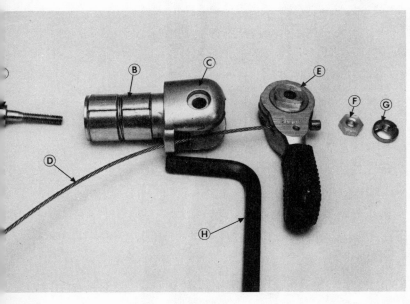

Fig. 223:
Step One

STEP TWO: Remove cable from front derailleur (Fig. 224).

STEP THREE: Remove rear derailleur shift levers and cable, and remove handlebar tape and end plugs. If tape can be reused, remove only as far as brake-lever body (Fig. 225).

STEP FOUR: Insert handlebar shift barrel into handlebar end, with cable partially installed as shown (Fig. 226).

STEP FIVE: Insert 6-mm. Allen wrench into barrel and tighten counter-clockwise, making sure axle holes are level as shown (Fig. 227).

Fig. 224: Step Two

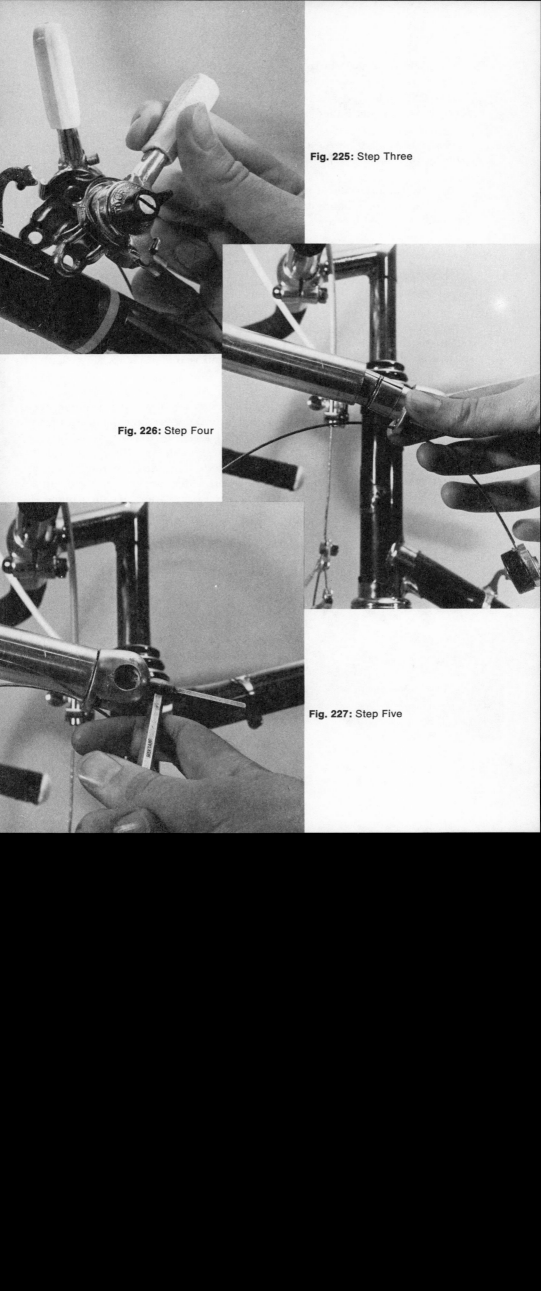

Fig. 225: Step Three

Fig. 226: Step Four

Fig. 227: Step Five

STEP SIX: Slide shift lever into milled section of housing. Note that flat lever flange fits into milled section of housing (Fig. 228).

STEP SEVEN: Insert lever-axle bolt into round countersunk hole in lever housing (*not* into square shank hole; see Step Eight) (Fig. 229).

STEP EIGHT: Insert lever-axle bolt on axle and thread down into octagonal-shaped hole that holds this nut in place. Tighten axle-lever nut from other side with screwdriver (Fig. 230).

STEP NINE: Thread on and tighten lever-axle locknut, using screwdriver. Slide steel tubing sheath over cables, and enough ⅛ or ³⁄₁₆-inch clear plastic tubing over sheath so that sheath won't rub on head tube (Fig. 231).

STEP TEN: Install cable sheath stop on down tube. Leave enough cable out so handlebars can turn unimpeded. Bring cable through metal sheath and cable stop, and install ends in front and rear derailleurs (Fig. 232). Check adjustment of derailleurs (see page 353).

STEP ELEVEN: Retape handlebars. You can either stop tape over derailleur cable sheathing just before you reach brake levers and let sheathing flop loose at this point, continuing beyond levers to top of bar without going over cable sheathing; or continue over cable sheathing till cable is covered up to near end of bars near stem. The latter method keeps cables from flopping around and looks a lot neater, but makes it difficult or impossible to remove handlebars when you bring your bike on a plane, as some airlines request.

Fig. 228: Step Six

Fig. 229: Step Seven

Fig. 230: Step Eight

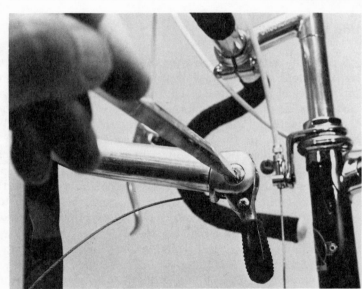

Fig. 231: Step Nine

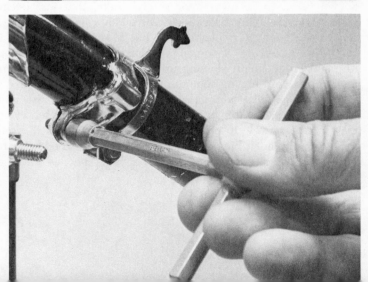

Fig. 232: Step Ten

BRAKES

Caliper Brakes

Caliper brakes have been around in one form or another for a long time, certainly (in an efficient form) since the early 1920s. With minor mechanical modifications and improvements, these are the brakes found on "lightweight" or "touring" and high-quality road (and many other types) of bicycles today.

How Fast Can You Stop?

Unlike the automotive industry, there has been practically no published research done by any bicycle firm or technical organization on the stopping power of all the various kinds of bike brakes under a wide range of conditions. The best I can offer you, at this writing, is my own experience. Using correctly adjusted Mafac center-pull brakes, which because they have soft blocks are the best I have used, I can stop within one foot for every mile per hour I am traveling, up to 12 miles per hour on a dry day, on dry concrete pavement, and on a flat road, with nothing on my bike but my own 160-pound self (that is, I am not carrying a load). Therefore, if I am traveling at 10 miles per hour, I should be able to stop within 10 feet, under controlled panic-stop brake-lever pressure, without skidding, and using both front and rear brakes.

Beyond 12 mph, however, I find it takes longer, exponentially, to stop, so that at 13 mph I can't stop in under 15 feet, and at 15 mph I have trouble stopping in 25 feet, and certainly in no shorter distance than that. So you need to be aware, for safety's sake, that just because you can come to a screaming halt in 10 feet when you're dawdling along at 10 mph, that when you're pushing hard at 15 mph you're lucky to be able to stop within 25 feet. Of course you don't *always* have to stop completely to avoid an accident; slowing up to half the speed you were at is often enough to avoid hitting something or it hitting you.

If you're pedaling a camping-gear-laden bike, it's also vital to remember that it will take longer to stop due to the greater tendency of the total mass of the bicycle to continue going forward, than it would the lesser mass of an unladen bicycle. I know I don't need to add this further warning about stopping on downhill runs at high speed—I know you know all about that. But just to make sure, I will say that if you can't stop on the flat within 25 feet at 15 mph, how soon could you stop at 45 mph going downhill? True, it's rare to have to stop completely on fast downhill runs, but you never know what's around that next blind turn; a trailer truck could be overturned in the middle of the road and you might need 60 or 100 feet to come to a dead halt (perhaps "live" halt would be more appropriate).

Remember, too, that stopping power is reduced when wheels are out of true; when you are using cheap center-pull or side-pull brakes (not Campagnolo or Shimano side-pulls; they're hardly inexpensive and are great); when brake cables are stretched so that you pull down on brake levers till they hit the handlebars and you still haven't put maximum pressure on brake shoes; when brake shoes are age-hardened; and, above all, when you're riding in the rain. You *can* stop in the rain, but allow 100 percent greater margin.

You may find combinations of front caliper brakes with rear coaster-brake hubs or two-, three-, or five-"speed" rear hubs. This combination is a good one if you like multiple-gear hubs and coaster brakes, but want good brakes. A coaster brake on the rear wheel alone is like a car with only rear brakes (which went out of style in the 1920s).

Caliper brakes operate very much like disc brakes on modern automobiles; that is, they squeeze down on both sides of the wheels so that a rubber pad, like an auto disc pad, grips the side of the rim and reduces forward wheel motion by pressure and friction.

Although there are dozens of makes of caliper brakes, there are only two basic types: center-pull (see Fig. 233) and side-pull (Fig. 234). Center-

Fig. 233: An elegant set of forged aluminum alloy center-pull caliper brakes comes on the beautifully handmade Panasonic top-quality bike. Adjustments are:
A. Brake cable locknut. Loosen to pull through cable slack; tighten.
B. Cable yoke.
C. Yoke pulley (a good idea that makes brakes work easier).
D. Brake shoe locknut. Loosen to move shoe up or down till it hits rim flat squarely and without rubbing on tire sidewall.

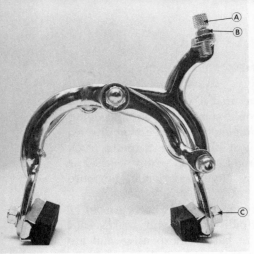

Fig. 234. Inexpensive side-pull brakes come on equally inexpensive ten- and three-speed bicycles. These brakes offer far less stopping power than good center-pull brakes such as the Gran-Compe, Fig. 233, and are almost useless in the rain. Adjustments are:

A. Cable slack take-up barrel. Turn counterclockwise to take up cable slack, bring brake shoes to within ⅛ inch of rim. Rim must be true.
B. Take-up barrel locknut. Turn down till it tightens on brake arm flat, as shown, after adjusting take-up barrel.
C. Brake shoe locknut. Loosen to move brake shoe up or down to bring it squarely on rim flat.

pull brakes are easier to adjust and tend to stay adjusted longer than the side-pull type, but they cost more and are found only on better bicycles.

Cantilever brakes are yet a third type, but they are used mainly on tandems, which require greater leverage for added stopping power. Cantilever brakes are heavy, must be brazed to fork blades, both undesirable. You don't need extra weight, and anything brazed on a frame weakens the frame at that point.

You can tell center-pull brakes by the wire that comes down over the brake and attaches to a piece of metal called a "cable anchor" (see Fig. 233). From the cable anchor another cable runs to both sides of the caliper brake assembly so that when the hand lever is squeezed, both sides of the caliper brake are pulled together.

Side-pull brakes, on the other hand, have a control cable that attaches directly to one of the caliper arms, usually the lefthand arm.

Most of the better center-pull and side-pull caliper brakes also come with a quick-release button, which is located either on the front of the hand lever (Fig. 235), or on the brake itself (Figs. 236 and 237). The quick-release lever button, when pushed in, releases the two brakes by opening up the caliper arms, only for the purpose of making it easier for you to get the wheel on and off. By no means should you think of the quick-release lever as another adjustment. It is there just so that you don't have to struggle so hard to get the tire and wheel out of the bike to fix a flat or make an adjustment on the wheel.

A quick-release on the brakes is helpful when it comes to removing the wheel with the tire inflated (Fig. 238). The tires are always wider than the brake-shoe spacing, so to remove the wheel without a release that spreads the brake shoes wider than the tire diameter means you will have to squeeze the tire past the brakes. This isn't so much of a problem on wheel removal, but when you try to put the wheel back in the dropouts, you still have to squeeze past the shoes, and in doing so it's easy to

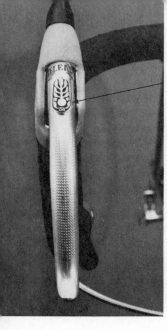

Fig. 235: Brake quick-release on brake lever (arrow). To release brakes so you can remove wheel easily, turn this release sideways. Other types of brake-handle releases work by pulling up, letting brake lever release further.

Fig. 236: Rear center-pull brake, showing quick-release and cable-slack take-up mechanism.

  A. Take-up barrel. Turn counterclockwise to remove cable slack.
  B. Take-up barrel locknut. Turn clockwise till it tightens down on brake fitting below it.
  C. Brake quick-release. Flip up to move brake shoes further out so wheel can be removed.
  D. Brake cable locknut. Loosen to take up cable slack when cable has stretched so far take-up barrel "A" won't take out slack. First, though, screw barrel "A" all the way clockwise. Pull excess cable through locknut D and retighten. Use brake "third hand," Fig. 243, to make brake adjustment easier.

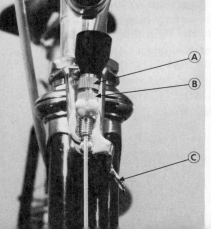

Fig. 237: Another type of front center-pull brake-adjusting barrel, which works similarly to adjustment-cable-slack take-up barrels described in Fig. 236.

  A. Cable take-up barrel
  B. Barrel locknut
  C. Quick-release lever. Flips up to release brakes.

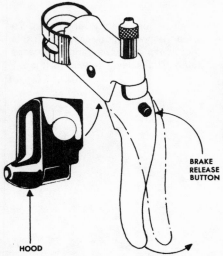

Fig. 238: Many center-pull brakes come with a rubber hood for hand comfort and buoyancy and a brake release button, which springs brakes apart to facilitate wheel removal. This Weinmann brake has both.

BRAKE
RELEASE
BUTTON

HOOD

force one of the brake shoes right out of its holder, leaving you without brakes on that wheel until you fiddle around long enough to replace the shoe in its holder.

Several new types of brakes have appeared on the market since the first edition of this book was published. While we mentioned earlier that side-pull brakes were inferior to center-pull because they did not "grab" evenly, we have since found three fairly expensive exceptions to this statement. Campagnolo has introduced excellent side-pull brakes (Fig. 39, p. 110) at a price steep enough to buy an inexpensive ten-speed. In my opinion, these new Campy side-pulls are designed for road racing, since, while having excellent stopping power, they are not as sensitive and require a firmer stopping grip on brake levers than do more conventional brakes, such as Mafac "Competition" center-pulls. I vastly prefer the Mafac center-pull brakes (Fig. 39) because they offer true fingertip-stopping in all but panic stops, whereas the Campagnolo brakes do not. Further, I and others have had trouble with Campy-brake shoe squeal, whereas this is not a problem with Mafac. By the time this book reaches your hands, Shimano will have on the market their own (less expensive) version of the Campy side-pulls (Fig. 239, 240, and 241). Both the Campagnolo and Shimano alloy side-pulls have good wet-weather stopping power and a quick-release arrangement on the caliper arm. Universal also makes good side-pulls for the more expensive bicycles.

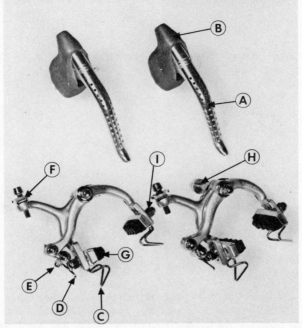

Fig. 239: These side-pull caliper brakes of aluminum alloy with drilled-out levers and rubber hoods are made by Shimano, and are similar to Campagnolo side-pulls. (A) Brake lever; (B) Hood; (C) Guard to help mount wheel; (D) Quick-release; (E) Cable locknut; (F) Adjustment barrel, to take up cable stretch and brake shoe wear; (G) Brake shoe; (H) Brake mounting bolt; (I) Brake-block mounting and adjusting bolt.

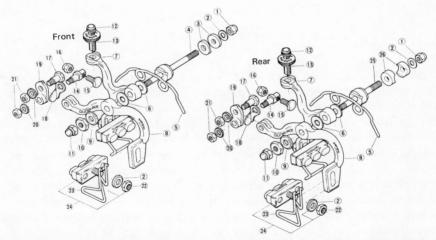

Fig. 240: Exploded view, Shimano Dura Ace alloy side-pull brakes. These brakes are quite similar to Campagnolo side-pulls, only a lot less expensive. Parts are: (1) Locknut for pivot bolt; (2) Washer (M6); (3) R-washer; (4) Pivot bolt; (5) Arm return spring; (6) Arm washer; (7) Brake arm "Y" shape; (8) Brake arm "C" shape; (9) Washer; (10 Locknut (M6); (11) Cap nut (M6); (12) Outer adjust bolt; (13) Outer adjust nut; (14) Inner fixing pin; (15) Wire fixing bolt; (16) Cap nut (M5); (17) Link pin; (18) Quick lever; (19) Link; (20) Washer (M5); (21) Nut (M5); (22) Shoe-holder fixing nut; (23) Tire guide; (24) Brake shoe assembly; (25) (rear) Pivot bolt; (26) R-washer.

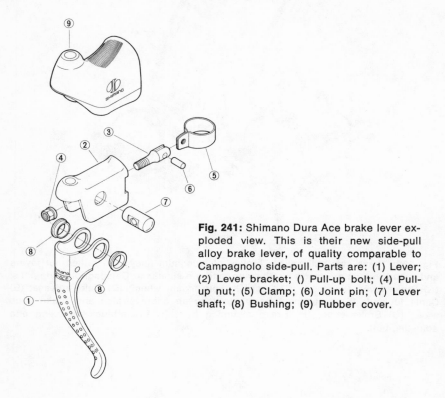

Fig. 241: Shimano Dura Ace brake lever exploded view. This is their new side-pull alloy brake lever, of quality comparable to Campagnolo side-pull. Parts are: (1) Lever; (2) Lever bracket; () Pull-up bolt; (4) Pull-up nut; (5) Clamp; (6) Joint pin; (7) Lever shaft; (8) Bushing; (9) Rubber cover.

Shimano also has on the market, but not as yet actively selling in the U.S. due to a lack of original-equipment manufacturer interest, what I consider to be the best brakes I have ever used on a bicycle. These are the Shimano hydraulic brakes (see Fig. 41 p. 112) mentioned earlier in this book in the chapter on safety. These brakes have a master cylinder and two brake cylinders, one between each set of caliper levers. As the master cylinder lever is squeezed, separate porting actuates the rear brake first, then a second later, the front brake. *One lever* actuates *both* front and rear brakes. Hydraulic power amplifies finger strength, so stopping power is more than ample under any conditions, even in the rain. I have used these brakes on my fairly heavy tandem, and they work safely under those adverse conditions, even including fast downhill riding, where ordinary caliper brakes would not offer sufficient stopping power. I would hope that someday these brakes will be available through your bicycle store. The brake lever fits under the flat section of turned-down bars. They are heavier than conventional-alloy caliper brakes, but they could be made in alloy, in which case they would be comparable in weight to these brakes. Shimano also has introduced both manual, cable-actuated, and hydraulic-disc brakes (Fig. 242). These are fairly heavy, though, and designed for the juvenile market.

Fig. 242: Shimano's new disc brake, cable-actuated. A hydraulic version is also on the market, both for juvenile bicycles. (A) Brake cable; (B) Brake disc; (C) Brake body; (D) Brake adjustment.

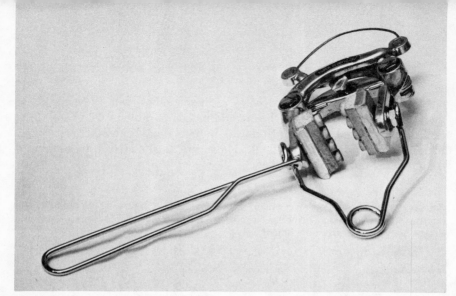

Fig. 243: "Third hand" is a simple steel spring gadget that holds brakes closed while you pull slack cable up to take out excess brake lever travel, and to bring brakes closer to rims for quick, reliable, positive stopping power.

Adjusting Caliper Brakes

To adjust caliper brakes, you will need a few simple tools:

· Metric socket wrenches; 6, 7, 8, 9, and 10 mm.
· "Third hand" to hold brakes closed while you adjust (Fig. 243)
· Small pair of cutting pliers

Replacing the Caliper Brake Pad

Eventually the rubber brake shoe on any caliper brake will wear out or, through age and lack of use, harden so that its characteristic rubbery friction is lost. If you're thinking about buying a used bike with caliper brakes, run your fingernail into the rubber brake shoe. If it feels hard and unresilient, fresh new shoes should be installed.

You can install the rubber shoe alone, which costs a few cents less than the rubber shoe in its metal holder. I prefer to buy a new block plus shoe because it doesn't cost much more, and you get a new nut and lockwasher in the bargain, which is important if threads on the old shoe are worn or partially stripped. The new brake block and shoe cost about seventy-five cents each, and you can save a couple of dollars in the twenty minutes or less it takes to replace all four brake pads.

To install a new brake shoe, squeeze the brake lever slightly, and press its quick-release mechanism if it has one (see Figs. 235, 236 and 237), so that the brakes open wide. This feature is designed to permit the brakes to open farther than usual in order to facilitate installation by making room for the side bulge of the tire to pass through the brake pads as the wheel is pulled from the fork. If you don't have a quick-release unit, disregard this step.

Next, using a small adjustable wrench or the proper-sized socket wrench, unscrew the nut holding the brake shoe on the caliper brake lever. Remove both brake shoes in this fashion.

Before replacing the new brake shoes, examine one. You'll notice that one end is closed and one end is open. *Always replace the brake shoe with the closed metal end toward the front of the bicycle* (Fig. 244). Otherwise, forward pressure as brakes are applied will push the brake pad out of the holder, and you will be left with no brakes just when you need them most.

Fig. 244: Brake blocks, as on this rear center-pull brake, are closed at front end and open at rear, so action of rim on brake can't force brake shoe out of brake block. When replacing blocks, make sure open end is toward rear of bicycle, as shown here. Note that shoes are ⅛ inch from rim, the correct position. Some blocks are closed at both ends.

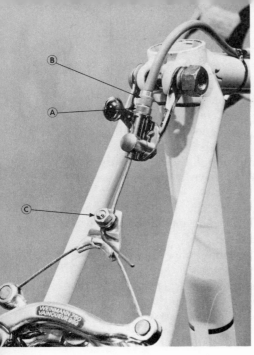

Fig. 245: When brake cables stretch you have to pull further on brake levers to stop. You should not have to pull levers more than one inch to come to a panic stop. If so, take up cable slack by loosening cable barrel (locknut "A" and turning cable barrel) adjusting housing "B" counterclockwise. Squeezing brakes together by hand will make it easier to move the adjusting barrel. If you can't take up cable slack as above, loosen cable locknut "C," pull excess cable through, and retighten locknut. You will probably need two 8 or 10 mm. wrenches, or one 10 mm. or 8 in. and one adjustable wrench, to make this adjustment. Use of a "third hand" (Fig. 243) to hold brakes closed while you're working on them will make things a lot easier. When you're through, brake shoes should be about 1/8 to 3/16 inch from wheel-rim flat.

Adjusting Center-pull Brakes

Brake cables stretch and brake shoes wear, so any make or kind of brake will need readjusting ever so often (Fig. 245). Just remember two things about brake adjustment: 1) brake shoes should always be between 1/8 to 3/16 of an inch, no more, from wheel rim; 2) brakes must grab evenly when you depress brake lever about one third of its total travel. One more point. The "safety" levers that come with some bikes aren't. Safety levers are extra brake levers in addition to standard levers on the rounded section of handlebars. "Safety" levers are under the top, flat part of the handlebars, where lever travel is very limited. Unless brakes are always almost touching rims, "safety" levers will stop you well enough for country riding, *but may not stop you well enough in an emergency.* So don't rely on them; in fact, take them off. For a few cents you can buy a shorter lever shaft to replace the longer one on safety levers and can remove this lever in a few minutes.

Also, no matter how well you adjust brakes, if the rims are badly out of round, it's obvious that brake shoes will grab the high spots and tend to miss the low spots, so you have uneven braking. And shoes can't be closer to the rim than the most out-of-round spot. So before you adjust brakes, true your rims. Refer to page 449 for rim-truing instructions.

Now let's get into adjusting center-pulls. Adjustment is a matter of taking up cable slack. You can take up cable slack somewhat by adjusting

Fig. 246: Use the thin hub wrenches to remove axle locknut and adjustable cone. Hold the lower wrench on the cone, turn the upper wrench to remove the locknut. In reassembly, turn adjustable cone with lower wrench till it's snug, back off one quarter turn, hold in that position with wrench, and tighten locknut with upper wrench. Check for binding or sideplay, and readjust as necessary as above.

the movable take-up barrel ("F" in Fig. 239, page 385). But after you're all out of adjustment there, you should loosen cable-stop bolt at the yoke (Fig. 246) and pull excess slack cable through. First, though, put a "third hand" on the brake to hold it closed (see Fig. 243). Pull cable just taut, tighten lock bolt nut (using socket wrenches on both ends) and remove third hand. Brake shoes should be about an eighth of an inch from rim. On the rear brake, the cable passes through a yoke fitting that's held by the seat-post lock bolt (Fig. 247). Sometime you will adjust the saddle, and when you do, this miserable little yoke will move, and if you tighten the seat bolt, leaving the yoke in the wrong position, it will act as though the cable was shortened and the brakes will drag. There should be a better arrangement. Back to the rear brake. Adjust it just like the front brake, as above. Check brake shoes, too, and if they don't hit the rim squarely, loosen the brake block bolt ("I" in Fig. 239 p. 385) and readjust

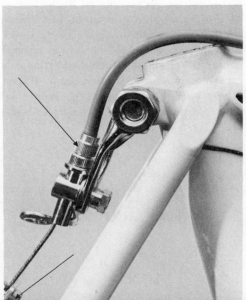

Fig. 247: Arrows are pointing at locations where you can take up the excess cable length on center-pull brakes. Rear center-pull brake anchor bolt assembly (at top) is fed through fixture attached to the seat-post adjusting nut, just visible at top of photo. When you loosen seat-post locknut to raise or lower seat, you should hold the hangar in the original position; otherwise, as you tighten seat-post locknut, the hangar will move out of position and cause brakes to bind on rim.

brake shoe position. You'll get fantastic stopping power if the brake shoe hits the tire, but the tire casing will give up the ghost real fast that way. It's a good idea to keep the brake shoe from touching any part of the tire. Perhaps I should be more positive. DON'T LET THE BRAKE SHOE TOUCH THE TIRE!

Installing a new cable is simple enough. Just remove the old cable by loosening the cable-lock bolt and nut and pull the cable through and out from under the brake lever. You will note that many brake levers have a brass ferrule, drilled and countersunk. The leaded stop end of the brake cable fits into the countersunk hole; that's what it's for. Shove the new cable, nonleaded end first, into the lever ferrule, up through the top of the brake lever, into the cable housing (spaghetti plastic-covered tubing) and back into the brake. Snip excess cable off neatly with cutting pliers. Perhaps a simpler way of inserting the cable in the brake lever is to leave the brake end loose and simply poke the brake end of the cable up through the top hole of the brake lever and pull the cable through till the lead ball end is about three inches from the brake lever top. You should then be able to fit the cable lead end into the brake lever shaft either by hand or by maneuvering it in with needle-nosed pliers. Later, should you wish to remove handlebars, as for shipping the bike, just squeeze brakes, slip off brake end of cable yoke, pull up brake lever end of cable and slip cable out of brake lever shift. Removing cables this way also makes it much easier to tape handlebars. An exception is Campagnolo brake levers; you must stick brake end of cable up through the lever axle hole because this hole is not open (split) on one side.

One trick I use to improve center-pull brake efficiency involves the fact that the yoke (the piece that fits on the stem through which cable passes from brake lever to front brake) bends slightly as you depress the brake lever. This bending takes up pressure that should be applied to the brake. A neat way out of this problem is to drill a hole in the stem, just above the brake, and pass the brake cable down through this hole. Use a brake cable slack adjustment fitting in the hole, both to hold cable tubing and to remove slack when it occurs. This also eliminates the yoke fitting, although you will need a spacing washer under the stem locknut. If you know your correct saddle height you can also eliminate the rear yoke fitting by drilling a hole through the seat post and fitting as noted above.

Adjusting Side-Pull Caliper Brakes

Side-pull brakes are adjusted in much the same manner as center-pull brakes. The brake cable is connected directly to the caliper arm instead of to a cable anchor, as in center-pull brakes. If you can't take up the slack in the brake cable and bring the brake pads back to around an eighth of an inch from the wheels by loosening the retaining nut on the adjusting barrel and turning the barrel, you'll have to loosen the anchor nut that holds the brake cable in place and pull the cable through a bit more. Be careful not to let the cable slip out of the anchor-bolt hole, because most cables will be frayed a bit at the end, and you'll find it all but impossible to put the cable back in the hole. This will call for a trip to the bike store for a new cable. Incidentally, some stores will try to sell you a complete new rig, the metal housing plus the cable for $2.50 or so, when all you need is a cable for about seventy-five cents. The professional shops, which do repair work on top-quality machines, will have the cables alone. Do not try to cut a cable before installing it—the cable wire ends will fray out, and you will wind up again having to buy a new cable. Bicycle repair shops have a special tool for cutting wire, but unless you want to spend the $5.00 or so that such a tool costs, stick to your old scissors or cutting pliers to cut the cable *after* you have it installed and the cable-bolt nut is tight. Make sure, when you buy a new cable for English bikes such as the Raleigh, that the cable has the correct leaded ends. Show the old cable to the salesman to make sure you get an exact duplicate. A good way to eliminate the frayed cable end problem is to sand and solder the cable with rosin core solder about a half inch on each side of where you trim off excess cable.

Caliper brakes can be adjusted as described on bicycles of any make— American, English, Japanese, Austrian, Dutch, and any others sold on the American market.

Hub Brakes

Hub brakes (Fig. 248) are usually found only on tandem bicycles used in mountainous terrain, where their superior braking leverage is required. Hub brakes are far heavier and more costly than caliper brakes and are unnecessary unless you have a tandem and plan a lot of riding in the Rockies, the Alps, or other mountain areas. However, a few words about adjustment may be useful.

Hub brakes use a brake "shoe" mechanism, much like conventional automobile brakes. To adjust them, it is vital that the metal clip which holds the cable anchor plate to the frame or fork be kept tight. If it is loose, the cable will not be able to pull the brakes tight enough for good braking.

Fig. 248: Typical internal expanding hub brake. (A) Brake shoes; (B) Brake shoe cam; (C) Cam spring; (D) Bearings; (E) Actuating arm; (F) Axle; (G) Brake drum; (H) Hub spoke holes. This hub brake is made by Jonas Oglaend, Sandnes, Norway, and is on some of the models this firm exports to the U.S.A. Advantages of hub brakes are: They do not heat up rim; there is less "fade"; they have excellent wet-weather stopping power. Although they are heavy compared with alloy caliper brakes, they are needed on heavy tandems.

Fig. 249: Hub brake installed. Notice clip at bottom center, removable so wheel is easy to remove; and adjustment barrel to take up cable stretch and brake shoe wear.

To adjust the brake lever which controls the hub brake, tighten the nut through which the cable passes until the brake binds (rotate the wheel to test), then slacken until the wheel revolves freely.

If the cable is too loose, loosen the locknut on the cable (located just under the clip securing the anchor plate to the bicycle frame), and rotate the adjusting nut until the play is removed. Then tighten the locknut (Fig. 249).

Caliper Brake Levers

Caliper brake levers are pretty much the same design, the difference being only a matter of shape, according to whether they are used on turned-down "racing" handlebars (see Fig. 61, p. 146) or on conventional "touring" handlebars (see Fig. 60, p. 146). If your brake levers are not located in just the right position for your hands and arm length, you may want to move them on the handlebars. The brake lever should be where you can get at it quickly. The reason for having the brakes adjusted, incidentally, so that the rubber shoes are about an eighth of an inch from the wheel rim, is that you will get fast results when you squeeze the brake lever. If the brake pad is too far away from the tire, it will take longer for your squeeze to stop the bicycle. In an emergency, this could be dangerous.

To move the brake lever on hooded levers on turned-down handlebars, pull up the rubber hood, and if you have a quick-release brake, push the release button and open the brake lever all the way. Underneath the lever, through the body of the lever mechanism, you will see a nut or pull-up bolt which tightens the clamps holding the brake-lever unit on the handlebars. By turning this nut counterclockwise, you will loosen the brake handles so that you can reposition them to suit yourself.

On "tourist" (conventional) handlebars, the pull-up bolt is on the outside of the pull-up grip. To get at the locknut that tightens the brake lever down on the handlebar, it helps if you can remove the cable from the brake lever. This is simplified on center-pull brakes by squeezing the brakes together, removing the cable from the yoke by slipping it off, and then pulling resultant slack cable by tugging on the cable at the brake lever. Then you'll see (on most) that where the brake-cable leaded end goes through the lever axle, there is a slot behind the hole which, if the cable is slack enough, lets you pull the cable head out from the axle. Now the cable is free and you can pull it up, cable cover and all, through the brake lever. On side-pull brakes, this can be done by removing the wheel and squeezing the brakes together to get enough slack to pull the cable through the slot at the brake-lever end. This can't be done, of course, if the brake-lever axles aren't slotted.

Replacing Brake Cables

Eventually your brake cable, like a shoelace, will wear and break. It is a good safety measure to replace frayed cables before they break so that you can always stop safely. The cable replacement procedure for all caliper brakes is pretty much the same. Loosen the cable-bolt nut where the cable fastens to the caliper cable anchor on center-pull brakes, or where the cable fastens to the caliper arm on side-pull brakes. Pull the cable out of the cable bolt and out of the cable housing.

Pull the cable out of the hand lever by pushing up from underneath. You'll see that the cable end comes out of a rotating slotted brass or steel cable holder in the handle. To replace the old cable with a new one, slide the *large* leaded head end into the larger of the two holes in the slotted cable retainer in the brake handle. Then push the brake cable through the housing into the cable-anchor bolt, and tighten the anchor-bolt nut slightly. Check to make sure the brake pads are about ⅛ to 3⁄16 of an inch from the wheel rims. If they are not, pull the cable through the cable bolt, or slacken it off as necessary. Remember, new cables stretch after a while, so it will be necessary to readjust brake shoe clearance as described above from time to time.

Note: On center-pull brakes, the rear cable-anchor bolt, and nut mechanism (see top of Fig. 247 for a partial view) are sometimes attached to the seat-post adjusting nut by a metal hanger. If you've adjusted the seat up or down, make sure that, in the process, the hanger is at the same angle as when you started. Otherwise the rear brakes will bind, because the cable will have been tightened by the hanger being too far up or down. The hanger should be parallel to seat stays.

Brake Tips: Do's and Don'ts

WHEEL RUB: If your wheel moves side-to-side, you'll find that you probably cannot adjust the brake shoe as close to the rim as an eighth of an inch. You should then realign the wheel as described on page 449 before adjusting the brake shoe clearance.

Untrue wheels will also cause excessive tire wear. As the rim brake grabs the distorted portion of the rim, it tends to grip more tightly there than on other parts of the rim. This can cause a skid mark, and the tire will wear excessively in that one spot.

CABLE SIZE: When you must buy a new cable, take your old cable and the old cable housing with you to insure an exact duplicate. Brake cables vary in diameter (thickness), and you must be sure to get a cable that will fit easily through the cable housing. If the choice is between a cable that fits stiffly or a little loosely in the cable housing, select the smaller of the two cables. When inserting the cable in the housing, coat it lightly with Lubriplate or another light grease so that it will slide in easily.

You should also check the cable housing carefully; if it's broken so that any part of the inside of the housing rubs on the cable, you will have a recurring cable breakage. If this is the case, replace the cable housing.

IF YOU CHANGE TIRE TYPE: As noted elsewhere, you may want to use tubulars for local trips and wired-on tires for distance tours. You will need two sets of wheels. Problem is that wired-on tires raise the rim brake flats about ⅛ to ³⁄₁₆ inch from where you had them on the tubular rim. If you change over to wired-ons, you will have to readjust brake shoes so they hit wired-on rim flats, and readjust them again when you change back. Well, it's not exactly a problem, just so you remember to make the adjustments.

CABLES MUST NOT KINK: Cables must be smoothly curved and aimed directly as possible at brakes to insure smooth operation. If brakes work hard (particularly rear brake) check cables. Cable position and length is a matter of experience. All I can say is you will have to develop a trained eye to know what works best. Always grease cable lightly with grease before inserting in cable tube.

Caliper Brake "Symptoms" and Cures

- *Front brake "drag":* If you can't eliminate drag by adjusting the brake shoes, check the front pivot bolt. This is the main bolt that holds the brakes to the frame. If it's bent, replace it.
- *Side-pull caliper brakes do not return to position, but "drag":* Lubricate the pivot points. If the arms drag (rub) on each other, bend the arms so that they clear each other. (Caution: Do not try to bend cast-aluminum brake arms, because they'll break off. Bend forged arms only.) Use an emery cloth or fine file to eliminate friction between the arms. If the arms do not pivot

freely, adjust the center bolt and the locknuts. Campagnolo and Shimano sidepull brakes have a marked tendency to drag on one side or the other so that one shoe is touching or dragging on the rim. You can eliminate this drag by first holding the brake either centered on the rim or away from the side that drags, then tightening the nut that holds the brake on the fork very firmly with a box wrench. *Don't try to center these brakes by adjusting brake spring tension; you'll only weaken the spring.*

· *Hand levers on handlebars bind:* Check to find the exact location of the binding. If sides of brake lever rub against the lever body, use a thin screwdriver to gently pry the lever inward (or bend the lever slightly inward). Check to make sure the cables aren't binding and that the cable housings (the spaghetti tubing through which the cables run) curve gradually from the levers to the frame and from the frame to the brakes without "kinks" at any point.

· *Center-pull brake arms do not pivot freely on trunnions (center bolt):* If the center bolt or trunnion fits too tightly, ream out a small hole in the arm with a drill. Or sand the trunnion to a smaller diameter. If the arms are too thick, file at the pivot area so that the pivot bolt sits against the trunnion without binding the arm. Loosen the pivot bolt; if the arm moves freely, the arm is too thick.

· *Uneven braking:* Check for out-of-round or dented rims. Sometimes the brakes will grab unevenly, and at the same time, "shudder" or "judder." Juddering means that the entire brake assembly is loose on the trunnion bolt holding it to the frame. The brake assembly must be rigid. Loosen the locknut, take up on the adjusting nut, and retighten the locknut. The brakes should have no front-to-rear play; they should pivot freely but not loosely. If the brakes still "judder," check the head bearing play on the front fork, and readjust (see page 380).

· *Squealing brakes:* Squealing is usually the result of vibration. Check the brake blocks for hardening due to old age. If the blocks have hardened, replace them with new rubber. Sometimes the only way to prevent looseness that causes squealing in the caliper-brake system is to cut away the rubber brake shoes at the front, causing them to "toe in" slightly. This puts pressure on the brake arms by causing them to bend slightly as the brake is applied. Also, check the brake shoes to make sure particles of grit are not embedded in the rubber, which is another cause of squealing.

PRECISION HUB MAINTENANCE

Precision-machined steel and alloy low- and high-flange hubs (Figs. 250 and 251) should be torn down and regreased every six months, or oftener if you have done a lot of riding on dusty roads or in the rain (Fig. 252). Spin the wheels every once in a while with your ear close to the axle and

Rear Hub

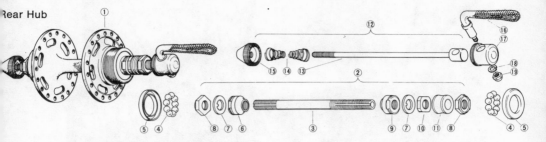

Fig. 250: Exploded view, typical hub. This is a Shimano alloy hub, but it is similar to Campagnolo and other high-quality alloy hubs. Parts are: (1) Complete hub; (2) Complete axle unit; (3) Axle; (4) Steel balls (¼"); (5) Dust cap; (6) Left-hand cone (0.59"); (7) Key washer; (8) Locking nut; (9) Right-hand cone (0.51"); (10) Locknut; (11) Spacer (0.47"); (12) Complete quick-release unit; (13) Mounting stud; (14) Volute spring; (15) Nut for mounting stud; (16) Quick-release lever; (17) Body with lever; (18) Spring washer; (19) Cap nut.

Fig. 251: Top, low-flange hubs. Bottom, high-flange hubs. Both are of aluminum alloy construction, type used on better ten-speed bicycles.

Fig. 252: Phil Wood sealed bearing hub. This elegant hub (front and rear types available) is exceptionally smooth-running and strong. Needs no maintenance for thousands of miles. High and low flange models are available.

listen for grating sounds, which indicate dirt in the bearings. Take the wheel out of the dropouts and spin the axle between thumb and forefinger to feel for roughness which also indicates dirt.

Tools Needed for Hub Maintenance

To disassemble most European alloy hubs you will need one 13 and 14 mm. and one 15 and 16 mm. thin cone wrench (see Fig. 253). For some Japanese hubs you will need a 16 and 17 mm. cone wrench. Use one wrench to hold the cone in place while you loosen the locknut (or tighten in on reassembly).

Hub Assembly and Disassembly (Front and rear derailleur bike only)

STEP ONE: Remove the wheels from the bicycle.

STEP TWO: Put one end of the wheel in a vise, gripping one of the locknuts. If this is a rear wheel, grip the freewheel locknut side. Remove quick release skewer first.

STEP THREE: If you are disassembling a derailleur-equipped bicycle wheel with a rear freewheel gear cluster, note very carefully the position of any spacers and washers before you disassemble. These spacers and washers must go back in *exactly* the same position to preserve the alignment of the gear cluster with the chainwheel (see page 412 for a discussion on alignment).

STEP FOUR: Remove the locknut, lock washer (the washer that fits into a spline on the axle), and the adjustable cone (see Fig. 250). Holding the wheel assembly *by the axle,* loosen the vise and set the wheel down on a rag or piece of paper on a workbench. Remove the axle and, at the same time, catch any bearings that come loose. Remove all bearings after removing the axle. If bearings are in a cage or retainer, pull off both retainers as you would a ring from a finger.

STEP FIVE: Clean the entire assembly—axle, bearings, hub cone, and hub cases and interior—thoroughly with kerosene.

STEP SIX: Inspect the balls for rust or cracks, the cones for galled spots (shiny spots indicating wear), and the axle-bearing surfaces. If any of the balls are rusty or cracked, replace the entire set of balls. Check the axle for alignment with a straightedge. If the axle shows signs of being out-of-round, replace it.

STEP SEVEN: With the wheel on its side on the table, put a layer of Lubriplate grease inside the hub case and lay the loose bearings in the

Fig. 253: Tools needed for hub disassembly and adjustment. Left, Campagnolo 13- and 14-mm. wrench; right, Campagnolo 15- and 16-mm. wrench.

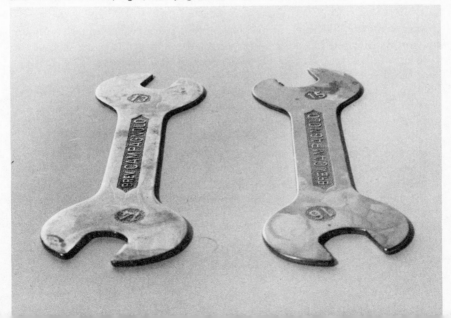

grease. The grease will hold the bearings in place until you insert the axle in place from underneath (which you should do next).

STEP EIGHT: Put a layer of Lubriplate Type A grease in the top hub race, insert the rest of the bearings in the race, and screw on the adjustable cone until it is snug. Then back it off a quarter-turn. Put the wheel back in the vise as described in Step Two.

STEP NINE: Insert the lock washer and locknut, and screw the locknut tight, while holding the adjustable cone in position with a cone wrench or cone pliers.

STEP TEN: Check the axle for side play by removing wheel from vise and by holding wheel at both sides of axle, moving axle up and down. If end play is apparent, loosen the locknut, tighten the adjustment cone with the cone wrench or cone pliers about an eighth of a turn, and retighten the locknut. Continue this procedure until the end play is removed.

STEP ELEVEN: Check for bearing tightness. Remove the wheel and axle from the vise. Twist the axle between your thumb and forefinger. If it feels tight or binding, loosen the locknut, back off the adjustable cone about an eighth of a turn, and retighten the locknut. Ideally, the wheel should spin so freely that the weight of the tire valve (if it is at the nine or three o'clock positions) is enough to move the wheel. At least, if you spin it, the wheel should come to rest gradually, and indicate a delicate enough balance so that the tendency is for the valve to come to rest somewhere between the eight and four o'clock positions.

STEP TWELVE: The above steps also apply if you have an American-made bicycle with caged bearings. However, if the retainer is worn so that the bearings fall out of it, replace the retainer and bearings. The retainer should have a part number stamped on it, which you should use in purchasing a replacement. When replacing caged bearings, make sure the correct side of the cage faces the cone. The balls should bear against the cup, not the cage itself.

STEP THIRTEEN: You may find it impossible to remove all end play and at the same time have the wheel turn freely, with the less-expensive American-made bicycle hubs. If this is your problem, a little end play won't hurt so long as the wheel turns freely. However, with precision-machined European hub assemblies, you should be able to adjust the cone for zero end play and at the same time achieve free wheel motion. This is what is meant by precision machining. Remember, if you own a more costly bicycle, you have paid a premium for performance. There is absolutely no reason why, with a little patience and care in adjusting the cones, you cannot get almost perfect wheel performance as far as the hub is concerned, i.e., no side play and no binding.

PEDAL MAINTENANCE

As you can imagine, a good deal of stress and strain is imposed on pedals. As you will see when you take a pedal apart, pedals use small ball bearings which, due to their location and use, are quite susceptible to wear and corrosion. This is why pedals should be disassembled, cleaned, and regreased twice a year, or more frequently if you do a lot of cycling.

The following tells how you disassemble and assemble various types of pedals.

First, become acquainted with the pedal parts, as shown in Fig. 254. Then take the pedal part, clean, and regrease as follows:

STEP ONE: Remove the pedals from the cranks. Remember, pedals always come off *opposite to the direction of crank turn.* On the right-hand side (chainwheel side), the pedal threads off counterclockwise. On the

Fig. 254: Typical precision alloy rattrap pedal. (A) Rattrap body; (B) Axle; (C) Ball bearings (they can roll and get lost on the floor faster than a drop of mercury); (D) Adjustable cone nut; (E) Splined washer; (F) Locknut; (G) Dust cap.

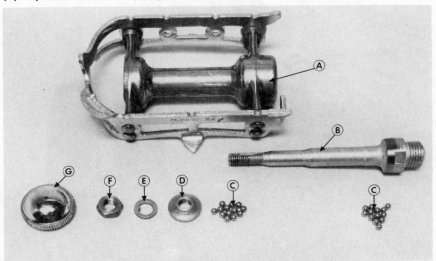

left-hand side, pedal threads off clockwise. If pedals are on tight, use penetrating oil to free threads and a long (10″) pedal wrench.

STEP TWO: Put the pedal in a vise, gripping the *flats* of the axle sides on the crank side with dust cap end up. The pencil points to a dust cap. Don't grip the threads in the vise. Turn the dust cap with a small screwdriver using the rattrap opening as a fulcrum, similar to where the pencil is located above. Be careful in removing the cap, so that you don't damage the knurled edges. There is a special wrench for dust cap removal; if you have a lot of bicycles to maintain it would pay to buy one. If you are working on the garden variety rubber-steel pedal (Fig. 255), you can get at the locknut, etc., by removing the rubber-tread locknuts on the crank side, and pulling off the entire rubber pedal assembly, after which follow the steps above and below, except the rubber treads should be replaced as above (Fig. 256).

STEP THREE: Remove the locknut, to which the pencil points in the photograph. On many pedals an 8-mm. socket wrench will do the job; for others you will need a 9- or 10-mm. wrench, or a small adjustable crescent wrench. I prefer wrenches that fit the nuts I am working on (Fig. 257).

STEP FOUR: Remove the splined washer (Fig. 258).

Fig. 255: Left, typical rattrap pedal with toe clip and strap. Right, rubber-tread pedal. Pencil points to tread axle nut. Removing both left- and right-hand nuts permits access to axle locknut, cone nut, and bearings.

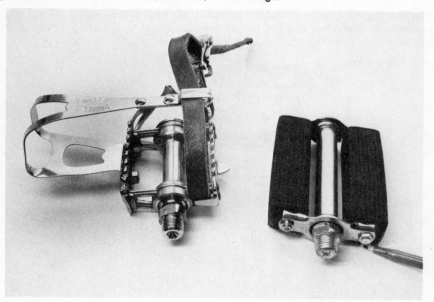

Fig. 256: Step Two

Fig. 257: Step Three

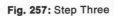

Fig. 258: Step Four

Fig. 259: Step Five

Fig. 260: Step Six

STEP FIVE: Remove the cone nut with a screwdriver. Count the balls so you know when you have the proper number back (Fig. 259).

STEP SIX: Holding the threaded portion of the pedal axle, loosen the vise and carefully pull the entire pedal out of the vise and hold it over a cloth rag on the bench top. If you are careful, you can remove the axle and leave the bearings in the races, and let them spill out on the cloth (Fig. 260).

STEP SEVEN: Clean the bearings, races, and axle in kerosene. Remove the toe strap from the toe clip, dunk the pedal body in kerosene, and clean off all road dirt, stuck-on tar, etc.

STEP EIGHT: Check the balls and races for cracks and rust. Replace balls as necessary.

STEP NINE: Put a light layer of grease, such as Lubriplate Type A (from auto supply stores) or Marine Lube grease (from boat stores), on races, and roll bearings around in a dab of grease till they're coated and clump together. Stick bearings back in the crank side of the pedal first. Make sure you have the correct count (see Step Five).

STEP TEN: Insert axle, threaded end first, into the crank side of the pedal; insert the remaining ball bearings in the dust-cap side; screw on the cone nut with a screwdriver until it's snug against the bearings (not tight), and back off about a quarter turn. Push on the splined washer and thread on the locknut. Put the pedal back in the vise, gripping the axle flats on the crank side as in Step One. Tighten the locknut. Remove from the vise and twirl the axle between thumb and forefinger to check for binding. Hold the pedal firmly and push the axle from side to side to check for looseness. If it is binding, loosen the locknut, back off the cone nut an eighth of a turn, retighten the locknut, and check again for binding. Repeat as necessary. If it is too loose so that you have sideplay, loosen the locknut, take up on cone nut an eighth of a turn, retighten the locknut, check again for sideplay, and repeat as necessary.

STEP ELEVEN: Put the pedals back on the cranks. Be careful to get the correct pedal on the correct crank, because the right side is threaded differently from the left, and if you're threading into a softer aluminum alloy crank you can strip threads easily. Also, be sure to thread on straight,

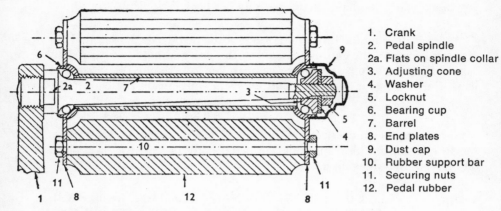

1. Crank
2. Pedal spindle
2a. Flats on spindle collar
3. Adjusting cone
4. Washer
5. Locknut
6. Bearing cup
7. Barrel
8. End plates
9. Dust cap
10. Rubber support bar
11. Securing nuts
12. Pedal rubber

Fig. 261: Standard assembly-line pedal used on British three-speed bicycles. See legend for part identification. Reprinted with the permission of Temple Press Ltd. from "The Cycling Book of Maintenance."

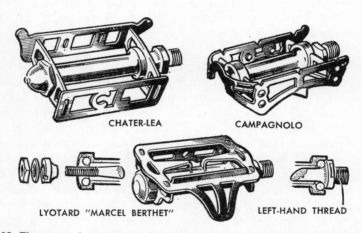

CHATER-LEA

CAMPAGNOLO

LYOTARD "MARCEL BERTHET"

LEFT-HAND THREAD

Fig. 262: Three popular rattrap pedal designs: top left, Chater-Lea; top right, Campagnolo; bottom, Lyotard "Marcel Berthet." Lip on the Lyotard makes inserting foot easier and faster.

using a drop or two of lube oil on threads. Don't get started cross-threaded. Alloy cranks are costly. English rubber pedals usually have "L" and "R" stamped in axle ends to denote left and right. French pedals (e.g., Lyotard) have "D" which means right, and "G," which means left, stamped on axle flats. Italian pedals (e.g., Campagnolo) have "D" for right and "S" for left stamped on axle flats. Remember, if in doubt, to try pedals gingerly; if they resist going into crank you are either using the wrong pedal or threading it on the wrong way. A good rule to remember is that pedals *always* thread on in the direction of crank rotation; the left-hand pedal threads on counterclockwise and the right-hand pedal threads on clockwise.

Standard rubber and rattrap pedals are shown in Figs. 261 and 262.

ALL ABOUT ALIGNMENT

A bicycle with all components aligned will ride easier, with less resistance; will steer accurately, even with "no hands"; and will not pull to right or left, which can be dangerous by causing wheel "wobble" at high speed downhill. Misalignment also causes poor braking, increased wear of tires and parts, and high-speed front-wheel "shimmy," which can lead to loss of control and accidents on fast downhill runs, as noted above.

Even a brand-new bicycle, right out of the carton, may be out of line if it's been mishandled at the factory, in shipping, or improperly aligned at the factory.

A check should include alignment of:

· Wheel tracking; are wheels straight behind each other?
· Chainwheels with rear gears
· Rear gears with rear derailleur
· Front derailleur with chainwheel
· Fork blades with steering head
· Steering head with main tubes
· Seat and chain stays with main tubes
· Dropouts parallel with each other
· Wheel position in dropouts—parallel to main tubes and to each other
· Wheels as to correct concentric and lateral trueness
· Frame main members (top tube, seat tube, and down tube)
· Rear derailleur wheels with each other

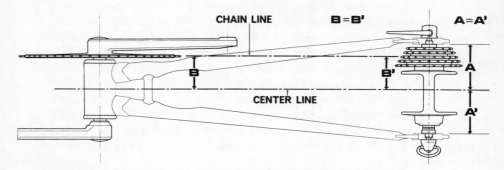

Fig. 263: Chainline should line up on a five-speed bicycle as shown above. Third rear gear should be parallel to centerline of front chainwheel. (Hub is "dished" to right so locknut to locknut centerline is between points A' and A. Distance between A' and A and entire hub should be equal.)

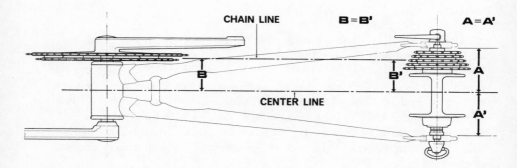

Fig. 264: Double-plateau chainwheel and chainline. Third rear gear should be parallel to an imaginary line centered *between* front chainwheels. On a *triple chainwheel* (not shown), chainline is aligned when third rear gear is aligned with center front chainwheel. To align, disassemble rear axle, and remove or add thin washers to right side, *under* locknut, as necessary. Make sure there is enough clearance between highest (small) rear gear and right-hand chainstay so chain won't rub on chainstay. Misalignment causes excessive wear of gear teeth, derailleur and chain, poor shifting, and "jumping" of chain off front gears. On twelve-speed bicycle, with double chainwheel and six rear gears, chainline is aligned when chain is between third and fourth rear gears and between the two chainwheels (this is, of course, an imaginary line and you would use a straightedge to determine this alignment). On eighteen-speed bicycles, with triple chainwheel and six-speed rear gear cluster, chainline runs from between rear third and fourth gears and center chainwheel.

To check gear alignment (Figs. 263 and 264), remove the chain. Lay a straightedge (a straight piece of 5-foot-long ³⁄₁₆ or ¼- by 1½-inch aluminum bar stock will be accurate enough) parallel to the rear gear and chainwheel involved (Fig. 265). There should be very little deviation from true, preferably none. If there is deviation, you can move the rear gears over to the *right* by *removing* one of the thin spacing washers from the right side of the axle. Remove the wheel, put the left side in a vise, unscrew the right side locknut, remove one washer and put the whole thing back together and in the bicycle and recheck alignment. To get at the right-side axle locknut you may have to take the hub axle apart, remove the left-side locknut, washer, and cone nut (be careful not to drop the bearings out of the hub on the floor, where you will never find them again). To move the rear gear to the *left, add* a spacing washer to the right side under the locknut. If this leaves you with less than an eighth of an inch of axle sticking out to put in the dropout, steal some space from the left side of the axle by readjusting lock and cone nuts. However, after you have lined up the freewheel gears with the chainwheel(s), you should then redish the rear wheel so it is centered on the faces of both axle locknuts. See page 413 for rim centering instructions.

Fig. 265: Check chainwheel and rear-gear alignment with straightedge laid between appropriate gears. See text.

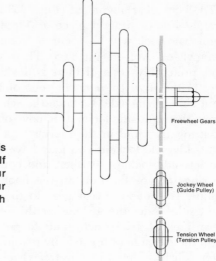

Freewheel Gears

Jockey Wheel
(Guide Pulley)

Tension Wheel
(Tension Pulley)

Fig. 266: Derailleur cage and wheels should be parallel to sprocket gears. If not, bend derailleur cage, derailleur mounting bracket, or dropout derailleur mounting "ear" back to parallel with large crescent wrench.

With a straightedge, make sure the rear derailleur cage and derailleur wheels are parallel to the rear sprocket sides (Fig. 266). If the derailleur is bent or not aligned, twist body gently with the rag-wrapped jaws of a large crescent wrench. But before you go this far, check to make sure the fault is not in the right-hand chain or seat stay, dropout, or bent derailleur mounting bracket, if this is how the derailleur is mounted. Better bicycles have a right dropout with a threaded "ear" to receive the derailleur and this can also be bent out of line. The mounting "ear" should be parallel to the dropout of which it is a part. If derailleur wheels are not aligned with each other (use a short piece of chain and sight down wheels), bend derailleur cage carefully to true them up.

Gears and Derailleur Alignment

Let's start with gears and derailleur alignment. As Fig. 263 shows, the chainline is in alignment on a five-speed derailleur bicycle when the center or third rear gear is directly in line with the centerline of the chainwheel.

On a ten-speed bicycle, the center (third) rear gear sprocket should line up *between* the two chainwheels, as shown in Fig. 265. On a fifteen-speed bicycle, with a triple plateau chainwheel, the center of the third rear gear sprocket should line up with the center chainwheel. The new twelve-speed bicycles make this alignment a bit trickier; these bicycles have a six-speed gear rear cluster and a double plateau chainwheel. These gears are aligned when a line drawn from the centerline of the double chainwheel to the centerline between the third and fourth gears of the six-speed gear cluster is parallel to the rear gears and to the chainwheel. Eventually there will, I suppose, be eighteen-speed bicycles, with a triple chainwheel and six-speed rear-gear cluster. For these bicycles, gears would be aligned on the middle chainwheel centerline and the centerline between the third and fourth gears of the freewheel.

Wheel "Tracking"

Wheels "track" in correct alignment when they are both exactly straight behind each other when the front wheel is straight. Rough-check wheel tracking on a rainy day or in light snow. Hold the wheel straight, stop pedaling so you don't wobble, coast twenty feet or so, and get off and look at your tire marks. Wheels should be one behind the other. If not, you have a dangerous bicycle that is hard to steer accurately, especially on downhill runs and on fast cornering. A better way to check wheel tracking is to hang the bike from the ceiling, tie the front wheel in line with the top tube with a shock cord, and place a straightedge alongside both rims. You may have to let air out of the tires so the straightedge will fit alongside rims. There should be no clearance, or very little—say about ¹⁄₆₄ inch between the straightedge and either rim.

Causes of poor wheel tracking are:

· Wheels not centered in dropouts (Figs. 267–268)
· Wheel rim(s) not centered (see page 449 on wheel truing)
· Fork blade bent
· Steering head bent
· and all of the other "bent" problems noted here (read on)

All of which means that the first check for bicycle alignment is wheel tracking, after which it's a case of finding out why wheels don't track and eliminating that cause.

If you have put the wheel in the dropouts carelessly so the wheel is "canted" or tilted to one side, the wheels won't track (Fig. 267). That should be your first check. Sometimes if the rear-wheel axle locknuts or quick-release skewer are not tight, as you pedal the rear wheel will be pulled to the right often enough so the tire rubs on the chainstays. Some better bicycles have a slender long bolt through the rear end of the drop-

Fig. 267: Rear wheel, when all the way back in dropouts and correctly "dished," should be centered between chainstays. Distance between stays and rim flats should be equal on both sides of rim.

Fig. 268: With wheel pulled all the way in fork dropouts, and wheel centered on hub (see page 449 for wheel truing), distance from left rim side to left fork and right rim to right fork should be equal.

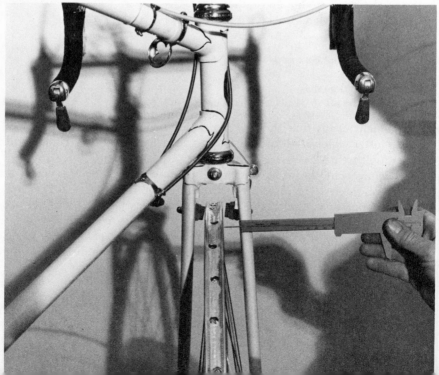

Fig. 269: Better bikes have axle-aligning bolts (A) in a threaded hole in rear drop-outs.

outs so you can center the axle in the dropout (Fig. 269) and keep it there. An alternative is to use a spacing slotted washer that fits in the dropout slot and can be lockbolted in place to hold the axle in alignment with the dropouts, seat, and chainstays. Either method will keep the rear wheel from sliding to the left as you put hill-climbing pressure on pedals.

Aligning Front Derailleur

To align front derailleur cage with chainwheel, please see page 412 for instructions (derailleur section).

Fig. 270: Check fork-blade alignment by putting straightedge against steering head and front-wheel rim. Straightedge should be parallel to both.

Aligning Fork Blades

Put the straightedge flat against the steering head and against the front wheel rim. If the rim is aligned, if the steering head is in line, the straightedge should lie parallel to the side of the steering head (Fig. 270).

(I wonder if, at this point, you get the picture regarding alignment? Alignment depends on everything. If one part is misaligned, and it can be one of a number of areas, the bicycle won't run true. You just about have to check alignment of everything if the wheels don't track.)

If a fork blade is bent, you may be able to bend it back. But if you're working on a fine bicycle, I'd take it to a good bicycle mechanic and let him align it, unless you are very good at working metal. *Above all, don't heat any metal* to straighten. It won't help the paint job, and you could ruin the frame. Most frame problems can be solved by pulling the offending member back to true, cold.

Head Tube Alignment

The head tube can either be bent sideways or twisted out of line. Check sideways alignment by putting a piece of string around the bottom of the head tube and tying both ends of the string taut to both rear wheel dropouts (remove the rear wheel). With a ruler, measure the distance between the string and the seat tube on both sides. Both measurements should be equal (Fig. 271). If not, it is possible to bend the head tube straight with a heavy metal rod in the head tube.

To check for head tube twist, tie *two* pieces of string, one wrapped around the *bottom* of the head tube and tied taut to both dropouts, and another piece wrapped around the *top* of the head tube and tied to the dropouts. With a ruler, measure the distance between both strings at the same place on both sides. There should be very little or no difference between both measurements. You can force the head tube to one side or another with a heavy bar placed on the correct side of the head and braced against the opposite side of the seat tube. But again, I don't

Fig. 271: Check head tube sideways alignment with piece of string around head tube bottom and tied to both rear dropouts. Distance between string and seat tube on both sides of tube should be equal.

advise you doing this; you could bend a main tube. Far better to let a good bike mechanic work on your frame. Another check for head alignment is to remove the bottom bracket assembly, and with a straightedge against the bottom bracket fixed cup and parallel to the head tube, to measure the distance from the straightedge to the head tube. Repeat on the other side. Both measurements should be equal.

Stays

For this check, the rear wheel must be accurately centered on the axle (see page 414). Assuming it is so centered, pull the wheel all the way back so that the axle is snug against both ends of the dropouts. With a ruler, check the distance from both sides of the rim to the seat stays (Fig. 272). Both measurements should be the same. Check the distance from rim to chain stays on both sides; again, both measurements should be the same.

Check chain stays by putting a straightedge against the right side of the head tube and the seat tube and measuring the distance from the right-side flat of the straightedge to the flat of the dropout. Put the straightedge on the *left* side of the head tube and the seat tube and measure the distance from the left-side flat of the straightedge to the left flat of the dropout. Both measurements should be at the same place on the dropout. Both measurements should be equal. If you have a bent stay, put the bicycle in a vise, bottom bracket hangar (axle, etc., removed) gripped between copper sheets or hardwood, and with a long steel bar braced at one end against the seat tube, and the other end against the offending dropout, bend as needed. Be careful! Do it slowly, a tiny bit at a time. Tape tubes so you don't mar finish.

Fig. 272: With rear wheel all the way back in rear dropouts and correctly "dished" (see page 449 for wheel truing), distance from left and right seat stays to left and right rim sides should be equal.

Seat Tube Alignment

Check alignment of the seat tube by putting a straightedge against the bottom bracket hangar and parallel with the seat tube and measure the distance from the straightedge to the seat tube. Repeat on the opposite side. Both measurements should be equal. If the seat tube is bent, it may be possible to straighten it by putting the frame in a vise, the bottom bracket gripped between copper or hardwood, and with a long steel pipe fitted all the way down into the seat tube, bending it as necessary.

Dropouts

Dropouts should be parallel to each other. Check by holding two straightedges on the outside faces of the dropouts and measuring the distance between the straightedges just above the dropout and about 18 inches above the dropout. Both measurements should be equal. If the dropouts are not parallel, align by twisting the dropout gently with a large crescent wrench.

A Precautionary Word

This section on alignment is designed more to help you trace down the cause of misalignment than it is to help you correct it. A fine bicycle frame deserves more help than you are likely to be equipped to give it. It *does* ease your mind when you can trace down a misalignment to something you can fix, such as off-centered rims. But bent tubes, etc., are something else again, and I do urge you to take the bicycle back to the bicycle shop you bought it from and let their mechanic take care of any frame straightening. And if you've had an accident with your bicycle, check the head tube where it meets the top and down tubes for wrinkled paint (a sign of frame buckling), and check the bottom-bracket bottom cup for bending where it meets the down tube.

Other causes of frame alignment problems are:

· Less expensive bicycles have high-temperature welded frames. Tube joints are heated red hot with a welding torch, and the frame tubes are welded together. If the frame is removed from the welding jig and thrown in a pile before it has had a chance to cool, joints may be hot enough to bend easily, and so a brand-new frame can be out of line.

- If you've shipped your bicycle and haven't blocked the front and rear drop-outs with wood or an old axle, the stays or fork blades can be bent in handling. (I know, it happened to me en route to Austria.)
- Your bicycle could have been run over if it was left in the driveway. In this case, I think you'll notice the sideways wobble.

CRANKS AND BOTTOM BRACKET

The bottom bracket and crank assembly (Fig. 273), located at the point where the seat and down tubes meet, is one of the most highly stressed parts of the bicycle. The entire assembly should be removed, cleaned, and regreased at least once a year. Side play must be removed by adjust-

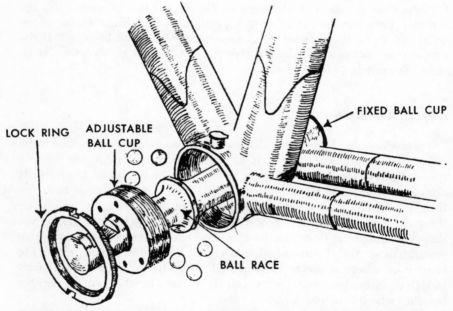

FIXED BALL CUP

LOCK RING

ADJUSTABLE BALL CUP

BALL RACE

Fig. 273: Typical three-piece steel cottered bottom bracket assembly. The oil cup is only found on less expensive bicycles, usually on three-speed models, almost never on ten-speeds. Oil is entirely unsuitable for the extreme pressures exerted through the pedals on bottom bracket bearings and cups. Grease will hold up under these pressures, and is far more resistant to being washed out by water. (Note axle flats for cotter pin to hold crank.) Reprinted by permission of Temple Press, Ltd., from *The Cycling Book of Maintenance.*

ing the adjustable (left side) cup and depending on your type of bicycle. Above all, the chainwheel assembly must spin freely.

Occasionally you should turn your bicycle upside down or hang it from the ceiling and, after removing the chain, spin the cranks and listen for grinding noises from the bottom bracket. If you hear any such racket, regard it as a signal that the axle and its bearings need cleaning and regreasing.

Crank and Bottom-Bracket Maintenance

The bottom-bracket assembly is the axle, bearings, cups and locknut, cranks and chainwheel(s) (Fig. 274). Bottom-bracket maintenance is too easily neglected because it is a bit more difficult to disassemble than, say,

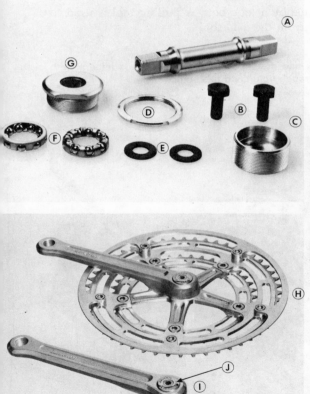

Fig. 274: Cotterless crank and chainwheel assembly: (A) Axle. Note that right side of axle is longer than left side. Long side is where chainwheel crank (H) goes on. (B) Crank locknuts; (C) Adjustable (left side) cup; (D) Lockring for adjustable cup; (E) Washers for crank locknuts; (F) Bearings in retainer. Note retainer has convex and concave sides. Retainer at right has convex side up, and this is side that fits into cups, so convex side always faces toward axle ends. (G) Fixed cup; (H) Chainwheel and right-hand crank; (I) Left crank; (J) Crank dust cap.

a wheel hub. Yet the bottom bracket takes a lot of wear and tear; it's close to the ground where it can pick up dust and dirt; and it can wear faster than need be if not maintained properly.

There are three types of bottom brackets: First, the one-piece unit (Fig. 275), which is a forged and machined bracket and crank set, with the cranks and bottom bracket all one piece. One-piece cranks are found on less expensive ten-speeds, some one- and three-speeds, and on juvenile bicycles. The second type is the three-piece cottered crank (see Fig. 273), which has a separate axle and cranks. The crank is held onto the axle by a wedge-shaped pin (Fig. 276) which is hammered or pressed into place and locked with a nut and washer. These cranks and bottom brackets are usually all steel, and are found on less expensive ten-speeds and on three- and five-speed internal-rear-hub bicycles.

The third type is the cotterless bottom bracket and crank assembly (see Fig. 274), made of aluminum alloy and found on high-priced ten- and fifteen-speed bicycles. The cranks are fitted onto tapered squared axle ends, and wedged in place by a lock bolt. A pulling tool is used to remove the press-fitted crank from the axle shaft.

Fig. 275: Typical one-piece crank and bottom bracket. Chainwheel is integral with crank and axle. Unit comes out through right-hand fixed cup.

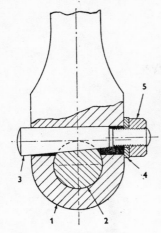

Fig. 276: Typical cottered crank. Reprinted with the permission of Temple Press Ltd. from *The Cycling Book of Maintenance.*
1. Crank (left-hand)
2. Bracket axle
3. Cotter pin
4. Washer
5. Nut

Each of these crank and bottom-bracket assemblies takes its own set of tools and methods of disassembly and reassembly. Let's start with the three piece, cotterless crank and bottom-bracket assembly (Fig. 277). Tools you will need are shown in Fig. 278.

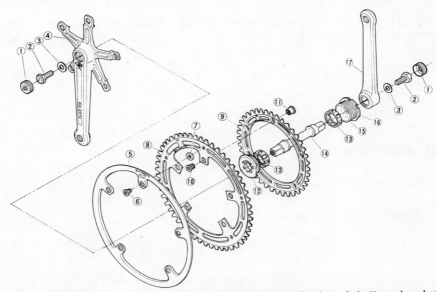

Fig. 277: Typical high-quality alloy cotterless chainwheel and bottom bracket assembly. This is a Shimano Dura-Ace unit. Parts are: (1) Crank arm cap; (2) Fixing bolt; (3) Fixing washer; (4) Right crank arm, 165 mm. (6½″) W; (4) Right crank arm, 170 mm. (6¾″) W; (5) Chain guard; (6) Guard fixing bolt; (7) Guard fixing spacer; (8) Chainwheel 52-teeth; (9) Chainwheel 39-teeth; (10) Chainwheel fixing bolt; (11) Chainwheel fixing nut; (12) Right-hand fixed cup (1.37 x 24); (13) Steel ball retainer; (14) Bottom bracket spindle 112 mm. W; (15) Left-hand adjustable cup (1.37 x 24); (16) Lock ring; (17) Left crank arm, 165 mm. (6½″); (17) Left crank arm, 170 mm. (6¾″). Note that cranks are available in 6½ and 6¾ inch lengths.

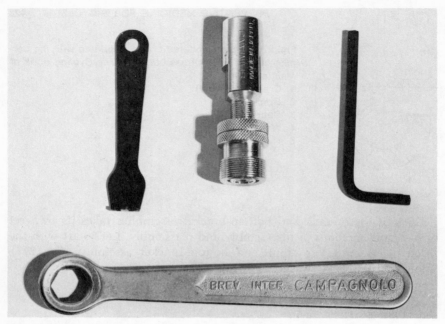

Fig. 278: Top, left to right: chainwheel pin tool; crank puller; dust-cap wrench. Bottom, crank locknut wrench.

Cotterless Cranks

Here are the steps in cotterless crank disassembly:

STEP ONE: Remove the dust cap and pedals (Fig. 279).

STEP TWO: Remove the locknut and washer (Fig. 280).

STEP THREE: Install the crank puller in the crank on left-hand side. It threads on clockwise. Before installing, make sure the crank-puller shaft ("A" in Fig. 278) is threaded *all the way back*. Make sure the crank puller is threaded *all the way in* the crank, so the pressure of pulling off the crank won't strip the crank threads (Fig. 281).

Fig. 279: Step One

Fig. 280: Step Two

Fig. 281: Step Three

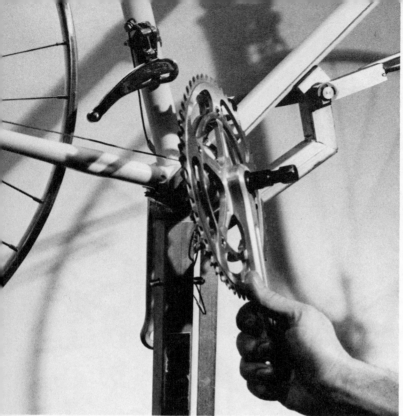

Fig. 282: Step Five

Fig. 283: Step Six

STEP FOUR: Turn the crank-puller outer bolt until it is flush against the axle shaft. Turn again one eighth of a turn. If the crank does not move, tap the crank-puller outer bolt two or three times sharply and try again. Cranks wedged on tightly will be hard to remove, and you may only be able to move the crank-puller bolt an eighth of a turn or less each time you tap it with the mallet. Do not try to force the crank off with the puller alone if it's wedged on tight; you may strip the aluminum crank threads.

STEP FIVE: When you have the left-hand crank removed, remove the right-hand crank and chainwheel (as one unit) as you did in Step Four (Fig. 282).

STEP SIX: With the bottom-bracket lock ring spanner, remove the ring, rotating it counterclockwise (Fig. 283).

STEP SEVEN: With the movable bottom-bracket cup wrench, remove the movable cup and catch the loose bearings in a rag.

STEP EIGHT: Pull the axle out through the left-hand bottom bracket hangar, remove the ball bearings from the right-hand fixed cup, and clean everything, including the chainwheel, in kerosene. Count all the bearings to make sure as you put them back that you haven't lost any. If the bearings are in a retainer and the retainer is worn, you can get by without the race if you can't wait for a replacement (remove the bearings from the race and replace without a retainer).

STEP NINE: Examine the balls and cup races for cracks and galled shiny spots indicating undue wear. Replace cups if necessary. (The right-hand cup can be removed by putting it in a large, sturdy vise and turning the entire bike frame.) But you must first be sure whether the fixed cup is a right- or left-hand thread, so you can turn it the right way. British thread dimensions call for a left-hand thread on the fixed cup and right-hand thread on the adjustable cup; both cups are threaded right hand on European metric threaded hubs. Right-hand threaded pieces thread *on clockwise;* left-hand threads *on counterclockwise.* (See Table 20 on page 342.) *Do not remove fixed cup unless it is cracked, worn or rusted.*

STEP TEN: Put a layer of grease in both cups; roll the loose bearings around in a dab of grease, or stuff grease into the balls in a race. Put the bearings back in the right-hand (fixed) cup. Put the axle carefully through; make sure the long (chainwheel) end of the axle goes first. Put the bearings in the adjustable cup, and thread cup on and up snug to bearings.

STEP ELEVEN: Snug up the adjustable cup with a wrench; back off an eighth of a turn.

STEP TWELVE: Thread on the adjustable-cup locknut and tighten with a spanner. Spin the axle between thumb and forefinger to check for binding; twist from side to side to check for sideplay. If binding, loosen the locknut, back the adjustable cup off an eighth of a turn, tighten the locknut and check again. Repeat as necessary. If the adjustable cup is too loose (indicated by sideplay), loosen the locknut, take up on cup an eighth of a turn, tighten the locknut and check. Repeat as necessary.

STEP THIRTEEN: Install the left-hand crank on shaft. Insert the washer and locknut and tighten the locknut firm with the locknut wrench. Install the right-hand crank the same way. Take up (tighten) both crank locknuts every 50 miles for 150 miles to make sure the crank does not work loose. A loose aluminum alloy crank on a steel axle will soon ruin the crank.

STEP FOURTEEN: Check the chainwheel bolts and nuts with special Allen and "T" wrenches to make sure they are tight. They can work loose. If you've changed chainwheels, check tightness three times at fifty-mile intervals.

Three-Piece Cottered Cranks

To disassemble three-piece cottered cranks, you will need these tools: Locknut spanner, ball peen hammer, small crescent wrench. Here are the steps in disassembly and assembly:

STEP ONE: Make up a piece of two-by-four about 40 inches high, notched at one end and held at that end in a vise. Loosen the cotter-pin nut three turns. Put the *bottom of the crank* in the V-cutout in the two-by-four, which is held in the vise with the other end on floor, and with a mallet, hit the cotter-pin nut squarely (Fig. 284). As the pin becomes loosened, turn pin nut two or three more turns and continue until pin is loose enough to tap out without damaging threads. You can buy a tool to press pins out, but unless you own a bike store, you won't need one. Take pins out as above on both cranks, and remove cranks from axle.

STEP TWO: From here on follow Steps Six through Twelve for cotterless cranks.

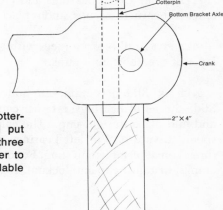

Cotterpin

Bottom Bracket Axle

Crank

2" × 4"

Fig. 284: To remove cottered crank cotter-pin, cut V-notch in two by four and put crank flat on top. Loosen pin nut three turns and hit nut squarely with hammer to loosen pin. A special shop tool is available to press out pins, but it's expensive.

STEP THREE: Examine axle flats, with a magnifying glass, if necessary, so that you can tell which side of the flat is beveled the most. In other words, the milled flat section of the axle is also at a slight angle, so more steel has been removed on one side and, gradually, less toward the other side. Check Fig. 276 closely. You will see that the cotter pin goes in threaded end first, with the flat of the thicker part of the pin fitting into the axle flat with the most steel removed. Pin must be flat so that it's snug against the axle. Then tap pin lightly into place.

STEP FOUR: Put the crank bottom back in the notched two-by-four and pound the cotter firmly in place from big end (not threaded end); thread on locknut. Tighten locknut carefully; it's very easy to strip.

One-Piece Cranks

STEP ONE: Remove pedals.

STEP TWO: With locknut spanner, remove adjustable cup and left-side locknut, and slide out over left crank. Remove adjustable cup and left bearings and slide out over left crank.

STEP THREE: Twist crank so you can slide it out of the bottom bracket hangar to the right. You should now have entire bottom-bracket crank assembly, including bearings, removed from bicycle.

STEP FOUR: Clean bearings and cups with kerosene, check for worn or cracked bearings or cups, and replace if necessary.

STEP FIVE: Fill bearing races with grease (Lubriplate Type A) and put a layer of grease in both cups.

STEP SIX: Slide left crank into bottom bracket hangar through right cup. Slide the set of bearings, retainer convex side to the right, over left crank and into place in right cup. (The convex side is like the bottom part of a spoon curvature.) Put left bearings, convex side to the left, in place and thread on adjustable cup snug. Follow Steps Eleven and Twelve, cotterless cranks, to adjust cup and locknut. Reinstall pedals.

THE HEADSET

Headset Maintenance

The headset consists of the front fork bearings and associated washers, adjusting nuts, cups, and cones. Once or twice a year you should dismantle the headset (Fig. 285) on your bike, clean it, and relubricate the bearings.

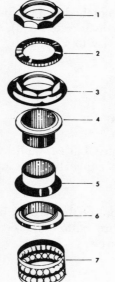

Fig. 285: Exploded view of typical headset. Bearings are usually loose, but in this new model Campagnolo headset, they are in a race, as they are on most American-made bicycles.
1. Locknut
2. Keyed washer
3. Adjustable cup
4. Top fixed cup in head tube
5. Bottom fixed cup in head tube
6. Crown fixed cup on fork
7. Top and bottom bearings

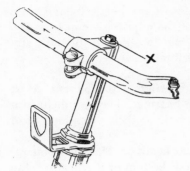

Fig. 286: Handlebars can be removed on any bicycle by loosening stem bolt "X" and pounding down with rubber or plastic-headed mallet.

To lubricate the headset, follow this procedure:

STEP ONE: Loosen the expander bolt. This is the head bolt on the handlebar stem (Figs. 286 and 287). When you have loosened it about a quarter of an inch, tap the bolt down with a rubber mallet or a block of wood and a hammer. You can either lift off the handlebars at this point and lay them, with brake cables still attached, over the top tube out of the way, or pull through brake cables as described on page 396 under the section "Replacing Brake Cables." You will then be able to move the handlebar and stem out of your way. Remove the handlebars by twisting and pulling upward at the same time. Alloy handlebars have Allen bolts and require a mating metric allen wrench. Use the Raleigh three piece set, from any Raleigh dealer.

STEP TWO: Remove the front wheel.

STEP THREE: With a large crescent wrench, monkey wrench, or smooth-jawed pliers, remove the locknut on the headset and the washer (Fig. 285). Or, if the locknut has holes and is round, use a center punch and a hammer, gently. Remove washer under locknut.

Fig. 287: Some stems have a recessed stem bolt, and to remove it you will need a 6- or 7-mm. Allen wrench, as shown (left).

STEP FOUR: Lay the bicycle on its side, with the headset lying on a large cloth to catch loose bearings. Remove the adjustable cup from the top of the headset, and pull the fork out from the bottom. Remove any loose bearings that are still in the top or bottom cones.

STEP FIVE: Clean the headset cones and bearings with kerosene. Most American-made bicycles do not have loose bearings. They are held in a retainer or cage, so you don't have to worry about their dropping out of the bicycle and getting lost.

This also applies to the new Campagnolo headsets. If, when you remove the caged bearing sets from the top and bottom of the headset, the bearing balls fall out of them, this means that the cage or retainer is worn and you should buy a new set of caged bearings. You can use loose balls if they are the same size as those in the retainer or cage set, instead.

STEP SIX: Check the cleaned bearings and cones for wear, galled spots, cracks, and rust, and replace any defective parts with new parts.

STEP SEVEN: Turn the bicycle upside down. Smear a layer of Lubriplate or Texaco Starfak No. 2 grease in the bottom cone, and replace the bearings. Insert the front fork. Holding the fork in place by hand, turn the bicycle over so that the weight of the bicycle is on the front fork (to hold bottom bearings in place).

NOTE: If caged bearings are used, place them in the cone so that the curved, outer part of the bearings face into the cup.

STEP EIGHT: Put a layer of grease into the top cup, insert the balls or caged bearing, and screw down the adjusting cup until it is hand-tight. Then, back off about a quarter-turn. Insert the front wheel.

STEP NINE: Adjust the headset by inserting the keyed flat washer and locknut, and tightening the locknut. Check the fork for play, vertically and horizontally, by turning it. If the fork feels stiff, loosen the locknut, back off the adjusting cup another quarter-turn, and retighten the locknut. If there is side or vertical play in the fork, loosen the locknut, tighten the adjusting cup a quarter-turn, and retighten the locknut. Repeat until the play is removed. The fork is ideally adjusted when it turns easily, and there is no vertical or horizontal play. *It is vital there be no sideplay in the headset.* If there is, the constant up and down pounding between cups and bearings will flatten and ruin bearings and probably cups as well.

Fig. 288: Here's how the top headset cup should look after you've replaced all the bearings and packed some grease around them.

STEP TEN: Reinstall the handlebars. Check the headset adjustment again by locking the front brake and rocking the bicycle back and forth. If sideplay exists, remove by backing off locknut, loosen adjustable cup about ⅛ turn, tighten locknut and check again. Reverse the process if the fork is too tight and binds. The fork should turn freely and yet have no sideplay. This is vital because if there is sideplay, headset bearings will be pounded and flattened under road impact. And a loose headset can contribute to high-speed wheel shimmy.

If, when you turn the fork from side to side, you find it still binds, or you can't seem to get the ideal adjustment, you have probably either put one bearing too many in one end of the headset, and consequently are short one in the other end, or you are missing a bearing, because it has rolled up into the fork and stuck there on a spot of grease. In either case, you will have to dismantle the headset, following Steps One through Six, above, before you can adjust the headset properly. I would like to be able to give you a bearing count so you would know how many bearings you should have, but there are far too many bearing sizes and consequently too many different numbers of bearings in various makes of bicycles to make this practical.

HOW TO LACE A WHEEL

For any of a number of reasons, you may want to "lace" up a wheel. Your rim may develop a flat spot after a hard jolt and rotate with an annoying "thump, thump, thump." You may wish to upgrade your wheels, change from steel to aluminum rims, change hubs, replace spokes, or simply build up a new set of wheels. You may wish tubular tires for local touring over good roads, and another set of clincher-tired wheels for long-distance touring over a variety of good and bad road conditions. So if you already have either a set of clinchers or tubulars, you can buy a pair of rims for one or the other, a set of good hubs, enough spokes and nipples, and build your own wheels.

If you have a bike shop build your wheels, you'll pay from $8.00 to $10.00 for lacing and truing to commercial standards, exclusive of parts. For a more exacting job to professional European road-racing standards, you'll pay more, because to lace and true to those requirements takes at least three hours. Bicycle shops that cater to the racing trade in this country charge around $20.00 for labor alone just to lace and true a set of racing wheels. It would, of course, be courting disaster for a racing cyclist, especially one who in Europe depends on his equipment for his livelihood (as much as $150,000 a year) to have anything but the most painstakingly accurately laced and trued wheels. In fact, there is at least one reported instance of a professional wheel builder in England taking forty hours to build a pair of wheels for European racing! I will say, categorically, and this is going to raise a lot of eyebrows, that any bike mechanic who claims he can build and true a wheel in fifteen minutes, and some do, can't possibly be doing anything more than a minimum job. That's the kind of wheel building that will buy you wheels that go untrue quickly, cause permanent flat spots in the rim and ultimate spoke breakage. I urge you to learn how to lace and true your own wheels, then you can be as finicky as you please, take all the time you want, and come up with wheels that will stay "true" to you indefinitely, with perhaps minor touching up after the first 200 miles.

We will discuss wheel lacing or building (they're synonymous terms) and truing, after which we will take up more exotic wheel building such as radial spoking, tying and soldering spokes, and various spoking arrangements.

Wheel building seems difficult, but once you get the hang of it, it's really quite simple. I still recall the time I saw a math prof busy with compass, protractor, and slide rule, figuring out all the spoke angles so he could lace a wheel; he computed spoke angles but not how to lace. Then I recall the time I was taught by an old-timer (who was taught by *his* grandfather) to lace a wheel. The lesson took exactly ten minutes. I have taught a twelve-year-old boy to lace a wheel in ten minutes, and *he* can still lace a wheel. Remember just one thing while you're learning. Forget about the maze and mess of loose spokes flopping around you as you lace, and learn to concentrate *only* on the spoke you're working with and its preceding spoke.

What Spokes to Use

I've nothing against other makes, but I prefer French-made Robergel spokes because they're stronger and used by racing cyclists in this country and abroad. You can buy Robergel spokes from Wheel Goods or Cyclo-Pedia by mail if you can't find them locally (see Appendix for addresses). Robergel spokes come in three types: "*Etoile,*" of stainless steel, plain gauge (not thicker or "butted" at the ends). "Etoile" spokes have a tensile strength of 14,930 to 16,360 lbs. per square inch. Robergel "Sport" spokes are butted stainless steel with a tensile strength of 19,900 to 21,300 lbs./sq. in. (Table 24). "Trois Etoiles" spokes are butted stainless chrome nickel, with a tensile strength of 17,068 to 18,500 lbs./sq. in. The "Trois Etoiles" spokes will stay better looking longer, but the "Sport" spokes are stronger and I prefer them. Other good spokes are "Berg-Union," made in Germany.

I don't recommend mixing makes of spokes in the same wheel. Different make spokes are made of different metals. High-quality spokes are of high-tensile-strength stainless steels, cheap spokes are little better than drawn wire. Mixing makes of spokes means that there will be variations in "modulus of elasticity" (stretch) and tensile strength at random places in your wheel, so it will be next to impossible to adjust spokes to keep wheel rim in perfect alignment, and even to keep the weaker spokes from breaking. And spoke nipples aren't always interchangeable either.

TABLE 24 · Robergel Spoke Lengths

INCHES	MILLIMETERS
10¹⁵⁄₁₆	278
11	280
11⅛	282
11⅝	295
11¾	298
11¹³⁄₁₆	300
11⅞	302
12	305
12¹⁄₁₆	306
12⅛	308

If you change to a low- from a high-flange hub, you may need longer spokes, unless you lace three cross, for example.

Table 25 gives spoke size in relation to hub size and whether spokes are crossed two, three, or four. This table is fairly accurate. The problem in accurate spoke-size selection will never be solved by any table, however, because there are dozens of makes of hubs, and even so-called standard high- and low-flange hubs do not have spoke holes spaced the same distance from the hub-axle housing. The problem isn't particularly great, though, since so long as you can get at least half the spoke threads in the nipple, the spoke can be made to fit. I just want you to know that this table is more of a reasonable indication than an exact specification as to which length spoke to order to lace your particular combination of rim and hub. For example, ferruled rims may take a slightly shorter spoke than a nonferruled rim using a washer over the spoke hole (see discussion of these rims below).

A wood-filled rim, such as a Milremo Weltmeister, uses a spoke about an eighth of an inch longer than a nonwood-filled rim, given the same hub; so you'd add an eighth of an inch to the spoke regardless of the number of spoke holes and crossing. This is because the nipple head seats on the rim section just underneath the tire, instead of in the center section of the rim (Fig. 289). Also, you will notice that the chart breaks down

TABLE 25 · **Spoke Length Selection Chart**

RIM (in.)		HUB	HOLES	CROSS	SPOKE LENGTH (in.) FRONT	REAR
TUBULAR TIRES	27 x 1⅛	Hi °	24	2	11⅝	11⅝
		Hi °	28	3	12	12
		Hi	28	3	12	11¹⁵⁄₁₆
		Hi	32	3	11¹³⁄₁₆	11¾
		Hi	36	3	11⅝	11½
		Hi	36	4	12	12
		Hi °	36	4	12¹⁄₁₆	12¹⁄₁₆
		Lo	28	3	12¹⁄₁₆	12¹⁄₁₆
		Lo	32	3	11¹³⁄₁₆	11¾
		Lo	36	3	11⅝	11½
		Lo	36	4	12¹⁄₁₆	12¹⁄₁₆
		Lo	40	4	11⅞	11¹³⁄₁₆

TABLE 25 · Spoke Length Selection Chart (continued)

RIM (in.)		HUB	HOLES	CROSS	SPOKE LENGTH (in.) FRONT	REAR
CLINCHER TIRES,			36	3	11	11
ENGLISH SIZES	26 x 1⅜		36	4	11¼	11¼
	26 x 1¼		40	4	—	11⅛
			36	3	11³⁄₁₆	11³⁄₁₆
			32	3	11¹³⁄₁₆	—
			40	4	—	11⅜
			36	3	11¼	11¼
			36	4	11½	11½
			40	3	—	11¼
			40	4	11⁷⁄₁₆	11⁷⁄₁₆
CLINCHER TIRES,	27 x 1¼	Hi	28	3	12¹⁄₁₆	12
LIGHTWEIGHT,		Hi	32	3	11⅞	11¹³⁄₁₆
HI-PRESSURE		Hi	36	3	11³⁄₁₆	11¾
		Hi	36	4	12⅛	12⅛
		Hi	40	3	11⅝	11⅝
		Hi	40	4	12	12
		Lo	28	3	12⅛	12⅛
		Lo	32	3	12¹⁄₁₆	12
		Lo	36	3	12	11⅞
		Lo	36	4	12⅛	12⅛
		Lo	40	3	11¹³⁄₁₆	11¹³⁄₁₆
		Lo	40	4	12¹⁄₁₆	12¹⁄₁₆
CLINCHER TIRES,	26 x 2.125	CB	36	3	10	10
U.S.A. SIZES		CB	36	4	10⅝	10⅝
		3S	36	3	10	10
		3S	36	4	10⅝	10⅝
	26 x 1.35	3S				
		CB	36	4	11⁷⁄₁₆	11⁷⁄₁₆
	26 x 1⅜	3S				
		CB	36	4	10⅞	10⅞
	26 x 1.75	3S	36	3	10⅝	10⅝
		CB	36	4	10⅞	10⅞
	26½ x 1½	3S/				
		CB	36	4	11⅛	11⅛

* Track rims: Hi = Hi Flange; Lo = Lo Flange.
3S is Three Speed; CB is Coaster Brake.

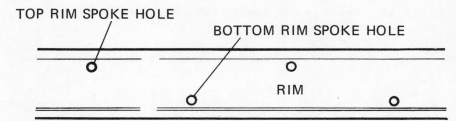

TOP RIM SPOKE HOLE

BOTTOM RIM SPOKE HOLE

RIM

Fig. 289: Spoke holes are drilled offset in rims, as shown in this exaggerated drawing. Note that valve hole is centered. Better rims also have spoke holes drilled at an angle, so nipples can follow spoke angle in tangential lacing, minimizing stress and spoke breakage potential. Some rims have first hole to right of valve hole on top, others on bottom as in drawing.

rims and hubs by country. U.S.A. rims and hubs given are the common garden-variety all-steel rims and low-flange hubs used on one-, two-, and three-speed hubs with and without coaster brakes. The 27-inch wheels are, however, presented first because these are, I hope, the sizes you are mostly involved with. In addition, if by some quirk of manufacturer, your spokes are too short or two long, Table 24 gives the size range of Robergel spokes in inches and millimeters so you can go up or down one size, as you need. If, as is the case in the smaller wheel sizes, you must use other than Robergel spokes, I suggest Berg-Union or Torrington. I have left out wheels smaller than twenty-six inches since they would be mostly for the juvenile market.

Strength of Wheels

Properly laced wheels, even the light tubular-tire rim type, are very strong. I ran into a parked car head on at about twelve miles an hour once, and the front wheel never even varied from true, yet I hit with sufficient force to bend a very strong Reynolds butted '531' tubing fork. (*I* varied from "true" for about ten minutes.)

A 40-spoke wheel weighing only 27 ounces was tested for maximum axle loading. The wheel sustained an axle load of more than 1,200 pounds, after which the wheel showed a permanent slight buckle. Since the buckling occurred at a pressure more than 700 times the weight of the wheel, it can be said that this wheel can safely sustain a working load of about 700 pounds at smooth riding conditions. Since the *average* cyclist weighs certainly no more than 180 pounds, we can assume this wheel is amply strong enough for racing on smooth roads and for touring even on fairly rough roads, such as cobblestone streets. But don't count on not putting a permanent crimp in your rim if you hit a pothole! In the section on safety where I discuss crash helmets I mention two of my own accidents, in one which I hit a crack in a bridge and the other in which I hit a parked car once again. Both times I used the same 3½ ounce Hi-E aluminum alloy hub, 32 spokes crossed three with an alloy rim. The second accident did put a crimp in the rim but the hub held up fine (I wish I had).

Wheel Lacing Steps

Let's start wheel building with a few basic observations about rims and hubs. First, to make life complicated, rims and hubs have spoke holes drilled off center. Fig. 289 shows that rim spoke holes are drilled so that every other hole is closer to one side of the rim than to the other side. Please keep that in mind as we proceed, because we'll come back to it. Next, study Fig. 290; note that hub holes are also drilled off center; i.e., the hubs in one flange are offset from the holes in the facing flange. If you poke a spoke down a hub hole from the top flange, straight up and down, it will land *between* the spokes in the bottom flange of the hub. Check this for yourself and bury it in your memory. Finally, and this is also important, pick up your hub and look at the spoke holes closely. You'll notice, as in Fig. 290, that if you have a fine hub such as a Cam-

Fig. 290: All wheel hubs have holes drilled off center with respect to holes in top and bottom flanges, as shown by spoke (A), which falls between spoke holes (B) and (C) below; and spoke (D), which falls midway between holes (E) and (F). Note also every other hole on *both* sides of the hub is countersunk. Spoke head goes in non-countersunk hole. Countersinking minimizes spoke breakage by spreading stress at spoke head bend over greater area, instead of at sharp right angle. See Fig. 291.

pagnolo alloy Record, Phil Wood, or Hi-E, every other hub hole is countersunk. This countersinking is to permit the spoke to bend gradually and to eliminate a sharp corner that would stress the spoke at this point, and contribute to premature spoke breakage. At first, though, because we're used to putting screw heads in countersunk holes, you may believe spoke heads should go into hub countersunk holes. Believe me, it's not so! You can bury spoke heads in countersunk holes for a sexier-looking hub, but you'll have busted spokes on the road if you do! Fig. 291 illustrates this point. (Some hubs have *all* holes countersunk.)

Before you start building a wheel, first make sure you have the right length spoke. Refer to the spoke chart on page 436 if you're not sure. Also, remove the freewheel gear cluster from rear wheels; you can't poke spokes in the rear hub with the freewheel in the way (which is why you should take a freewheel-removing tool as well as spare spokes on trips). You may also find it difficult or next to impossible to poke spokes through hub holes if they are drilled too small to accommodate the spoke. Most dealers, if they stock Robergel "Sport" spokes, only have them in .080-.072 gauge. This means the butted ends are .080, and the rest of the spoke is .072 inches. The nearest fraction equivalent to .080 is ³⁄₃₂-inch (or 2.032 millimeters). So you would drill out a too-small hole with a ³⁄₃₂-inch drill. Actually, I'd rather see you use a metric drill, 2.05 mm., to be exact, which gives you a snugger fitting hole only .018 mm. larger than the butted section of the spoke. Be sure to drill straight, and remember, once you've drilled out your hub, always replace spokes with the same diameter spoke.

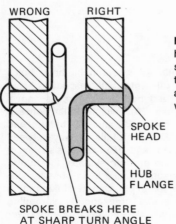

WRONG   RIGHT

SPOKE HEAD

HUB FLANGE

SPOKE BREAKS HERE
AT SHARP TURN ANGLE

Fig. 291: Left, wrong way to put spoke in wheel hub, which stresses spoke at sharp noncountersunk hole. Right, correct way to insert spoke so that head is flush against rim and spoke shaft angles out against countersunk side of hole, which reduces stress and breakage at this point.

If you use a smaller gauge spoke you will invite spoke breakage, as the spoke bounces around the larger spoke hole under stress. If you have a drill press you should recountersink holes, or countersink every other one on both sides if not already so countersunk. If you can't find metric drills locally (see page 337 for a discussion of the metric system), you can get them from either of the two metric mail-order supply houses listed in the Appendix.

A few definitions, so we're talking in the same language:

- *Rim* is the round steel or alloy part the tire goes on.
- *Spoke head* is the section of the spoke with the curved area and flat head (flat on the bottom). The other end of the spoke is threaded.
- *Spoke nipple* is the short, tubular, internally threaded piece that holds the spoke on the rim.
- "*Spoke head up*" means that in referring to the hub, the spoke head faces up, as shown in the Step One drawing (Fig. 292).
- "*Top rim hole*" means rim hole closest to upper edge of rim.

Before you start, you might consider drilling a one-inch hole in your wooden work bench to fit the axle of the hub so the hub assembly will stay put as you stick spokes in the wheel. And, while I'm thinking of it and before you despair, remember that, as I said, lacing a wheel is simple. It just *seems* difficult; it surely is hard to write about how to do it so that it comes out as easy as it really is.

Since most wheels on ten-speed bikes have 36 spokes front and rear, I'll assume this is what you're about to lace. You have a naked hub and rim, and a fist full of the right diameter and length spokes and nipples. You can get fancy later on and lace up 24-, 28-, 32-, or 40-spoked rims and hubs, and lace them radically or 3 or 4 cross as your heart desires. For now, we'll stick to 36 holes, crossed 4.

STEP ONE: Grab 9 spokes, threaded ends down. Hold the hub in one hand, the spokes in the other, and stuff a spoke down every other *non-countersunk hole,* so the spoke head faces up. If none of the holes are countersunk, stick a spoke in every other hole. Do the same for the bottom flange, with the hub in the same position as when you started. You should now have a hub that looks like the drawing above (Fig. 292).

STEP TWO: Sweep up all the spokes on both flanges into two bundles, hold them so they don't fall out, turn the hub over, and repeat Step One. When you're through, the hub will have all 36 spokes in it, with every other spoke head alternating, on each side of both hub flanges as shown in Fig. 293.

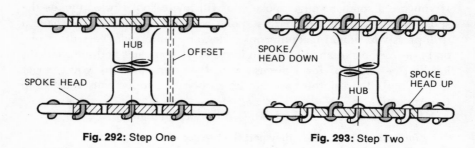

Fig. 292: Step One   **Fig. 293:** Step Two

STEP THREE: Sweep all the spokes as far away from the spoke hole as possible. Take any head-up spoke from the top flange (spoke head up means the spoke head is facing upward, on top of the flange), and put it in the first hole to the *right* of the valve hole. This rim hole must be a top rim hole (a top rim hole is the hole closest to the top of the rim). However, some rims are drilled so that the first hole to the right of the valve is a bottom rim hole (hole closest to the bottom of the rim). If so, start lacing with the first hole to the *left* of the valve hole. On this spoke and from here on thread a nipple four turns on each spoke as you lace it into the rim (Fig. 294).

STEP FOUR: Count off five spokes to the right (not counting the valve hole), including the hole you spoked in Step Three. This must also be a top rim hole. Into this hole put the next head-up spoke to the right of the one you spoked in Step Three. Continue this sequence until you have laced all head-up spokes in the top hub flange. The wheel will now look like Fig. 295, with three holes between each spoke, the center of the three empty holes being a rim top hole, the other two, rim bottom holes. (This happens to be a 32-hole rim and hub so only 8 spokes are showing. You should show 9 spokes.)

STEP FIVE: This is a critical step, so take it slowly and repeat it if you don't get it at first. Take the partially spoked rim and hub, and, keeping the same side up, *twist* the rim so the spokes are at an acute angle, just grazing the outside of their adjacent spoke holes. Depending on how the rim has been drilled, twist the rim either left or right, just so no spoke crosses over the valve hole (Fig. 296). Hold the hub as you twist the rim.

Fig. 294: Step Three

Fig. 295: Step Four

Fig. 296: Step Five

Fig. 297: Step Six

Fig. 298: Step Seven

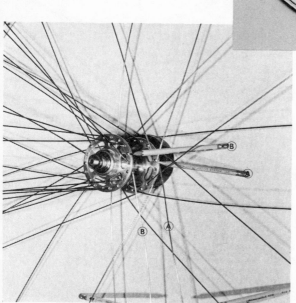

Fig. 299: Step Seven

STEP SIX: Another critical step. Take any head-down spoke from the top hub flange (the wheel should still be in the same position as when you started) and, going in the *opposite direction* from the spokes laced so far, cross *over* three and *under* the fourth spoke, as shown above, then stick it in the rim and thread on a nipple four turns. Remember Step Four? You had three empty spoke holes between each spoke. Right? I hope you did, anyway. If not, stop now and go over the preceding steps to check what you did wrong. Let's assume all is well. The spoke we are lacing in Step Six should go into a center (top rim hole) rim hole (Fig. 297). You are lacing Spoke "A." Note that it crosses *over* spokes B, C, D, and *under* E, and winds up in a top rim hole. Continue lacing all head-down spokes in the top flange, cross *over* three and *under* the fourth spoke, as above. When you are finished, spokes will be in groups of two, with one bottom rim spoke between each group of two. (If you wish to lace in a "cross three" pattern, pass the spoke *over* two and *under* the third spoke.)

STEP SEVEN: This is a most critical step. Turn the wheel over, with all unlaced spokes in the top flange. Straighten spokes out, sweep all but one out of your way. Take an old spoke, put it straight up alongside any head-up spoke in the top flange, with the threaded end resting on the bottom flange facing you. Notice that just to the left of this trial spoke is another head-up spoke, offset, to the left (naturally) in the bottom flange (see Fig. 290). We will call the bottom reference spoke in the bottom flange Spoke "A" and the spoke above and to its right, Spoke "B." Referring to the photo at left, bring spoke "B" parallel but angled to the left of spoke "A" below it. Refer to Fig. 298. Put spoke "B" in the first empty rim hole to the left of spoke "A," thread on a nipple. Now you will have (you *better* have) your first group of three spokes, with one empty spoke hole on either side. Step Seven is so critical I have taken extra photos from various angles to demonstrate it. Fig. 299 shows a close-up of the hub, with key spoke "A" at the bottom on the hub and key spoke "B" at the top of the hub. Fig. 300 shows key spokes "A" and "B" as they enter the rim. Fig. 301 is another view of Step Seven, with pencils on spokes "A" and "B." An important point to remember is that spoke "B" is parallel to spoke "A," is offset to it, and goes next to it in the rim, just above (to the left) of spoke "A."

Fig. 300: Step Seven

STEP EIGHT: Now, if all is well so far, the rest is simple. Just take the next head-up spoke, count off two *empty* (*EMPTY*) spoke holes to the *left* (*LEFT*), stick this spoke into *that* top rim hole, and thread on nipple four turns. Repeat until all head-up spokes are in the rim with nipples on. Now you will have all spokes in groups of three (Fig. 302) and are ready for the final step.

STEP NINE: Take any of the remaining spokes (they will all be head down, with heads *under* the top flange) and bring it around to the right, crossing *over* three and *under* the fourth spoke and stick it in the only hole it will fit into. If you're not sure which hole this is, please repeat Step Seven, only with head-down spokes, referencing a head-down spoke in the bottom flange and being sure that the parallel head-down spoke in the top flange also goes in a direction opposite to *its* reference spoke below. Confused? Well, actually I don't blame you. Let's take it from the top. First, find any head-down spoke in the bottom flange. Then find the first head-down spoke in the top flange offset to the right (counterclockwise) of your reference head-down spoke below, and put it in the first empty spoke hole to the right (counterclockwise) of spoke "A." Refer to Step Six drawing to refresh your memory as to what crossing over three and under four is all about. Continue as above, lacing up the remaining head-down spokes. Now the wheel is laced, spokes are in groups of four as shown above, and we are ready for the exacting job of "truing" the rim. Finished wheel is shown in Fig. 303.

Varieties of Wheels

As you will note from Table 25 on page 436, wheels can be laced with various spoking configurations. You can buy tubular tire, rims, and hubs drilled in multiples of 4, from 24 to 40 holes. And spokes can be crossed over three or even two, or not crossed tangentially at all but spoked radially, that is, straight up and down. They can even be laced tangentially on the driving side (the freewheel side) and radially on the other side; some racing cyclists prefer this combination, with 24 spokes, although it's rare in this country.

Wheels can also be tied and soldered, with 40 or 50 turns of thin steel wire wrapped around spoke intersections, and the wire soldered. Tying spokes in this manner makes a stiffer wheel, and reduces spoke breakage by cutting spoke "whip" under stress.

Fig. 301: Step Seven

Fig. 302: Step Eight

Fig. 303: Step Nine. VOILÀ!

Radial Lacing

Some cyclists prefer a radially laced front wheel and a tangentially (conventionally) laced rear wheel. Because radial spoking offers little resistance to forward power thrust, it's not practical for rear wheels. Radial spoking does offer less wind resistance because the spokes are in line behind each other, whereas tangentially laced spokes angle out more and so offer greater wind resistance. Radial spoking gives you a strong, rigid wheel for a front wheel only.

Crossing three instead of four spokes means that spokes are shorter, and again, offer a stiffer ride.

High- vs. Low-Flange Hubs

High-flange hubs provide a stiffer ride than low-flange hubs because they take shorter spokes. There's less spoke to absorb road shock. But I do not recommend using a 40-hole lacing with low-flange hubs, because this would put holes too close together and make a weaker hub. But that's my opinion, and if you wish to lace up a 40-hole rim and low-flange hub, by all means try it out. If you're a 200-pounder carrying 26 or 30 pounds of gear on tour over rough roads, I definitely would use a 40-hole rear wheel with *high*-flange hub, and a 36-hole *low*-flange front wheel and hub. If you're lighter, say from 150 to 180 pounds, on tour with normal camping gear of about 30-35 pounds, I'd stick to a 36-hole high-flange rear and a 36-hole low-flange front arrangement. If you're lighter, a 32-hole front and rear low-flange hub should hold up. This assumes all the wheels recommended above are crossed four. If you're a real lightweight, say 100 to 115 pounds, you may get by with a 28-hole, crossed four, low-flange hub front, and a 32-hole, crossed four, low-flange hub rear. Spoke breakage isn't all just spoke configuration, though. It's also how even spoke tension is, and how much tension is applied. Too little tension permits excessive spoke play in the hub, and whipsawing can break spokes at the bend near the hub hole. If you're lacing a 36-hole rim, cross four, in a low-flange hub, and *rim* holes are not drilled at an acute enough angle to permit the nipple to follow the spoke line, you will have stress and possible breakage at the nipple. If, as you apply tension, the spoke winds up with a twist, you can have spoke breakage at the twist. As you apply spoke tension in truing, watch that spokes stay put. If not, hold spokes with a smooth-jawed pair of pliers as you tighten the nipple.

Speaking of nipples, use short nipples for lightweight rims and long nipples for heavier rims, such as clinchers and touring tubular rims.

Here is a rather general recommendation for wheel-lacing configuration, subject to modification as personal experience warrants, and as to weight and style of riding:

TABLE 26 · **Wheel-Lacing Configuration**

TYPE OF RIDING	FRONT WHEEL	REAR WHEEL
MASSED-START RACING	28	36
TRACK SPRINTS	36 or 32	36
DISTANCE TIME TRIALS	36	36
SHORT TIME TRIALS	28 or 32	28 or 32
PURSUIT	28 or 32	28 or 32
GENERAL RIDING	36	36
TOURING, HEAVY RIDER, LUGGAGE	36	40

Remember, as one final observation, that reliability is more important than lightness, particularly when it comes to racing.

HOW TO "TRUE" A WHEEL

When we finished instructions for wheel lacing, you were left with spokes hanging loose. An accurately trued and tensioned wheel is vital to spoke life, for all the reasons noted above. You should also know how to true a wheel that has come untrue, because continued riding of an out-of-line wheel can put a permanent crimp or flat spot in the rim, and you will need a new rim. Braking is also safer with true rims because brake shoes can grab the rim evenly all the way around, and because brake shoes can be adjusted closer to the rim for minimum brake-lever travel and maximum stopping power. In other words, never ride very far with untrue rims; they're bound to be unfaithful.

Tools you will need for truing a wheel are shown in Fig. 304. They are: "A," truing stand; "B," vernier caliper gauge; "C," spoke wrench; "D," ratchet screwdriver; and, "E," rim-centering gauge.

It will be helpful before starting step-by-step truing instructions to establish a common vocabulary of truing terms, so we all talk the same language:

- *Concentricity* is the degree to which the wheel is perfectly round.
- *Lateral trueness* is the degree to which the wheel is centered over a point on the axle and remains on that point, with no side-to-side untrueness.

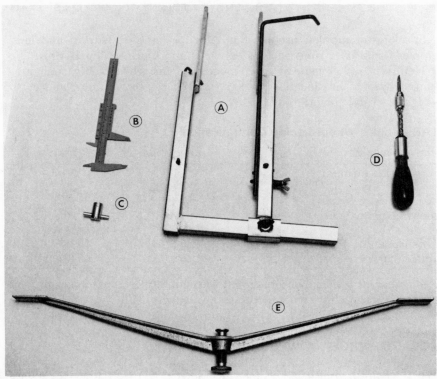

Fig. 304: Tools for truing include: (A) Wheel-truing stand; (B) Inch-metric vernier caliper and depth gauge; (C) Spoke wrench; (D) Ratchet screwdriver; and (E) Rim-centering gauge.

- *"Dishing"* applies to the rear wheel only, and means that the rim is "dished" or moved to the right so as to be centered *between* axle locknuts rather than on the hub alone. "Dishing" is well illustrated in Fig. 305. The rim is centered between A and A', and you will notice that the space between the axle locknuts is the same on *both* sides of the rim. Notice also that the rim is *not* centered on the hub alone, as evidenced by the fact that more of the hub is on the left than on the right side of the rim. "Dishing" is vital not only to rear wheel alignment, but also to the alignment of the rear wheel with respect to the frame and to the front wheel. Please study Fig. 305 until you are sure you understand the concept of "dishing." Remember that dishing is necessary because the extra width of the freewheel gear cluster adds a dimension to the rear wheel which the front wheel doesn't have; and so the rim must be centered on the total dimension, which *includes* the freewheel, just as the front wheel must be centered on *its* total width, which includes only the hub and axle locknuts.
- *"Centering"* is what you do to the front wheel; although of course, it's done to the rear wheel too, only we use the word "dishing" for the latter to stress

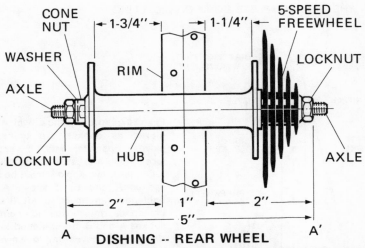

DISHING -- REAR WHEEL

Fig. 305: Rear wheel must be "dished," or moved to the right, so the rim is centered over the axle locknuts, as shown. Note that the distance on both sides of *rim* is equal (2 inches), yet hub is 1¾ inches on left and 1¼ on right side of rim.

that the rim is moved to the right side of the hub. The front wheel is centered on its hub. See Fig. 306; note that the rim is centered on the hub.

• *"Tension"* is the degree to which spokes are tightened. Too much tension can cause broken spokes; so can too little. Tension of *front* wheel spokes should be equal on all spokes; on *rear* wheels, tension of right-side spokes is a bit more than left side because the rim is pulled (dished) over to the right.

• *The rim gauge* (see Fig. 304) helps you center the rim, or "dish" it accurately.

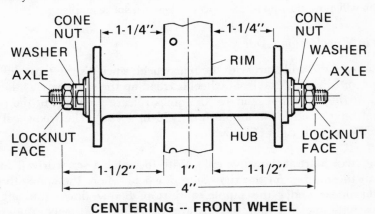

CENTERING -- FRONT WHEEL

Fig. 306: Unlike rear wheel, front wheel is centered on hub and between axle locknuts. Dimensions in Fig. 305–306 are illustrative only and do not necessarily apply to your wheels.

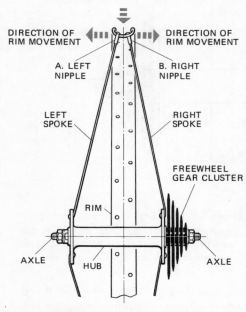

DIRECTION OF RIM MOVEMENT

DIRECTION OF RIM MOVEMENT

A. LEFT NIPPLE

B. RIGHT NIPPLE

LEFT SPOKE

RIGHT SPOKE

FREEWHEEL GEAR CLUSTER

RIM

AXLE

HUB

AXLE

DIRECTION OF RIM MOVEMENT

Fig. 307: Arrows show which way rim moves as spokes are tightened. Rim moves opposite way if spokes are loosened. Note that to remove out-of-roundness, *two* spokes must be tightened, spokes A and B. If spoke A alone is tightened, rim moves to left. If spoke B is tightened, rim moves to right. If both spokes A and B are tightened to the same degree, rim moves only downward.

- *Direction of rim movement* is which way the rim moves (left or right, up or down, with respect to the hub centerline) as you tighten or loosen a spoke nipple. Please study Fig. 307 until you understand in which direction the rim will move as you tighten a particular spoke nipple. Remember that the rim will move the opposite way as you *loosen* a spoke nipple.

Steps in Wheel Truing Are:

STEP ONE: We will start with the rear wheel, since it's the most difficult. Except for "dishing," the front wheel is trued up the same way as the rear wheel. If they're still on, remove the quick-release skewer. Put the wheel in the truing stand (or in an old fork held in a vise). The freewheel side should be on your right (Fig. 308).

STEP TWO: Start at the valve hole. With the ratchet screwdriver, speed-turn all the nipples on the right side down to where the spoke threads just disappear under the nipple, and stop. Screw down the left-side nipples until the last four threads are visible on the spoke, under the nipple. When you do the front wheel, screw down all the nipples until the threads are just covered.

STEP THREE: Measure the distance between axle locknuts. Now is when we learn to use the rim-centering gauge. Please study Fig. 305 again. (Dimensions are illustrative only, and do not necessarily apply to your rim.) You will see that the measurement between axle locknuts is five inches. The rim is one inch wide. There are two inches on either side of the rim, between the locknut faces and the edges of the rim. Two plus two plus one equals five inches. So you can see the rim is *not* centered between the hub flanges, because there are 1¾ inches between the left hub flange and the left rim edge, and only 1¼ inches between the right rim edge and the right hub flange. The rear wheel is "dished" to the right. To adjust the rim-centering gauge to your rear wheel, measure the distance between axle locknuts with the vernier calipers. You can buy a surprisingly accurate pair of these calipers for around $3.50 from one of the metric supply houses listed in the Appendix. I prefer the one from Ametric. They are inside, outside, and depth vernier calipers, in both inch and metric. Metric measurements are so much easier to use that I also urge you to convert your thinking to that system. Let's say the distance between locknut faces is 120.3 mm. (for inch comparison, see Step Five) (Fig. 309).

STEP FOUR: Measure the width of the rim with the vernier gauge. Let's say it's 19.4 mm. wide.

Fig. 308:
Step One

Fig. 309:
Step Two

STEP FIVE: Subtract the first measurement from the second and divide the answer by two. For example:

TABLE 27 · **Measuring Hub Width**

	MILLIMETERS	INCHES, FRACTION	INCHES, DECIMAL
Locknut to locknut width:	120.3	4¾	4.750
Hub width:	− 19.4	−⁴⁹⁄₆₄	− .76242
Subtracting:	100.9	3⁶³⁄₆₄	3.988
Dividing by two:	50.45	1¹²⁷⁄₁₂₈	1.994

As you can see, the metric system is much easier to work with and more accurate. Good bikes are almost all made to metric measurements. A reminder: the measurements above are hypothetical, and may or may not apply to your wheel and hub. You will have to measure the ones you are working with.

STEP SIX: Put a reasonably flat strip over the rim-centering gauge, and with the vernier depth gauge set to 50.45 mm. (or 1¹²⁷⁄₁₂₈ inch) adjust the rim-gauge centering screw to 50.45 mm. If you can't find a flat metal strip, set the gauge on a flat surface and look at the setting, as in Fig. 310.

STEP SEVEN: Put the rim gauge on *both* sides of the rim to check how far off you are on dishing the rim to the right. Remove the wheel from the truing stand for checking, and then put it back. The rim-gauge screw is hollow, so it fits over the axle and axle locknut and permits the rim-gauge set screw flat to rest on the axle locknut face (Fig. 311).

STEP EIGHT: Set the lateral movement indicator on the truing stand so it touches the worst bump on the left side of the rim. (Or, if you're using an old fork, anything that will stay still and indicate will do, such as a pipe cleaner wrapped around the fork blade.) When you find the worst left-side bump, stop there and find the spoke nipple just to the *right* of the bump. (Also at this point, study Fig. 307 to review rim-direction movement. Note that when spokes "B" or "D" are tightened, the rim moves to the right, and vice versa when spokes "A" or "C" are tightened.) Tighten this spoke nipple one turn to pull rim to the right. Then find the next worst bump and tighten the spoke nipple to the right of *that* bump one turn. Repeat this process once around the left side of the rim. Fine truing will come later.

Fig. 310: Step Six

Fig. 311: Step Seven

STEP NINE: Move the indicator so it touches the right side of the rim, and repeat Step Eight. Continue until you have removed all the right-side bumps.

STEP TEN: Check rim centering with the rim gauge, as in Step Seven. If the rim is too far to the left, tighten *all* the spoke nipples on the *right* side one-half turn; if the rim is too far to the right, tighten all the spoke nipples on the left side one-half turn (Fig. 312).

STEP ELEVEN: With wheel in truing stand, repeat Steps Eight and Nine, except this time turn the spoke nipples one-quarter turn as you continue to pull out major lateral untrueness once around; one-quarter turn the second time around; one eighth turn succeeding times around.

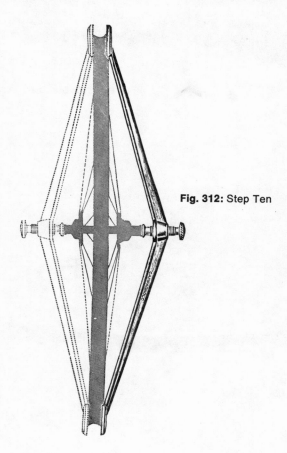

Fig. 312: Step Ten

STEP TWELVE: Now, with the wheel back in the truing stand, move the indicator so it touches the *outside circumference of the rim,* so we can remove out-of-roundness. Referring again to Fig. 307, notice that when spokes "A" *and* "B" are tightened, the rim moves toward the hub; this is also true when spokes "C" and "D" are tightened. In other words, in removing concentric untrueness, *both* spokes at the points of major concentric highs must be tightened to pull the rim down. Rotate the rim, watch the indicator till you find the highest out-of-round spot, and tighten both left and right spokes at that spot one-half turn the first time; one-quarter turn the second time around; one-eighth turn third and succeeding times around.

STEP THIRTEEN: Repeat Step Seven, except turn the nipples one-eighth turn.

STEP FOURTEEN: Remove the wheel from the truing stand, and put the axle end on a wooden bench, holding the rim with both hands on either side of rim. Press the rim sharply and hard down on the bench, to stress the rim, and seat in the spoke heads and nipples. You may hear popping sounds as spokes seat in. Rotate rim one-quarter turn, change grip, repeat rim press, and go around the rim twice.

STEP FIFTEEN: With the wheel in truing stand, touch up lateral and concentric untrueness, turning nipples one-eighth turn. If you can't move a nipple, loosen the spoke nipple on the *opposite* side. Example 1: if you find a small lateral bump on the left side, and the right-side nipple is too tight to move, *loosen* the left-side nipple at the bump one-eighth turn. Example 2: you have a concentric high bump and both nipples at the bump can't be tightened anymore. Instead, loosen both nipples at the point on the rim *opposite* the bump one-eighth turn (on the other side of the rim). On a rear wheel, as stated earlier, right-side spokes should all be slightly tighter than left-side spokes. Spokes on each side should show the same tension as other spokes on the same side. Don't try to pull a high or low spot out by tightening a nipple all at once; you'll have a highly stressed spoke that will very likely be short-lived, perhaps when you're careening downhill. Later, as you ride on your trued wheels, you may hear "twanging" sounds as the spokes seat in more. Or you'll likely hear that sound on a new bicycle, no matter what the price. Your rims will need touch-up truing for each 50 miles till you hit about 150 miles, after which rims should remain true, barring accident.

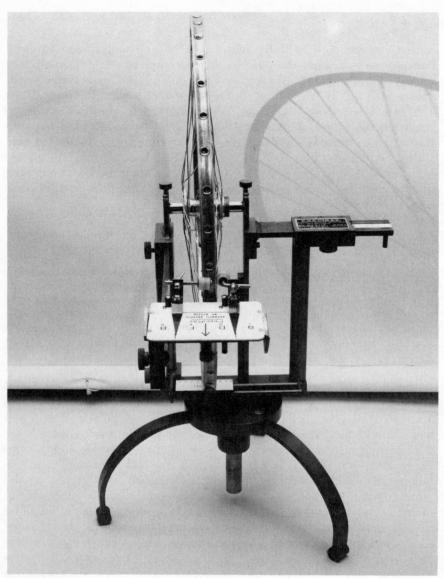

Fig. 313: A trend in cycle maintenance is for bicycle clubs to buy the more costly tools, such as bicycle stands, for club member use. I would also recommend purchase of the wheel-truing machine above, made by PreciRay of Belgium, available through Holdsworth (see Appendix). The PreciRay machine enables even an amateur to true a wheel accurately in about ten minutes, after a bit of practice. And the PreciRay could pay for itself in a bike shop by cutting wheel-truing time drastically. Racing team mechanics use this machine, as do bicycle manufacturers.

A WORD ABOUT LUBRICATION

Although there are very specific instructions about when to lubricate various parts of the bicycle elsewhere in this book, it might be helpful for you to review this general summary of lubrication instructions.

Front-Wheel Hubs

- If the hub has an oil fitting, squirt in about a half-teaspoonful every thirty days. Use SAE 30 oil.
- If the hub has a grease fitting, add one or two shots of a multipurpose grease such as Lubriplate Snowmobile grease, which is especially good for winter cycling, or Texaco Starfak No. 2.
- Twice a year, disassemble, clean, and relubricate with grease.

Coaster-Brake Rear-Wheel Hubs

- Grease all new bicycle hubs immediately upon purchasing, with two or three shots of Marfak No. 2 grease or, if an oil fitting, with two tablespoonfuls of No. 20 oil.
- Thereafter, lubricate as above every thirty days.

Multispeed Internal Gear Rear Hubs

- Add a tablespoonful of No. 20 good-quality motor oil to the hub immediately upon purchase (oil may have evaporated during shipment and storage), and thereafter every thirty days.

Chains

- Every couple of weeks, oftener if you're on tour or ride a lot, remove the chain, agitate it in kerosene, and relube with Chainlube (from a motorcycle store), then reinstall chain. Clean old grease and dirt from the freewheel and chainwheels before reinstalling chain.

Headset (Fork Bearings)

- Twice yearly, remove the headset locknut, adjusting cup and bearings, clean, and relubricate with Lubriplate Snowmobile or Texaco Starfak No. 2 grease.

Bottom Bracket (Chainwheel Axle)

- Pedals are attached to pedal cranks, which are fitted to the axle, which is supported in the bottom by bearings and ball caps. Once a year, remove bottom bracket bearings, following instructions on page 420; clean all parts and relubricate with Lubriplate Snowmobile or Texaco Starfak No. 2 grease. The first time you relube, roll up a piece of an aluminum beer can to fit snugly inside the inner diameter of the bottom bracket to seal out dirt dropping down the seat and the tubes. Pack the bottom bracket well. If you do this, you can relube the bottom bracket every two years instead of yearly. Note: Another excellent bike bearing grease is distributed by Phil Wood to bicycle stores. Phil makes sealed bearing hubs and has gone to some trouble to select a grease that is highly resistant to being washed out by water.

Cables

- Once a month, squirt a few drops of light oil, such as Lubriplate Spray-Lube "A," which comes in a handy "Spra-Tainer," on brake and gear change cables where they enter spaghetti tubing. Lubricate cable tubing before installing new cable.

On the Road

On bike trips, especially if you ride over dirt roads, check hub and bottom bracket bearings at the end of the day for dirt and sand pick-up. Spin wheels and remove chain and spin bottom bracket, listen and "feel" for gritty sounds. Clean and re-lube hubs on the spot if they get dirty; clean bottom bracket assembly if you have the tools, or do it at the next bike shop, if you hear a lot of grinding noise, or feel it as you spin cranks with chain dropped off. Spray Chainlube on chain every few days.

Derailleur Mechanisms

- Every thirty days or so, put a few drops of a light oil on the moving parts of derailleur gear shifters, front and rear, including idler wheels of rear derailleurs and gear-shift levers.

- Once every six months, dismantle rear derailleurs, clean and regrease idler wheels with light grease such as Lubriplate Snowmobile, and oil other working parts.

Freewheels

- Every thirty days put a few drops of light oil, no heavier than No. 5 motor oil, into the freewheel mechanism on derailleur-equipped bicycles. *Do not use heavier oil. Do not attempt to dismantle the freewheel.*
- Every six months (more often if you have been riding in dusty conditions), remove the freewheel, soak it in kerosene, and relubricate as above. (Review freewheel maintenance instructions on pages 369–370.)

Pedals

- On conventional pedals squirt a few drops of No. 30 oil in *each* end of the pedal every thirty days.
- On rattrap pedals, dismantle the pedals every six months (according to mileage), clean the parts, and repack with grease such as Lubriplate Snowmobile. See page 403 for instructions. This applies to rattrap pedals particularly. Do not oil rattrap pedals.

  Bear in mind that one key to long life for a bicycle is cleanliness. After every long ride and once a week in the cycling season, wipe off all dust, dirt, and road soil from the frame and wheels and around the caliper brakes and pedals.

THREE-SPEED AND COASTER-BRAKE HUBS

There are four makes and a wide variety of one-, two-, three-, and five-speed integral rear hubs in common use on bicycles in this country. There is even an adapter kit to convert multispeed integral rear hubs into a six- or nine-speed machine, using a derailleur. A Japanese manufacturer makes a twelve-speed combination rear hub and derailleur which, if used with a double front chainwheel, will give you twenty-four speeds, and with a triple front chainwheel, thirty-six speeds. I don't know what you'd do with more than twelve or fifteen speeds, but if you want them, they're available. More on these combinations later in this chapter.

I am not going to attempt to give you detailed take-apart and assembly instructions for all these hubs; there are simply too many makes and

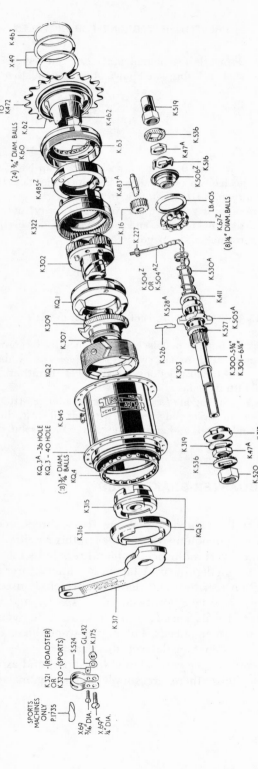

Fig. 314: Sturmey-Archer three-speed hub and coaster-brake combination. This drawing is shown here to convince you not to take any three-speed hub apart. Let your bicycle dealer fix these. Of course, if anything mechanical poses a challenge to you, go right ahead and take it apart, but save the pieces.

LEGEND

Part No.	Description
GL432	Shakeproof Washer
K16	Planet Pinion
K47A	Cone Locknut
K60	Right-Hand Ball-Ring
K62	Sprocket Dust Cap
K67Z	Ball Retainer—(8) 1/4" Ball
K175	Nut for X69A Bolt
K227	Locknut
K300	Axle 5¾"
K301	Axle 6¼"
K302	Planet Cage
K303	Axle Circlip
K307	Brake Actuating Spring
K309	Thrust Washer
K315	Left-Hand Cone
K316	(Chromium) Dust Cap for Left-Hand Cone
K317	Brake Arm
K318	Brake Arm Locknut
K319	Lock Washer
K320	Clip for Brake Arm (Sports)
K321	Clip for Brake Arm (Roadster)
K322	Gear Ring
K411	Thrust Washer
K462	Driver
K463	Driver Circlip
K466	Sprocket 16 Teeth
K472	Sprocket 22 Teeth
K483A	Planet Pinion Pin
K485Z	Gear Ring Pawl-Ring
K504Z	Gear Indicator Rod and Coupling. For 5¾" Axle.
K504AZ	Gear Indicator Rod and Coupling. For 6¼" Axle.
K505A	Clutch
K506Z	Cone
K516	Right-Hand Cone Locking-Washer
K519	Right-Hand Axle Nut
K520	Left-Hand Axle Nut
K526	Key
K527	Clutch Sleeve
K528A	Thrust Ring
K530A	Clutch Spring
K536	Serrated Axle Washer
K645	Lubricator
KQ1	Planet Cage Pawl Ring
KQ2	Brake Band
KQ3	40 Hole Shell and Left-Hand Ball Cup Assembly
KQ3A	36 Hole Shell and Left-Hand Ball Cup Assembly
KQ4	Ball Retainer—(18) 3/16" Ball
KQ5	Brake Arm/Left-Hand Cone/and Dust Cap Assembly
LB405	Dustcap
S524	Nut for X 69 Bolt
P1735	Strengthening Pad—For Sports Machines only
X49	Sprocket spacing Washer (1/16")
X69	Clip Screw, 3/16" Diameter
X69A	Clip Screw, 1/4" Diameter

models to make this practical. Hubs are a rather complicated assemblage of gears and mechanisms. (If Fig. 314, page 462 doesn't scare you off, nothing will!) Many require special tools to assemble or disassemble, and the majority of bicycle dealers are competent to deal with most of them.

This section, therefore, will be limited to routine hub maintenance, adjustment, and tips on correct usage. If you follow these instructions, your hub should last the life of the bicycle and seldom, if ever, need to be taken apart. However, if you really want to disassemble your rear hub, either out of curiosity or because you can't find a bicycle mechanic who knows how to fix it, you can obtain step-by-step illustrated assembly and disassembly instructions, complete with a list of spare parts, from the hub manufacturer or the bicycle manufacturers.

Bendix Rear Hubs

Bendix coaster-brake and multispeed hubs are used on Schwinn and some other makes of American bicycles, so we'll start with these hubs.

Bendix Automatic Coaster Brakes

The Bendix automatic coaster brake is a two-speed unit which contains both coaster brakes and a set of internal gears. This type of hub permits the cyclist to change gears by back-pedaling slightly, or to brake by back-pedaling, both without removing hands from the handlebars. It is well suited for a young rider, up to age twelve. There is a 32 percent decrease in gear ratio between high and low gears on this hub—enough to enable a young rider to negotiate moderate hills fairly easily.

There are two types of Bendix coaster-brake two-speed hubs. The standard model is marked with three yellow bands around the hub shell. The other, which is marked with three blue bands around the hub shell, is the overdrive automatic unit. This has a direct drive and a high gear with a 47 percent gear ratio increase, which makes cycling a bit easier on hills. It is used on Schwinn Sting-Ray bicycles, among others.

Lubrication

Because all the working parts are inside the hub, these hubs don't require much maintenance, beyond regular lubrication about every month, and after long trips. Use a fairly light oil, equivalent to No. 20 SAE viscosity motor oil. Squirt about a teaspoonful into the hub through the hub hole provided for this purpose.

Also, once a year you should take the bicycle into the dealer and have him disassemble and regrease the hub and check for any worn or broken parts.

Since coaster brakes (*unlike* caliper brakes) need grease for proper operation and for long life, if you've made extensive tours in hilly country involving a lot of braking, it's a good idea to have your dealer disassemble the hub and regrease it when the tour is over, rather than wait until the year is up.

If the hub does not shift properly, makes grinding noises, shifts into low without back-pressure, or if the brakes fail, this means that new internal parts may be necessary. These can be installed by your bicycle dealer.

No routine operating adjustments are required on any Bendix hubs, making them even better for children and more child-proof than other hubs, which have wires attached to them.

All you need to remember, if you remove the rear wheel, is to refasten the coaster-brake clamp arm which clamps onto the rear fork stay.

Sturmey-Archer Multispeed Rear Hubs

Sturmey-Archer multispeed rear hubs are perhaps the most widely used of all hubs. They are used on Raleigh bicycles and other brand-new bicycles made by Raleigh such as Robin Hood, Hercules, and private label brands.

There are three- (Fig. 314), four-, five-speed and combination coaster-brake and three-speed Sturmey-Archer rear wheel hubs in use today. All of them have a number of things in common, one of which is that proper gear shifting is greatly dependent upon proper adjustment of working parts.

Lubrication is also very important. In fact, oil can evaporate from a hub between the time the bicycle leaves the factory and when you buy it, so be sure to have the dealer add a tablespoonful of *light* oil to the hub before you ride off.

When changing gears with any Sturmey-Archer hub, ease pedal pressure slightly, and change gears quickly.

Sturmey-Archer Trouble-Shooting

PROBLEM: Gears slip; they won't stay in the gear selected.

SOLUTION: Adjust the indicator rod. Check your hub so you know which type you have, and follow the instruction on the indicator rod adjustment for your particular hub.

TCW, AW, AB, AG, and SW Hub Indicator Rod Adjustment

STEP ONE: Put the gear-shift lever in No. 2 position (or S5 five-speed hubs in third gear) (Fig. 315).

STEP TWO: Unscrew the locknut (A, Fig. 315)

STEP THREE: Adjust the knurled section of the cable (B, Fig. 315) until the end of the indicator rod is exactly level with the end of the axle (B, Fig. 316). Check the location of the indicator rod through the "window" in the *righthand* nut on the axle (B, Fig. 315).

STEP FOUR: Tighten the locknut.

STEP FIVE: If you can't obtain enough adjustment with the cable connection at the hub, unscrew the nut and bolt holding the cable on the top tube (X 90, Fig. 317) and move the cable forward or rearward, as required. This step is known as "changing the fulcrum point" of the cable.

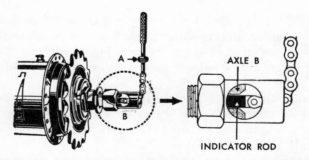

Fig. 315: Cable adjustments for SW-TCW hubs, including locknut (A), and knurled section of cable (B). Indicator rod should be where shown for proper hub operation. Courtesy of Raleigh Industries, Limited

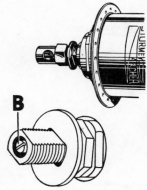

Fig. 316: Rod (B) on a Sturmey-Archer hub should line up with end of axle for proper cable adjustment of Sturmey-Archer hubs.

AM, ASC, and AC Sturmey-Archer Hub Indicator Rod Adjustment

The only difference between indicator rod adjustment for these hubs and other Sturmey-Archer hubs lies in the location of the indicator rod adjustment indicator. On AM, ASC, and AC hubs, the indicator rod is in the correct position when the end of the rod is level with the end of the axle on the *lefthand* side of the hub. This is the side opposite the chain, or left side as you face the front of the bicycle.

Adjustment of the indicator rod should be made as shown above.

If gears still slip or change noisily after the indicator rod has been adjusted, wear on the internal parts in the hub is indicated. Take the bicycle to your dealer for repairs, or, if you wish to make them yourself, write to the bicycle manufacturer or see your dealer for assembly and disassembly instructions and the special tools that are needed.

Cable Change on Sturmey-Archer "Sportshift"

Sturmey-Archer also makes a gear-shift mechanism for their three-speed hubs, which is mounted on the top tube. Follow these steps to change cables:

STEP ONE: Loosen the locknut on the hub cable at the hub, and unscrew the knurled ferrule until the cable is free at the hub end.

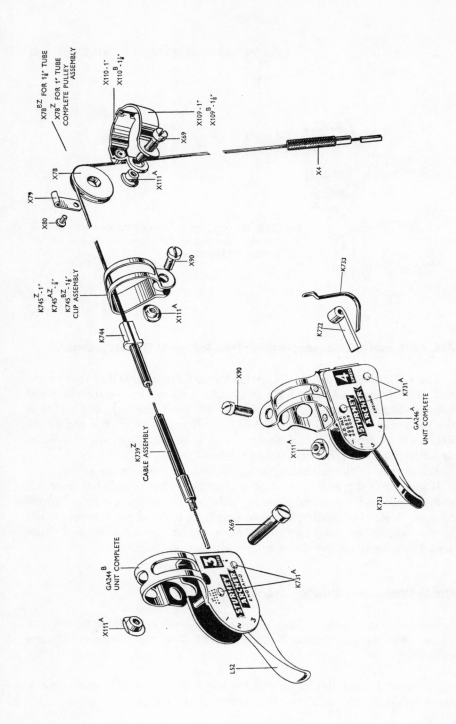

X78 BZ FOR 1⅜" TUBE
X78 Z FOR 1" TUBE
COMPLETE PULLEY
ASSEMBLY

X110 - 1"
X110 B - 1⅛"

X109 - 1"
X109 B - 1⅛"

X69

X78

X111 A

X79

X30

X4

X90

K745 Z - 1"
K745 AZ - ⅞"
K745 BZ - 1⅛"
CLIP ASSEMBLY

X111 A

K744

K733

K722

K739 Z
CABLE ASSEMBLY

X90

X111 A

X111 A

K731 A

GA246 A
UNIT COMPLETE

K723

X69

GA244 B
UNIT COMPLETE

K731 A

X111 A

L52

Fig. 317: Trigger control gear-shift lever for three- and four-speed Sturmey-Archer hubs. If you cannot get enough adjustment with the cable locknuts at the hub, loosen nut X90 and slide clip assembly further forward about a half-inch, and retighten.

Code No.	Description	3-SPEED UNIT	4-SPEED UNIT	Description
K739Z	Trigger Cable assembly—Give length of both inner and outer cable	GC3B	GC4A	Trigger Control complete less pulley
K744	Fulcrum Sleeve	GA244B	GA246A	Trigger Unit
K745Z	Fulcrum clip complete 1" diameter	L52	K723	Trigger Lever
K745AZ	Fulcrum clip complete 7/8" diameter	K731A	K731A	Pivot Pin
K745BZ	Fulcrum clip complete 1⅛" diameter	L55	K722	Trigger Pawl
X90	Clip Screw	L56	K738	Trigger Spring
X78Z	Pulley complete for 1" tube	X69	X69	Clip Screw
X78BZ	Pulley complete for 1⅛" tube	X111A	X111A	Clip Screw, 1/4" Diameter
X69	Clip Screw			
X78	Pulley Wheel only			
X79	Pulley Arm			
X80	Pulley Arm Screw			
X110BZ	Clip with Pulley Stud (1⅛" tube)			
X109B	Half-clip (1⅛" tube)			

STEP TWO: Remove the center screw from the control unit (gear-shift unit) and remove the cover from the plastic cover plate.

STEP THREE: Push the control lever to the No. 3 position, and remove the old cable. Pull the old cable through the slot of the cable anchorage and over the pulley wheel to remove the entire cable.

STEP FOUR: Readjust the cable by moving the lever to the No. 2 position and adjusting the cable ferrule at the hub end until the indicator rod is in the correct location for the type of Sturmey-Archer hub involved. (TCW, AW, AG, AB, and SW hubs have a different adjustment from AM, ASC, the AC Sturmey-Archer hubs. See page 471 for details.)

Here are common symptoms of Sturmey-Archer hub problems, their causes and their solutions. If hub needs disassembly, I recommend you let your bicycle shop do it.

PROBLEM: Sluggish gear change.
CAUSE: Cable binding or worn toggle link chain.
SOLUTION: Lubricate or replace cables. Lubricate gear-shift unit.

PROBLEM: No gear at all; pedals turn, wheel doesn't.
CAUSE: Internal pawls stuck or held in place by too heavy oil.
SOLUTION: Add light oil. If this does not free up, dismantle hub. Clean parts. Reassemble and oil again.

CAUSE: Bent axle.
SOLUTION: Dismantle hub. Replace axle.

CAUSE: Distorted axle spring.
SOLUTION: Replace spring (requires hub disassembly).

PROBLEM: Hub runs stiffly, drags on pedals when free-wheeling, wheel seems to "bind."
CAUSE: Chain stay ends not parallel. When the axle nuts are tightened, this causes the axle to be "sprung" out of true, which, in turn, makes the internal hub parts "bind."
SOLUTION: Straighten the chain stay ends, or add packing washers on the left-hand side to align. You may also need a new axle.

CAUSE: Corrosion of hub working parts due to nonlubrication.
SOLUTION: Disassemble the hub. Check and replace worn parts. Relubricate. Follow lubrication instructions above.

PROBLEM: Slips in any gear.
CAUSE: On S5 hubs, this could be a kinked gear cable. On other hubs, internal parts are worn or incorrectly installed.
SOLUTION: Replace cable or reassemble hub with new parts as needed.

PROBLEM: On TCW (coaster-brake and three-speed) hub combinations *only,* brakes are noisy or "shudder" when applied.
CAUSE: Loose brake arm clip.
SOLUTION: Tighten clip nuts and bolts.

PROBLEM: On TCW hubs only, internal brakes in hub "grab" on application.
CAUSE: Lack of oil in rear hub.
SOLUTION: Add good quality *thin* oil, SAE 20 or thinner.

General Instructions

Sometimes even when you take the steps to correct any of the problems listed above, you will still not have corrected them. If this happens to you, there is probably wear in the internal parts of the hub. I do not recommend that the average bicycle owner attempt to replace any of the interior parts of these hubs. But, if you want to anyway, trouble-shooting charts and hub assembly data can be obtained from the manufacturers.

In any case, do not attempt to adjust the rear wheel cones on multi-speed hubs. If the wheel binds, or shows side-play, and you think that cone adjustment is the answer, let your dealer do it. Some hubs have factory-adjusted cones, and you can ruin the hub if you try to adjust them yourself, without following a detailed instruction manual.

Sturmey-Archer Trigger (Gear-Shift) Control Maintenance

There isn't much that can go wrong with a gear shift (Fig. 318) unless you bend it accidentally. If you do, it should be replaced.

Cables do fray, wear, and break, however, and you should know how to replace the gear-shift cable (or cables, on an S5 five-speed hub).

Trigger Control Cable Replacement, Three- and Four-Speed Hubs

STEP ONE: (Note: You do not have to remove the control mechanism from the handlebars if you can pull the lever back far enough to permit the cable nipple to pass between the pawl and ratchet plate.) Remove the inner wire from the indicator chain at the hub.

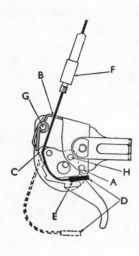

Fig. 318: Typical Sturmey-Archer gear shift. To remove control wire, it is not necessary to remove control from handlebar if the lever can be pulled back far enough to allow cable nipple to pass between pawl and ratchet plate. Procedure is (1) detach inner wire from indicator chain at hub, and (2) outer casing from fulcrum clip. Pull cable ferrule (F) upward until screw engages that of control casing at (B), then unscrew ferrule. Pull lever right back beyond bottom gear position to stop (A), push inner wire through to detach nipple from ratchet plate, then pull wire out between pawl and ratchet at (C) and finally through threaded hole (B).

To fit control wire, pull lever right back beyond bottom gear position to stop (A) and insert wire through threaded hole (B) and between pawl and ratchet plate at (C). Wire nipple (D) is then fitted into notch (E) and cable ferrule (F) screwed into (B) until it rotates freely. Keeping tension on wire, push lever forward into top gear position. Control is then ready for reconnection.

STEP TWO: Remove the outer wire casing (the spaghetti tube) from the fulcrum clip on the top tube (or, if it is a woman's model, from the top of the two down tubes).

STEP THREE: Pull the cable ferrule upward (so that the metal sleeve is entering the gear shift) until the ferrule screw (which you can't see because it's in the control casing) engages the control casing. Then, unscrew the ferrule.

STEP FOUR: Pull the control lever back beyond the bottom gear position as far as it can go. Push the cable (inner wire) through so you can remove the cable nipple (leaded end) from the ratchet plate, then pull the wire out between the pawl and ratchet and through the threaded hole.

STEP FIVE: To replace an old cable with a new one, reverse Steps One through Four, above.

Fitting Gear-Shift Cable to Frame (Sturmey-Archer)

When you install a new cable and its spaghetti cover on the bicycle frame, be sure to have the cable and cover long enough so you can turn the handlebars through their full movement in both directions. However, do not overdo it. Make it just long enough for adequate handlebar movement.

Standard control wire length for most bicycles with Sturmey-Archer multispeed hubs and handlebar controls is 54½ inches with a spaghetti cover length of 17½ inches. For controls mounted on the top tube, standard lengths are thirty-two, thirty-four, and thirty-six inches.

For Sturmey-Archer Five-Speed Hubs

When installing new cables on Sturmey-Archer five-speed rear hubs (Fig. 319), follow this procedure:

STEP ONE: For the righthand gear-shift lever, follow the same procedure as for standard handlebar flick control. Screw down the locknut (Fig. 319).

STEP TWO: For the lefthand lever, push the lefthand lever to the forward position, and screw the cable connector to the bellcrank (the metal connecting piece between the cable and axle, held onto the axle by a nut). Screw the cable connector (1) to the bellcrank just two or three turns, no more.

STEP THREE: Push the lefthand lever to the backward position, and screw the cable connector until all cable slackness is eliminated.

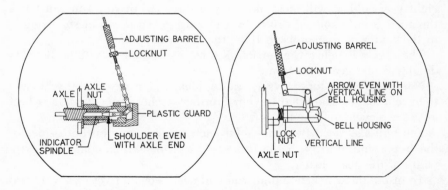

Fig. 319: Right- and left-hand gear-shift cables for Sturmey-Archer five-speed hubs.

STEP FOUR: With light pressure, push the bellcrank arm forward and, at the same time, turn the wheel backward or forward. If the gears are not fully engaged, the bellcrank arm will move farther forward.

STEP FIVE: Screw the cable connector as far as possible, and secure with the locknut.

How to Convert Sturmey-Archer SW or AW Hubs to Nine-Speed

If you're going on a tour, particularly if you are going to carry a load of gear and will have to climb hills, you can buy either a lightweight, ten-speed, derailleur-equipped bicycle with a wide range of gear ratios (see page 179 for discussion of gear ratios) or install a conversion kit on your Sturmey-Archer rear hub to give you a wider range of gears in both directions.

To convert your Sturmey-Archer rear hub to a nine-speed gear, you can install a Cyclo-Benelux Conversion Kit, which costs about $12.00. You will also need a three-gear sprocket, costing $3.75.

Since the Cyclo-Benelux Conversion Kit comes with complete installation instructions, which are fairly easy to follow, I will not repeat them here. A word of warning, though. Be sure to order the correct conversion kit for your hub. You can order a kit from any of the bicycle mail-order shops listed on page 497. But you must specify whether your hub is an AW or SW model, and tell the bicycle shop whether you have a threaded or a splined driver. If your Sturmey-Archer three-speed hub is more than eight years old, it will most likely use a threaded driver. You can tell a threaded from a splined driver by checking to see if a split snap ring is in the center of the sprocket. If so, the driver is splined.

The Cyclo-Benelux Conversion Kit comes complete with a Benelux derailleur and gear-shift lever.

Note: Some rear fork stays are quite thick, which means you will have to have a longer axle fitted to your Sturmey-Archer hub. This job is best left to a bicycle mechanic.

You will also need two one-eighth-inch washers, one on both sides of the hub spindle, to push the fork stays out to accommodate the extra width of the gear cluster.

To install the conversion unit, you will need a chain rivet removing and installing tool (which costs about $1.75 and can be bought at any bicycle store or from any bicycle mail-order house), and an additional four to six extra links for your chain. Make sure you buy links that are the same make as your chain.

To determine how many extra links to add to your chain, see the discussion on chain length on page 372.

General Instructions on Maintenance, Adjustment, and Alignment of Hubs

Sturmey-Archer Hubs

For efficient cycling with minimum effort, as well as for proper operation of the rear hub, it is important that the rear sprocket of any rear hub, whether coaster brake or multispeed, line up with the front chainwheel.

For more information on alignment, see the discussion on page 412 in the section on derailleurs.

To align Sturmey-Archer rear hubs, all you need do is change the rear sprocket a little, which is easy. You have an alignment adjustment of between 1½ inches and 1¾ inches in ⅟₁₆-inch increments. To change alignments simply follow these steps:

STEP ONE: Pry off the locknut (circlip) with a small screwdriver. (This is the round springlike clip that fits into a groove around the sprocket side of the hub—outboard of the sprocket.) Snap this ring out.

STEP TWO: Slide the sprocket off the hub, along with the washers on either side of the sprocket. To change alignment, you have a number of choices:

1. Face the concave side of the sprocket toward the outside of the hub. Put all the washers on one side or the other, or one washer on each side.
2. Put concave side toward the hub, washers as above. This gives you a total of six adjustments.

Incidentally, if you wish to change the gear ratio, up or down, on any Sturmey-Archer hub, simply ask your bicycle dealer to send to Raleigh of America in Boston for the sprocket with the number of teeth you desire. A larger sprocket with more teeth will give you a larger ratio (less speed in all gears but more hill-climbing ability), while a smaller sprocket will give you more speed, but hills will be more difficult to negotiate (all other factors, such as your physical condition, being equal, that is).

Shimano Multispeed Hubs

A number of American bicycle manufacturers use Japanese-made Shimano multispeed rear hubs. The Shimano hub, in my opinion, is every bit as good as any American or European multispeed hub and is a good deal easier to repair. If you plan to remove this hub, and disassemble and reassemble it, you will, however, need two special tools—a split snap ring remover and a ballcup remover—which you will have to order through your bicycle store.

The Shimano 3.3.3. three-speed hub is the most widely used of the Shimano units. Shimano publishes well-illustrated, easily understood, step-by-step disassembly, repair, and reassembly instructions. Repair parts are available in this country. However, since many of the bicycles sold in discount houses and department stores (American and foreign-made) use Shimano hubs, you may find that bicycle dealers are unwilling or unable to service them. This is why a knowledge of how to maintain them well is essential. Lubrication is very important. Use a light oil, adding about a teaspoonful every thirty days and after each long ride.

There are two types of Shimano gear-shift levers for this hub, both positive "click-stop" types. The first is a handlebar "twistgrip" similar to a motorcycle speed control, and the second is a lever, usually mounted on the top tube.

To remove a frayed wire from the handlebar twistgrip:

STEP ONE: Loosen the locknut on the handlebar twistgrip and remove the ferrule and wire.

STEP TWO: Remove the cable cover from the fulcrum stopper on the top tube.

STEP THREE: Unscrew the locknut on the bellcrank on the rear wheel and unscrew the knurled cable nut from the bellcrank lever. At this point, the cable and cable cover should be removable from the bicycle. Install the new cable and cover, reversing Steps One, Two, and Three.

STEP FOUR: The adjustment for both the twistgrip and the lever-type control should start with the shift in the "N" position. At this position, the red "N" on the bellcrank should be centered in the "window" of the bellcrank or, on older models of this hub, the arrow indicator should be centered over the indicating line on the bellcrank.

STEP FIVE: If the centering in Step Four cannot be made, move the fulcrum stop on the top tube forward or backward, as necessary, to make more or less cable slack as needed; then readjust at the bellcrank end by loosening the cable locknut and screwing the cable ferrule in or out as required. This step applies for both twistgrip and lever-type controls.

Note: Wire cables on any bicycle will stretch in time, so you will find it necessary to readjust the shift cable from time to time, as per Step Five.

PROBLEM: In the "H" shift position, the pedal skips or won't turn.
CAUSE: Pawl is worn or installed backward.
SOLUTION: Disassemble the hub and install new pawl and pawl spring (a job for the bicycle mechanic).

PROBLEM: Pedal skips at "N" position.
CAUSE: Planet cage pawl worn or broken, or pawl spring broken.
SOLUTION: Disassemble hub and replace defective parts (a job for the bicycle mechanic).

PROBLEM: Gears are stuck or do not change smoothly.
CAUSE: Broken parts are caught up in hub mechanism.
SOLUTION: Complete hub overhaul (a job for the bicycle mechanic).

PROBLEM: Hub is noisy.
CAUSE: Rusty mechanism due to lack of oil.
SOLUTION: If rust has proceeded far enough, a new hub may have to be installed. Try oiling the hub first. If this doesn't work, disassemble the hub and look for rusted parts. Install new parts as needed (a job for the bicycle mechanic).

PROBLEM: Erratic shifting.
CAUSE: Control cable not set correctly.
SOLUTION: Adjust as described under Steps Four and Five above.

The Shimano click-stop shift lever is used on a number of 20- and 24-inch-wheel bicycles, as well as on 26-inch-wheel machines. It is described as a "Three on the Bar" shift by American advertising writers. To change the cables on the "stick" shift, follow these steps.

STEP ONE: Pry out the plastic dust cover on the round section at the bottom of the lever, which will reveal a screw in the center of the space.

STEP TWO: Remove the lever hub screw. The factory has this screw down rather tight, so use a good screwdriver and apply some elbow grease. Be careful not to lose the spacing washers under the nut, and to replace them in the same order.

STEP THREE: With the lever screw removed, the lever handle and wire will come off the lever slip in one piece. Remove the metal dust cover. Remove the cable nipple (leaded end) from its seat in the lever handle, and remove the cable and cable cover, replacing them with the new cable and cover by reversing the above steps.

The Shimano Combi-12 uses a combination four-speed derailleur and three-speed rear hub, for a total of twelve gear changes (twenty-four gear changes if a double chainwheel is used, thirty-six if a triple chainwheel is used).

Full instructions on the care, adjustment, and alignment of derailleurs are given on page 353. Since the three-speed section of the Combi-12 is identical to the standard Shimano 3.3.3. three-speed hub, maintenance and adjustment instructions already given in this section for this hub apply to the Combi-12 hub unit. Cable-changing procedures for both lever gear shifts have already been described.

There is, however, a difference between the derailleur lever on the Combi-12 and the conventional derailleur gear-shift levers. Standard levers have no click stops. The rider must adjust the lever position so that the derailleur is not pushing the chain part way off a cog and causing a grinding noise from the rear wheel while under way. The Shimano lever has click stops, so fine adjustment of the lever cannot be made to prevent the chain from running part way off a cog and causing a grinding noise.

Most youngsters today seem to be able to cheerfully ignore all sorts of mechanical noises which would annoy experienced adult cyclists. The only time young folks complain about their bicycles is when the wheels stop turning, which is too late. Therefore, the Shimano click-stop lever shift is a real boon for the adult who has to fix his child's bicycle. Once the cable adjustments are properly made so the click stops and you move the derailleur to the correct position for each hub external gear, you don't have to make any further adjustment of the lever. All you have to do is watch out for later stretching of the cable. When it stretches—and it will —you'll need to readjust the cable position as follows:

STEP ONE: A stretched wire will cause an inaccurate setting of the click stop on the three-speed hub. Put the gear-shift lever in *top* position. If speed change cannot then be made to the *second* position, readjust by loosening the wire adjusting nut at the bellcrank and loosen or tighten the knurled ferrule on the cable as necessary. Then retighten the locknut.

STEP TWO: Make sure the indicator on the bellcrank is pointing directly to the red indicator line, with the three-speed lever in the "N" position.

To adjust the derailleur wire:

STEP ONE: Put lever in *top* position. If the cable is not tight (taut), cable tension is correct.

STEP TWO: Now move the pedals (the bicycle should be upside down or hung from the ceiling) and change the gears through the four gear changes. Make sure the derailleur moves the chain from highest to lowest gear and back, smoothly.

STEP THREE: If the lever cannot be put into the *second* position easily, tighten the wire by loosening the locknut at the clamp on the seat stay and adjusting the knurled ferrule as necessary. Retighten the locknut.

STEP FOUR: Check adjustment by moving the lever to *top* position, as you turn the pedals. If the lever won't go into *top* position easily, loosen the wire slightly. Now, move the lever through all the gear ranges and adjust the cable as needed, if there is any noise in any of the gear-click stops.

Torpedo Duomatic Hubs

Some American and imported bicycles are fitted with a West German-made two-speed hub with a foot-operated gear change and back-pedaling brake. This hub, which is called a Torpedo Duomatic, is similar in design to the Bendix automatic two-speed hub with coaster brake, and requires the same type of maintenance. Just follow the same instructions as for the Bendix unit (see page 464).

I do not recommend your trying to dismantle this hub, unless you make sure you have complete step-by-step illustrated instructions, which can be obtained through your bicycle dealer.

Torpedo also makes a two-speed hub without the coaster brake, for use with caliper-brake-equipped bicycles. Maintenance instructions for this hub are the same as for the Bendix automatic hub; just feed it some light oil once a month after long trips, and if any strange sounds come from it, rush the bicycle to the nearest bicycle shop. If your mechanic can't (or won't) fix the hub, write to the Torpedo distributor or the bicycle manufacturer for the name of the closest *bicycle store* (not discount or department store) that can do this work.

As on most of the multispeed rear hubs used on bicycles in this country, the sprocket on the Torpedo hub can be easily changed to one with more teeth for touring in hilly country, or to one with fewer teeth for faster riding where the going is flat and easy. If you do change sprockets, remember that you must order the same make of sprocket as your hub, because sprockets are not interchangeable from one make of hub to the other.

Apropos of changing parts, parts from different makes of bicycles and bicycle components are more likely *not* to be interchangeable, except for mundane things such as tires, seats, and spokes. Be careful about ordering everything else!

A Word of Warning

Before you take your multispeed rear hub to a bicycle shop, phone the shop to make sure it has the parts on hand or can assure you it is willing to go to the trouble to order them for you from its wholesaler. The problem is that hardly any bicycle shop can afford to carry the tremendous number of parts it would take to be able to service all American, English, and Japanese hubs that are popularly used in this country.

A related problem is that not all wholesalers carry all parts, and if the bike shop proprietor can't find what he needs from his own wholesaler, the chances are very good that he'll tell you they aren't available. If this happens to you, keep calling dealers until you find one who says he can and does repair the type and make of hub you have.

If you have a three-speed or coaster-brake hub, do not take the hub apart; you will find a mess of gears and sundry other parts all over the place, and it isn't worth the trouble. The only maintenance needed by Sturmey-Archer, Bendix, and other multispeed and coaster-brake hubs is a monthly oiling with a medium-weight (20 SAE) oil.

English and some American bicycles (Figs. 115, 116) have oil fittings on the hub so that you can squirt oil into the wheel bearings from time to time. The better European hubs do not have such fittings, because they are precision machined and designed to be taken apart from time to time for cleaning and greasing.

All hubs, oilable or not, should be torn down, cleaned, and regreased approximately twice a year, and those with oil fittings should be oiled once a month, depending on how frequently the bike is used. Oil isn't as successful a lubricant as thin grease, because oil is easily washed off bearings by water (as when you ride in the rain). Also, oil is too thin to stand up under long, hard, dusty rides.

Fig. 320: New Tokheim five-speed gear shift unit "Gear-maker." Unit shifts so that gears move, chain stays in place. Gear ratios, with a 44 or 50 width chainwheel, are about the same as a 10-speed medium to wide range gearing.

Fig. 321: Tokheim "Gear-maker" five-speed twist grip shift lever mounts on handlebar end. Shifting is positive click-stop mechanism; chain always lands exactly on gear shifted to so shifting is fool-proof, especially for younger cyclists.

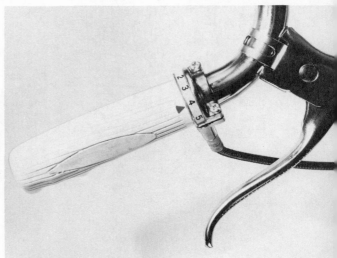

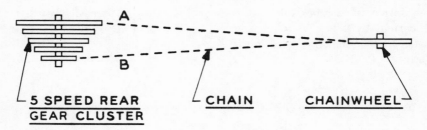

5 SPEED REAR GEAR CLUSTER — **CHAIN** — **CHAINWHEEL**

Fig. 322: Here's what happens to chainline in conventional derailleur system. As you shift rear derailleur to big or small gears, chain assumes increasingly greater angle, with greater wear and tear on chain and gears.

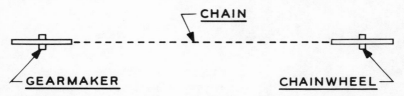

CHAIN

GEARMAKER — **CHAINWHEEL**

Fig. 323: Tokheim unit chainline does not change when gears are shifted. Instead, gears move in and out and chainline remains accurately aligned with chainwheel and rear gears for minimum chain and gear wear.

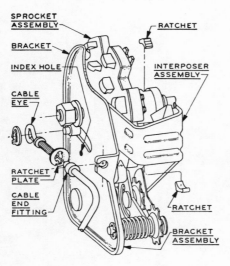

SPROCKET ASSEMBLY
BRACKET
INDEX HOLE
CABLE EYE
RATCHET PLATE
CABLE END FITTING
RATCHET
INTERPOSER ASSEMBLY
RATCHET
BRACKET ASSEMBLY

Fig. 324: To adjust Tokheim unit, shift to fifth gear, and, by adjusting cable, line up index holes as shown above.

New Tokheim Gear-Maker Transmission

About the time I was finishing up the revision of this book, Tokheim Corporation, Fort Wayne, Indiana, announced a new type of transmission gear-shifting device. This unit, the "Gear-maker" (Fig. 319), is designed to replace internal three- and five-speed rear hubs and five-speed derailleur systems on utility-type bicycles. For such application, the Gear-maker has a number of advantages. For example, children will often have trouble shifting a conventional derailleur accurately. The Gear-maker unit will shift positively into any gear selected, via a click-stop handlebar twist grip shift unit (Fig. 320) so the rider can't have the chain between gears where it grinds and wears both out faster. Under power shift, as going uphill, the unit also shifts under conditions that would cause conventional derailleurs to strangle on their own gears. And to shift down for fast getaway at a stoplight, you just pedal backward while shifting to desired gear.

Since the *gears* move but the chain stays in the same place, the chain is alway aligned with the chainwheel, reducing chain and gear wear, as illustrated in Figs. 321 and 322. An added safety feature is the fact that chain can't hang up in gears, or between spokes and gear or stays and gear to cause an accident, as with improperly adjusted or used derailleur systems. So for certain types of riding such as the juvenile trade or utility cycling, the Gear-maker does offer an improvement over internal hubs, which are so difficult to keep in adjustment.

Maintenance of the Gear-maker is simple. Gear cables will stretch and this unit is no exception. To compensate or take up cable stretch, all you do is shift the unit to fifth gear, adjust cable until an index hole in the bracket plate (Fig. 323) is lined up with an index hole in an "interposer" and retighten cable locknut. It's as simple as that. The Gear-maker requires only occasional cleaning and lubrication. The unit, incidentally, uses a ⅛-inch chain, thicker than the conventional ³⁄₃₂-inch chain used on derailleurs, so it will be a bit stronger than derailleur chains. You can't remove the rear wheel without "breaking" the chain by removing the master link with a screwdriver (pry it off) but this is no particular problem since you can or should be able to repair most rear tire flats by removing the tire from one side of the rim, pulling out the tube at the puncture, repairing it and shoving everything back together. The Gear-maker, at this writing, can't be installed on conventional bikes because it takes a wider spacing between stays, which must be built in at the factory (never force stays apart to fit a wheel; if you have to, something is wrong). It also takes its own hub, which is laced and maintained like any other derailleur-type hub, including dishing. Also at this writing, a number of bike manufacturers, in this country and abroad, are going to be equipping models with the Tokheim Gear-maker, so you should know how to do the simple maintenance required if your bike, or your child's, has one on it.

Appendices

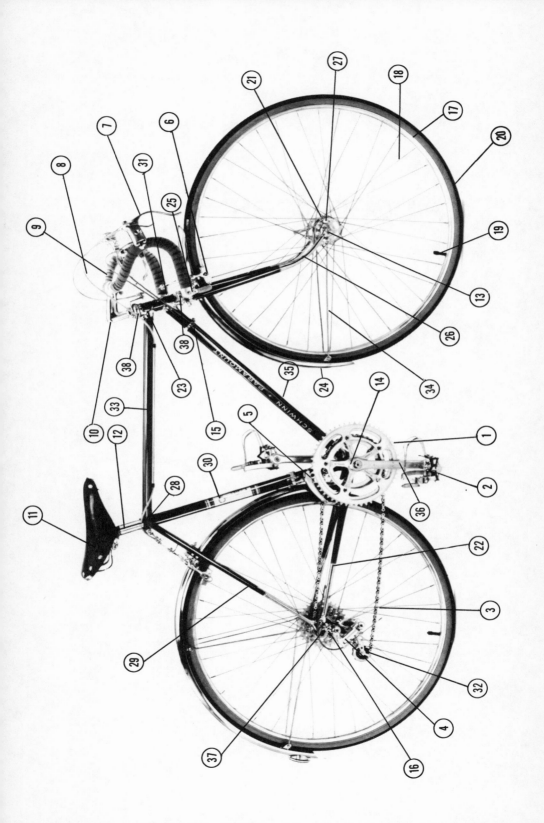

Fig. 325: KEY TO BICYCLE PARTS

1. Chainwheel
2. Pedal
3. Chain
4. Rear derailleur
5. Front derailleur
6. Caliper brake
7. Brake lever
8. Brake cable
9. Handlebars
10. Handlebar stem
11. Seat (saddle)
12. Seat post
13. Quick-release skewer (for instant wheel removal)
14. Bottom bracket
15. Gear-shift lever for rear derailleur
16. Freewheel gear cluster
17. Rim
18. Spoke
19. Valve
20. Tire
21. Hub (high-flange type)
22. Chainstay
23. Lug
24. Fender
25. Fork crown
26. Fork
27. Front wheel dropout
28. Seat cluster lug
29. Seat stay
30. Seat tube
31. Head tube
32. Tension roller, rear derailleur
33. Top tube
34. Fender brace
35. Down tube
36. Cotterless crank
37. Rear wheel drop out
38. Headset (top and bottom)

A CYCLING DICTIONARY
OF TERMS

ALIGNMENT   Applies basically to bicycle frame. Dropouts should be parallel; fork blades and stays parallel to top tube; top tube centered between stays; head tube parallel to fork blades; fork blades parallel to each other; stays parallel to each other; seat tube parallel to bottom bracket sides, for example.

ANKLING   Technique of pedaling, in which the foot follows through 180 degrees or more.

BOTTOM BRACKET ASSEMBLY   Axle, bearings, right fixed cone, left adjustable cone, adjustable cone locknut.

BOTTOM BRACKET HANGAR   Short round tube, usually from 68 to 72 mm. long, to which is welded or brazed the seat and down tubes and chainstays, and which accommodates the bottom bracket assembly.

BRAKE LEVERS   Levers mounted on handlebars to actuate caliper brakes.

CABLE   Wire to brakes or derailleur gears.

CALIPER BRAKES   Hand brakes. Actuated by handlebar mounted levers.

CHAIN   Articulated drive unit which transmits power from chainwheel to rear wheel.

CHAIN STAYS   Section of frame from bottom bracket to rear wheel dropout.

CHAINWHEEL   Large wheel with gear teeth on right crank, which delivers power from crank, through chain, to rear wheel. Chainwheel can be single, double, or triple wheel.

COASTER BRAKES   Foot-activated internal hub rear brakes.

COTTERPIN   Holds cranks on bottom bracket axle in cottered crank designs.

CRANK   Steel or dural member, one end of which is threaded to receive pedal, other end of which is fastened to bottom bracket axle. Righthand crank (facing forward) also is fitted with chainwheel.

CYCLOMETER   Bicycle odometer for measuring mileage. Mounts on lower front fork.

DERAILLEUR   From the French "to derail." A mechanism to derail or move chain from one gear to another on either rear wheel or chainwheel.

DERAILLEUR CAGE   Holds rear derailleur idler and jockey wheels.

DOWN TUBE   Part of frame extending from steering head to bottom bracket.

DISHING   Truing rear wheel so rim is centered exactly between outer faces of cone locknuts; necessary because of added width of freewheel. In dishing, rear rim is more toward right of hub centerline, whereas front-wheel rim is centered on hub centerline.

FORK CROWN   Flat or slightly sloping part at top of fork, just under steering head.

FRONT FORK   Part holding front wheel dropouts, which is turned by handlebars to steer bicycle. Included in this unit is steering head (inside head tube of frame), fork blades (round or oval depending on whether a track or road bike), and fork tips.

FRONT DROPOUT   Lug brazed to front fork bottom tips into which front wheel axle fits.

HANDLEBAR STEM   Steel or dural piece, top section of which holds handlebars, bottom part of which fits into top of fork.

HEAD TUBE   Large-diameter tube holding front fork and fork bearings, into which is brazed or welded top and down tubes.

HUB   Front or rear wheel unit drilled to receive spokes and machined to hold axle and bearings.

JOCKEY SPROCKET   The top of the two rear derailleur idler wheels. This wheel moves the chain from one rear wheel gear to another.

MUDGUARDS   Fenders.

MUDGUARD STAYS   Fender braces.

PANNIER   Saddlebag for mounting on rear of bicycle, usually in pairs for balance. Smaller units may also be mounted on the front of bicycle.

QUICK-RELEASE SKEWER   Mechanism to permit removal of front or rear wheels in seconds.

RATTRAP PEDALS   Steel or aluminum alloy body, steel axle, cones, and bearings of open design. For racing or touring, usually with toe clips and straps to hold foot in place and permit 360° pressure on pedals.

REAR DROPOUT   Lug brazed or welded to seat stays and chain stays into which rear wheel axle fits.

RIM   Wheel, less spokes and hub.

SADDLE   Seat.

SEAT CLUSTER   A three-way lug into which is brazed or welded top and seat tubes and seat stays.

SEAT POST   A hollow cylinder made of dural or steel, the top end of which holds seat, the bottom section of which fits into seat tube.

SEAT STAYS   Part of frame extending from just under seat to rear wheel dropout.

SEAT TUBE   Part of frame in which seat is placed and which extends from under seat to bottom bracket.

STEERING HEAD   That part of fork just above crown. Threaded to receive headset locknuts and splined or flattened on one side to receive headset washer.

TENSION ROLLER   Bottom of the two rear derailleur idler wheels. This wheel keeps correct tension on the chain.

TIRES, TUBULAR   Ultralightweight track- or road-racing tires. "Sew-ups" with tube sewn in all around inner periphery of tire.

TIRES, WIRED-ON   Conventional tire, with wire bead that holds tire seated on rim section. Open so tube can be easily removed.

TOE CLIPS   Cage on pedals, to hold feet in position, keep them from sliding off pedals.

TOP TUBE   Horizontal frame member between seat tube and head tube.

TRUING   Also "centering" of rim between axle locknuts. Also concentric (roundness) and lateral (side-to-side) alignment of rim.

VALVE   Where air is put into tire.

VARIABLE GEAR HUB   Rear hub containing two, three, or five internal gears and as many gear ratios, shiftable from external gear lever mounted on handlebars or top tube.

CYCLING ORGANIZATIONS

Amateur Bicycle League of America
Box 669, Wall Street Station
New York, New York 10005

The ABL is the governing body of bicycle racing in the United States, and is a member of the U.S. Olympic Committee, an affiliate of the Union Cycliste International (the world governing body of racing), and an allied member of the Amateur Athletic Union of the United States.

American International Cycle Club
P.O. Box 96
Silver Springs, Maryland 20907

Arranges charter flights and tours, provides group insurance, offers discounts on bikes and parts to members (according to brochure).

American Youth Hostels, Inc.
20 West 17th Street
New York, New York 10011

Sponsors bicycle trips and tours both in the United States and abroad. Maintains hostels throughout the country, where members can stay at very reasonable rates. Provides touring information and maintains a stock of cycle camping gear sold from its catalog. Furnishes list of hostel locations and planned tours to members. Holds membership in International Youth Hostel Federation. Clubs located in principal cities throughout the United States. Membership: From $4.00 to $7.00, depending on age; family membership, $10.00.

Association Cycliste Canadienne
Mr. Kenneth V. Smith
BP 2020 succursale D.
Ottawa, Canada (Ontario)

The governing body of competitive cycling in Canada.

Bicycle Institute of America
122 East 42nd Street
New York, New York 10017

Furnishes booklets, pamphlets, and information to those interested in starting cycling clubs and racing events, and in promoting bikeways (bicycle paths), locally and at the state level. BIA is the cycling trade association.

British Cycling Federation
26 Park Crescent
London W.1
England

Governs bicycle racing in England, although the BCF also offers assistance to members who wish to cycle-tour by providing itineraries, routes between youth hostels abroad, maps, accident insurance, and general advice. Membership: $4.50 if over eighteen, $3.00 under eighteen.

Bicycle Touring League of America....
c/o Dr. Roland Geist
260 W. 260th Street
Bronx, New York 10471

Sponsors adult-oriented bicycle tours in Europe and suggests tours in U.S.

Canadian Youth Hostels Association
268 First Avenue
Ottawa, Ontario, Canada

Similar in scope and function to American Youth Hostels, Inc. The international card issued by the AYH or the CYH enables you to use the facilities in hostels in all European countries.

Committee for Safe Bicycling, Inc.
c/o Dr. Paul Dudley White
264 Beacon Street
Boston, Massachusetts

An organization devoted to making cycling safer, an activity sorely needed, what with all the new cyclists on the highways today. I urge you to support this organization. No specific dues, but any contributions will be thankfully accepted.

Cyclists' Touring Club
Cotterell House
69 Meadrow
Godalming, Surrey
England

Similar in scope and purpose to the League of American Wheelmen, Inc., but furnishes infinitely greater touring service, including maps, guides, lists of hostels, and guided tours of England and Europe. Publishes bimonthly magazine, *Cycle Touring*, free to members. (See list of publications.)

Eastern Cycling Federation
Ernest McAdams
Doylestonian Apartments
403 South Main Street
Doylestown, Pennsylvania 18901

Eastern Intercollegiate Cycling Association
William Lambart
3210 Byrd Place
Baldwin, New York 11510

Federación Mexicana de Ciclismo
Cd Confederación Deportiva Mexicana
Av. Juarez 64-311
Mexico DF, Mexico

The governing body of competitive cycling in Mexico.

International Bicycle Touring Society
846 Prospect Street
La Jolla, California 92037

Plans and conducts bicycle tours throughout the world. Operates famed "Huff- 'n-Puff" tours.

International League for Cycle Touring
c/o Alain Leroux
700 Avenue des Platanes
Bat. 17 B2, 50000 Saint Lo
France

League of American Wheelman, Inc.
19 South Bothwell
Palatine, Illinois 60067

Current membership over 10,000; members in every state and in Canada, Germany, Italy and many other countries. The L.A.W. Bulletin is free with membership dues. If you're interested in cycling you owe it to yourself to join the L.A.W. Individual membership (sixteen years old and up), $5.00 per year. Family membership, $8.00 a year, includes parents and unmarried children to age twenty-one. Besides informative magazine, L.A.W. (the nation's oldest cycling organization) helps promote cycling activities nationally, organize clubs locally. Membership in the L.A.W. is your entry to a fraternity of cycling enthusiasts around the globe. Sustaining membership $15.00.

National Bicycle Dealers Association
29025 Euclid Avenue
Wickliffe, Ohio 44092

The trade association of retail bicycle dealers.

Olympic Cycling Committee/U.S. Olympic Association
Alfred E. Toefield
87-66 256 Street
Floral Park, L.I., New York

Scottish Youth Hostels Association
7 Bruntsfield Crescent
Edinburgh 10, Scotland

Will help plan tours in Scotland and provide list of youth hostels for cycle tourists.

U.S. Bicycle Polo Association
Carlos F. Concheso
P.O. Box 565
FDR Station
New York, New York 10022

Affiliate of U.S. Polo Association. Governs and regulates bicycle polo tournaments, helps organize chapters. Organized 1942, now has 18 chapters. For information, write to national headquarters listed above.

BICYCLE SUPPLY SOURCES

L. L. Bean, Inc.
Freeport, Maine 04032

The old standby. High-quality camping equipment at quite reasonable prices.

Big Wheel, Ltd.
310 Holly Street
Denver, Colorado 80220

Thomas Black & Sons
930 Ford Street
Ogdensburg, New York 13669

The U.S. member of Blacks of Greenock, Ltd., well-known and old British supplier of tents and sleeping bags for expeditions, including British Mount Everest teams and North and South Pole explorations. Lightweight tents, sleeping bags, general camping gear. Catalogue.

H. W. Carradice
North Street, Nelson
Lancashire, England

Cycle bags, panniers, straps, and carriers.

Cyclo-Pedia
311 North Mitchell
Cadillac, Michigan 49601

Publishes comprehensive list of bicycles of all types, as well as bicycle accessories, parts, and supplies. Catalogue price: $2.00.

Eco-Cyclery
5907 Todd
Oxford, Ohio 45056

Catalogue

Evian (G.B.), Ltd.
69 Manor Park Road
Harlesden, London NW 10
England

Derailleurs, parts for same, chainwheels and bottom brackets, freewheels, fork ends, frame fittings, cables, tools. Catalogue.

Gerry Division of Outdoor Sports Corporation, Inc.
5450 North Valley Highway
Denver, Colorado 80216

Another source for highest quality tents, sleeping bags, panniers, just about everything a touring, camping cyclist could want except the bicycle.

I. Goldberg & Sons
429 Market Street
Philadelphia, Pennsylvania 19106

Free camper's catalogue.

Chuck Harris
Ultra-Light Shop
Box 308
Brinkhaven, Ohio 43006

Makes tiny, lightweight rear-view mirror you clip on eyeglass temple or cap visor. A major contribution to cycling safety.

Hi-E Engineering, Inc.
1247 School Lane
Nashville, Tennessee 37217

Hi-E builds top-quality wheels to order for the discriminating, fussy cyclist. Ultralightweight wheels for racing or careful touring; heavier duty for touring with a load. Firm also markets their own sealed, lightweight front and rear hubs, and mail orders other parts such as hubs, tires, saddles, spokes, derailleurs, and a host of other cycling parts and accessories. HI-E also makes aluminum-frame bicycles to custom order. Catalogue.

W. F. Holdsworth, Ltd.
132 Lower Richmond Road
Putney, S.W. 15
England

Complete list of cycling accessories and gear. If you're planning a European trip, you may want to order abroad for pickup in England to save shipping expense.

Ron Kitching, Ltd.
Cycling Center
Hookstone Park
Harrogate, England

Ron Kitching, Ltd., is a wholesaler *only* of bicycles and bicycle parts. He publishes a fascinating catalogue with everything you could possibly want to buy for bicycling, totaling 272 pages in the last edition. It sells for $2.40, and includes a separate 176-page price list. You can buy anything in Kitching's Handbook from W. F. Holdsworth, Ltd., or R. E. W. Reynolds. But please *don't* order direct from Kitching's; you'll only delay things. First check parts-importing problems (page 141). Try not to buy anything you can get in the States; you may pay more for it if you import the item yourself because of shipping costs and, possibly, duty.

Metropolitan New York Council
American Youth Hostels, Inc.
535 West End Avenue
New York, New York 10024

Catalogue of camping needs, including cycle camping. Prices are quite reasonable and gear is pretested by AYH members, which is as good a qualification as any.

Recreational Equipment, Inc.
1525 11th Avenue
Seattle, Washington 98122

Camping gear, *including* good cycling knickers, which are almost impossible to find in the U.S. (for comfortable, dressy cycling). Every kind of packaged food you can dream of, and some you can't. Catalogue.

R. E. W. Reynolds
159–161 Wellingborough Road
Northampton, NNI 4DX
England

When we asked this firm if they are interested in bikes, parts, and bike-clothing mail-order business with U.S. customers, they wrote right back and said not only are they interested but, in fact, "we dote on it." So you should receive good and prompt service. Catalogue.

Stuyvesant Distributors
8 East 13th Street
New York, New York 10003

Bicycles (Masi, Anquetil, Bottechia, Atala), parts, tools, clothing, accessories. Catalogue.

The Touring Cyclist Shop
P.O. Box 378
Boulder, Colorado 80302

Owner Hartley Alley has designed the most practical set of multi-pocket, quick-release panniers on the market. Firm also markets carriers, lights, cadence counters, small day-trip bags, and a host of other hard-to-come-by quality accessories. Not cheap, but when you're in the middle of nowhere, you want things to work. And the price differential between the best and the worst bike accessory is, over all, minute, all things considered. Mr. Alley is an experienced cycle camper and tourer who learned how to design bags the hard way.

Wheel Goods Corporation
2737 Hennepin Avenue
Minneapolis, Minnesota 55408

This firm specializes in mail-order bicycles and bicycle parts. Its new sixth edition, 160-page catalogue ($3.00) and separate price list includes everything bicycling: bikes, tools, replacement parts, tires; you name it and Wheel Goods will likely have it.

Youth Hostels Association
29 John Adam Street
London, W.C. 2
England

Forty-eight-page cycling and camping equipment catalogue, including panniers and carriers, tents and sleeping bags.

CUSTOM FRAMES

Firms specializing in building custom frames or complete bicycles to order (besides Reynolds and Holdsworth above) include those listed below. To order a frame, see page 501 for measuring instructions:

Bob Jackson
148 Harehills Lane, Leeds LS8 5BD
England

Jack Taylor (especially for lightweight tandems)
Church Road
Stockton-on-Tees, England

Harry Hall Cycles
30 Cathedral Street
Manchester 4
England

Rene Herse
12, rue de President Wilson
92 Levallois-Perret
France

A custom bicycle builder par excellence. Monsieur Herse makes a unique folding 10-speed touring bicycle of Reynolds '531' tubing and lightweight components (plus standard ten-speed touring bicycles). Probably the best and costliest bicycles in the world. Very limited, handmade production.

Alex Singer
53, Rue Victor-Hugo
92-Levallois
France

Another very fine custom bicycle builder. Makes very elegant touring bicycles with his own design annular sealed bearing bottom bracket, ultralightweight bolted on carriers that can be removed. Will make about any type bicycle with any kind of brazed on fitting you wish. Has many U.S. customers, is used to shipping bikes to this country. Write to proprietor E. Csuka. (I have an Alex Singer, and it's very, very good, but since a lot of hand work went into it, it seems expensive, until you consider the labor involved. A life-time investment, in my opinion; but so is a Rolls Royce.)

FOR METRIC SUPPLIES

Both firms below supply, on a mail-order basis, just about every hard-to-find-size metric nut, bolt, measuring tool, drills, wrenches, cutting and reaming tools, fasteners and thread inserts. There's also British stuff, the British Standard Whitworth thread you'll find on some English bicycles. Especially useful is a caliper vernier inside, outside, and depth gauge of plastic for measuring bike parts, and a metric screw gauge, to make sure you get the right size replacements.

Ametric Supply Co.
2309 W. Leland Avenue
Chicago, Illinois 60625

Metric Multistandard Components Corp.
198 Saw Mill River Road
Elmsford, New York 10523

BICYCLE MAGAZINES

American Bicyclist and Motorcyclist
461 Eighth Avenue
New York, New York 10001

A monthly publication for the bicycle dealer. Little of interest to the cycling fan, unless he wants to start a bicycle shop. Subscription for a non-industry affiliated subscriber: $18.00 per year, for U.S. industry subscriber, $6.00 per year.

Bicycle International
7555 Woodley Avenue
Van Nuys, California 91406

Published bimonthly. U.S. subscription: $5.00 a year.

Bicycle Journal
P.O. Drawer 1229
Fort Worth, Texas 76101

For the bicycle dealer exclusively. Subscription: $5.00 per year.

Bicycle Spokesman
19 South Bothwell
Palatine, Illinois 60067

Published bimonthly. U.S. subscription: $7.00 per year.

Bicycling!
55 Mitchell Blvd.
San Rafael, California 94903

Now under new management, this old magazine should show new life. Published monthly. U.S. subscription, $8.00 per year.

Bike World ·
P.O. Box 366
2562 Middlefield Road
Mountain View, California 94040

Published bimonthly (February, April, June, August, October, December). U.S. subscription: one year, $3.00; two years, $5.00.

Cycling
161–166 Fleet Street
London, E.C. 4
England

Primarily for cycle-racing enthusiasts, although it also contains excellent articles on touring in England and Ireland and on the Continent. Published every Thursday. Subscription: one year, $24.00.

Cycling Today
P.O. Box 96
Silver Springs, Maryland 20907

Publication of American International Cycling Club, same address. Free with $15.00 annual dues.

Cycle Touring
69 Meadrow
Godalming, Surrey
England

Free to members of the Cyclists' Touring Club (same address as publication). Subscription $2.80 for six issues yearly, postage paid. December, February, April, June, August, and October. Well worth the money if you plan to cycle-tour abroad.

The Hosteler
20 West 17th Street
New York, New York 10011

Published by American Youth Hostels, Inc. Has news of AYH bike tours and trips in this country and abroad. Published ever so often, usually two or three times a year. (Local AYH chapters, the big ones, have their own house organs.) (See Bicycling Organizations.) Free to members.

International Cycle Sport
Kennedy Brothers Publishing, Ltd.
Keighley
Yorkshire
England

An excellent publication covering the European and English competitive scene. Monthly. Suscription: $20.00 per year.

The L.A.W. Bulletin
356 Robert Avenue
Wheeling, Illinois 60090

Organ of the League of American Wheelmen. Subscription with dues (see Bicycling Organizations). Invaluable aid in knowing which organized bike tour goes where and when. Nationwide coverage. Articles by experienced cyclists.

Le Cycliste
18, rue du Commandeur
Paris 14e, France

For the Continental cycling enthusiast, or for those who read and understand French. Even if you don't read French, this is a charming little publication, mostly on cycle touring in France, which should prompt you to learn the language just to read the material that goes with the beautiful illustrations. Subscription: $15.00 per year.

Popular Mechanics
Box 646
New York, New York 10019

Has a monthly column on bicycles and bicycle maintenance called "The Bicycle Shop." Subscription: U.S. only, $5.00 per year. Published monthly. Single copies $.50.

The Wheelmen
c/o G. Donald Adams
214 Maywinn Road
Defiance, Ohio 43512

Publication of The Wheelmen, an organization devoted to the restoration and riding of early bicycles, and to the "encouragement of cycling as a part of modern living." *The Wheelmen* Magazine is published twice a year, in summer and winter. Subscription is included in annual dues of $5.00 to The Wheelmen; or individual copies are available at $1.00 a copy. A wonderful publication for those interested in old bicycles. To join The Wheelmen, send dues to Mrs. Donald Cottrell, 6239 Anavista Drive, Flint, Michigan 48507.

BIBLIOGRAPHY

BOOKS AND PAMPHLETS

Baranet, Nancy Neiman. *The Turned Down Bar*. Philadelphia: Dorrance & Company, 1964.

Benedict, Ruth and Ray. *Bicycling*. New York: A. S. Barnes and Company, 1944.

Bowden, Ken, and John Matthews. *Cycle Racing*. London: Temple Press Books, Limited (42 Russell Square, London, W.C. 1), 1965.

English, Ronald. *Adventure Cycling*. London: Nicholas Kay Limited (194–200 Bishopsgate, London, E.C. 2), 1959.

English, Ronald. *Cycling for You*. London: Clutterworth Press, 1964.

a'Green, George. *Story of the Cyclists' Touring Club*. London: Cyclists' Touring Club, 1953.

Kraynick, Steve. *Bicycle Owner's Complete Handbook*. Los Angeles: Floyd Clymer Publications, 1960.

Moore, Harold. *The Complete Cyclist*. London: Sir Isaac Pitman & Sons, Ltd., 1960.

Morehouse, Laurence E., and Augustus T. Miller. *The Physiology of Exercise*. St. Louis: C. V. Mosby Company, 1959.

Murphy, Dervla. *Full Tilt: Ireland to India on a Bicycle*. New York: E. P. Dutton & Company; Inc., 1965.

Pullen, A. L. *Cycling Handbook*. London: Sir Isaac Pitman & Sons, Ltd., 1960.

Shaw, R. C. *Teach Yourself Cycling*. London: The English Universities Press, Ltd. (102 Newgate Street), 1963.

Simpson, Tommy. *Cycling Is My Life*. London: Stanley Paul & Co., Ltd. (178–202 Great Portland Street), 1966.

Way, R. John. *Cycling Manual*. London: Temple Press Books, Limited, 1967.

Bicycle Clubs Directory. New York: Bicycle Institute of America (122 E. 42nd Street, New York, New York, 10017).

Bicycle Dealer's Source Book. Dayton, Ohio: National Bicycle Dealers Association, 1967.

The Bicycle, Its Care and Maintenance. London: Iliffe Books Limited. (Dorset House, Stamford Street, London, S.E. 1), 1961.

Bicycle Riding Clubs. New York: Bicycle Institute of America.

Bicycle Touring Atlas. New York: American Youth Hostels. 1969.

Bike Racing on the Campus. New York: Bicycle Institute of America. (122 East 42nd Street, New York, N.Y. 10017.)

Bike Trails and Facilities (information kit). New York: Bicycle Institute of America.

Bike Trails and Facilities: A Guide to Their Design and Construction. West Virginia: American Institute of Park Executives, Inc., Walter L. Cook. (Oglebay Park, Wheeling, W.Va.), May, 1965.

Cycling Book of Maintenance. London: Temple Press Books, Limited, 1961.

Cycling Guide. Pennsylvania: American Youth Hostels, Inc. (2200 Pine Street, Philadelphia, Pa. 19141.)

Cycling in the School Fitness Program. Washington, D.C.: American Association for Health, Physical Education and Recreation, 1963.

The Family Hosteling Manual. New York: American Youth Hostels, Inc.

Gear Ratios. Cyclo-Gear Company, Ltd.

A Handbook on Bicycle Tracks and Cycle Racing. Dayton, Ohio: The Huffman Manufacturing Company, 1965.

Hostel Guide and Handbook. New York: American Youth Hostels, Inc. (20 West 17th Street, New York, N.Y. 10011), 1967–1968.

Know the Game Cycling. London: Educational Productions Limited (17 Denbigh Street, London, S.W. 1), 1964.

Miroir du Cyclisme. Published monthly.

Miroir Spring. Published weekly. Both of the French publications above are published by Editions "J" at 10, Rue des Pyramides, Paris 1, France. Send to publisher for rates.

Public Safety Memo 92, Bicycles. Chicago: National Safety Council, 1965.

Reynolds '531' Cycle Tubing (technical booklet). Reynolds Tube Company Limited.

Safe Bicycling. Boston: Committee for Safe Bicycling, Inc., 1965.

Traffic Accident Facts. Chicago: National Safety Council, 1967.

MAGAZINE ARTICLES

DeLong, Fred. "The Care and Use of Lightweight Bicycles." Philadelphia: Philadelphia Council, American Youth Hostels, Inc.

———. "Handlebars and Riding Position," *Bicycling!* (formerly *American Cycling*), April, 1966, p. 16.

———. "What Bicycle for Touring?" *American Cycling* (now *Bicycling!*), May, 1967, p. 12.

———. "What Length Cranks?" *American Cycling* (now *Bicycling!*), September, 1967, p. 14.

Duex-Roves, "Winter Cycling," *American Cycling* (now *Bicycling!*), December, 1966, p. 9.

Hartke, Vance. *The Congressional Conference on Bicycling in America.* Congressional Record, September 20, 1966.

Kepner, Paul R. "Cadence Chart." *Cyclo-Pedia*, 1967, p. 63.

St. Pierre, Roger. "Equipment Review: Witcomb Cycles and Jacques Anquetil Cycles," *American Cycling* (now *Bicycling!*), August, 1967, p. 17.

———. "Road Test Raleigh RSW-16," *American Cycling* (now *Bicycling!*), June, 1967, p. 17.

Thomas, Vaugh. "Scientific Setting of the Saddle Position," *American Cycling* (now *Bicycling!*), June, 1967, p. 12.

Wolf, Spence. "Derailleur Maintenance," *American Cycling* (now *Bicycling!*), November, 1966, p. 23; December, 1966, p. 25.
———. "Front Hub Bearing Maintenance," *American Cycling* (now *Bicycling!*), September, 1966, p. 23.
———. "Tire Care," *American Cycling* (now *Bicycling!*), June, 1966, p. 19.

"The Bike's Comeback," *Sunset*, July, 1965, ER-191.
"Bikeways," *American Bicyclist and Motorcyclist*, February, 1967, p. 76.

INDEX

Eugene A. Sloane